CW00686547

Faith Map

Resources for children based on the Sunday readings

Year A

Written by
Maurice Billingsley
Rachel Denton
Yvonne Fordyce
Jill Ormondroyd
Stephanie Thornton
Kathryn Turner

Edited by Yvonne Fordyce and Jane Williams
Design by Active Noise
Illustrations by Louise Hilton

© Redemptorist Publications
Published by Redemptorist Publications in 2007
A registered Charity limited by guarantee.
Registered in England 3261721

ISBN: 978-0-85231-337-4

All rights reserved. No part of this
publication may be reproduced, stored in a retrieval system
or transmitted in any form by any means, electronic, mechanical,
photocopying, recording or otherwise,
without prior permission in writing from Redemptorist Publications
(except where indicated).

Printed by Cambridge University Press

Redemptorist
PUBLICATIONS
Alphonsus House Chawton Hampshire GU34 3HQ
Telephone 01420 88222   Fax 01420 88805
rp@rpbooks.co.uk   www.rpbooks.co.uk

Introducing FaithMap Year A

FaithMap is interactive, fun and engaging for children of all ages and abilities. It is a valuable resource for anyone involved with children's liturgies, Sunday schools or children's groups. It can also be used in primary schools for assemblies or class teaching and by parents who want to explore the Gospel message at home with their family.

Designed for a range of ages, FaithMap offers a choice of two approaches: "Young Ones" and "Juniors", plus additional suggestions for children with learning difficulties.

FaithMap is based on the Catholic Lectionary for Year A (on the majority of Sundays this coincides with the *Common Worship* Lectionary), covering all possible Sunday celebrations in Year A. Each week the Sunday Gospel is explored through five sections.

1. **Introduction** to the theme of the day with a Leader's Reflection.

2. **Arrival:** Gather around a focal point, which reflects the theme of the day. The Sunday Gospel is read from the Lectionary or the Children's Lectionary.

3. **Response:** Suggested questions for discussion to find out what the Gospel is asking of us. A story or real-life experience follows, to link up with the Gospel and to help the children understand its message.

4. **Activity:** A practical section with a photocopiable template and suggestions for activities suitable for a range of abilities. Tips for those with learning difficulties are included.

5. **We Come Together** to share, pray and sing, offering the opportunity for parents to join in the group's activities. The Gospel message is highlighted, and work from the activities shared in a short prayer time to end the meeting.

There is also a photocopiable **Family Sheet** for each week, which the children can take away with them and use during the week. This takes the learning experience home, back to the heart of the family for ongoing discussion and daily prayer. It includes a weekly thought for parents, and a picture symbol to mark/colour each day when the suggested action is completed.

It's a rich resource giving you all the information, ideas and material you need to run successful sessions with children. Use some or all of the sections, and feel free to add your own ideas to help bring the Gospel message alive.

We hope that you and the children in your care will enjoy using **FaithMap**.

Contents
Roman Catholic

Contents
Anglican

FaithMap follows the Catholic Lectionary. Often, the readings on which the text is based are the same as those given in the *Common Worship* lectionary. This list, therefore, only indexes those Sundays on which this happens. On occasions when the Catholic and *Common Worship* lectionaries do not match up, the user may wish to consider working from the Catholic provision for the day.

1st Sunday of Advent

1. Introduction to the theme of the day

"Stay awake – you do not know the hour"

Aim: We think about Jesus' second coming, what will it be like?

Leader's reflection: During the first two weeks of Advent we are looking forward to Christ coming – not as a baby, but at the end of time, in glory. Belief in the "Parousia" was one of the sustaining features of the early Church, which lived in daily expectation of its occurrence. In our times, although we are told "you do not know the day", our anticipation is less urgent. Nonetheless, when it does occur, there will be no chance of our missing out – "All things will be brought together in him."

2. We arrive
We sit in a circle ready to listen to the Gospel.
Has anyone anything they would like to tell us about last week's Family Sheet?

Focus
Advent wreath ready to light one candle, purple fabric for Advent, statue of Jesus:
Christ the King would be best, but the Good Shepherd or the Sacred Heart could be used.

Gospel: Matthew 24:37-44
Read from the Lectionary or Children's Lectionary.

3. We respond
What is the Gospel asking of us?
When Jesus was on earth as a man, he was not very famous. Even after the resurrection only a few people knew that he was God. Before he ascended to heaven, he told his apostles that he would come back to earth one day in all his glory, and this time everybody would recognise him. What will that be like? How will we recognise him?
Work in age groups if appropriate, then come together as a group to end the session.

Young ones

Story: The angels' workshop

Aelred was Jesus' guardian angel. He was a very young angel and had a lot to learn. Every now and then he went back to the angel school in heaven for a few days, so that he could learn new things.

Today his class were going on a special trip to the wardrobe department. That was the place where they made all the outfits for the angels. Aelred had been there once before when he was measured up for his guardian angel clothes, but today their teacher was going to show them something different.

She took them through the sewing rooms where there were lots of angels busily stitching together all the different outfits and wing shields for the different sorts of angels, and then they all trooped into a place that Aelred had never seen before. It was a vast hall, so big and bright that Aelred could not see the walls, they were too far away, and the ceiling was so high it almost hit the stars.

Rows and rows and rows of angels were sitting behind sewing machines and tables, busily working. The first strange thing that Aelred noticed was that they all seemed to be making the same thing. White dresses!

Wherever he looked there were white dresses. Some angels were cutting white dresses out, others were sewing white dresses together, whilst others were matching white dresses with haloes from a great pile in the middle of the room and then hanging them together on long racks of hooks which were lowered from the ceiling. Once each rack was full, an angel at the end rang a little bell, and the rack was pulled up to the ceiling while everybody clapped and cheered. Then Aelred noticed something he hadn't spotted before. All the way up to the ceiling there were racks and racks of white dresses, all with their haloes hanging next to them, shining brightly in the starlight. There were trillions of them. "Who are they all for?" he gasped.

"They are for people," his teacher explained. "At the end of time, Jesus will go back to earth and pick up all the good people and all his friends and bring them back up here with him. There will be a big party, which will last for ever. These dresses are for all those people."

"But there are so many!" exclaimed Aelred.

"Well, yes," explained his teacher with a smile on her face, "Jesus has lots of friends!"

Who is a friend of Jesus?
What plans has Jesus made for his friends?
What do you think heaven is like?

Juniors

Story: Good and evil in fiction

Epic adventures depicting the fight between good and evil are very current in junior fiction. Obvious examples include *The Lord of the Rings* (J.R.R. Tolkien), Harry Potter (J.K. Rowling), the Dark Materials trilogy (Philip Pullman), the Narnia stories (C.S. Lewis), the Wind on Fire trilogy (William Nicholson). Apart from the first and last of the Narnia stories, none of these is a direct allegory of the Christian story, but they might still be used to "warm up" the spiritual imagination. The instructions given below should enable you to locate two passages, one in *The Return of the King* and the other in *The Last Battle*. Refer to junior activity for suggestion as to how best to use them.

Lord of the Rings *Return of the King*: "The Battle of Pelennor Fields", towards the end of the chapter. Eomer, a warrior, is about to make a last stand against the powers of evil, when he sees the ships bearing Aragorn (the as-yet-unrevealed king) from the Paths of the Dead. "And then wonder took him … and upon his brow was the star of Elendil."

The Chronicles of Narnia *The Last Battle*: "Night falls on Narnia"; start reading at the end of the previous chapter. "He (Aslan) went to the Door and they all followed him … And all these ran up to the doorway where Aslan stood."

4. Activity

Young ones

You are going to dress a paper doll for the party at the "End of Time". Roughly cut out one of the dolls on the template, stick it onto card and then cut it out accurately. Colour in the hair, eyes, nose etc. Cut the outfit out of paper, taking care with the tabs, and decorate. (We will all be dressed mainly in white at the "End of Time", so don't over-decorate!)

Juniors

The passages given in the junior story section both have the flavour of the "Parousia": the second coming of Christ, and the last times. Read either or both of them, and then invite the children to have a go at writing their own imaginative description, or drawing it.

Tips for learning difficulties

Juniors – Some children might prefer to make a collage of a procession or battle using cut-out people from magazines, or even to enact it using toys, Lego models etc.

Young ones – sequins, ribbons, silver foil etc. could be provided to stick on the white dresses as decoration.

5. We come together

Parents can be invited to join in at this stage.

Focus

Form a procession around the room, singing the hymn and carrying the paper dolls, writing and pictures. These can all be placed in front of the statue which could be decorated with flowers as well.

Gospel

Jesus said, "One day I will come back to the earth in glory. You don't know when that will be, so stay awake and be ready."

Prayer

Jesus, we look forward to the "End of Time". Then you will come again in glory. Make us ready to be with you for ever. Amen.

Share

The juniors can read their descriptions of the "End of Time".

Sing

"Look at the sky"
"Mine eyes have seen the glory"

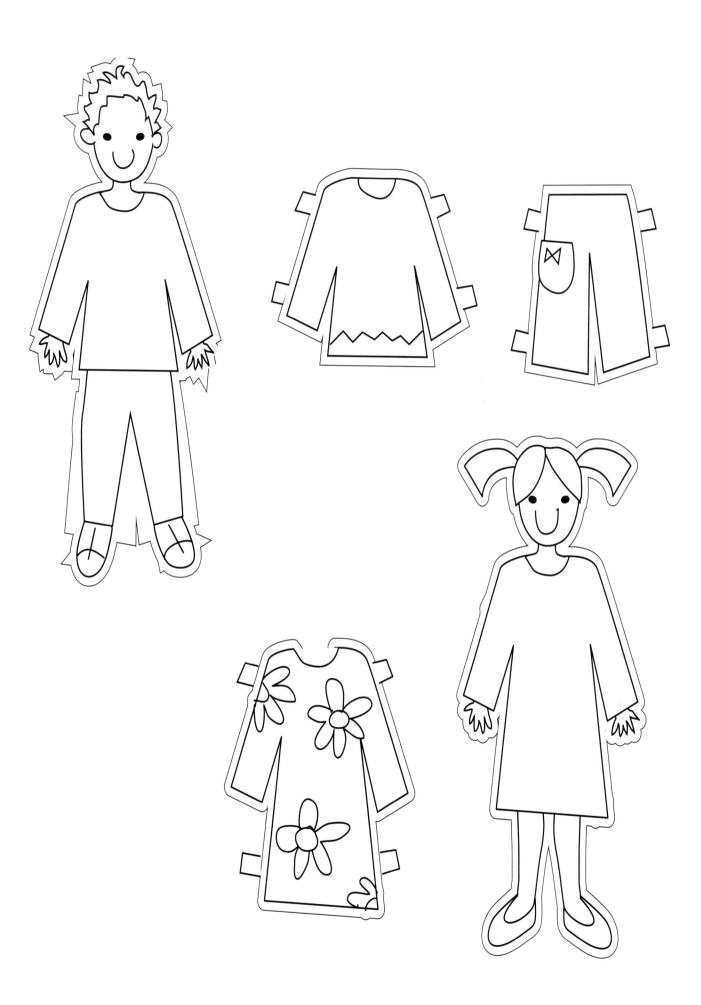

2nd Sunday of Advent

1. Introduction to the theme of the day

> ## "Get ready for the king's coming"

Aim: To lead the children to a closer understanding of what we need to do to welcome the king.

Leader's reflection: The Gospel throughout Advent is a call to conversion. Today's Gospel focuses on clearing away the "mess" and getting ready for something special to happen. Getting ready for the Lord's birth is like getting a house in order for a much-loved visitor, like a grandparent. Through all the work and excitement of tidying up and putting things straight, we are making the gift of welcome, creating a real spirit of Christmas.
How can we get ready to welcome Jesus?

2. We arrive
We sit in a circle ready to listen to the Gospel.

Focus
Two candles on the Advent wreath to be lit, and three brushes: a paintbrush, a dustpan and brush, a hairbrush. As you light the first candle, recall what the first week of Advent was about. As you light the second, wonder what this week will be about. What are the brushes for?

Gospel: Matthew 3:1-12
Read from the Lectionary or Children's Lectionary.

3. We respond
What is the Gospel asking of us?
Work in age groups if appropriate, then come together as a group to end the session.

Young ones

Story: Sarah gives the Queen a special welcome

Sarah was in hospital. She had had an operation on her back to help her to walk properly. Sarah had always had to get around with a wheelchair. Now she had managed to walk with a frame, then on crutches and today she was going to walk with sticks. The doctors hoped she'd soon be able to walk without anything to help her.

Chris, her physio, came. He'd got the sticks.

"Come on," he said. "Let's get going."

Sarah leaned on the sticks. They didn't take the weight off her legs like the crutches, she felt very wobbly.

"Come on, Sarah," shouted the other children in the ward. "You can do it."

After a while she got the hang of it and walked up and down the ward.

"Well," said Chris, "that's enough for one day – no sticks when the Queen comes?"

Sarah didn't know anything about the Queen's visit. She wanted to know all about it. "Yes, she's coming to open a new part of the hospital and she's going to come around the wards while she's here. We've all got a lot to do to get ready. No trolleys out of place, no litter, fresh paint... the works."

Sarah decided to do what she could to help. She tidied up her own corner. She made a card to thank the Queen for coming and she decided that when the Queen came she would be walking without sticks. It took a lot of hard work. When Sarah got to the end of each day she was tired out. She got rid of one stick and then the other. She walked from bed to bed, without her sticks. She walked down the corridor, very close to the wall, without her sticks, every day she got a little better.

Then it was the special day. Sarah and her family waited to see if the Queen would come to "their" ward. The door opened and there she was.

"Isn't she small?" said Sarah's mum. "Isn't she old?" said Sarah's dad.

She was, but she was smiling. She had nice things to say to the nurses and to the other children. When she got near to Sarah, she stopped.

"Is this Sarah?" she asked. "The girl who has been working so hard to walk without sticks. Show me how you're getting on."

Sarah couldn't believe it. She picked up the card she'd made, stood up and walked across the ward to the Queen.

"I can't curtsey," she said, "but this is for you, thank you for coming."

You could see the Queen was pleased.

"Well done... and thank *you*," she said.

How can we get ready for the coming of our king at Christmas? Think of all the special things we are doing to get ready for Christmas. How do these things help us welcome Jesus?

Juniors

Story: Simon takes up the challenge

Simon had been with his family to listen to the Baptist talk before. He was more than a little afraid of this strange figure of a man who was dressed very oddly and by all accounts ate even more oddly.

The Baptist didn't seem to be afraid of anyone. He told soldiers what they must do; he shouted at groups of Pharisees and Sadducees. He had only one message and it was "Get ready."

Today Simon listened more carefully. Get ready for what?

"Repent, for the kingdom of heaven is close at hand," John shouted.

Simon tugged at his father's sleeve.

"What does he mean... the kingdom?"

"He's talking about a great leader, he will set up a kingdom and he's coming soon. Yes, John is right, we need to be ready. Today I shall be baptised. There are many changes I must make."

When John stopped talking Simon's father hurried towards the water. Simon followed him. He'd never been so near to the Baptist; suddenly Simon wasn't afraid of him.

"You too?" asked the Baptist. Simon nodded. "You'll have to become better, more hardworking, listen to your parents and no fighting." Simon nodded again.

The Baptist lowered him into the water.

"Listen," said John when Simon came up gasping, "this is water to wash you because you are sorry and ready to try again, but the one I'm talking about will baptise with the Holy Spirit and fire. Be ready for him and his kingdom."

"He is a king then?" said Simon.

"Oh yes," said John. "A powerful king. I am only his servant and not even fit to undo his shoes for him."

Let the children suggest the sorts of changes our king expects.
He wants nothing less than our total service. He expects the subjects of his kingdom to be kind to each other; to think of what other people would like before thinking of what they want; to try hard to say only encouraging things, and to care for his world.

4. Activity
Young ones and Juniors

Use the crown template to make a crown for each child. You will need four shiny pieces of paper to be jewels for the crown. Ask the children to think of four things they could do to prepare for the king's coming (thinking back over the day may help). These actions should be written on the reverse of the jewels and glued to the crown. No one else will know the promised changes.

Tips for learning difficulties

Concentrate on decorating the crown and wearing it to show that Jesus, our king, is coming.

5. We come together

Parents can be invited to join in at this stage.

Focus

Children and parents may gather around the Advent wreath and the crowns made by the children. When everyone is gathered begin with the sign of the cross.

Gospel (read by one of the children)

John said, "Repent, for the kingdom of heaven is close... I baptise you with water but the one who is coming is more powerful than I am. I am not fit even to undo his sandals. He will baptise you with the Holy Spirit and with fire."

Be quiet for a few moments. Think of the changes you promised today, hidden under the jewels of your crown.

Prayer

Our king, we have made some promises to you today. Help us to keep them and work for your kingdom. Amen.

Share

The work and ideas from the activities.

Sing

"Sing we the king who is coming to reign"
"I give my hands to do your work"

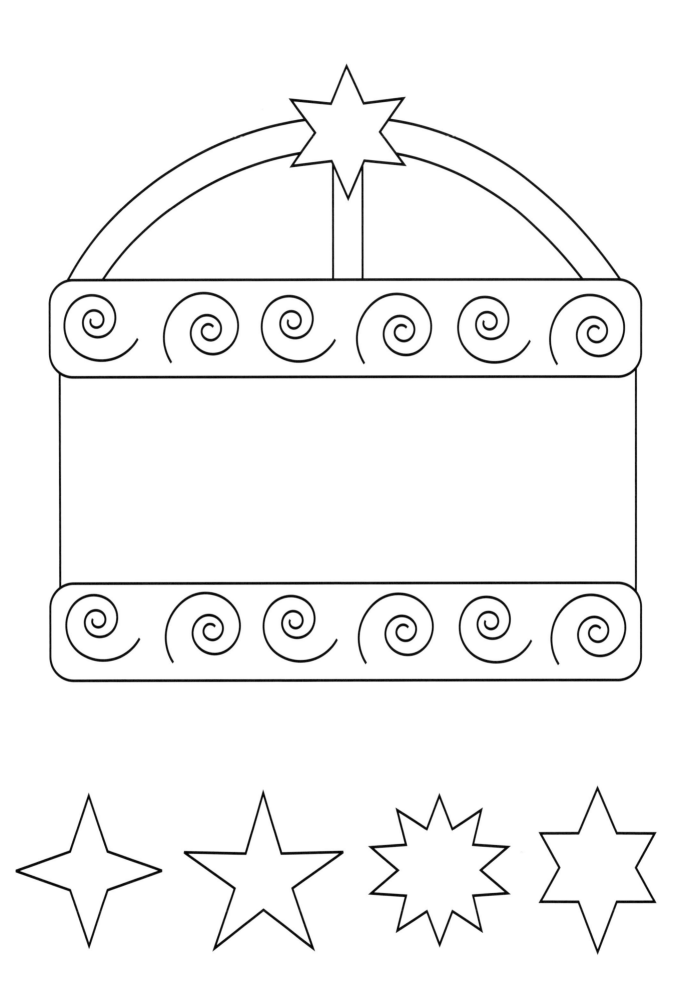

3rd Sunday of Advent

1. Introduction to the theme of the day

"Rejoice, the Lord is near!"

Aim: To encourage the children to keep on with their preparations for the Lord's coming.

Leader's reflection: We all have our doubts. John the Baptist had his doubts: "Have we got to wait for someone else?" Our doubts honestly admitted bring a great gift from Our Lord. "Go back and tell John…"; "Thomas, see here are my hands…"; Jesus always encourages his followers. His message is one of "hang in there, don't give up".

2. We arrive
Greet the children by name, sit in a circle to listen to the Gospel.

Focus
Advent wreath, three candles to be lit, purple cloth.

Gospel: Matthew 11:2-11
Read from the Lectionary or Children's Lectionary.

3. We respond
What is the Gospel asking of us?
Work in age groups if appropriate, then come together as a group to end the session.

Young ones

Story: A birthday surprise

Luca was waiting for his birthday. There was still a week to wait. He had heard whisperings and knew they were about his birthday presents and his party. He had handed out invitations to his friends at school, they were all coming. There was going to be a magician to entertain them.

Best of all, his uncle and aunt and his cousins were coming to stay. They would be bringing cards and presents from his grandparents.

The day finally came. The postman brought cards to open. His parents and sister gave him presents. His friends came to the party with more cards and presents. The birthday tea was great, the magician amazing. But his uncle and aunt did not arrive.

"Where are they?" Luca demanded. "We got their rooms ready, we've saved them some party food."

"I don't know," said Dad. "I tried Uncle Tony's mobile – it's switched off. I left a message. They'll be in touch."

The evening dragged.

"They're not coming, are they?" Luca said.

"Go on waiting," said Mum. "We don't know why they're late yet, they'll come, they'll let us know."

Eventually Luca went to bed. It had been a good birthday, but he *had* been looking forward to his *family* celebration.

The visitors had still not arrived in the morning.

"Don't give up hope, Luca," said Dad. "You get off to school and wait and see."

All day Luca tried to think about school and work and his friends but he kept on hoping. Finally it was time to go home.

There was Dad by the school gate, and with him... yes, it was. It was his uncle.

"Made it at last," said Uncle Tony. "Bet you thought we'd all got lost."

"I didn't give up hoping you'd be here," said Luca. "What happened?"

"Well, you've got a new cousin. Your aunt had a baby girl yesterday, on your birthday. I was stuck at the hospital. We're going to call her Lucy!"

Sometimes waiting can be very hard. Have you had to wait a long time for something special?
John the Baptist knew that Jesus would come, but didn't know exactly when. However, he carried on with his work, preparing people to welcome Jesus. Christmas is not far away; how can we continue with our preparations thinking of others before ourselves?

Juniors

Story: Simon has a problem

John the Baptist and his friends, including Simon's father, were confused by what they heard that Jesus was doing. Was this really the great leader they had been expecting? He did not seem to be setting up his kingdom with fire and authority. He wasn't sorting out the rulers and forcing people to be his subjects.

John, who by now had been put into prison, begged his friends to find out if this really *was* the king they were waiting for.

When Simon's father told him about John's doubts, Simon could not believe it.

"But the Baptist was so certain, he told me about the king who was so powerful when he baptised me. We must find out about this Jesus – there's no point in getting ready for a kingdom when the king isn't coming."

When the messengers came from John, Jesus understood exactly how he was feeling. John was in prison, he couldn't see for himself how Jesus' work was going.

"Watch what I'm doing today, talk to the people who are listening to me and those who can see again, or hear or walk. Then go back to John in his prison and tell him all about it. Encourage him; he is in a lonely place."

Simon's father went back to tell John what he had seen and heard with the other messengers, but Simon stayed to listen to Jesus.

Jesus talked about John.

"You went to see John because he was a prophet, speaking God's truth, not because he was wearing special clothes, a prince from a palace. He is the special messenger sent from God to prepare you for my kingdom."

"Yes," thought Simon. "We got ready for the king's coming and I have seen the king's power. He doesn't rule his kingdom by force but by kindness. John was right, this is the king to follow."

Why were John's friends worried? What had they expected of Jesus? What sort of person did they actually find? What sort of people would Jesus like us to look out for this Christmas?

4. Activity

Young ones and Juniors

Colour in the heading on the template page.

What happens in Jesus' kingdom? Draw pictures or write in the missing word.

Can you put your name on the line at the bottom of the page?

Could you give this worksheet a border of Advent candles to make it special?

Tips for learning difficulties

Enlarge the heading "Be very happy" – colour this in while talking about the things that make the child happy and thanking God for them.

5. We come together

Parents can be invited to join in at this stage.

Focus

As at the start but with the children's work (or selected samples) on display.

The children and their parents may gather around the focus. Start with the sign of the cross and lighting the candles.

Gospel (read by one of the children)

Jesus said: "The blind see again, and the lame walk, lepers are cured and the deaf hear. The dead are lifted to new life, the poor hear the Good News. Trust me, you will be very happy."

Prayer

Keep us close to you while we look forward to your coming and work to get ready for it.

"Our Father..." Amen.

Share

The work and ideas from the activities.

Sing

"Rejoice in the Lord always and again I say rejoice"

Be very happy!
The Lord is near

The _____ can see.

The _____ can hear.

The _____ can walk.

The _____ are cured.

The _____ are raised to life.

The _____ hear the good news.

_____ will go on getting
ready for Jesus' coming.

4th Sunday of Advent

1. Introduction to the theme of the day

"Looking forward"

Aim: To learn to look forward, without fear.

Leader's reflection: Joseph's mind must have been confused. He was formally betrothed, he was to marry, big changes in themselves. He finds his "wife to be" already pregnant. A kindly man, trying to avoid trouble he decides on a private solution, not a public divorce. He sleeps on his decision, dreams of an angelic message and on waking does what has been asked of him in his dream. How far ahead did he look? How worried was he? In fact he took the one step asked of him, he took Mary to his home and got on with his life. Perhaps we should follow his example and take just the one clear step and give up the fear and worry about tomorrow's problems.

2. We arrive

We sit in a circle ready to listen to the Gospel.
Has anyone anything they would like to tell us about last week's Family Sheet?

Focus

Purple cloth, Advent wreath, four candles ready to light.

Gospel: Matthew 1:18-24

Read from the Lectionary or Children's Lectionary.

3. We respond
What is the Gospel asking of us?

Work in age groups if appropriate, then come together as a group to end the session.

Young ones and Juniors

Story: Mary and Joseph trust in God

All the preparations for the wedding were made. New clothes for the bride and groom, special food and wine for the wedding feast, the guests invited... Joseph had prepared his own house specially to welcome Mary. Both of them and their families were looking forward to their special day.

Then the bombshell dropped. Mary's father came to speak to Joseph. He was struggling to find the right words. In the end he just came out with it.

"Mary is expecting a baby," he said. He tried to tell Joseph Mary's story of the angel who had come to her. "Mary's baby is to be special, the one we have all been waiting for. Mary had to do what God wanted."

Joseph could not believe it, it was too fantastic for words. "I need to think about all of this," he said.

"But what will you do, what about the wedding?" said Mary's father.

Joseph went over and over what he had been told. How could the baby be God's? How could he believe such an amazing story? What was he going to do?

Eventually he made his decision.

"I can't marry her now. But I can't hurt her, she obviously believes she saw an angel who gave her a special message. I shall find a way of ending it all, but privately. I don't want people pointing at Mary or laughing at her. I shall talk to her father about it tomorrow."

That night Joseph went to sleep. With his decision made, he got to sleep.

It was that night he had the dream.

It seemed to him that an angel had come to him too. God's messenger was shining, beautiful and very close. Joseph had no doubts that this was truly an angel from God. He was afraid, just as Mary's father had said Mary had been.

"Don't be afraid, Joseph," said the angel. "Don't be afraid to take Mary to your home as your wife. The child she will have will truly be special. God's Holy Spirit of power makes all this possible. Mary will have a son. He is to be called Jesus and he will save his people from their sins. Do you remember what the prophet said? 'A young woman will have a son; they will call him Emmanuel, a name that means God is with us.' That young woman is Mary, she has said 'yes' to God. Don't be afraid."

When Joseph woke up, he remembered everything that he had dreamed about. The angel and his message were very clear. Joseph was certain. He had a job to do, he had to be a father to this special child. He would not look too far ahead but he was glad to take the first step. He would marry Mary and take her to the home he had got ready for her.

Can you put yourself into the shoes of Mary and Joseph? They were looking forward to a new life together. Then everything was changed. How do you think they felt? Would they be afraid, happy, confused?

Do you think about the future? Are you ever afraid of what might happen or are you excited? How far ahead do you look? Sometimes we worry about things which never happen.

Joseph just took one step when God's messenger spoke to him. He got on with marrying Mary.

4. Activity
Young ones and Juniors

Each child will need a copy of the activity sheet and a piece of blank paper on which to draw themselves (rear view). You might provide material or tissue paper, wool etc. to make clothes or hair. Use the drawings to make a large collage of children looking forward. Add a caption, e.g. "We are looking forward to Jesus' coming."

There are two activities to complete today.
1. Can you complete the story we had in today's Gospel, filling in the speech bubbles and colouring the pictures?
2. Draw yourself looking forward – you won't need to draw your face! You might want to use some wool for hair and some material for your clothes. When you have finished, cut out your drawing and add it to a big picture where everyone is looking forward.

If you have time, you might use the Advent "getting ready" colours, of purple and pink, to make a border for your big picture.

Tips for learning difficulties

Have a figure already cut out to be dressed to represent the child. Put glue on the figure, press small pieces of material onto the glue.
Concentrate on talking about "tomorrow" and the good things the child may be expecting to happen then, while doing the sticking.

5. We come together

Parents can be invited to join in at this stage.

Focus

The collage made by the children and the Advent wreath. Parents and children may gather around the focus. Light the candles again. As you light each one the children may say:
"We are looking forward to Jesus' birthday."
Make the sign of the cross.

Gospel

One of the children to hold up the completed activity sheet while the Gospel is read.
"When Joseph woke up from his dream he did what the angel had told him. He took Mary to his own house."

Prayer

Thank you, Lord, for coming to us and giving us Christmas to look forward to. Like Joseph, help us to be ready to do what you ask. Amen.

Share

The work and ideas from the activities.

Sing

"Emmanuel, Emmanuel, his name is called"
"Light the Advent candle four"

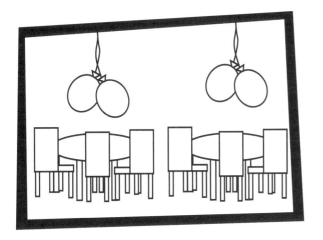

The Nativity of Our Lord

Christmas Day

1. Introduction to the theme of the day

"Welcome"

Aim: To know that at Christmas we welcome Jesus to his world.

Leader's reflection: Being truly welcome, in a relationship, to a place, or a party, is one of the great joys of our lives. When we recognise Jesus among us and make him truly welcome that joy is enhanced, perfected. Christmas is a welcoming time, welcoming the baby and making each other welcome.

2. We arrive
We sit in a circle ready to listen to the Gospel.
Has anyone anything they would like to tell us about last week's Family Sheet?

Focus
A crib or picture of the nativity.

Gospel: Matthew 1:1-25 (vigil); Luke 2:1-14 (midnight); Luke 2:15-20 (dawn); John 1:1-18 (day)
Any or all of these Gospels can be read from the Lectionary or Children's Lectionary.

3. We respond
What is the Gospel asking of us?
Work in age groups if appropriate, then come together as a group to end the session.

Young ones

Story: Light in the church

It was the first time that Will had ever been to church when it was so dark. The only light seemed to be coming in from outside each time the door opened and more people came in, and from the red light shining high up in front of the altar. Then the lights on the Christmas tree were switched on.

Will thought it looked very beautiful shining in the darkness of the building.

"Come on," said Mum, "we'll sit here near the crib that the Flower Guild has decorated."

"There are Mary and Joseph and some shepherds and sheep. Oh look, there's lots of straw and a cow... but there's no baby there," said Will with disappointment.

"No," said Mum, "Father Tony will bring the baby in and put him in the manger when our service begins."

Will thought for a bit.

"Why is it so dark?"

"Jesus was born at night in a dark stable," said Mum. "We're remembering what happened and who was there to welcome him. When we welcome him, the world lights up, you'll see."

The bell rang, Father Tony came in. He was carrying the baby. He took the baby to the manger.

"It's a special night," said Father Tony, "we are going to bless our crib and let the light of Jesus shine right through our church."

Father Tony put the baby in the crib and said some prayers. He lit the lantern which was hanging over the manger. Then he went to the altar. He lit a candle from those on the altar and two of the servers lit candles from his. The servers came to each row in turn. Mum gave Will a candle and when the server reached their row, each person lit a candle from the person next to them.

Light spread through all the church.

"Now," said Father Tony, "we have filled this church with the glory of light, just as Jesus has come to fill our hearts with light when we welcome him. Let us pray."

Can you tell me the Christmas story we heard in the Gospel? What happened first? Who were the people who came to welcome Jesus on his birthday?

How do you think those people celebrated the first Christmas?

How do we celebrate Christmas: do we have special people to welcome, what do we do to make people feel welcome?

How do you feel when people are pleased to see you?

Juniors

Story: The first Christmas

You have all seen or taken part in a Nativity Play, and you know this Gospel story very well.

Share the retelling of the Gospel, allowing each child to contribute as the story unfolds, or use drama and mime.

Listen to the children's ideas, and discuss them. Encourage each of them to focus on one welcoming activity they could do today.

Think quietly for a moment of all the people who had a part to play in that first Christmas. What sort of welcome do you think each of them gave to Jesus? Now it is Christmas and we are welcoming Jesus to his own world, what sort of welcome can we give?

4. Activity

Young ones and Juniors

Look at the people on the template page who are part of the Christmas story. Under each one, write down how they welcomed Jesus. Draw yourself and write down how you welcome him. Colour the pictures.

Tips for learning difficulties

Ask the child to draw a picture of themselves; talk about how Christmas is celebrated in the children's families and the happiness that is shared at this time of the year.
The expression drawn on the face will be a guide to further discussion.

5. We come together

Parents can be invited to join in at this stage.
Invite everyone to take a few moments to be quiet.

Focus

The crib or picture and a lighted candle.

Gospel

When the angels had left them, the shepherds said, "Let us go to Bethlehem and see what has happened for ourselves."
So they left their sheep and hurried to the town. There they found Mary and Joseph, and the baby lying in the manger. They explained what they had heard and seen and everyone who heard it was astonished. As for Mary, she treasured all the things she heard and thought about them. The shepherds went back to the fields glorifying and praising God.

Prayer

Father, we are filled with joy at the birthday of your Son. Help us to be welcoming to everyone at this time, spreading your light through our celebration of Christmas. Amen.

Share

Talk about some of the ways of welcoming Jesus at Christmas.

Sing

"The light of Christ is come into the world"
"Emmanuel, Emmanuel. His name is called Emmanuel"
"Away in a manger"

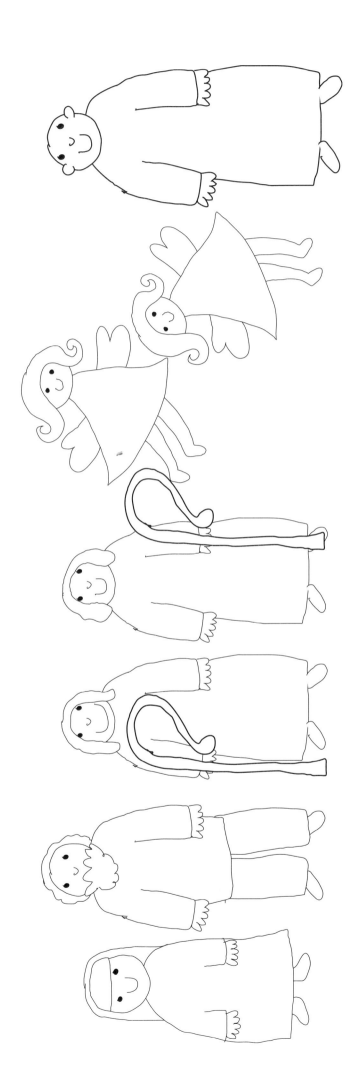

The Holy Family of Jesus, Mary and Joseph

The 1st Sunday of Christmas

1. Introduction to the theme of the day

"Holy Family!"

Aim: To try to understand that we need to be able to rely on each family member.

Leader's reflection: Our families are based on relationships. These may be of choice or by accident of birth. These relationships best mirror the Holy Family when they are loving and reliable. Our children should be able to rely on the love within their families and, conversely, they too should learn the need to be reliable, trustworthy. You will need to talk this week about the Holy Family as refugees. The children may have their own ideas about asylum seekers and refugees and some will be part of our parish communities. Take time to talk this through with them.

2. We arrive
We sit in a circle ready to listen to the Gospel.
Has anyone anything they would like to tell us about last week's Family Sheet?

Focus
In the centre a lighted candle is placed. Some pictures of rich and poor people can be put around the candle as a focus for today's theme.

Gospel: Matthew 2:13-15. 19-23
Read from the Lectionary or Children's Lectionary.

3. We respond
What is the Gospel asking of us?
Work in age groups if appropriate, then come together as a group to end the session.

Young ones

Story: A strange new country

Marta had joined their class in school, but Year 1 were puzzled. Marta did not say anything and she liked best to sit with her back to the wall in the library corner.

Their teacher explained that Marta did not speak any English and she had been badly frightened in her own country. Her house had been burned down and some of her friends had been killed. Marta's family had escaped to England with nothing but a few special treasures in a bag carried by her father.

"Perhaps Marta likes to sit in the library corner because she feels safest there. We shall all be very kind and smile and wait until Marta understands that we care about her. Do your best to look after her."

The children in Year 1 did their very best. They tried to get Marta to play, they asked her to sit with them, they talked to her (their teacher said that was how she would learn English).

One day Jack was talking about his family. He had brought photographs to show everyone of their holiday in Jamaica. Marta came close. Jack showed her the photo he was holding.

"That's my dad, that's my little brother and that's my mum with the big hat."

"Family," said Marta.

It was her first word in school. Year 1 were very pleased.

How do you think Marta felt about her family? What do you think she felt about being in England? What helped to make her feel safe? What makes you feel safe?

Juniors

Story: Joseph trusts in God and leads the way

The Holy Family of Joseph, Mary and Jesus became a refugee family in our Bible story today. They left their country because they were not safe at home and Joseph trusted God to look after them. Can you put yourself in Mary's shoes?

Mary was hurriedly packing as much as she could, wrapping clothes inside blankets, remembering the precious gifts she had been given by those wise men. She must not forget food... what could she take, how much could they carry?

Joseph had said they must go, and go now, quickly. God had told him that they were not safe here any longer, so they should escape to Egypt.

Mary was not entirely sure where Egypt was or how long the journey would be. She knew that she had no home here any more and that she had no home in Egypt either.

But she had Joseph, she could rely on him, and she had the baby to keep safe.

It was a long journey. Looking back, all Mary could really remember was the tiredness and the fear. She seemed to be always looking over her shoulder.

Was anyone coming? How long before they would be safe from pursuit?

But Joseph was there, sharing her fears and her hopes for the future, loving her and the child. She relied on him, just as the child relied on her for warmth, food and protection.

Think about your family. Who do you rely on? Who relies on you? We trust people to do what they say they will do, to be trustworthy.
Think about your parish family and your school family in the same way.

4. Activity

Young ones and Juniors

Using the template, draw the Holy Family leaving Bethlehem. Find the way for the Holy Family to reach safety in Egypt and colour the picture.

Think hard about the decision Joseph had to take to keep his family safe. Can you act out the story?

Tips for learning difficulties

Talk through the activities. Enlarge the picture to colour.

5. We come together

Parents can be invited to join in at this stage.

Focus

Parents and children may gather together around the focus of the children's work and the open Bible.

Gospel

Act out the Gospel – as practised during the activity time.

Prayer

We remember all those families forced to leave their own countries in fear. Give them people who can be trusted to help them. Help us to be trustworthy, always ready to help other people especially those in our own family. Amen.

Share

The work and ideas from the activities.

Sing

"Kum ba ya"

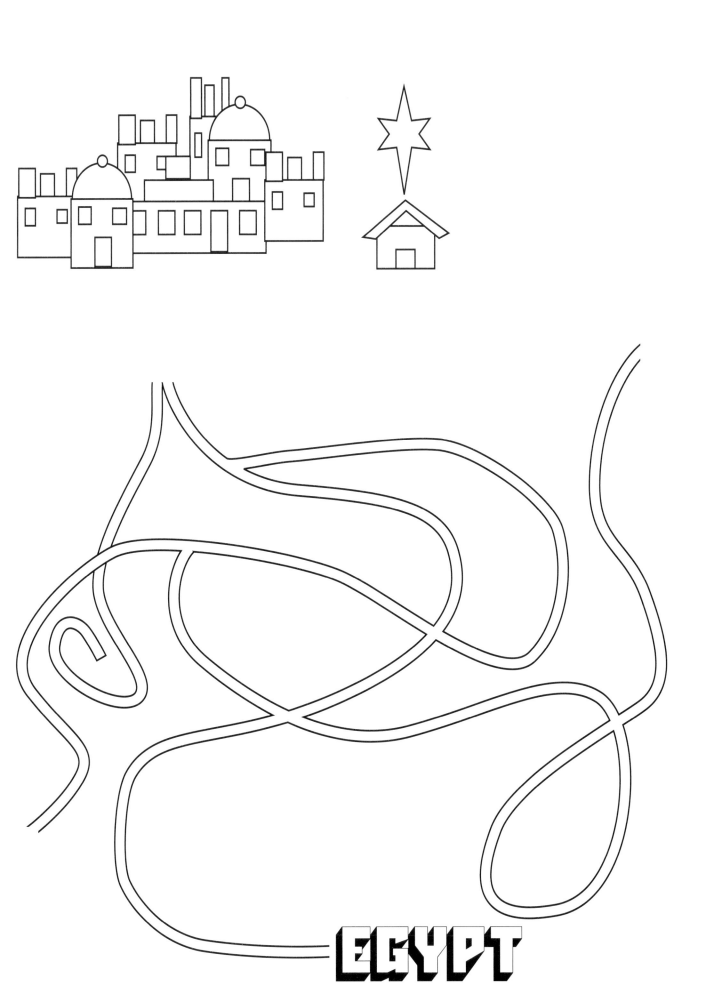

EGYPT

Solemnity of Mary, Mother of God

1. Introduction to the theme of the day

> ## "Mary treasures everything in her heart"

Aim: To reflect on Mary as the perfect model for the disciple.

Leader's reflection: Mary is often described as the perfect disciple. Her whole life was spent in loving service of her God: listening always to his will for her and willing to respond even when what God asks seems to make little sense. When God invites her into the wondrous work of the incarnation of Christ, her first response is puzzlement: how can this be? Yet, even without a clear answer, she agrees: "Let what you have said be done to me."

This willingness to take the risk of acting comes from her disposition of listening; of contemplating; pondering things deeply in her heart. It is from this depth of faith, this storing up of insights and experiences, that she was able to discern what was genuinely of God, and to act freely and generously in what was asked of her.

This is a model that all disciples can develop within themselves: building up a practice of pondering the word of God; reflecting on experience in the light of that word; and acting in love and obedience to the fruits of that contemplation.

2. We arrive

We sit in a circle ready to listen to the Gospel.

We wish everyone a Happy New Year!

Today is what we call the Octave of Christmas: the eighth day after Christmas Day. In Jewish tradition, this is the day a baby boy would be given his name, so we remember the Holy Name of Jesus today. And, at the beginning of a New Year, we pray that the world might have the peace that Jesus came to give.

Focus

White cloth, candle, Bible open at today's Gospel, a picture of Mary holding Jesus.

Gospel: Luke 2:16-21

Read from the Children's Lectionary or Bible.

3. We respond
What is the Gospel asking of us?

As the group is likely to be small this week, one story is offered with a variety of discussion ideas, and activities. Choose the ones most suitable for your group.

Young ones and Juniors
Story: Benjamin and the baby

Benjamin was excited. His father had promised that tonight he could go out with him to watch the sheep. This was the first time and Benjamin felt very grown up. The night was dark and cold and the stars shone bright and clear. Benjamin enjoyed listening to the stories the older shepherds told about the constellations. After a while, his father said he could sleep and he would wake him to take his turn watching the sheep in a couple of hours.

But, just as Benjamin drifted off to sleep, he felt a massive tingling all through his body. He jumped up wondering what on earth had happened and looked up to see magnificent lights in the sky. From the expressions on the other shepherds' faces, Benjamin knew that this had not happened to them before and joined them staring at the heavens.

To his amazement, he heard singing – the most beautiful voices making music that seemed to fill him right up with the sound. They sang of a baby that had been born in the nearby town of Bethlehem, and how this was a great king, but that they would find him lying in a manger.

As the singing faded away, Benjamin wondered if it had been real but knew that all he wanted to do was to go and find this baby. The shepherds agreed that some of them must go, and others should stay to keep the sheep safe. Benjamin and his father were among those to go, but, before he went, Benjamin asked if he could take a gift and chose one of the lambs that he had reared at home. Benjamin tucked it under his arm telling the lamb that it was going to see a king.

When they arrived, Benjamin was just a little disappointed. He had expected a palace and lots of gold but found a stable and, just as the angels had said, a baby wrapped up in swaddling clothes and fast asleep in a manger.

What he couldn't explain was that the baby seemed to have a glow about him, and the lady, who Benjamin guessed was his mother, looked very happy as she welcomed these strangers into her temporary home.

The shepherds told their news and the mother seemed to come alight with joy. She told them that even before the baby had been born she had known that her baby was special; well, even more special than all babies are! And to think, she had said, that angels had shared the good news of his birth with the shepherds! That was truly wonderful.

After the shepherds had spent time talking to Mary and Joseph, they got ready to go back to their fields. Benjamin came forward and shyly gave the lamb to the baby's mother.

"I looked after this lamb myself," he said. "It was very small, but I fed it and kept it warm, and... I'd like the baby to have it. I know it's not much use, but ..."

"A lamb is a lovely present!" said Mary. "We can use the wool to make cosy clothes for the baby, thank you."

As they left, Benjamin looked back and saw Mary looking fondly at her baby. She glanced up and caught his gaze.

"I hope you'll meet my son again," she said, "when he is bigger."

Young ones

Did anyone play a shepherd in their Nativity Play? What did they have to do? Why were the shepherds important in the Christmas story? (Prompt: they were the first people to hear the Good News of Jesus' birth – and did something about it!)
Would they like to have been shepherds in Jesus' time?
(Talk about the cold, fear of wolves, etc.)

Juniors

The shepherds heard the song of the angels and went to find the baby. They heard a message from God – what did they do? What did they find? Was it what they expected? What made them believe that what they heard was right, that this was the Saviour the angels had promised?
How do they think Mary reacted? What might have puzzled her, or given her food for thought when the shepherds came to see her son?

4. Activity

Young ones

Using the template page, colour in the picture and add some shepherds. Encourage them to talk about the characters and the Christmas story as we have heard it so far. How does it help us to know that Jesus is special: the son of Mary and the Son of God?

Juniors

Invite the children to colour in the picture but also to add some of the things that Mary might have wondered about: Gabriel's message; why did they have to travel all the way to Bethlehem; why did angels appear to the shepherds; what did their message mean; what would her son become; would he be happy; was his life in danger and so on.

Talk about how Mary would have thought of all these things during all the years that Jesus was growing up, trying to understand what God was doing through him.

Tips for learning difficulties

Talk about the characters in the Christmas story in relation to the child's own family. Perhaps the child or helper could draw a similar picture using their own family and compare it to the Holy Family.

5. We come together

Parents can be invited to join in at this stage.

Focus

Light the candle. Invite those gathered to become still, to look at the candle and think about the start of a New Year.

Gospel

In the Gospel, we hear that, after the shepherds had heard the angels sing about the Good News of Jesus' birth, they hurried to Bethlehem to see if the message was true. There they found Mary, Joseph and the baby Jesus lying in a manger, just as they had been told.

For Mary, these were yet more signs of how special her son was and, like any mother, she treasured all the wonderful things that people said about her son. Unlike other mothers, though, Mary's son had a special destiny; he was the Son of the Most High. Mary could not possibly understand all this at the time, but held all these things in her heart and pondered them over the years to come.

Prayer

(Use this prayer or make up your own prayer based on the "Share" ideas below.)
Hail Mary, full of grace, the Lord is with thee.
Blessed art thou among women
and blessed is the fruit of thy womb, Jesus.
Holy Mary, Mother of God,
pray for us sinners now
and at the hour of our death. Amen.

Share

Mary has a special place for Christians. Because she said yes to God, the great work of salvation could begin, not as people thought, by a great warrior coming into the world, but with the birth of a tiny baby. This baby needed all the love every baby needs, all the care and guidance that a mother can give.

God placed a great trust in Mary when he gave her his Son to care for. Mary listened to God and did all she could to ensure that his plan could be fulfilled. Even when things seemed to become dark and dangerous, she believed that God would honour his promise to her and to the world.

Sing

"Oh Mary, when our God chose you"
"While shepherds watched their flocks by night"
"O little town of Bethlehem"

2nd Sunday after Christmas

The 2nd Sunday of Christmas

1. Introduction to the theme of the day

"Adopted!"

Aim: To develop the children's understanding of their place within the loving family of God.

Leader's reflection: St Paul tells us that God chose us before the world was made to be his adopted children. Today's Gospel tells us that: "to all who did accept him, he gave power to become children of God".
As we cannot help loving our children despite their failings, so God cannot help loving: it is what God is.

2. We arrive

We sit in a circle ready to listen to the Gospel. Has anyone anything they would like to tell us about last week's Family Sheet?

Focus

The Gospels and a lighted candle.

Gospel: John 1:1-18

Read from the Lectionary or Children's Lectionary.

3. We respond
What is the Gospel asking of us?

Work in age groups if appropriate and come together as a community to end the session.

Young ones
Story: Charlie's new family

Charlie (whose name was really Charlotte) had come to live with Mr and Mrs Ellis. Her little brother, Dewi, had come too. Life had been very difficult for Charlie. Her dad was in the army and her mum had left home so long ago that Charlie could hardly remember her. She'd been living with her gran, but Gran had got too old to cope with two small children. Dewi didn't talk much and when he got upset he threw things about and screamed.

Charlie had got to know the Ellises quite well; she called them Auntie and Uncle, although she knew that they were not really her own family. She'd been out with them and they'd come to Gran's house and she'd even been to stay with them for a week or so at a time, but now she and Dewi were coming to stay for good.

When bedtime of that first day came, Dewi was difficult. He wanted Gran and he didn't know how to tell anyone so he started screaming. He wouldn't drink his milk and when he was in his cot he wouldn't lie down. Charlie felt very unhappy; she didn't want to upset Auntie and Uncle, and Gran had told her to be good and look after her brother.

Auntie said, "Well, I think what Dewi needs is to be here with you and me. Let's bring him here and we'll all sit on your bed, have a cuddle and look at some stories."

"He doesn't mean to be naughty," said Charlie. "He's probably missing Gran."

"Don't you worry," said Auntie. "He'll soon learn that we love him and however he feels we'll go on loving him."

When they were all snuggled together on Charlie's bed, Dewi calmed down. Charlie held his bottle of milk and he drank it. His eyes started to close.

"There," said Auntie. "In a minute or two we'll pop him in his cot."

Then she looked at Charlie,

"I'm so glad that you've come here to stay. I've really looked forward to having you with us."

Charlie didn't know what to say. In the end she said,

"I'm glad I'm here because I know that I feel safe with you and Uncle, but I feel a bit mixed up because I'm used to being with Gran and I love her."

"I expect that's how Dewi feels too, mixed up. Well, we're part of your family now and you and Dewi and Gran are part of our family. We've made a whole new family together. We shall all look after each other. Now, I'd better get this brother of yours into bed. Snuggle down, call me if you need anything and God bless."

Charlie slid under her duvet and was soon fast asleep.

Have you ever been to stay with someone without your mum or dad?
Sometimes children have to go to live with other families who are not their own. Can you think why? Sometimes they stay with those families for good. We call this being adopted. **(Tread carefully here if you don't know the history of the children in the group.)**
God "adopts" us: we are not his sons and daughters as Jesus is, but God chooses us to be his children and live in his family. God cannot help but love us and want the best for us. How can we love him as a part of his family?

Juniors
Discussion around *The Jungle Book* by Kipling.

Do you know the story of Mowgli, the central character in Kipling's *The Jungle Book*?
(See if any of the children can tell you some of the story... They'll almost certainly know it from the film.)

Mowgli knew all the animals of the jungle, the sounds they made, what they ate, where they lived. The animals adopted him and looked after him; he became quite like them. But did Mowgli ever really become one of the animals? How does the story end?

In the Gospel, St John tells us that Jesus is God's only Son. We can't see God, but we know what God is like because Jesus shows us.
St John also says that we can become God's children, part of his family. Why does God want us to be part of his family? How can this happen?
What does becoming one of God's children mean for us?

Let the discussion flow but encourage the children to see that it is the love of God that drives our adoption into his family, that unlike Mowgli and the animals we really become part of this family of love.

4. Activity

Young ones and Juniors

Use the template of a picture of Jesus with group of children.
In the space draw a picture of yourself. Put your name in the space in the sentence. Colour the picture.

Tips for learning difficulties

If using a pencil and colouring presents a problem, have people already cut out to make a circle. Put a photo of the child into the circle.

5. We come together

Parents can be invited to join in at this stage. Take a few moments to be still.

Focus

The children's activity sheets and a lighted candle.

Gospel

Jesus says,
"I came into the world and to those people who accept me I give the power to become the children of God... No one has ever seen God, it is the only Son who is nearest to the Father's heart who has shown us what he is like."

Prayer

Dear God, thank you for coming to the world. We are glad that your love makes us your children. Amen.

Share

Talk about how God has adopted us into his family. We are a family now in the Church.

Sing

"The love of God is truly wonderful"
"He's got the whole world in his hands"

"_____ is a member of God's family."

The Epiphany of the Lord

1. Introduction to the theme of the day

> "Bethlehem: the town where Jesus was revealed to the world"

Aim: To reflect on the fact that Jesus was born in a real place in real time.

Leader's reflection: One of the most wonderful aspects of our faith is the incarnation. This is our belief that God became fully human: the Word was made flesh and lived among us; Jesus is fully human and fully divine.

After two thousand years and living so many hundreds of miles from the places where Jesus lived and breathed, it is often easier for us to focus on the fact that Jesus is divine, someone who may have lived a long time ago but who ultimately is of heaven and far removed from us.

For people who visit the Holy Land, one of the overwhelming aspects of their stay is the fact that they are walking on the very soil upon which Our Lord walked; they are seeing the very scenery that he saw and used in his teaching; they experience something of the way of life that has echoes of that which Jesus would have recognised.

The town of Bethlehem still exists: Manger Square marking the spot where people have traditionally held that Jesus was born. In real buildings set in a real landscape, we have a tangible reminder that Jesus was fully human, born in a simple outbuilding, the fullness of God making his home among his people.

2. We arrive

We sit in a circle ready to listen to the Gospel.

Has anyone anything they would like to tell us about last week's Family Sheet?

Focus

White or gold cloth, candle, Bible open at today's Gospel, a picture of Bethlehem, perhaps from a Christmas card, and a photo of the town as it is today.

Gospel: Matthew 2:1-12

Read from the Lectionary or Children's Lectionary.

3. We respond
What is the Gospel asking of us?

Work in age groups if appropriate. Alternatively, choose the discussion ideas, story and activity most suitable for your group. Come together as a community to end the session.

Young ones

Story: Hassan's big adventure

Hassan was tired. It had been a marvellous adventure but he was ready for it to end. His mother had said that it was a great honour that Caspar had wanted Hassan to come on the expedition and help to look after the camels. The three wise men had kept looking at maps and the stars, always expecting to find a baby king in a grand palace.

As Hassan was not needed for a while by Caspar, he decided to explore the market in this little town of Bethlehem. He saw many different things to buy and watched women choosing the best meat and vegetables for their families' meals but that made him feel lonely and homesick. He spotted a boy about his own age who was minding some sheep and a couple of lambs. The boy stood up and looked at him and smiled.

"Hello," he said. "You're new here, aren't you?" Hassan nodded.

"Would you like some halva? Mum made some today. Here, have some."

Hassan took the halva gratefully. It was getting dark and he was feeling hungry.

"I'm Benjamin," said the boy. Hassan told Benjamin his name and why he was there.

"And the wise men are trying to find out where the new king has been born."

"A new king!" exclaimed Benjamin. "Well, I saw one last week and he wasn't in the palace. The angels told us to go and look in a stable! It was definitely him."

Hassan was amazed that Benjamin had seen angels. "We've been following a star but it disappeared... it was just there and..." And, as he looked up, there was the star they had been following! Benjamin laughed.

"It must be the same king! Angels – and now a star; come on, let's see where it goes!"

Hassan and Benjamin ran through the evening crowds, Benjamin whooping all the way. "Yes, it's going to the same place! Come on, Hassan. Come and see the king!"

They reached the stable and went in. The baby's mother looked up and smiled as she recognised Benjamin. Hassan felt shy but Benjamin drew him close to the manger. "Look," he said, and just as Hassan looked over the edge, the baby opened his eyes and smiled at him. "He's just learnt to do that," said Mary, proudly.

At that, there was a great commotion outside. Hassan turned and saw Caspar peering through the door.

"Here he is!" Hassan cried excitedly. "Here's the king we came to see!"

And at his words, the rest of the party came in and fell to their knees in wonder.

They had come all this long way, and here in a simple stable in the middle of a small town was the king they had come to see.

What do you remember about Hassan's story? Who had he come to see? What had guided him? Who had come with him?

Juniors

Story: The town of Bethlehem

The town of Bethlehem is a place of pilgrimage for people from all around the world. **Do the children know anyone who has ever been there?** Find pictures of contemporary Bethlehem to share with the children, of Manger Square and some of the pilgrims who have made their way there. If you can find pictures of what Bethlehem might have looked like in biblical times, use them to see what has changed and what has stayed the same. **Think about why buildings are built as they are** (to protect from heat and strong sunlight).

There are increasing numbers of craft items from Bethlehem, often made from olive wood. If you have some examples, let the children look at them and handle them. **Talk about the age of olive trees, of how hard the wood is and how difficult it is to carve, but how it lasts a very long time.**

If appropriate, you may want to talk about the wall that is being built around the town and think about how it affects the people who live there. **What must it be like to have to go through checkpoints to go to hospital or work?** Talk about how the Muslim and Christian families largely live in peace with each other, with respect for the holy ground where Jesus was born.

4. Activity

Young ones

Each child can be given a template of a house to cut out to which they can add windows and doors. The houses can then be pinned to a board to create a collage of Bethlehem.

Juniors

Some juniors may want to make houses but others could be invited to add details such as people (in traditional Middle Eastern dress), donkeys, sheep, market stalls and so on. These can be added to the collage.

A large star could be hung over the collage, perhaps with the title: **Bethlehem – Birthplace of our Saviour!**

Tips for learning difficulties

Colour or paint the background to the town (a hairdryer may be needed to dry paint), or help with colouring, or use scraps of material to give texture to the scene.

5. We come together

Parents can be invited to join in at this stage.

Focus

Light the candle. Invite those gathered to become still, to look at the collage and think about today's feast.

Gospel

In today's Gospel, we hear how a prophecy made by the prophet Micah many years before the birth of Jesus came true. Bethlehem was not an important town, but it was the place where Jesus was born and where the wise men came and found him. They had followed a star for many miles, and thought that they would find the new king in a palace. But God chose to come into the world in a stable in a small insignificant town in a small country in the Middle East.

Prayer

Lord Jesus, a star guided the wise men to Bethlehem, where they saw your glory. Guide us to see your light and your truth and help us to follow you more faithfully in all we do and say. Amen.

Share

We have been thinking about how wonderful it is that our God whose home is in heaven should come to a small town in the Middle East to be born. Bethlehem is still a real place that people can go and visit (name anyone who has been there) and pray at the exact spot where it is believed that the stable stood, where Jesus was born.

In prayer in that place we are linked over 2000 years to that first Epiphany when the baby Jesus was revealed to the world as the new king, and, even more wondrous, the Son of God.

Sing

"We three kings"
"O little town of Bethlehem"

The Baptism of the Lord

1. Introduction to the theme of the day

> " **This is my Son, the Beloved** "

Aim: To learn about the baptism of the Lord. Jesus, the Son of God, came to carry out God the Father's work. The Father anointed his beloved Son, Jesus, with the Holy Spirit and with power to bring healing and peace to all the nations.

Leader's reflection: Christ, the perfect image of God. When someone believes in us we feel better and we actually do better when more is expected of us. The Father believed in his Son, Jesus. He was confident that Jesus' life would be fruitful. When we were baptised, the Father had similar hopes and expectations that his life in us would bear fruit. He believes in us. Our task, simply, is to appreciate that belief and allow it to bear fruit in us. Baptism is the sign of God's free gift of his love for us — once and for all. While we continue to accept his gifts of grace, especially in the sacraments of the Eucharist and Reconciliation, we will steadily grow in union with Jesus and our own lives will bear the fruits of the Holy Spirit. Our heavenly Father believes in us as he believes in his Son. He hopes that each one of us will achieve our true purpose in life. He loves us personally. The difference between Christ and ourselves is not the Father's love for us but our ability to accept that love. He has great expectations for what he would like to do through us because we have been baptised with the same baptism which Jesus received.

2. We arrive

We sit in a circle ready to listen to the Gospel.
Has anyone anything they would like to tell us about last week's Family Sheet?

Focus

Symbols of baptism — water, oil, white garment, baptismal candle.

Gospel: Matthew 3:13-17

Read from the Lectionary or Children's Lectionary.

3. We respond

What is the Gospel asking of us?

Work in age groups if appropriate, then come together to end the session.
Who has been to a baptism? What happens? Who gets baptised? Do we baptise our pets? Only human beings get baptised. It is a special gift which God has given only to us. When Jesus was baptised, he was showing us that he is human just like you or me.

Young ones

A play: Come to the baptism party

John baptised Jesus in the River Jordan. When Jesus came up out of the water, the Spirit of God came down like a dove and rested on him. A voice said from heaven, "This is my Son. I love him very much."

Talk about the Gospel:

1. Where was Jesus baptised?
2. Who baptised him?
3. What relation was he to him?
4. Why did the people come to the River Jordan to be baptised?
5. When were you baptised?

Juniors

A play: Jesus is baptised

John the Baptist was baptising people in the River Jordan. When Jesus asked him for baptism John felt unworthy and embarrassed. "You should be baptising me," he said. Jesus answered, "This is God's plan for me — we will do it this way." As he stood up in the water the Holy Spirit settled on him like a dove and a voice from heaven said, "This is my own dear Son whom I love very much."

Talk about the Gospel:

1. What sign appeared so that John knew that Jesus was the Son of God?
2. Why did Jesus come for baptism? (He does not need to be cleansed of sin, but is baptised to fulfil God's saving plan. Jesus is the Son of God; the Spirit of God rests on him: he will begin his ministry with the Father's authority and love.)
3. When and where were you baptised?

Role-play a baptism

Use the Rite of Baptism. You will need a narrator, priest, parents and baby doll, godparents and congregation.

Sing and clap "Walk in the light" or another song with a baptismal theme. Encourage the children to talk about their own or family baptisms they have attended. Talk about baptism as it is celebrated at the Easter Vigil.

Role-play a baptism

Dress a doll in a white garment: clean and blameless.
A jug of water: washes us, helps us grow.
Oil: to give strength.
Baptismal candle: the light of Christ coming into our life.
Leader talks through and explains the ceremony of baptism, involving the children where possible.
Sing and clap "Walk in the light", or another "light" song.

4. Activity

Young ones

Using the candle template, decorate it with your name and write "I was baptised on..."
Ask someone at home to help you fill in the date.

Juniors

Cut out circles of card, 7cm in diameter. Write a prayer around the edge: "How I can show Jesus' light to others." Make a slit in the centre and place a votive candle into the card.

Tips for learning difficulties

Using the candle template, colour the flame, or use glitter glue, and write your name on the candle.

5. We come together

Parents can be invited to join in at this stage.

Focus

White garment, bowl of water, oil, baptismal candle to be lit.

Gospel

This Sunday we leave Christmastide behind and look ahead to a new year. Jesus is leaving behind his old life and starting a new one, teaching people about God. He wants to mark the change and so goes to John the Baptist and asks to be baptised. John realises that here is the one that he has told people about: the one whose sandal John does not feel worthy to undo.

Jesus insists and, as he emerges from the water, the Spirit of God comes upon him and God declares that Jesus is his beloved Son.

Prayer

Lord Jesus, you were baptised and God said you were his Son. Thank you for sharing your life with us in our own baptism. Help us to grow strong in faith and love, and be worthy of the name Christian. Amen.

Share

The work from the activities. The decorated candles and some prayers from the older ones may be read.

Sing

"All over the world the Spirit is moving"
"The light of Christ"

1st Sunday of Lent

1. Introduction to the theme of the day

> **"The desert is a place of silence and solitude, a place which we can all make for ourselves when we need to"**

Aim: We begin Lent – a time to get ourselves ready for the great feast of Easter. In today's session, find ways of allowing God to get close. We invite Jesus into our lives.

Leader's reflection: Genesis tells us that sin enters the world through disobedience to God. Adam and Eve, in eating the forbidden fruit, are ashamed of themselves and afraid of God. They hide from God. God searches for them and they are banished from the garden into the wasteland. We live in a world where survival is a struggle; where relationships are fragile and where faithfulness to God's word will always be a challenge.

The promise of salvation enters the world through one man's obedience: Jesus of Nazareth. Like God in the Garden of Eden he comes to look for those who have hidden themselves from God. "I have come to seek out and to save the lost." Jesus is the saviour. Before he begins his mission Jesus is faced with a series of temptations in the wilderness. He uses the power of God to confront the devil. By Jesus' obedience to God we are saved.

2. We arrive

We sit in a circle ready to listen to the Gospel.
Has anyone anything they would like to tell us about their Family Sheet last week?

Focus
Light a candle. If possible, make a small sand dune on a tray, and use this to support the candle. Use purple fabric and purple items.

Gospel: Matthew 4:1-11
Read from the Lectionary or Children's Lectionary.

3. We respond
What is the Gospel asking of us?
Work in age groups if appropriate, then come together to end the session.

Young ones

Story: Peace and quiet

Henry was a small brown honeybee. He lived with his friends in a big hive at the bottom of the garden. He enjoyed flying around with the other bees and visiting all the flowers. He was a very happy bee.

One day when he was out flying amongst the foxgloves, he met another bee.

The bee was called Bruno. Bruno was bigger than Henry; he was furry with a black and yellow coat. Henry had never seen a bee like him before.

"Where do you live?" he asked Bruno.

"Come and see," buzzed Bruno, and off they flew together.

Bruno was a bumblebee. He lived by himself in a little nest amongst the dandelions. His home was very pretty and very cosy, but soon Henry noticed something else.

As they sat outside drinking their nectar juice, he noticed how very, very quiet it was. It was so quiet that Henry could hear the breeze ruffling through the dandelion leaves, and he could hear the birds singing way above in the apple tree, and, if he listened very carefully, he could even hear the dew dropping off the top of the grass stalks.

"This is so quiet," whispered Henry. "In the hive, the other bees are buzzing all the time, you cannot hear anything except for the buzzing. But here it is so nice to be able to hear the breeze ruffling through the dandelion leaves, and the birds singing way above in the apple tree, even the dew dropping off the top of the grass stalks." Bruno smiled quietly to himself and buzzed a little tune. "I like it too," he said.

Jesus went into the desert so that he could talk to God. The desert is very quiet and Jesus could concentrate here. He could think about his Father, God. Talk with the children about what it is like in the desert: quiet, empty, no houses, no trees, no electricity etc.

Juniors

Story: The life of Charles de Foucauld

Charles de Foucauld was a French nobleman, a soldier and a Jew, born in 1858. He was a successful man, but not a happy one, and he spent his early days searching for something to give meaning to his life. He read of the simple life led by Jesus of Nazareth and determined to follow him. At the age of 28 he converted to Christianity. He wanted to imitate Jesus as far as possible and so he decided to be a monk in the poorest monastery that he could find – a Trappist monastery at the top of a snowy mountain. After some time, he found even this life too comfortable, so he became a hermit and began to live in a shed at the bottom of a monastery garden. In 1905, Charles moved to a central part of the Sahara Desert. The desert was very bleak and inhospitable but Charles remembered the time that Jesus had spent in the desert and decided he wanted to spend his whole life there.

Although everybody else thought that he was crazy, he went to live in the desert and stayed there for nine years.

Charles' legacy to the Church was the foundation of an order of monks and nuns called the Little Brothers and Sisters of Jesus. These people live together in poor communities trying to imitate the life of Jesus. They take very ordinary and humble jobs – in factories or hospitals, as cleaners or care assistants – and live and work with the poorest of people. Although they do not talk to people in sermons, or preach to them about God, they try to show Jesus' life by the lives they lead themselves.

Another suitable story:

The Island of the Blue Dolphins by Scott O'Dell is a book based on a true story of an Indian girl who was abandoned on a fierce and desolate island off the coast of California and survived alone for eighteen years.

Before he started his ministry, Jesus went into the desert to pray. The desert is a very lonely place, very bleak and dangerous. There is a tradition throughout the Bible of people looking for God in the emptiness of the desert. While Jesus was there, he resolved the way he was going to live his life from then on.

During Lent we are given a new opportunity to resolve to live our lives in a different way, following Jesus more closely.

Find some pictures of desert landscapes – sandy, stony etc. Spend some time looking at these and discussing how it might feel to be alone in such a place. Invite the children to make their own desert by sitting in a space on their own and closing their eyes.

Encourage them to think about the 40 days of Lent ahead. Invite them to think of three ways in which they want to live their lives differently. Use the template to record these.

4. Activity

Young ones

If you have access to a sand tray or plastic sheet and a sackful of sand, a desert can be made. Use a doll to show Jesus praying, a few pebbles for boulders and twigs for brush. Otherwise, using the template of the desert, mount it onto stiff card and make a large picture together. Stick on sand and small stones. Add a figure of Jesus to the scene.

Juniors

Make a collage of desert landscapes using pictures cut from magazines and newspapers. News items on conflicts in the world are a likely source. Also advertisements for four-wheel-drive vehicles, chocolate bars etc. Has the desert landscape changed much since Jesus' day? How would you prepare if you were to go out into the desert today?

Tips for learning difficulties

Children with learning difficulties might enjoy running their hands through sand, gravel and pebbles and experiencing the differing sensations. They could compare the dryness and roughness of these materials with the wetness and smoothness of water.

5. We come together

Parents can be invited to join in at this stage.

Focus

Our candle is lit; purple fabric during Lent; desert pictures, desert scenes.

Gospel

The Spirit led Jesus into the desert to be tempted by the devil. After spending 40 days and nights without food, Jesus was hungry. Then the devil came to him and said, "If you are God's Son, order these stones to turn into bread."
But Jesus answered, "Scripture says, 'Man cannot live on bread alone, but needs every word that God speaks.'"

Prayer

Sit in a circle around the candle very quietly. Encourage the children to listen to the quietness first of all, reminding them that a desert is usually a very quiet place, and then to listen to all the sounds and noises in the room, and outside the room. When they are ready, invite them to thank God or to pray for the sounds they can hear, e.g. Thank you, God, for the wind blowing outside; We pray for all the people who are driving today that God will keep them safe on their journeys. Juniors could respond to each prayer with the Taizé chant "Wait for the Lord".

Share

Share the work from the activities.

Sing

"Be still for the presence of the Lord"
"Wait for the Lord"

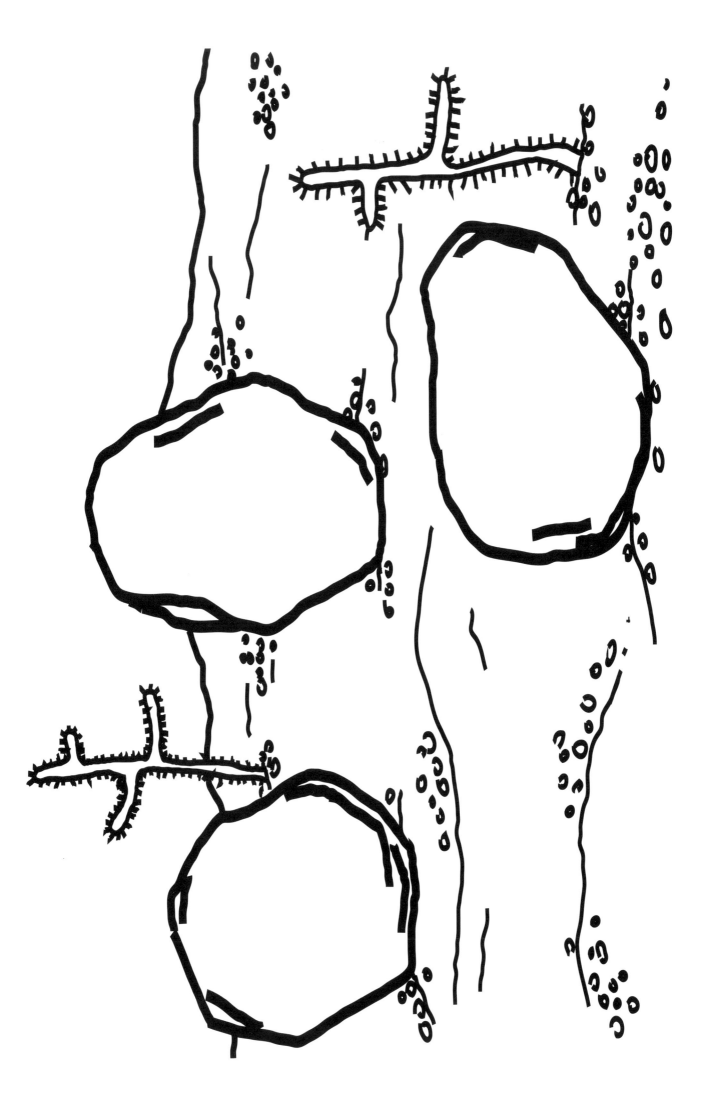

2nd Sunday of Lent

1. Introduction to the theme of the day

> **"Jesus shows his closest friends who he really is. Who do we show ourselves to?"**

Aim: To help the children understand that Jesus showed his true self to his closest friends. Who do we show ourselves to? God knows our deepest thoughts. Meet him in our own private space.

Leader's reflection: Life is described as a journey. Although we know the beginning and the end it also involves a search. We have to discover the paths that lead us to what we seek. Some lead us to dead ends, but we learn that it is important to keep going. The call of Abraham, the father of God's chosen people, meant a complete change of direction, leaving his country and family home. He travels hopefully, rooted in the conviction that God's purposes are being furthered.

Jesus changed direction when he left Nazareth to work as a wandering prophet. As his ministry develops Jesus becomes increasingly aware that to carry out his Father's mission will bring him face to face with a violent death.

Jesus did not face this knowledge alone. The story of the transfiguration enables Jesus to make the journey to Jerusalem in the declared love of the Father. Jesus is the one who is to suffer but he is named and owned by the Father. We are all directed to listen to him. We are helped to make difficult decisions, knowing that we are loved and supported. In the death of Christ, God demonstrated the extremes of his love. It helps us to travel hopefully.

2. We arrive

We sit in a circle ready to listen to the Gospel.
Has anyone anything they would like to tell us about their Family Sheet last week?

Focus

Light a candle. If possible use spotlights or torches reflecting off a white background to light up the area around the candle. Use purple fabric.

Gospel: Matthew 17:1-9

Read the Gospel using the Lectionary or Children's Lectionary.

3. We respond
What is the Gospel asking of us?

Work in age groups if appropriate, then come together to end the session.

Young ones

Story: The unhappy caterpillar

Catherine was a caterpillar. She was brown and very hairy, and very wrinkly. She lived in the cabbage leaves at the bottom of the garden, and she was very unhappy. "I am so ugly," she would sigh. "I am brown and hairy and wrinkly."

She would gaze at the birds in the sky high above her. "I wish I was blue and yellow like a bird," she sighed.

She watched the bright red ladybirds running around on the leaves about her. "I wish I was bright shiny red like a ladybird," she sighed.

She watched the bright orange goldfish shimmering in the pond. "Oh how I wish I was gold and could shimmer for everyone to see me." But she couldn't. She was just a brown, hairy, wrinkly caterpillar.

One day, after she had eaten a lot of cabbage, she felt very sleepy. She wove herself a little nest and she settled into it, and she slept, and she slept, and she slept. She slept for a very long time.

When she woke up she felt very strange inside. She felt all glittery and shimmery and excited. She stretched herself out and she stretched and she stretched and she stretched! She stretched much further than she had ever stretched before. To her amazement, as she stretched, she became blue and yellow and bright, bright, red, and glittery, shimmery gold. She had turned into a butterfly. "Oh look!" she gasped. "I was beautiful inside after all!"

Use a large ball – a football, a spacehopper or exercise ball is ideal. Ask the children to describe the outside of the ball – round, shiny, colour, pattern etc. – then ask them what it is like on the inside of the ball – dark, empty (there are no correct answers). The person that we are on the outside does not always show what we are really feeling inside. You are going to think about your outsides and your insides. The leader might start, "On the outside I have a happy face; on the inside I am excited because I am going to my mum's house for tea this afternoon."

Juniors

Story: St Thérèse of Lisieux

Jesus shows his closest friends who he really is, but tells them not to tell other people. The person that we are on the outside does not always show what we are really like inside. Today we are going to think about both – our outside person and our inside person. How do they fit together?

When we read the lives of the saints, we can usually only see them from the outside. We have to try to work out, from what they said and did, what they were like on the inside. St Thérèse of Lisieux was a girl who was born in France in the nineteenth century. At the age of 15 she became a nun in an enclosed order. She died at the age of 24. The life that Thérèse lived does not seem to be very special, but what makes her so special for us is her autobiography. Thérèse wrote down the story of her own life from the inside. In it she tells all about her "inside" person. She tells us how much she loved God, but more importantly how much God loved her. She tells us that she lived her life just by trusting God and letting him love her.

Although the life she lived was very humble and hidden, as a result of her book she is now a very popular and famous saint, and she has been made the patron saint of France. Her book is called *The Story of a Soul*. Although it is difficult in places, it is well worth reading.

Another suitable story:

Skellig by David Almond describes the meeting of Michael, Mina and an angel whom they find in Michael's garage. As they begin to share with each other some of the secret difficulties in their lives, their friendship grows.

4. Activity

Young ones

Using the template of two figures draw an outside and inside picture of themselves. The children will begin to understand that people have feelings which they do not always show.

Juniors

Use the template of the cube. On one side, the children should draw six "sides" of themselves which are public, e.g. brother, friend, good at sports etc. On the other side they should draw six private faces, e.g. scared of the dark, child carer, hate cabbage etc. Nobody else will see this side. They should then fold it into a cube so that the private faces are inside.

God knows all about that inside space, and it is often here that we find it easiest to talk to him. Spend some time this week quietly with God, talking with him about these six secret faces.

Tips for learning difficulties

Children can use larger cube templates, ready cut and scored. If pre-warned, carers could provide photographs for use on the outside of the cube, and a selection of simple pictures depicting happy, sad, excited etc. for the inside.

5. We come together

Parents can be invited to join in at this stage.

Focus

Our candle is lit, purple fabric during Lent, other lights or torches if used.

Gospel

Peter, James and John were with Jesus on a high mountain when Jesus was transfigured. His whole body lit up with shining light. They heard the voice of God saying, "This is my Son whom I love," just as he had spoken when Jesus was baptised. Knowing that God's love was deep inside him, Jesus was able to make the difficult journey to Jerusalem. Jesus knows that he belongs to God, his Father, who will support him all the way.

Prayer

The children can present their pictures/cubes to the group.
Young ones can respond with
Thank you, God, for _____. For the bits we can see and the bits we can't see.
Juniors can respond by adapting the chorus of "We behold the splendour of God" to each individual –
We behold the splendour of God, shining on the face of _____
We behold the splendour of God, shining on the face of us all.

Share

Share the work from the activities.

Sing

"Shine, Jesus, shine"
"We behold the splendour of God"

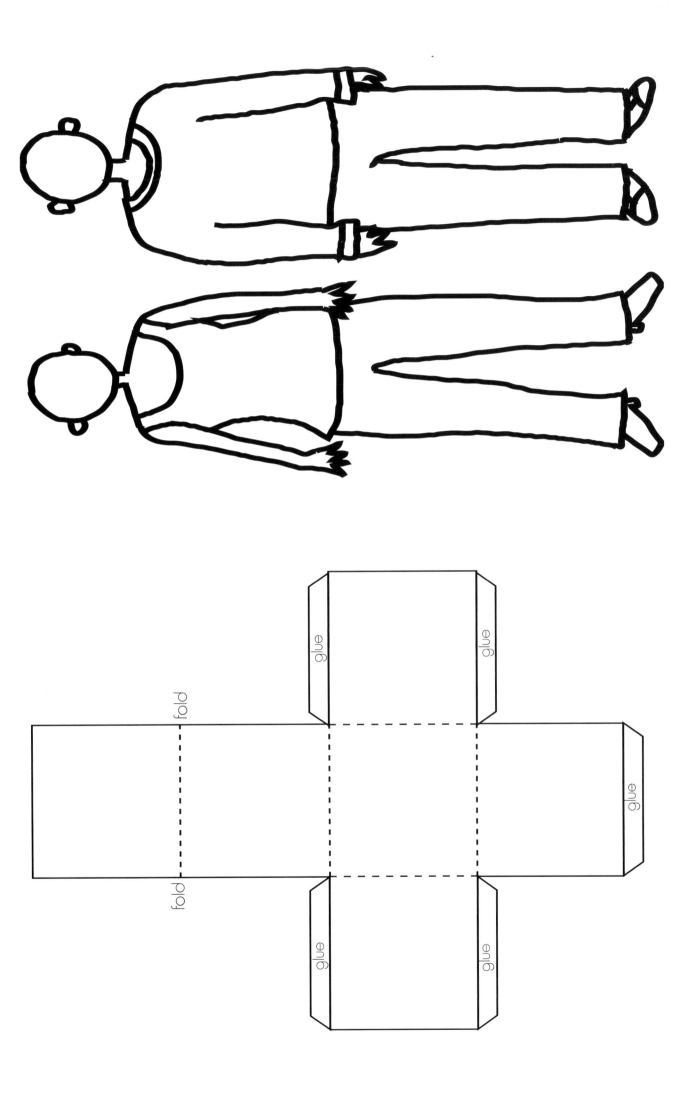

glue

glue

fold

glue

fold

glue

glue

3rd Sunday of Lent

1. Introduction to the theme of the day

> ## "The love of God is poured into our hearts"

Aim: To understand the measure of God's love.

Leader's reflection: In the Gospel story John tells his readers who Jesus is: he is the Messiah and the Saviour of all peoples. First we see Jesus weary and thirsty, a Jew, asking a Samaritan for a drink. The woman is confused, especially when Jesus says that if she knew his identity, she would be asking him for living water. In her conversation with Jesus she sees him as a man of power, calling him "sir", then as a prophet, since he knows of her husbands and her quest for the "right man". They move on to talk about worshipping God in Spirit and truth. Jesus owns up to this woman that he is the Christ. In telling her this he gives himself away to her. He gives her the living water. She does not keep her experience a secret. She turns her experience of Jesus into a message for others. Many believe in Jesus because of her story; many more believe in him when they meet him for themselves. Her past does not hinder her from being a messenger of the Good News.

God's love is endless, like an everlasting fountain of water.

God's love comes to us in unexpected ways.

2. We arrive

We sit in a circle ready to listen to the Gospel. We may have something to discuss from last week's Family Sheet.

Focus

Purple fabric during Lent. A candle, a lava lamp, continually moving. Or use a picture of a famous fountain, or a familiar one in your neighbourhood. Ask them to think about fountains, or other types of water geysers, showers, hosepipes, mountain springs, leaks in a pipe, and so on.

Focus on the idea of water flowing without interruption, spraying out over everything and everyone.

Gospel: John 4:5-42

Read from the Lectionary or the Children's Lectionary.

3. We respond

What is the Gospel asking of us?

Work in age groups if appropriate, then come together to end the session.

Young ones

Can you remember being very thirsty? Perhaps you were on the beach, and it was very hot, and you felt thirsty. You needed a drink! How did your mouth feel? All dry, and then you got a drink and it was lovely.

In today's Gospel, Jesus says that he has a very special kind of drink to give us. What is it? He says, if we drink his special water, we will never be thirsty again. Jesus' water isn't like the water that comes from the tap. What could it be? The special water Jesus wants to give us is God's love.

God's love is like water from a fountain: because it flows and flows and never stops. And it makes us feel wonderful.

Story: Geoffrey's secret friend

Everybody was horrid to Geoffrey. Well, he was a very horrid little boy. He pinched your arm and he broke your toys. Nobody wanted to play with him. Poor Geoffrey! How sad he was. Nobody liked him. He wanted so much to have friends.

Then one day, something very strange happened to Geoffrey. He found a secret friend. When I was young, my secret friend was a huge teddy bear called Sebastian. He wore blue shorts and a scarf round his neck. Sebastian went everywhere I went. He was my best friend. Nobody else could see him. But it didn't matter: I knew he was there, so I was never lonely. But Geoffey's secret friend wasn't like Sebastian. Sebastian was often naughty. It was always his fault when we got into trouble with Mummy. It was his idea to draw on the wall. It was his idea to splash my sister in the bath.

But Geoffrey's secret friend wasn't naughty at all. He was very good, and very kind. He went everywhere Geoffrey went. He loved Geoffrey. Whatever Geoffrey did, however bad and horrid he was, his secret friend still loved him. It made Geoffrey feel all warm inside, knowing that his special friend always loved him.

But Geoffrey's secret friend was no pushover. He didn't laugh, when Geoffrey did something bad. It made him sad. He said to Geoffrey, "You made Robert cry. That wasn't nice. Why did you do that? Don't you think Robert would like you to be nice to him, the way I'm nice to you?" Geoffrey thought about this. Bit by bit he began to change. and began to realise that he didn't pinch anyone any more, and he didn't break their toys. Everyone began to like him. He was so happy.

Geoffrey's secret friend never ever left him. Who do you think he was?

Juniors

Can you ever remember being very thirsty? What was it like? And then you got a drink: what did it feel like?

Your body needs water, or it will get ill, or maybe even die, just the way plants do if you forget to water them. In today's Gospel story, Jesus is hot and tired and thirsty, and he asks a woman for a drink of water. But then he says something very strange: he says he can give her a special kind of water so that she will never be thirsty again.

What could he mean? Jesus isn't talking about ordinary water, the kind that comes out of taps or wells. He's talking about something very special: something that is like water, but invisible. What could it be?

The special water Jesus wants to give the woman is God's love. He is telling her that God's love is like water coming out of a fountain or a stream: it will keep coming and never stop. Like water, God's love makes our hearts feel alive and wonderful, the way water makes your mouth feel refreshed when you're thirsty.

A person without God's love is like a thirsty person: they need something to make life better. Jesus is telling us that God wants to give us his love. All we have to do is to ask him for it. And that is what Jesus is inviting us to do today: reach out and ask God to give us his love.

Story: The power of love

This is a true story. Once, there was a very ugly girl. She wore dull clothes, and she hardly ever smiled. She was always grumpy and rude.

Now, at this girl's school, there were four boys. These boys talked about this girl. One boy, Jack, said: "She can't help it, she was just born like that." Another boy called Tom said: "I bet she could change! I bet if we all pretended she was clever and pretty she would stop being so rude and grumpy." Well, the other boys laughed at him, but they agreed to see if he was right or not.

For the next month, the four boys pretended that the plain girl was very pretty, and they pretended that she was fun, instead of grumpy. At first, the girl was very suspicious.

She thought to herself: "What are they up to?" But the days went on, and the boys were nice to her, and she began to have fun and to smile. And as she started to feel happier, she stopped being rude, and she took more care with her appearance. In fact, she became quite pretty.

Gradually, other boys and girls began to want her as a friend too: she became quite popular. Tom won his bet. Because he and his friends pretended that the girl was lovely, she turned into a lovely person. If you think about it, Tom and his friends pretended to love that plain girl, and their pretend love made her beautiful. In the end, they started to really love her.

Being loved makes everyone beautiful. Feeling loved makes you beautiful.
Do you know anyone sad or dull who needs some love to feel beautiful?

4. Activity

Young ones

Using the fountain template, paste it onto some background card or paper. Make the water flow by pasting slivers of blue, water-coloured sellophane flowing up and out of the statue. Follow the curve down into the water below – a never-ending flow of water. Write the title of the picture "God's fountain of love for ever".

Juniors

Using the fountain template colour the picture and with coloured pencils draw the flow of water up out of the statue and back into the water. Write in words on the streams of water describing God's love for you, e.g. never-ending, drowning, cooling, calming etc. Write the title at the top of the sheet: LORD JESUS, LET ME STEP INTO YOUR FOUNTAIN OF LOVE FOR EVER. Bring the picture "alive" by using a faint shine of glitter on the water.

Tips for learning difficulties

Focus on the fountain of water, imagining running into the water. Children who haven't seen a fountain will probably have seen and been sprayed by a shower, or a hosepipe, and may understand these images. Asking children to pretend that the water is God's love may convey the key idea.

5. We come together

Parents can be invited to join in at this stage.

Focus

As at the start of the session: light the candle – and/or the lava lamp.

Gospel

Jesus said: "You don't know what God wants to give you, and you don't know who is asking you for a drink. If you did, you would ask him for the water that gives life. No one who drinks the water I give will ever be thirsty again. The water I give is like a flowing fountain that gives eternal life."

Prayer

Let's see if we can feel God's love for us right now. We have lit the candle, and now sit quietly, and see what happens.

- Look at the candle flame. It burns and burns and burns. Just watch the flame and feel peaceful.
- Now shut your eyes and think about water. Make a picture of water in your head, water coming out of a fountain, a huge and lovely fountain of warm water flowing and flowing.
- The water is God's love. Imagine yourself stepping inside the fountain, letting all that love fall all over you.
- How does it feel, being covered in love like that?

Children repeat after the leader the following prayer:

Lord Jesus, let me step into the fountain of your love for ever. Amen.

Share

Share the work from the activities.

Sing

"Spirit of the living God, fall afresh on me.
Spirit of the living God, fall afresh on us.
Spirit of the living God, fall afresh on them."

4th Sunday of Lent

1. Introduction to the theme of the day

> ❝Jesus brings light to the world❞

Aim: To know that Jesus changes the way we see the world.

Leader's reflection: John's story in today's Gospel tells how a blind man comes to see the light, both physically and spiritually. When Jesus' disciples first see the blind man, they presume that his affliction is a result of sin. But Jesus sees this roadside beggar who has always inhabited a world of darkness as the one who will display the work of God and point to who Jesus really is. The blind man returns home a new man. He knows that "the man called Jesus" has given him his sight. Others refuse to recognise him. The Pharisees know Jesus but doubt his power to heal especially as in doing so he had not "kept" the sabbath. They become more blind as the formerly blind man grows in insight and identifies Jesus as a prophet. The parents know their own son, but fear the Jewish leaders, so make the son speak for himself: "I only know I was blind and now I can see." The story of the blind man speaks to us of God's choices. Because God sees the heart, he chooses differently from the way that we do. The man born blind is the one who points to the Son of Man, the light of the world. In our baptism we have been chosen to point to Jesus by the witness of our Christian lives. Our greatness lies in the fact that we have been chosen, not in ourselves alone. We allow God to work in us.

2. We arrive

Welcome the children by name. Recap on the last week – has anyone anything they would like to tell us about last week's Family Sheet?

Focus

Light a candle, and sit quietly for a moment with the room light low so that the candle stands out more clearly. During Lent, use purple material and a vase of spring flowers.

Gospel: John 9:1-41

Read from the Lectionary or the Children's Lectionary.

3. We respond
What is the Gospel asking of us?

Work in age groups if appropriate, then come together to end the session.

Young ones

Shut your eyes. Keep them shut! Can you remember how the candle looked?
What about the room? Keep your eyes shut: can you point to the door? Can you remember what colour top the person next to you is wearing? Don't look!
Now, keep your eyes shut: one of the grown-ups is holding something up.
What is it? We can't see, with our eyes shut. The blind man in today's story could never see anything, till he met Jesus. How boring and difficult his life must have been.
Now open your eyes and look round again. Have a good look: notice all the colours and shapes in the room, and people's faces. Jesus wants us to open our eyes in a very special way. He wants us to notice how beautiful the world is, and be glad and thankful to God our creator.

Story: Grumpy Mrs Gumpy

Down our street there was a grumpy old woman. Everything made her cross. If you gave her a hat for a present, she said it was the wrong size. If you said, "What a lovely day!" she would say: "I bet it'll rain later."

One day, the people in the house next to Mrs Gumpy moved out, and some new people came. The new family had a little girl called Anna. Anna was the happiest person in the world. If you gave Anna a hat, she put it straight on her head and loved it. If the sun was shining, she took her shoes and socks off and danced in the garden.

Mrs Gumpy watched Anna over the garden fence. "That child," she thought, "dancing in the garden! I bet she'll cut her toes, dancing in the garden like that." She called out: "Watch out, Anna, it's going to rain." But Anna only laughed. She said: "Look at the sky, Mrs Gumpy! It's beautiful and blue, and the sun is shining and dancing on the leaves of the apple tree. Don't you want to dance too?"

Mrs Gumpy looked at the leaves on the apple tree. The sun was shining on them, and the breeze was making the leaves wave and dance in the light.

And Mrs Gumpy thought: "Yes! The sunshine is beautiful." She went indoors, and baked some cakes, and took them round to Anna's mother. She and Anna's mother had tea in the garden, and Anna danced in the beautiful sunshine, and Mrs Gumpy was as happy as she could remember.

What do you think is beautiful?

Juniors

Shut your eyes, and keep them tight shut. Imagine what it would be like, being blind, not being able to see the world around you. It's very hard for people who can see to understand what it's like, being blind. Could you find your way round this building, with your eyes closed? Keep your eyes closed and try to remember where everything is in this room.
Now open your eyes and look around. Did you remember how everything looks? What things did you not notice?
In today's Gospel story, Jesus healed the blind man so that he could see the world around him. Jesus gave that man the very precious gift of sight. That must have been amazing enough for the man. But Jesus gave the man much more than ordinary eyes. He gave him eyes that could see God. Because as soon as he could see, that man recognised that Jesus was the Lord.
Most of us have got ordinary eyes that work very well. We can see everything all round us. Jesus wants to give us special eyes, to see the world he has created, and to see God. He wants us to learn to use those special eyes properly.

Story: There is always something beautiful to look for...

There's an old saying: two men looking through prison bars; one sees mud, and the other sees stars. What it means is that it doesn't matter where you are, you can choose what to see in the world. If you were looking out of a prison window, you could choose to look down into the gutter and see all the dirt and the rubbish. Or you could choose to look up to the sky, and see the beauty and mystery of the stars.

My friend Jack always sees what's wrong with the world. Jack always thinks things are going to go wrong. He's never happy; presents are not quite right; neighbours are a problem; people ignore him; there's always something to complain about.

Everybody is a bit like Jack sometimes. Some days we just feel sad, with nothing good to look forward to. But really, all the good things are still there.

My best friend Kate knows a clever trick: on days when she is so sad that the world looks bad, she tells herself that the good things are still there. She stands very still with her eyes shut, then opens them and looks for the first beautiful thing she can see. The day then starts to be happy again.

What do *you* see that cheers you up?

4. Activity

Young ones and Juniors

Use the template of the blind man looking happy. Draw in the figure of Jesus beside him. Draw in a speech bubble and write the words: "Jesus, help me to see your light in the world."

Play "My grandmother went to market." Sit in a circle with the vase of spring flowers in the centre. The first person says: "I can see a vase." The second person says: "I can see a vase and some flowers." The third person says: "I can see a vase and some flowers and some stalks." The game continues, each person adding another word, until the list is so long, your memory fails.

Discuss the gift of sight: the harder we look the more we find; how others see things differently; how important it is to take time to look. Use the template. Draw yourself beside the "blind" man who is happy at meeting Jesus. Write what makes you happy at knowing Jesus.

Tips for learning difficulties

Help the child understand what the blind man's life was like, and hence how great was the gift that Jesus gave him. The very young and those with learning difficulties often have problems in spontaneously paying careful attention to anything. They get distracted and lose concentration. Doing is easier than being passive for these children: encouraging them to describe things, such as the candle, or what it's like when your eyes are shut, will help their concentration.

5. We come together

Parents can be invited to join in at this stage.

Focus

As at the start of the session, light the candle.

Gospel

One day as Jesus walked along he saw a man who had been blind from birth. Jesus spat on the ground. He made some mud and smeared it on the man's eyes. Then he said: "Go and wash off the mud in Siloam pool." The man went and washed. When he had washed off the mud, he could see.

Prayer

Let's see if we can use our special eyes right now. Let's look at the candle flame carefully.

- Look at how the flame burns: sometimes it's very still, and sometimes it twists and turns. Sometimes the flame is big and strong, and sometimes it nearly blows out. Sometimes it's all yellow, sometimes there are other colours there too.
- The more you look at the candle, the more you will notice about it, and the more beautiful and interesting it will turn out to be.
- Everything you see every day is like the candle. If you take the time to look properly at the world, you will see what a beautiful world God has made for us. If you look properly at people, you may see their kindness and goodness. Just as God is in you, so he is in them.
- The beauty of the world, and the good in people are God's light. How do you feel when you see God's light? What can you do to make it burn brighter?
- Loving Jesus helps us to see the world in a new and better way. Children repeat after the leader the following prayer: Lord Jesus, help me to see your light in the world, and to make it burn brighter. Amen.

Share

Share the work from the activities.

Sing

"God made me"

5th Sunday of Lent

1. Introduction to the theme of the day

> ## "Jesus the resurrection and the life"

Aim: To understand the power of Jesus in enriching and renewing our lives, and the constant presence and care of God. Seeing the world anew makes life more vivid.

Leader's reflection: In today's Gospel we hear how the death of Lazarus left a large absence in the lives of those who loved him. By the time Jesus arrives at the house, Lazaus has been buried in the tomb for four days. Both Martha and Mary profess their faith in Jesus even though they regret the lateness of his arrival. John tells us that through the death of Lazarus the Son of God will be glorified. Just as in last week's Gospel the blindness of the man showed Jesus as the light, so the death of Lazarus serves to show Jesus as the life. The great miracle is that while he is dead, Lazarus hears the word of Jesus and obeys it. Jesus has the power to call us out of our tombs – for the Christian life only begins when we, even though we are dead, hear the word of God and obey it. When Lazarus emerges from the tomb he is wearing the shroud of a dead man. Obeying the words of Jesus to unbind him, the community plays its part in helping Lazarus unwind and emerge into the light of his new life.

We can be "dead" in the midst of life – hoping for a word and a community that will put us together again. The Gospel challenges us to take responsibility for our brothers and sisters who, like Lazarus, are loved by Jesus. If we see someone "buried alive" we are invited to call them and help them go free.

2. We arrive

We sit in a circle ready to listen to the Gospel. Has anyone anything they would like to tell us about last week's Family Sheet?

Focus

Purple fabric and spring flowers. Light a candle; perhaps you could also lay out four flowers: a bud, a full bloom, a dead flower and a dried flower. Younger children don't really understand the nature of death. You might ask them to compare the the bud, the bloom and the dead flower. What about the dried flower: is it dead or alive? (Don't give an answer: leave it as half dead but half alive.)

Gospel: John 11:1-45

Read from the Lectionary or the Children's Lectionary.

3. We respond
What is the Gospel asking of us?

Work in age groups if appropriate, then come together as a group to end the session.

Young ones

What makes a flower alive? How about a person? What makes a person alive? Can you make the dead flower alive again? How surprised all the people were, when Jesus made a dead man alive again.
How did Jesus make Lazarus come alive again? He prayed to God. He was very sure that God was listening, and that God would help him. Jesus wants us all to know that God is listening when we pray, and that God will look after us.

Story: A squirrel to the rescue!

There used to be an old farmhouse, up in the forest, a long way from the town. A man lived there, all by himself: he was a forester, and he looked after the woodland. His name was Henry. Henry liked the woods. But he was very lonely. Much as he loved his work, he had no one to talk to. He wished something would happen.

One day, Henry woke up and felt sure something special was going to happen. He put on his boots and his coat, and he went for a walk in the woods. Everything looked the same, but then he noticed a little squirrel. It was a baby squirrel, too small to look after itself, and it had fallen out of its nest and broken its leg. He took it home, and he made a little bed for it in a shoe box, and tucked it up under the end of a great big red woolly scarf. Henry brought food for the baby squirrel: milk, and nuts and berries from the forest. He called the squirrel "Edgar". Edgar the squirrel grew bigger and stronger, but his broken leg never mended properly. Edgar couldn't climb trees or look after himself; he had to live with Henry always.

Henry had saved Edgar's life, and Edgar loved him. But Edgar changed Henry's life too. Edgar went everywhere with Henry. The forest was new and exciting for Edgar. He showed Henry things Henry had forgotten. He showed Henry things he had never thought of looking at. He made Henry look at the forest the way a little squirrel sees it. Henry wasn't lonely any more. He wasn't bored, either. He looked at the forest in a new way and his work became fresh and exciting once again.

What makes you feel happy and excited?

Juniors

What makes a flower, or a person, alive? Can you make this dead flower come alive again? But remember nothing is impossible for Jesus. He could even make a dead man come alive again.
What does Jesus want us to understand, from this story about raising Lazarus from the dead?
First, Jesus wants us to see that he is special, that he is sent from God. He is not just an ordinary person like you or me. He has a special connection to God. Secondly, Jesus wants us to understand that his special connection to God comes from trusting God. He is very, very sure that his prayers will be answered, and that there is nothing God can't do, if it is right. Jesus wants us to learn to trust God that way, too.
Lazarus was like the dead flower, and God made him alive again. People who don't know Jesus are a bit like the dried flower: they are still beautiful, but there is something missing. They are not so lovely as the living flower. Without God's love there is something missing. Trusting God fills up that gap and makes us as lovely as the whole flower. It makes us properly alive.

Story: It's great to be alive!

Have you ever noticed how you feel, if you expect something bad to happen, and then it doesn't happen? Maybe you think your parents are going to be very cross about something, but then they aren't cross at all. Or maybe you knocked something over, and you thought it would break, but it landed safely?

Just when you think something bad will happen, you feel all scared and upset. But when it's OK, you feel great. You feel much better than usual. Everything seems nicer and happier than usual. Have you noticed that? You feel more alive, more special, because something bad has not happened.

There was a man called Anthony who liked to go climbing. Anthony had an accident on a mountain. He fell off a high place and got stuck half-way down. He couldn't move, and he thought he would die, but he was rescued.

The next day, all the world looked wonderful! The mountains seemed more beautiful than ever, the people seemed kinder, and even the water tasted better. Anthony realised that he felt much more alive than usual, and that it was a wonderful feeling. He thanked God that he was alive. He wished he could feel that way every day. But the feeling wore off, and Anthony felt ordinary again.

Anthony thought and thought how to get that wonderful feeling back. He read books and he asked other people, but no one had the answer. Then he realised that he had had the answer all the time. He was alive every day, but until he nearly fell off the mountain he just hadn't noticed how good that was. Now, Anthony thanks God every day for just being alive, and the world is always a beautiful place for him.

4. Activity

Young ones

1. Use the template of the rainbow. Draw in the things you would like to thank God for. Say a thank you prayer out of your head.
2. Draw a picture of something beautiful. Say a prayer about it.
3. Draw a picture of something that makes you feel alive. Say a prayer about it.

Juniors

Colour the rainbow template. Make up three prayers and write them under the rainbows. Cut out the shapes. Paste on to card and use as bookmarks. You may want to write a prayer for someone special and give them it as a bookmark.

Tips for learning difficulties

Young children and those with learning difficulties do not understand the idea of death. They often believe that dead people or pets can come back to life. The story of Lazarus is less startling and less miraculous for them than it is for the older child. An emphasis on trusting God and having faith in prayer is easier for such children to understand.

5. We come together

Parents can be invited to join in at this stage.

Focus

As at the start of the session, light the candle; lay out four flowers: a bud, a full bloom, a dead flower and a dried flower.

Gospel

Jesus said: "Didn't I tell you that if you have faith, you will see the glory of God?" Jesus looked up toward heaven and prayed: "Father, I thank you for answering my prayer. I know that you always answer my prayers. But I said this so that the people here would believe that you sent me." When Jesus had finished praying, he shouted, "Lazarus, come out of the tomb!" The man who had been dead came out.

Prayer

Let's make up a prayer together.

✦ Let's thank God for listening to our prayers: Lord, we are so happy because you are listening to us.
✦ Let's tell God how glad we are that we can trust him: Lord, I know I can always trust you.
✦ Let's tell God how grateful we are that he makes us feel alive: Lord, thank you for my fingers and toes, my eyes and my nose, for making the world a beautiful place.
✦ Let's make up our own prayers. What do you want to thank God for today?

Share

Share the work from the activities.

Sing

"Thank you God for... right where we are"

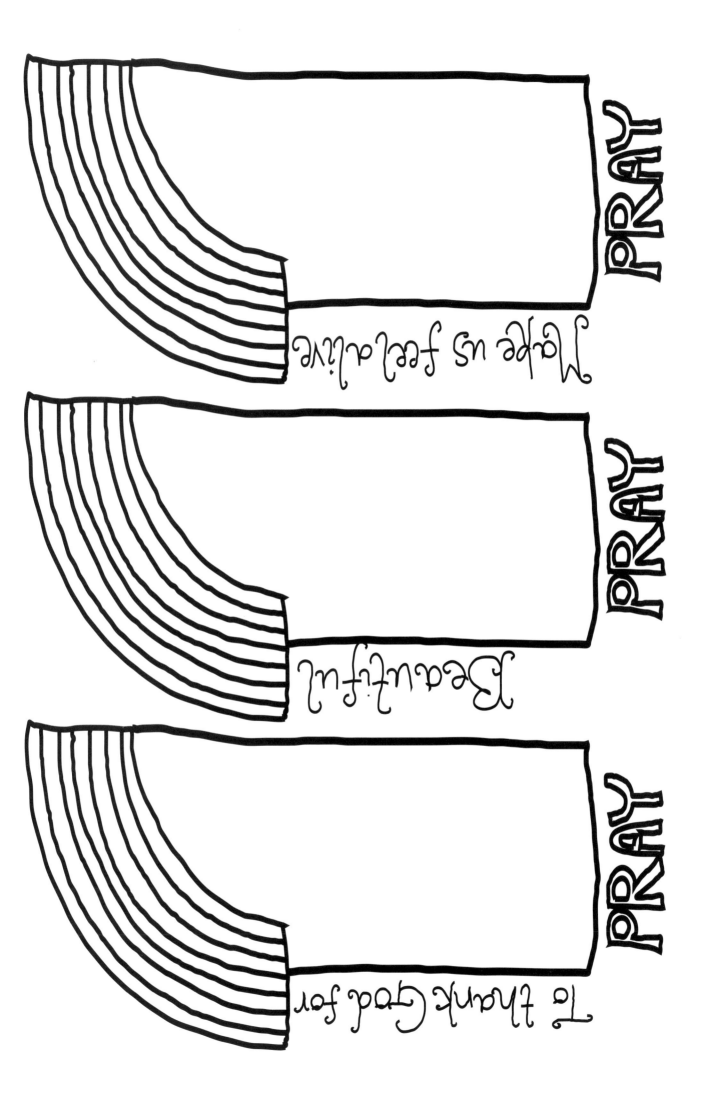

Passion Sunday (Palm Sunday)

1. Introduction to the theme of the day

> ## "Blessed is he who comes in the name of the Lord"

Aim: To explore the themes of triumph and disaster, and the presence and support of God in both.

Leader's reflection: Jesus knows the road he must take. He organises his own "grand entrance" into Jerusalem, riding astride a donkey, cheered on by palm-waving well-wishers. A countryman from the north, known as the prophet, Jesus of Nazareth has come to confront established authority.

By the time the Passion gets under way there is nothing to shout about. Processions that follow condemned criminals are shabby affairs. All Jesus' disciples deserted him. When we speak of the Passion of Jesus we usually mean the suffering and death inflicted on him. But the Passion is not just something that is done to Jesus by others, it is the power within Jesus, his passion, that enables him to face the violence and pain. His ardent love insists that he face the ultimate test of love: the cross. The cross of Jesus stands at the centre of the Christian story as the sign of the lengths love will go to in its passion for others. Jesus loves us so much that he thought we were worth dying for. We honour his death as the supreme act of love: the love of one who "did not cling to his equality with God but emptied himself" to become as we all are; and to show that in spite of our sins and stupidities, God loves us.

2. We arrive

We sit in a circle ready to listen to the Gospel. Has anyone anything they would like to tell us about last week's Family Sheet?

Focus

Candle, red fabric, palms.

Gospel: Matthew 26:14 – 27:66

As the whole of today's story and activities are based around the telling of the story of Holy Week, leaders might choose not to read formally from the Lectionary.

3. We respond

What is the Gospel asking of us?

Work in age groups if appropriate, then come together as a group to end the session.

Young ones

Imagine how happy all the people were, following Jesus on the donkey and shouting "Hooray!" Shout "Hooray!" now, and even louder: "Hooray!" What a lovely day that must have been!

But then the soldiers took Jesus and they crucified him, and the sky went black. Poor Jesus. What a horrible day that was. Sometimes God wants us to do lovely things, like the happy day on the donkey. But sometimes God needs us to be brave, and to do very difficult things. Jesus let the soldiers arrest him so that he could do what God wanted him to do, and save us all.

Can you think of any happy things God wants you to do? When does God want you to be brave?

Story: A birthday surprise

It was Mummy's birthday. Susie wanted to make her something very special for her birthday present. So she got up very early, and she got out all her paints and crayons and scissors and glue, and she started to make a present. It was exciting, being the only person awake, and making something special for Mummy.

But Susie had some problems. She tried to paint a beautiful picture of her house, but it all went wrong. Then she tried to do a lovely drawing of the garden, but that went all wrong too. Then she tried to paint her family: Mummy and Daddy and her baby brother. But it came out all wrong, and then she spilled the paint tray over the table.

Susie was very upset. She cleaned up the mess with a cloth, but all her pictures were spoiled: all the paint ran in together.

Then Mummy got up, and came to see what was happening. Susie was very sad. She said: "I wanted to make you such a lovely present, but now it's all spoiled."

"No it isn't," said Mummy. "Look! Your painting is beautiful."

She held up the paper on the top of the pile. All the paint had run in together, and made a beautiful picture like the sun coming up over the trees in the garden. Mummy liked the picture very much, and they put it on the wall in the kitchen. So you never can tell: sometimes things turn out really well, just when it all looks spoiled.

What do you like to make for your mummy or daddy?

Juniors

There's a famous poem, by a man called Rudyard Kipling, called "If". It has these words in it:
"If you can meet with triumph and disaster, and treat those two imposters just the same..."
Then, Kipling says, "you'll own the earth and everything that's in it".
Kipling's poem makes a very important point. What matters is not whether things go really well, or whether they turn out badly; all that matters is that you do your best.
Imagine Jesus riding into Jerusalem on the donkey, with all the people cheering and singing.
What a triumph that seemed to be.
He was coming to Jerusalem like a king. But then he was arrested by the soldiers, and crucified like a criminal.
What a disaster that seemed to be.
It must have seemed as if everything had gone horribly wrong. But both the triumphant ride into town and the crucifixion were God's will. Jesus obeyed God's will just the same and did his very best, in triumph and disaster.
Jesus was ready to do anything God wanted him to do. He calls us always to try to know how God would like us to behave, and to try to do what God wants us to do: always to do our best.

Story: Maggie in a muddle

Have you ever had a really bad day? The sort of day when everything goes wrong? It happened to a girl called Maggie.

One Tuesday morning, Maggie decided to get up early and lay the table for her family for breakfast. But she dropped a cup, and it broke on the kitchen floor. Then she went shopping with her dad. There was an old lady in the shop, who was in a wheelchair, and she couldn't reach the tins of baked beans. Maggie tried to help her. But all the tins fell down with a great crash. Maggie went home, and she started to play with her little sister. They were pretending that the arms of the sofa were horses, and they were pretending to have a race. Maggie's little sister got very excited, and she fell off her horse and bumped her head.

Maggie was pretty fed up. What else could go wrong? She went to her room and sat on her bed and felt miserable. But then her mother came up to see her, and gave her a great big hug. "Thank you, Maggie," she said. "You've tried so hard to be helpful all day. You're a lovely girl." Maggie smiled and stopped feeling sad. She went downstairs, and helped her mother make the tea. Just as the toast was all ready and buttered, it slid off Maggie's plate onto the floor. Her mother laughed. "It's just one of those days, Maggie," she said. So they made some more toast and ate it with honey and jam.

4. Activity

Young ones

Use the template of Jesus on a donkey. Colour the picture. On the palm trees write:
a) doing God's will; b) loving the poor; c) always forgiving.
Write a heading: "ON THE WAY TO JERUSALEM".

Juniors

Have ready an A3-size piece of thin card that is red on one side and yellow on the other. Cut out a cross shape as follows:

> Divide the width into three equal lengths and mark with pencil lines.
> Divide the length into four equal parts and mark with pencil lines.
> You should have twelve squares measuring approximately 9.9cm x 9.9 cm.
> Cut out a cross shape along the pencil lines, discarding the top square on the right and left and discarding the bottom two squares on the right and the left.

Write on the middle square: "Dear Jesus, thank you that you died for me. Amen."

All the children write their names on the other squares. Fold the squares up with the yellow on the inside so that you have a red cube. This activity could easily be done with all ages writing their names on the cross.

Tips for learning difficulties

Explain to the children that it was a very sad day for Jesus' mother Mary, and for all of his friends. Jesus was a very good person, he was God's Son, but some people didn't like him and put him to death on the cross. We know that Jesus was helping all of us to be friends with God for ever and ever.

5. We come together

Parents can be invited to join in at this stage.

Focus

As for the start of the session and add the red cube from Juniors' activity.

Gospel

They brought a donkey, and Jesus got on its back. People put clothes on the road, and branches they had cut from trees. Some people walked ahead of Jesus and some behind. They were all shouting: "Hosanna, for the son of David! God bless the one who comes in the name of the Lord. Hooray for God in heaven above!" ... The soldiers nailed Jesus to the cross. At noon the sky turned black and stayed that way until three o'clock. Then Jesus shouted: "My God, my God, why have you deserted me?" Then he died.

Prayer

✦ Let's think of some things God would like us to do. What can you think of?
✦ What would God like us to do for each other? Be kind? Share? What else can you think of?
✦ What would God like us to do for ourselves? Be happy? Talk to him? Feel his love for us? What else can you think of?
✦ What would God like us to do for him? Help him make the world a better place? What else can you think of?

Children repeat after the leader: Lord, tell us what you want us to do. Amen.

Share

Share the work from the activities. Look at the red cube. The colour red reminds us of the suffering and death of Jesus. Everyone was sad when Jesus' body was laid in the tomb. We have a "tomb" (our red cube) to lay on our focus area. Will it be the same when we come back after Easter? How will it be changed?

Sing

"Jesus, remember me when you come into your kingdom"

Easter Sunday

1. Introduction to the theme of the day

> ## "Alleluia! Christ is risen from the dead!"

Aim: To explore this day of new life, a new world through trust in Jesus.

Leader's reflection: The Father's undying affection for Jesus sweeps death aside as he claims his beloved Son again. Nothing can come between them. We believe that God's graciousness will be extended to ourselves; that we will participate in Jesus' resurrection on the last day. Today the challenge of Easter is to understand the history of human suffering in the light of Jesus' resurrection. This means that we have to take God's part in protesting against the violence and the suffering that are accepted so readily as inevitable. The truth that God raised Jesus from the dead gives hope and help to all those who want that miracle repeated in the midst of life. Jesus' words, "I am the resurrection and the life", mean that God's work continues today.

We can all catch something of the reality of the resurrection when we experience new life in the midst of hopelessness: tired hospital workers nursing the dead back to life; men and women who risk their lives protesting against violence inflicted on their fellow humans; beloved disciples who see in the dark what no one else sees. It is Easter in our midst; it is the refusal to accept that anyone should be left for dead.

2. We arrive

We sit in a circle ready to listen to the Gospel. Has anyone anything they would like to tell us about last week's Family Sheet?

Focus

White fabric (for joy); spring flowers; eggs; water; coloured eggs. Light a night light for every child. "Alleluia! Jesus is alive for ever" – on a banner.

Gospel: Matthew 28:1-10

Read from the Lectionary or Children's Lectionary.

3. We respond
What is the Gospel asking of us?

Work in age groups if appropriate, then come together to end the session.

Young ones

How surprised the women were, when they couldn't find Jesus in his tomb.
It was scary. But Jesus had done just what he had said he would do: he had come back to life.
Nothing is too difficult for God. Nothing can really kill Jesus or take him away from us. He will always be here, looking after us; that's God's promise. Today, God wants us to trust him and feel safe, and to cheer and shout and be very glad, because Jesus has come back to us for ever.
How loudly can you cheer for Jesus? How safe do you feel with Jesus?

Story: Who's scared?

Tim was scared of the dark. He didn't like being all alone in his bedroom, with all that dark.
You never knew what might be hiding in the corner, or under the bed. He was sure there was something scary hiding in the dark. Every night, at bedtime, Tim got worried and miserable.

Then, one day, Tim's friend John came to stay. John wasn't scared of the dark. John had a camp bed, and a sleeping bag in Tim's room.

At bedtime, Daddy read the boys a story, said a prayer with them as usual, and then he put out the light. Tim began to feel scared of the dark.

He asked John: "Are you scared?" John said: "No, Jesus is here too, so we're all safe, just like last night."

Tim hadn't thought of that. Then he remembered; last night, he thought he saw a monster in the corner, but in the morning, he was still safe.

"Wherever I am, Jesus is always there too," thought Tim. Suddenly, Tim stopped feeling scared. He felt very, very safe.

Tim was never scared of the dark again.

What makes you scared?
Is Jesus there with you, looking after you in scary places?

Juniors

Imagine how surprised and afraid the women must have been, when they went to the tomb and found that it was empty. They thought of everything that might have happened, except the right answer. They couldn't believe that Jesus could keep his promise to come back from the dead, until an angel told them.
Jesus has risen from the dead! He kept his word. God brought him back to life, so that we can know that we can trust him, and know how powerful he is.
God wants us to know that he can give us the same strength. He can make us so full of life if we trust in Jesus. Alleluia!

Story: Say a prayer: help is at hand

What a lot of time we waste worrying. Have you ever noticed that worrying never really helps? If you worry when the teacher asks you to read or answer a question in class, it just makes you feel bad, and you get so nervous you do worse. If you worry whether someone wants to be your friend, it's the same thing: it makes you nervous, and you can't think what to say.

Martin was a real worrier. He worried about everything. He worried that people didn't like him. He worried about his schoolwork. He worried about playing football. He worried about walking home from school. He worried in case he didn't clean his teeth properly. In fact, Martin worried all the time, and it made him miserable.

The strange thing was that nothing really bad ever happened to Martin.
He had some friends at school. He was quite good at schoolwork, and nothing bad ever happened playing football or walking home from school. His teeth were perfect – not a single filling. He was making himself miserable worrying about nothing.

One day, someone at school did do something that seemed nasty. He said, "Martin, you're a real worrypot!" Martin got worried at once – maybe people didn't like worrypots. That night, at bedtime, Martin's mother gave him a cuddle and read him a story. Martin told her what the boy at school had said, and that he didn't want to be a "worrypot". His mother gave him a big hug. "Well," she said, "let's ask Jesus to help you with that, in our prayers tonight." So that's what they did. Martin asked Jesus to help him feel safe whenever he started to worry. After that, Martin didn't worry so much any more. Everything began to be much more fun.

4. Activity

Young ones

Use the template of the vase of flowers. Colour them in using spring colours: yellow, red and purple. Write a message on the vase:

To: _____ (name of someone you want to cheer up)

Love from: _____ (your name)

Leaders, meanwhile, make enough tissue paper flowers, one for each child, to use in the final "prayer" session.

Juniors

Sow some cress seeds on moist paper towel placed in a plastic beaker. Discuss what you expect to happen – the "dead" seeds come to life.

Have eggs as examples of new life. Show the children how to boil eggs with onion skins for a deep mahogany colour or tie ferns or flowers to the egg with thread before boiling to give a tracery effect. Talk about other symbols of Easter: lilies, Easter bunnies, Easter baskets.

Tips for learning difficulties

Focus on the joyful celebration associated with Easter. For the very young, or children with learning difficulties, the idea of resurrection may be hard to understand. These children will grasp the more concrete idea that Easter celebrates something very lovely that God has done for us. What do they think is lovely? What gifts do they think God has given them?

5. We come together

Parents can be invited to join in at this stage.

Focus

White fabric (for joy); spring flowers; candle alight, as at the start of the session.

The purple cube, the "tomb" which was used at last Sunday's lesson. Open the cube to show the bright happy colour of the yellow cross with the words "Jesus is alive" written on a piece of paper.

Gospel

The women went to the tomb. An angel said to them: "There is no need to be afraid. I know you are looking for Jesus, who was crucified. He is not here because he has risen, as he said he would. Come and see the place where he lay, and then go quickly and tell his disciples: 'He is risen from the dead and now he is going to Galilee. You will see him there.'" The women were amazed. They ran to tell the disciples.

Prayer

(As each line of the prayer is said, the children stick a tissue paper flower on the yellow cross to show that they are really happy.)

Alleluia! Jesus is alive for ever.

Hooray for springtime!

Thank you, God, for the daffodils and other spring flowers.

Jesus gives us new life.

Jesus gives us new hope.

Thank you, God, for young creatures: baby lambs and rabbits, baby birds, tadpoles and newts.

Jesus – you make us come alive.

Alleluia! Jesus is alive for ever. Amen.

Share

Share the work from the activities.

Sing

"If you're happy and you know it, clap your hands"

2nd Sunday of Easter

1. Introduction to the theme of the day

> ❝ God is full of surprises ❞

Aim: Our faith is a sign of God working in our lives, because we have not seen Jesus, but we believe in him.

Leader's reflection: During Jesus' public ministry the disciples could not see for themselves the whole truth about Jesus. They came to that truth only after the resurrection when they received from Jesus the Spirit of truth. Then they could remember with understanding the mighty deeds and words of Jesus.

In today's Gospel John builds a bridge between those who saw Jesus and those who did not: "Happy are those who have not seen and yet believe." That blessing is directed at us: we believe in Jesus without seeing him.

Seeing did not necessarily lead to believing; but the apostles saw and believed and shared with us their Christian faith. It is a great chain of faith which is linked to the person of Jesus himself. The Spirit which Jesus gives is a present reality in the Church. The Spirit is the life of the Church, the power which keeps the memory of Jesus alive, and which enables each of us to have a living relationship with God. We gather together as a sign of our belief and a declaration of our love in Jesus.

2. We arrive
We sit in a circle ready to listen to the Gospel. Has anyone anything they would like to tell us about last week's Family Sheet?

Focus
White fabric; white eggs; spring flowers; candle.

Gospel: John 20:19-31
Read from the Lectionary or Children's Lectionary.

3. We respond
What is the Gospel asking of us?
Work in age groups if appropriate, then come together to end the session.

Young ones

God can do incredible things when we least expect it. He can make sick people better. He can solve difficult problems... he was even able to bring Jesus back to life after he died.
If we ask God to help us, and if we believe that he can, he will!
Do you talk to God often? What do you ask him? Does God ever help you in surprising ways?

Story: Surprise! Surprise!

It was Jane's birthday and she was very excited. She imagined all the presents she would get, and the cake she would eat. She thought of all her friends congratulating her and singing "Happy Birthday" to her. She was looking forward to this special day.

But, that morning, when she went downstairs to eat breakfast, her family wished her a happy birthday but that was all. And when she went to school, nobody said much about her birthday, not even her friends. As she sat on the bus going home, she felt very sad. "It doesn't *feel* much like my birthday. No one wants to celebrate with me."

When Jane arrived home, she opened the front door. "SURPRISE!" they all shouted. Everyone was there... Mum and Dad, brothers and sisters, friends, teachers, neighbours.
They had not forgotten at all.
They had just wanted to surprise her with a party, with cake and sweets, and with many, many presents. Jane was so happy. It was a lovely surprise!

Juniors

Thomas only believed that Jesus was alive when he was able to see him with his own eyes. If we had been alive 2,000 years ago, we too could have seen Jesus for ourselves.
But today we must look harder in order to see Jesus. We will listen to his word when we go to church and receive him in the Eucharist. We will find him in pictures and books, and in the readings. We will see his actions in people who do good works. Jesus tells us that we are more fortunate than Thomas, because we can see Jesus in so many different ways. God sent the Holy Spirit to be the power in our lives to remember Jesus and his teachings. As Christians we take Jesus with us wherever we go.

Story: The life of St Thérèse of Lisieux

St. Thérèse of Lisieux was a Carmelite nun living in France 100 years ago.
She believed that God loved her very much. When she was very young, she went to see the Pope to ask him if she could become a nun. Everyone knew she was too young to enter into a convent, but Thérèse knew that God would surprise them all. And God did, because Thérèse was allowed to enter into the convent at the age of only 15. In the convent, Thérèse's life was simple, unselfish and obedient.

However, when she was only 22 years old, she became very sick. She knew that she was going to die. But she

believed that God loved her and would take care of her, even though at times she felt alone and afraid. Today she is a saint because, even though she could not see him or touch him, she never doubted that God was her best friend.

During the two years of her illness, her Superior ordered her to keep a diary. It was published after her death at the age of 24 and became popular with both Christians and non-Christians. *The Story of a Soul* was a spectacular success and a number of miracles and favours were attributed to her heavenly prayers.

Encourage comments relating the story to the Gospel.
St Thérèse believed that every person and every situation offers a meeting with Jesus. There is no need to look for Jesus in the extraordinary, when he is all around us in the ordinary.
How does this make you feel? Do you agree with the belief of St Thérèse?

4. Activity

Young ones

Use the template and carefully colour the eyes the same colour as your own. Colour the rest of the face like yours, putting freckles on the nose if you have them, glasses, bumps and bruises.
Write under the eyes the good things you can see around you.

Juniors

Colour the template. Imagine Jesus coming to your front door, under the eyes write a description of how you welcome Jesus. Describe the scene, what he looks like and perhaps what he says to you.

Tips for learning difficulties

Ask the children if they understand what a surprise is. Ask them to talk about the times when they were surprised.

5. We come together

Parents can be invited to join in at this stage.

Focus

As for the start of the session. Light the candle and display some, or all of the pictures.

Gospel

Today we hear how the disciples thought that Jesus was dead. But then, all of a sudden, they see him again, alive and well. They cannot believe their eyes! Thomas, however, does not believe that such a surprise could happen. He doubts that God would do such an amazing thing. But Jesus reminds him that everything and anything is possible with God.

Prayer

Say together – or one person can lead.

Dear Jesus, thank you for so many lovely surprises in our lives. You give us many wonderful things which we do not expect: you give us family who love us, friends who care for us, teachers who help us. We know that you are working in all these people who look after us. Help us to see you in all good people so that we can love you and know you more. Amen.

Share

Share the work from the activities.

Sing

"Open your eyes you Christian people"

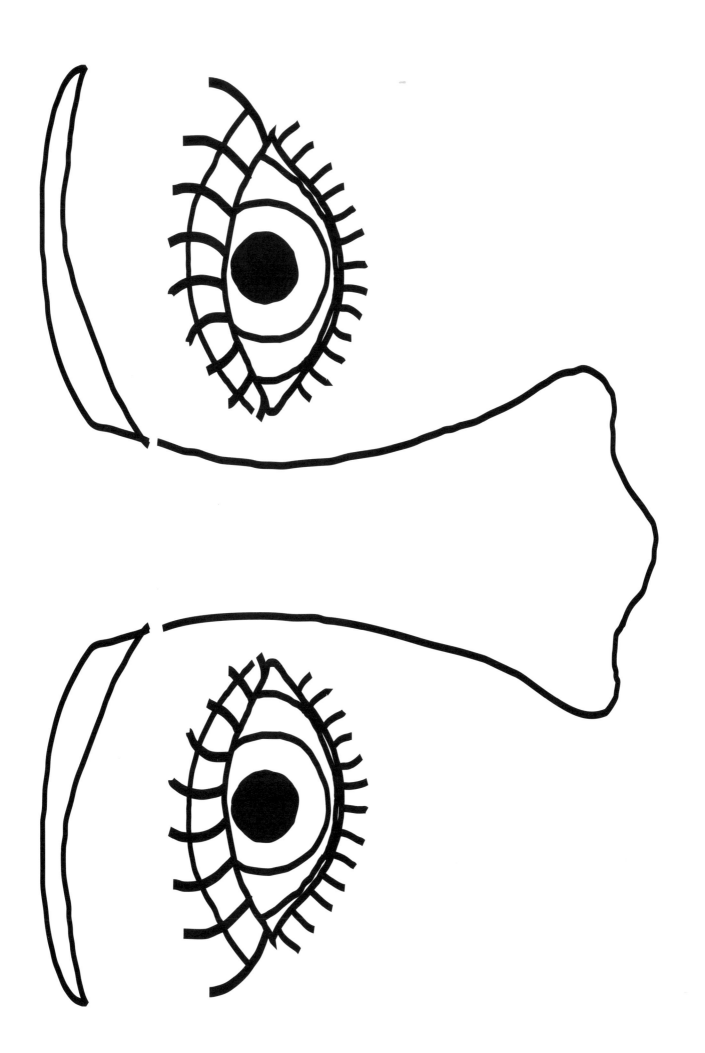

3rd Sunday of Easter

1. Introduction to the theme of the day

> ## "When we share we discover God"

Aim: To understand the Gospel reading that while on the road to a village called Emmaus, two of Jesus' followers, who are sad and lonely, start to share with each other. Through talking, walking, eating and sharing together, through being generous and unselfish, they start to see Jesus with them and they discover that God never leaves us.

Leader's reflection: The two disciples had left Jerusalem as the place where their hopes met with final defeat. When they recognise the stranger as the risen Jesus, their hearts burn within them and they can see a new future. They take the light of Easter Sunday back into the darkness of Good Friday. The risen Jesus makes sense of everything that went before. In his word and in the breaking of the bread, the past is brought up to date. When we gather to celebrate the Eucharist each week, we too listen to the word of God and break bread together. Jesus comes among us not as a stranger; rather he comes to give us new hope to face the future with faith in him. Whatever our way of life, young or old, we are invited to tell our stories to the Lord, to listen to him as he speaks his word, and to recognise him in the breaking of bread.

2. We arrive

We sit in a circle ready to listen to the Gospel. Has anyone anything they would like to tell us about last week's Family Sheet?

Focus

White fabric; spring flowers; candle; soda bread; a jug of red juice.

Gospel: Luke 24:13-35

Read from the Lectionary or Children's Lectionary.

3. We respond
What is the Gospel asking of us?

Work in age groups if appropriate, then come together to end the session.

Young ones

Story: A fairy tale

Luke and Maria lived in the mountains with their poor old grandfather. One day, they decided to go for a walk. Their grandfather knew that they would not be home until late, so he gave them each a little food to eat on the way. He placed two wrinkled apples, some hard bread and a piece of old cheese in a bag for them, because he had no other food to give them. Luke and Maria knew that he was too poor to give them anything else, so they thanked him and left for the walk.

On the way, they discoverd an old lady. She was crying, and when they stopped to ask her what was wrong, she replied, "I am so hungry. I have not eaten for days and I think I will die." Luke and Maria felt so sorry that they gave her all the food they had, little though it was. She ate it all and thanked them for their kindness.

Having no other food, Luke and Maria were very hungry when they returned home.

They explained to their grandfather what had happened and told him who they had met. They opened their bag to show him, and, to their surprise, they discovered sweet fruit and roasted meat, soft bread and delicious cheese inside. They were truly astonished. But their grandfather just said, "Your kindness has been rewarded. The lady you met was a kind fairy. Because you were good to her, she has in turn been good to you."

Jesus wants us to be generous people because when we are good and share, God is with us. To share our toys, sweets and books is not easy. But when we do, we will have many friends who want to share with us too! Is it easy or difficult to share? What things do you like to share with others? Who do you like to share things with?

Juniors

When Jesus' disciples were walking along, they were very sad about the death of their friend. However, when they started to talk and listen to each other, they felt much better afterwards. Sometimes we keep our worries and feelings to ourselves and do not want to share them with others. But if we tell someone who loves and cares for us, these fears can be eased.

It is said: "A problem shared is a problem halved." What does this mean?

Who do you like to talk to when you are sad? How do you feel afterwards?

Story: The road to Emmaus

Turn the Gospel story into a play, or allow children to mime the actions while the leader retells the story.

Characters: 2 disciples; 1 stranger (different children could play the parts in each act)

Act 1: On the Road
- Disciples walking along, talking together with sad faces.
- A stranger joins them, wondering at their downcast faces.
- 1 disciple explains what has happened.
- Stranger explains the message from the prophets.
- Disciples cheered now, with the stranger's conversation.
- Late evening; invite stranger to their home.

Act 2: At the Meal
- At the table, stranger takes bread and blesses it, breaks it and hands the bread to the disciples.
- Disciples recognise Jesus, stand, astonished, and Jesus disappears.

Act 3: Go and Tell
- Disciples understand; chat excitedly with each other.
- Leave immediately in haste, longing to tell the good news to their friends.

4. Activity

Young ones

Use the template and fill in the faces to show if the people are happy or sad. The children should draw happy faces when there is sharing and sad faces when there is selfishness.

Juniors

Look at the word ALLELUIA. It means "Praise the Lord." In today's Gospel the two disciples returned to Jerusalem praising the Lord.

Have some sunflower seeds, yogurt or plant pots, potting compost and talk about the "dead" seeds. Plant them and take them home to watch the new life. Use the growing plant as a teaching aid now and then in the weeks to come.

Tips for learning difficulties

Make sure that everyone understands what it is to share. Do an exercise where the teacher has a number of sweets and keeps them all. Then share them out and show the difference between being selfish and generous.

5. We come together

Parents can be invited to join in at this stage.

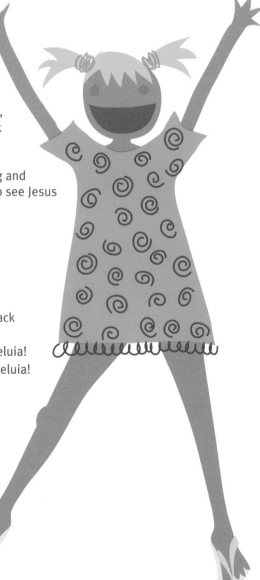

Focus

White cloth over a small table or box; the lighted candle; soda bread; jug of red juice and three plates ready for a meal.

Gospel

While on the road to a village called Emmaus, two of Jesus' followers, who are sad and lonely, start to share with each other. First, they talk and share their worries with each other. They share a long and tiring journey by walking together. And finally, that night, they sit down together to eat and share their food. Through talking, walking, eating and sharing together, through being generous and unselfish, they start to see Jesus with them and they discover that God never leaves us.

Prayer

(At the end of each sentence all say together: Alleluia.)
Christ is risen. Alleluia!
May we all have the courage to let go of things that are holding us back from growing. Alleluia!
Let us pray that we will grow to trust Jesus a little more each day. Alleluia!
Let us pray that we will never be afraid to follow Jesus day by day. Alleluia!
Amen.

Share

Share the work from the activities.

Sing

An Alleluia song, e.g.
"Alleluia, alleluia, give thanks to the risen Lord"

4th Sunday of Easter

1. Introduction to the theme of the day

> ## "Jesus is like a good shepherd"

Aim: To understand the work of a shepherd and how this relates to Jesus as the Good Shepherd.

Leader's reflection: Today's Gospel gives us an image of Jesus as someone who hopes that people will come to recognise his voice. Many do not want to hear the truth from Jesus. He was insulted and tortured but he did not retaliate with insults and threats. He put his trust in the Father. In spite of the treatment he received he always refused to give back as he had received. This was Jesus' way of being human. As Christians we are all called to be fully human like Jesus. Jesus came so that we could "have life and have it to the full"; to share in his way of being human; to speak our truth quietly and insistently, even when the opposition is strong. Jesus wants us to meet meanness with generosity and to have a heart that can see the muddle and conflict in people's lives. The voice of Jesus forever calls us. It is the voice of the one who loves us with an everlasting love: the shepherd who is willing to die for his sheep.

2. We arrive

We sit in a circle ready to listen to the Gospel. Has anyone anything they would like to tell us about last week's Family Sheet?

Focus
Use white fabric and models of a shepherd, fold, sheep or goats.

Gospel: John 10:1-10
Read from the Lectionary or the Children's Lectionary.

3. We respond
What is the Gospel asking of us?
Work in age groups if appropriate, then come together as a group to end the session.

Young ones

Jesus tells us that he loves us and cares for all of us very much. He says that, even though there are millions of people in the world, he knows each one by name.
He also asks that we follow him and stay close to him. We do that by being good, kind and generous, by not fighting or being disobedient.
Do you want to follow Jesus?
How are you going to follow Jesus this week?

Story: Lost and found!

One day, there was a little girl called Mary who went shopping with her mummy. Mary was very excited about going to the supermarket because she knew that if she was good, her mummy would buy her some sweets. When they arrived at the supermarket, Mary's mum went to buy some fruit. But Mary ran straight to where the sweets were. When she had found the sweets that she wanted, she started to look for her mummy so that she could buy them for her. But Mary's mum was nowhere to be found. Mary looked and looked, but she could not find her mummy. She started to cry. Suddenly she heard a voice. "There you are, Mary. I was looking for you everywhere." Mary's mum hugged her and wiped away her tears.

"I thought I had lost you. I looked for you up and down every aisle. I was really worried. Let's stay very close so that we don't lose each other again."
Mary was so happy to be safe with her mum once more.

Juniors

Shepherds are people who look after animals like sheep, goats and cows. Early in the morning, the shepherd leads the animals out of the farm and brings them to find grass to eat and water to drink. They keep watch too at all times to see that all the animals are safe. If any wander away and get lost, the shepherd looks for them until they are found. And at the end of the day, the shepherd brings all the animals home so that they can sleep safely during the night. Jesus says he looks after us like a good shepherd who cares for his own animals.
Jesus tells us that there are good shepherds and bad shepherds. Good shepherds are people who help others and are patient and caring. However, people who are selfish, who tell lies and say bad things about others would make very bad shepherds. Who are the good people in your life who look after you and care for you? Do you want to be like them?

Story: A true account of the Masai people of Africa and their cows

In Africa there are people called the Masai who have many cows. The Masai people depend on their cows for everything: they eat their meat and drink their milk. Their clothes are made from cow skin. Even their mud houses use cow manure to make the walls strong.
The more cows a Masai man has, the richer he is. To a Masai man, his cows are more important to him than his children and wives! The Masai man knows each one of his cows, even though to us the cows can all look the same. If one is missing, he realises immediately and he goes looking for it until it is found.
Sometimes the rains fail and there is no grass for the cows to eat. The cows become weak from hunger, but even then the Masai man will not sell them for money because he never wants to lose his cows.
In Africa, God is like the good Masai man who always cares for his animals.

Encourage comments relating the story to the Gospel.

4. Activity

Young ones

Using the template of the shepherd and sheep, colour the picture. Give the sheep names, including your own. Use collage materials to bring the pictures to life using cotton wool for the sheep.

Juniors

Draw in two prayer boxes in the spaces at the bottom of the picture. In one, write a prayer on how you can care for your family like God cares for you. In the other, write a prayer for people who do not know God. Colour the picture and name the sheep that Jesus the Good Shepherd is guarding.

Tip for learning difficulties

Have a picture of a shepherd and some sheep/cows/goats so that they can be explained to help the children fully understand the job of a shepherd.

5. We come together

Parents may be invited to join in at this stage.

Focus

As at the start of the session; light the candle.

Gospel

Jesus said, "My sheep listen to my voice; I know them, and they follow me. I give them eternal life, and they shall never die. No one can snatch them away from me. What my Father has given me is greater than everything, and no one can snatch them away from the Father's care. The Father and I are one."

Prayer

Jesus is the Good Shepherd. He looks after us and takes care of us. He knows who we are.
Let us pray that we will listen to the voice of Jesus.
Response: Lord, hear our prayer.
Let us pray that people who have strayed like sheep will come back to the shepherd.
Response: Lord, hear our prayer.

Share

With eyes closed try to recognise the voice of friends. Share the work from the activities.

Sing

Choose any Good Shepherd song –
a familiar version of "The Lord's my shepherd"
"Loving Shepherd of thy sheep"

5th Sunday of Easter

1. Introduction to the theme of the day

"There are many rooms in God's house"

Aim: To know that we are all welcome in God's house.

Leader's reflection: In today's Gospel John describes the profound loss that the disciples are experiencing when Jesus leaves them. Which direction do they take? Jesus simply points to himself: "I am the Way, the Truth and the Life." God is as inseparable from Jesus as the Father is inseparable from the Son. Jesus is the face of God; the heart of God; the word of God. The one who walked the roads of Palestine and ate with sinners is God's gift of his true self to us. Jesus is the Life, and we all have our life in him. The disciples learn from the early division in the community that they all have to work together to find a way forward. Jesus trusts his followers down the ages to face the confusion and complexity of the world. Jesus, as the Way, the Truth and the Life, wants us to put our faith to work.

2. We arrive
We sit in a circle ready to listen to the Gospel. Has anyone anything they would like to tell us about last week's Family Sheet?

Focus
Light a candle; white fabric for Eastertide; spring flowers; a globe or world map; dolls dressed in national costume.

Gospel: John 14:1-12
Read from the Lectionary or the Children's Lectionary.

3. We respond
What is the Gospel asking of us?
Work in age groups if appropriate, then come together as a group to end the session.

Young ones

God makes many different types of people. Because everyone is different, each one of us is asked to follow God in many different and unique ways. But all of us are also God's children and one day we will all live with God together in peace and happiness in God's home.
Do you know people who come from different countries and speak different languages?
Do you know people who go to different churches from you?
How has God made your friends different from you? God asks us to be friends with all types of people, to live together with them in peace and respect.

Story: A legend from India

Once upon a time, all the colours in the world started to argue, each one thinking that they were the best, the most important, the most useful. Green said, "I am the best. Look, I am everywhere... in trees, grass, leaves. Obviously I am the most important."

Blue interrupted, "You are only thinking of the earth. Look at the sky and the sea. Blue is everywhere, much better than green."

Yellow laughed, "You are all so serious. Look at me. I bring warmth, light and life. The sun, moon and stars are all yellow. Without them there would be no fun at all."

Orange then stood up, "But what about me. I may be hidden but I am still the most important. I am in carrots and pumpkins, oranges and mangoes. Without me there is no health or strength. No, I am the best of all."

Red could stand it no longer. He shouted, "I am the king of colours. Red: the colour of life's blood, the colour of danger and passion." Purple disagreed, "Nonsense. I am the best, the colour of royalty and power, the colour of kings and bishops and leaders. It is I who am ruler of you all."

Indigo could hold its tongue no longer. "Think of me. I am the colour of silence. I am peace and prayer. Without me there is chaos."

They continued to argue and argue, their voices booming across the sky. When all of a sudden, there was an almighty FLASH... and thunder rolled from the heavens. Rain poured down and the colours crouched in fear. "Foolish colours," the rain said, "fighting amongst yourselves. Don't you know that God made you all, that each has a purpose unique and different? God loves you all, God needs you all. So join hands and come with me." The colours joined and stretched out across the sky. A beautiful rainbow of colour appeared, each colour united now in their diversity. For separate they were pretty. But together, they were radiant.

Juniors

God wants all of us to know him and love him. Jesus said if we want to know God we should listen to what Jesus said and learn from what he did. We can find out what Jesus said and did by reading the Bible. What is your favourite Bible story about God?
Other people come to know God through different ways: through their way of life or culture. There are many ways to meet God. We are invited to know God more through sharing our own experiences of him with others and through listening to and learning from each other.

Story: What makes a refugee?

In the world today many people have to leave their countries and live in other places. It may be because there is no food in their own country. Or sometimes there is war and if they stay they will be killed. Some people have to leave their homes because other people will not allow them to pray or to say what they think.
When these people arrive in a new place, they can feel very frightened. They are scared because they had bad experiences in their own countries and they are in a new place where they know no one and cannot understand the language. People like these are called refugees. Refugees need our help and understanding. They are different from us, but God wants us to welcome them because they are our brothers and sisters.

Encourage comments relating the story to the Gospel.

4. Activity

Young ones

Use the template of six faces and colour each as if they come from different parts of the world. Write the name of the country under each face. Find the countries on a map or globe.

Juniors

Using the world map or globe, highlight the countries that have a refugee problem. Fill in the faces on the template according to the country you have chosen, and write their names underneath (remember they won't sound very English!).

Try speaking in a different language to each other. How do you feel when you don't understand?

Tips for learning difficulties

Show a picture of different coloured people dressed according to different cultures with a map of the world. Ensure they can appreciate the unique differences between people.

5. We come together

Parents may be invited to join in at this stage.

Focus

As for the start of the session; light the candle.

Gospel

Before Jesus leaves his friends, he tells them that he will prepare a place for each one of them in his Father's house. Jesus has prepared places for everyone in heaven. For men, women and children; for people of all colours and nationalities. Indeed, there is room for everyone in God's kingdom. All of us are welcome!

Prayer

Dear Lord, no one is a stranger to you. Look with kindness on those who are lonely and are separated from their homeland.

Response: Lord, in your mercy; hear our prayer.
Dear Lord, sometimes people have no friends and everyone ignores them. May they find a place of welcome in the family of God's people.

Response: Lord, in your mercy; hear our prayer.
Dear Lord, help us always to respect other people as part of your family.

Response: Lord, in your mercy; hear our prayer.
Amen.

Share

Share the work from the activities.

Sing

"He's got the whole word in his hands"

6th Sunday of Easter

1. Introduction to the theme of the day

"The hope that we have"

Aim: To understand that the meaning of Easter continues to unfold as the Easter season follows its journey to Pentecost. The ascension of Jesus will be celebrated during the week and in the Gospel Jesus prepares his disciples for what is to come. He will soon leave them, but they must not be afraid or lose hope. The words of Jesus invite his disciples, and us as well, to look to the future with confidence and hope.

Leader's reflection: Today's Gospel is taken from John's account of the last meal shared together by Jesus and his disciples. If the language seems difficult or convoluted to a modern reader it must be remembered that phrases such as "Spirit of truth", "I am in my Father and you in me and I in you", and others, were written for a particular community and chosen to convey images and meanings which would be specially significant to them. John is also striving to refute contemporary groups, such as the gnostics, who were seeking to bring Jesus and his message into their own system of beliefs. If we look at the other two readings we find, in Acts, the Holy Spirit coming down on the people of Samaria, only after Peter and John have arrived and confirmed the truth of what the people now believe. In the letter of Peter we hear him encouraging people to be strong in their beliefs and actions, even if they are challenged or made to suffer. Today, we can draw comfort and confidence from the fact that these writings have brought the true message of Jesus to us. They have survived over 2,000 years and not lost their authority. To receive that message so clearly today is a reason for joy and hope.

2. We arrive

We sit in a circle ready to listen to the Gospel. Has anyone anything they would like to tell us about last week's Family Sheet?

Focus

White fabric for Eastertide; candle; spring flowers; a Bible.

Gospel: John 14:15-21

Read from the Lectionary or the Children's Lectionary.

3. We respond

What is the Gospel asking of us?

Work in age groups if appropriate, then come together as a group to end the session.

Young ones

Jesus was having a meal with his friends but he knew that soon those people who hated him would come for him. So he told his friends not to worry, whatever happened, he loved them and he would always be with them.

1. How do you feel if someone you love promises you something very special?
2. How do you feel when you are looking forward to a birthday or a special treat?
3. How do we feel when Jesus tells us that he will always love us and be there for us when we need him?

Story: A birthday surprise!

Charlie and Chloe were five-year-old twins. They were the best of friends. Now they were at school they played with lots of other children. They wanted the whole class to come to their sixth birthday party in four weeks' time.
Mum said: "Impossible! Not enough room."
Dad said: "Thirty children, just like you, it's the stuff nightmares are made of."

Charlie and Chloe chatted and had cuddles with their mum and dad. They smiled and said lots of "pleases". Very soon, Mum and Dad made a promise that their sixth birthday would be the best ever.

Invitations went out to all their friends. Everyone was getting very excited, that is, all except Charlie and Chloe. There was no sign of party preparations anywhere: no chocolate crackolates, no special crisps, no fizzy drinks, no birthday cake, no balloons, no "pass the parcel" wrapped. But they had been promised the best party ever.

The night before the party, Charlie and Chloe said a "trusting" prayer to Jesus: short, but to the point. "Dear Jesus, when you told your friends not to worry, you made a promise to always love them. Please remind Mum and Dad about their promise to us. Thank you for loving us all. Amen."

The party day arrived. Charlie and Chloe were in the car with Mum and Dad. They drove towards the supermarket, past the swimming pool and playground and turned into a car park by a large barn of a building.

The name on the colourful board right across the front said: "PLAYBARN" for the best parties ever!

Charlie and Chloe scampered in to join their friends after giving their mum and dad the biggest hug ever.

Juniors

In his last meal with his disciples Jesus tries very hard to explain that, although he will soon be taken from them, he will not leave them to face the future alone. The Father's love will be brought to them by the Holy Spirit and will keep Jesus with them in a way they do not understand now, but will understand when the Holy Spirit comes.

1. If someone you love very much said they were going to have to go away how do you think you would feel?
2. If the person you love very much told you not to worry, that they promised to come back soon, how would you feel then?
3. How important would the promise be to come back, while they were away?
4. Hope is very important throughout our lives. Whatever happens to us we can hope for peace and love because Jesus promised that he would love us and bring the Father's love to us. Without hope we would spend our whole lives waiting and worrying, but because of Jesus' promise we have hope for the future.

Story: An event in the life of St John Baptist de la Salle

St John Baptist de la Salle was a French priest who lived from 1651 to 1719. He founded a congregation of Brothers who taught as schoolteachers in Christian schools during the great Paris famine of 1709. The food supplies of the community got very low.

John Baptist de la Salle remained calm and left it all in God's hands. The following morning, on his way to say Mass, he met a person who asked, "Sir, may I know where you are going?"

"I am going to celebrate holy Mass, and pray to God that he send our community what we need to survive the day as we have no food and foresee none coming," replied John. Touched by his words, the person replied, "Go in peace: I will provide for you myself." That person kept his word, sending money to the community, satisfying the pressing need. St John Baptist de la Salle prayed with confidence, as we are encouraged to do in today's Gospel.

4. Activity

Young ones

Each child draws round their hand, colours in the outline and cuts it out. These are all stuck on a large sheet of paper round a coloured circle in the centre to create a large collage: "Our Flower of Hope". Alternatively, write these words in the centre of the flower on the template. Colour the "petal" hands and write the children's names on the petals.

Juniors

Jesus asked his friends to go out into the world and teach everyone about his message of love and hope. Everyone who receives Jesus' message has a duty to carry it to others so that the message of Jesus spreads to all people in all nations.

Design a maze with LOVE and HOPE in the centre. At the places where the path is blocked write the name of something that gets in the way of Jesus' message, e.g. GREED, HATE, SELFISHNESS.

Tips for learning difficulties

Have petals ready to colour and paste onto the centre circle of the Flower of Hope.

5. We come together

Parents may be invited to join in at this stage.

Focus

As for the start of the session. Add the collage "Our Flower of Hope" or the individual flowers. Light the candle.

Gospel

One day Jesus said to his disciples: "I will not leave you on your own. I will ask my Father to send you a helper who will stay with you always. The Spirit of God will be with you and in you, though others will not be able to see him or know that he is there. Soon the world will not see me, but you will know that I am truly about."

Prayer

Jesus, I hope you like the flowers we have near the special book which brings us good news.

Jesus, I hope I can bring your love to someone this week by being kind and caring.

Jesus, I hope I can always remember that you love me and want me to be happy. Amen.

Share

Share the work from the activities.

Sing

"Alleluia, alleluia, give thanks to the risen Lord"

The Ascension of the Lord

1. Introduction to the theme of the day

"Baptised into a worldwide family!"

Aim: To reflect on Jesus' command to go out to all nations and baptise them in the name of the Father, and of the Son and of the Holy Spirit.

Leader's reflection: It is interesting to note that Jesus' earthly mission was confined to the area we now know as the Holy Land. It is unlikely that Jesus travelled more than 200 miles from his home town. In these days of global travel that may not seem far but, bearing in mind that it would have been largely on foot, it was probably a considerable distance.

So it could seem odd to command his disciples to do what he himself had not done, but Jesus knew that the disciples would shortly receive a gift that would inspire and empower them to go beyond the boundaries of land and people and take the Gospel and the gift of baptism with them.

We are the recipients of these gifts and, in our turn, are commissioned to go out of our church hall, or wherever we meet, and continue the great work of teaching others about God, helping them to build a close and loving relationship with Jesus and to discover and develop the gifts given to them by the Holy Spirit.

2. We arrive
We sit in a circle ready to listen to the Gospel. Does anyone have anything interesting to tell us about what happened to them during the week?

Focus
White or gold cloth, candle, Bible open at today's Gospel.

Gospel: Matthew 28:16-20
Read from a Children's Bible or Lectionary. Use the introduction and conclusion from the Mass.

3. We respond
What is the Gospel asking of us?
Work in age groups if appropriate. Alternatively, choose the discussion ideas, story and activity most suitable for your group. Come together as a community to end the session.

Young ones

Story: Mateo and Maria are baptised

Mateo and Maria were very excited. They had come to live in (name country) with their parents. They had travelled a lot and lived in several countries. Although none of the family had been baptised, they had gone to lots of different churches around the world. One day, Dad had said, "Now that we are a bit more settled, I wonder if it is time that we were baptised." The more the family talked it over, the more they thought that it was time that they became part of the church family.

Mum and Dad went to special meetings called "Journey of Faith". They told Mateo and Maria that they talked about the readings from Mass and learned about what things meant. Mateo and Maria met with Sister Rosa who told them more about Jesus and what it meant to be baptised.

One day, the family travelled with people from their parish to the cathedral and shared a service with many other people who had decided they wanted to become part of God's family. They had to sign their names in a special book and the woman there told them that their names would be there for ever! Then they were introduced to the bishop who shook their hands and said how pleased he was to see them all.

Then the great day arrived, or rather the great evening, because they were going to be baptised at the Easter Vigil (the night before Easter Sunday). Sister Rosa explained that this was the holiest night of the year and that this was when people all around the world would be baptised too. When they went for the practice in the morning, she told them that people in Australia would already be celebrating their Easter Vigil, then people in India and so on until it was their turn that night.

The children saw the Easter candle being lit and then joined Mum and Dad as Fr Joe poured water over their heads and baptised them.

Everybody was so happy for them. At the party afterwards, they met people from all around the world and realised that they really were part of a huge family, God's family.

Are there different nationalities in your community? Where were people baptised? Was anyone baptised in your church this year? Where did their families originally come from?

Juniors

Discussion: Christians throughout the world

Jesus still calls some people to take the Good News out to the world. **What are they called?** (Missionaries)

Can the children think of any people who spread the Good News?

Are there missionary orders close by? Invite them to come and talk to the children about their work, where they live, where others in their order live and work. **Who was their founder?**

There are Christians throughout the world. If you have children whose families originate in other countries, invite them to tell the group (or try to find out) the names of the people who first brought the Gospel to that land. Think about some of the sacrifices made by the missionaries, but also of the great gift they gave to the country they went to.

Talk about the work of contemporary missionaries and their work with hospitals, schools and support for human rights.

4. Activity

Young ones

Using the template, colour in the picture and use to make the centrepiece of a collage. Have ready posters from CAFOD or Christian Aid or newspaper cuttings, to give as examples of different nationalities. Copy, or cut out and paste, children or adults from Asia, India, S.America, N.America and Europe. Draw arrows to link the people with their country.

Add a large bowl of water to symbolise baptism.

Talk about how people from all over the world are doing what Jesus commanded: being baptised in the name of the Father, the Son and the Holy Spirit. Think about the different languages that are used; different costumes; different climates; but always the same sacrament.

Juniors

The children could also help with the young ones, and add, if possible, some translations of the words of baptism for the children to include on the picture, for example:

I baptise you au nom du Père et du Fils et de du Saint-Esprit (French)

I baptise you im Namen des Vaters und des Sohns und des heiligen Geistes (German)

I baptise you no nome do Pai e do Filho e do Espírito Santo (Portuguese)

I baptise you en el nombre del Padre y del Hijo y del Espíritu Santo (Spanish)

 The children or people within your parish may be able to supply others.

Tips for learning difficulties

Use a globe or a world map to talk about different countries, climates, food, clothes. A selection of dolls in national costume, actual examples or pictures, may help to explain the subject.

5. We come together

Parents can be invited to join in at this stage.

Focus

Light the candle. Invite those gathered to become still.

Gospel

In the Gospel, Jesus knows that he is about to leave the disciples to return to the Father, and he wants them to carry on his mission. He had focused his work on the Holy Land but now was the time to look further, to take his message of Good News out to the world.

The disciples are not quite ready; they will need the power of the Holy Spirit in order to do what Jesus asks. But he makes them a promise: that he will be with them always.

This is the promise Jesus makes to us too.

Prayer

Lord Jesus, you want the whole world to hear the Good News of love and peace that you came to bring.

Thank you for the work of all the people who travelled far and wide so that we could hear your Gospel and be baptised into the family of God. Amen.

Share

During our session, some of us listened to a story about two children who were baptised with their parents and thought about people who may have recently been baptised (include names).

We thought about the work of the missionaries who risk their lives to take the Good News out into the world. We tried to say the words of baptism in different languages (The children might like to try out the translations, or add their own.)

Sing

"Blessed are they who are poor in spirit" (select verses)

"Seek ye first the kingdom of God"

7th Sunday of Easter

1. Introduction to the theme of the day

"Life is this"

Aim: To bring the children to understand that the Easter season draws towards its close in this final Sunday before Pentecost. Jesus prays for his friends so that they will be prepared for what is to come. Most importantly he wants them to know what life really is, not just life lived on earth but life lived onwards beyond death. Eternal life is "to know you, the only true God, and Jesus Christ whom you have sent".

Leader's reflection: As with last week's Gospel the language of this Gospel reading is not straightforward. It is probably better to think of it as a prayer rather than as statements or instructions. The prayer, addressed to the Father, emphasises the unity of the Father with the Son but it goes further, it emphasises the continuation of the Father's message of love and salvation which will be taken into the world by the apostles. They will be "in the world" whilst Jesus will not: "I am not in the world any longer, but they are in the world." Eternal life belongs to anyone who knows the Father through the Son. The power to fully understand this will come to the apostles at Pentecost, that is why Jesus prays rather than teaches. By the work of the apostles and all those who have carried Jesus' message the prayer of Jesus becomes a prayer for all those who have received life and faith through the Holy Spirit.

2. We arrive

The children sit down in a circle. The leader picks up the Lectionary and passes it to a child who passes it on until it has gone round the circle and has come back to the leader. While the Lectionary is being passed the leader says, "We welcome your word, Lord, please let it enter our hearts and minds and live within us."

Focus
White fabric; spring flowers or pot of seedlings; candle.

Gospel: John 17:1-11
Read from the Lectionary or the Children's Lectionary.

3. We respond
What is the Gospel asking of us?
Work in age groups if appropriate, then come together as a group to end the session.

Young ones and Juniors

To be read to all ages together – the theme being growing up from young ones to juniors to adult leaders.

Story: A lesson on life

There was once an old woman who loved gardening and of all the things she grew she loved vegetables most of all. She planted the seeds in the spring and cared for the plants as they popped above ground and she watched as they grew into the most delicious vegetables. At night, when the old woman was asleep, the vegetables in the garden would argue about which one the old woman loved most. The cabbage said he felt her great love in the way she watered him, the Brussels sprouts jostled each other on their stalk trying to say they were loved most because they had the best spot in the garden and the turnip, from just underground, said he was too shy to come above ground in case the old woman embarrassed him by showing all the vegetables how she loved him best. Finally one night an angry onion shouted, "Shut up all of you. Tomorrow I will stop all this constant arguing and ask her myself which of us she loves best."

Next day the old woman came into the garden and, as soon as she was near enough, the angry onion shouted, "Hey, you, old woman, which of us do you like best?" The old woman jumped back and dropped her watering can and ran back into the house shouting, "Help, somebody, there's a talking onion in my garden."

That night a friendly old owl landed among the vegetables. The owl said, "You must understand that vegetables, like everything else, are born, grow and die. But they should know that they are loved because someone gave them life, cares for them and brings them to their final purpose, to be part of a lovely meal. All vegetables are loved differently because they taste different but no vegetable is loved more than any other and it doesn't help anyone to shout at the gardener who looks after you and cares for you. Know that you are loved, know what vegetables are for, stop arguing and be the best vegetable that you can manage is my advice."

And that is what they did. I wouldn't like to finish up as part of a nice meal and nor, I think, would you, but then I am not a carrot or a cabbage. I do get angry sometimes though, and I do argue and I do sometimes forget that I am loved. So I too can take the advice of the owl and try to be the best vegetable, sorry, I mean the best person that I can be.

Young ones

Jesus prayed for his friends.

He wanted them to know the Father as well as he knew the Father, and know that life can only be lived properly by knowing the Father's love. Anyone who knows that really understands Jesus' message and will have life for ever.

1. Is it important to pray for the people you love?
2. Is it important to pray for other people even if they are not your friends?
3. Sometimes people can get mixed up about what life is really all about. Some people want lots of money or lots of friends or to own lovely things. These are all very important but, even if you have all of these things, life can be very, very sad and empty if there is not love as well.

Juniors

Jesus' prayer was that his friends would come to understand what life was really all about, as well as Jesus himself understood it. Jesus prayed that they would come to know that true life, eternal life, was "to know you, the only true God, and Jesus Christ whom you have sent". Jesus prayed that now that his friends knew that what he had been teaching came from the Father, they would be "in the world" and take his teaching out to the world.

1. Everyone dies; no one lives life on earth for ever. That is a hard thing to understand and accept. But Jesus, before he suffered and died, prayed that those who knew him would have eternal life. Is it good news to know that there is a life after death?
2. Of all the things that people can have on earth, which things can people take with them after they die?
3. Do you think it would help people to live a good and caring life to know that beyond this life is a life lived in the love of the Father?
4. What would you say is the most important thing about living?

Leader comment

In our lives we will all be different and many different things will happen to us but we can know that we are all loved and that, whatever happens to us, our real work is one day to be happy with all those people loved by God in heaven. We must try to keep that in our minds as we grow up and grow older. We needn't keep asking God, "Do you love me?" Jesus has told us we are loved, we are loved no matter what happens to us in our lives.

4. Activity

Young ones

May is a month full of life and beauty. Spring is turning into summer and so much new life is around us. Lambs are in the fields, trees are covering themselves with leaves and many flowers have pushed up from the cold winter ground and are now blossoming. Using the template, decorate the cross with flowers and make the star representing Jesus as bright as possible. Draw some flowers growing around the base of the cross.

Juniors

Use the template as above, then finish the following sentence and write it underneath the decorated cross. "The best thing in life is _ _ _ _"

Tips for learning difficulties

However young you are, making faces is fun. Learning difficulties almost never affect this. Making faces, and thinking about how the faces we wear affect others, works with everyone. Mime different moods and guess which is which.

5. We come together

Parents may be invited to join in at this stage.

Focus

As for the start of the session. Light the candle.

Gospel

Jesus looked up to heaven and said, "Father, I have finished the work you sent me to do, and have told my friends all about you. They know that you sent me and through your power I have been able to do many wonderful things. They have listened to me teaching and they truly believe in you. Through their faith and love the world will see the glory of God. Father, I pray that you keep them safe and watch over them always."

Prayer

Choose a different child to read each line.
You lived and died and know what life is like.
You suffered and were hated so you know life can be difficult.
You met and talked to people who were sinners, so you know people can go very wrong.
But you told your friends to tell everyone that you loved them and you brought them the Father's love.
You told us through your friends that love waits for us.
Help us to remember that future love as we live our lives and grow up and grow old. Amen.

Share

Share the work from the activities.

Sing

"Lord of all hopefulness, Lord of all joy"

Pentecost Sunday

1. Introduction to the theme of the day

" **Jesus keeps his promise** "

Aim: To teach the meaning of Pentecost. Pentecost brings us to the end of the Easter season. Jesus calls the Holy Spirit to come to his friends so they can believe what Jesus had told them, and not only believe it themselves, but help others to believe. Suddenly, and for the first time, death is not the end of life. He is risen and we, and all those who believe, can rise after death and live an eternal life of love.

Leader's reflection: We have finally arrived at the end of the Easter season and the end, almost, of the Gospel of John. The Gospel of John is so different from the three synoptic Gospels. It was written for a particular community to help them to understand that faith in Jesus as the Son of God leads to eternal life. It is not so much history, as very early Christian theology. Those for whom the Gospel was written are "in the world" but are not to see themselves as belonging to the world which surrounds them. The mission of their community is simple but overwhelming: to change the world. The Pentecost event in John centres on their authority for such action, a direct commission from the risen Christ, "As the Father sent me, so am I sending you." Jesus also tells of the means by which they will fulfil their mission: "Receive the Holy Spirit." Jesus is faithful to his promise to be with his people and we find his people are to be the whole world. Those who have heard and believe this promise have a duty to change the world. They have a duty to let everyone know that there is a life beyond death, a life of love, given by the Father, made known through Jesus and brought by the Holy Spirit. The message has survived over 2,000 years and not lost its authority. To receive that message so clearly today is a reason for joy and hope.

2. We arrive

We sit in a circle ready to listen to the Gospel. Has anyone anything they would like to tell us about last week's Family Sheet?

Focus
Red fabric/wear red clothes; red candles; balloons for the Church's birthday; white flowers; a dove.

Gospel: John 20:19-23
Read from the Lectionary or the Children's Lectionary.

3. We respond
What is the Gospel asking of us?
Work in age groups if appropriate, then come together as a group to end the session.

Young ones

After Jesus was put to death by the Romans his friends were frightened. They hid from the people who had killed Jesus. Then suddenly Jesus was among them alive and risen from the dead. He had come back to them just as he had promised. He wanted his friends to tell everyone that death was not the end of everything and that the Father's love went on for ever. The Holy Spirit came to Jesus' friends to give them the courage and strength to spread Jesus' Good News to everyone they met.

1. What sort of news is good news?
2. Do you think that when people hear good news they like to share it? Why?
3. It is sad when someone you love dies, but if you know that there is love and life for them in heaven with Jesus, is that good news among the sadness?

Story: Flowers for ever!

Denise loved flowers; she loved all sorts of flowers. Daffodils and roses, lilies and daisies, she even liked flowers that were weeds such as dandelions and buttercups. Denise was only four years old.

Then one day she got a present, it was a tiny present which looked small even in her small hand. It was a seed. Denise and her mum planted the seed in some soil in a small plastic cup with holes in the bottom so the water wouldn't fill it up. They put the cup on a saucer to stop the water dripping out onto the window sill where the plant could get plenty of light. Guess what? The seed became a little plant and grew and grew. Denise and her mum had to keep changing the pot to a bigger one. The plant grew and grew until it was as tall as Denise herself.

Then one day it opened and it looked just like the sun, it had a dark centre with bright yellow petals all around it. "It looks like the sun," said Denise. "It's beautiful."

"That's what it is," said Mum. "It's a sunflower." Denise loved the sunflower more than any other flower in the world. She loved taking care of it and just looking at it.

Then autumn came and the sunflower began to die. "Save it, Mummy," said Denise. "Don't let it die." But Mum said, "It's autumn, Denise, it's time for the flowers to die. Don't worry, Denise, I promise the sunflower will be back. It's dead now but that won't be the end of it, you wait."

Months went by until spring. Then her mum took her to a drawer in the kitchen. "Look what I took from the sunflower when it died." It was a seed, a sunflower seed off Denise's own sunflower. "Now we can plant it and care for it and watch it grow. It will die like the other one in the autumn because plants die then, but if you keep a seed and plant it and care for it you can have sunflowers each year for as long as you like."

And that's just what Denise did.

Juniors

The friends of Jesus had many enemies in Jerusalem, people who had not liked what Jesus had been saying. Jesus' friends were afraid that now Jesus had been killed by the Romans they, themselves, might be in great danger. Then, suddenly, Jesus was among them in the place where they were hiding. Jesus had risen from the dead and was still with them just as he had promised. Death and burial had not been the end of everything for Jesus and death would not be the end of everything for his friends. They understood that believing in the Father's love, and Jesus as his Son, could really bring eternal life. Jesus brings the Holy Spirit to them so they will have the strength, courage and love to take his message out to people, even the people who hated Jesus and had him crucified.

1. Is it hard to believe that there is a life after death?
2. Jesus understood how hard it would be for people to believe his message. He said to his friends, "You believe because you can see me. Blessed are those who have not seen me and yet believe." Do you think praying to Jesus helps people to believe?
3. If someone you love died how important would it be to believe in Jesus' message that people live in heaven in love and happiness after death?

Story: The life of St Aloysius Gonzaga

St Aloysius Gonzaga is the patron of youth and religious novices. He was a gifted Italian and died at the age of 23 years. Aloysius went to great lengths to help the victims of the great plague which ravaged all of Italy. He was struck down with the plague himself and prepared for his death on 20 June 1591. His superior, Fr Jean Casminata, visited him one last time. Aloysius told him, "I am leaving, Reverend Father."

Fr Casminata asked, "Where are you going?"

"To heaven if my sins don't keep me away from it," answered Aloysius.

Fr Casminata exclaimed: "Look at that! Our brother Aloysius speaks of going to heaven as if he is planning a walk to our country house in Frascati!"

Do you know someone you have loved who has died and is now living in heaven with God in love and happiness?

4. Activity

Young ones

Give each child a small seed. Ask them to look at the seed. It looks dried up and dead but if it is planted and looked after it will grow. Inside the dead seed there is new life waiting to come out. Give them something to take the seed home in and ask them to plant and grow the seed to see what the new life will turn into – perhaps a sunflower. Plant some cress on some damp kitchen paper and check its growth next week.

Alternatively, use the template picture of a pot and draw the seed in dark compost, with water and sunlight nearby.

Juniors

Pentecost is the Church's birthday. Wrap nine empty cartons in wrapping paper. Design a different label for each one, representing the nine fruits of the Holy Spirit (Galatians 5:22-23): love, joy, peace, patience, kindness, goodness, faithfulness, gentleness, self-control.

Tips for learning difficulties

Attach some dove mobiles to a coat-hanger. Allow the breeze to blow through them. Explain the gentleness of the Holy Spirit.

5. We come together

Parents may be invited to join in at this stage.

Focus

As for the start of the session. Light the candle. Display the work from the activities, including the nine fruits of the Holy Spirit.

Gospel

When the day of Pentecost came, all the believers were gathered together in one place. Suddenly there was a noise from the sky that sounded like a strong wind blowing, and it filled the whole house. Then they saw what looked like tongues of fire which spread out and touched each person there. They were all filled with the Holy Spirit and began to talk in other languages, as the Spirit enabled them to speak.

Prayer

Today we celebrate the coming of the Holy Spirit. May we go out in peace to all the world to continue the work of Jesus. Amen.

Share

Share the work from the activities.

Sing

"Spirit of the living God" or another Spirit song.

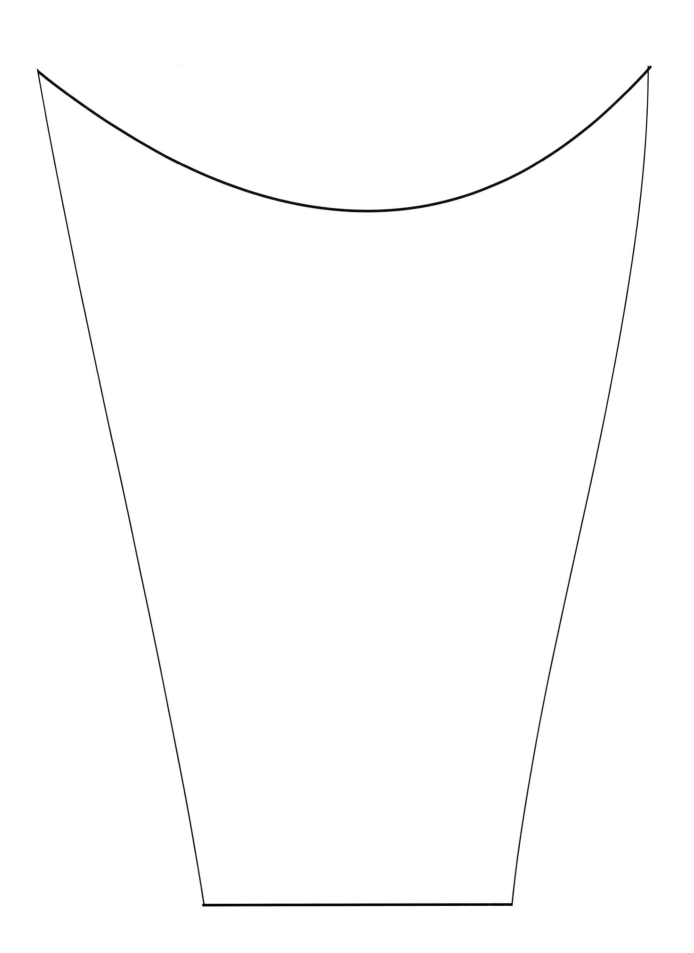

2nd Sunday in Ordinary Time

The 2nd Sunday of Epiphany

1. Introduction to the theme of the day

"Here is the Lamb of God"

Aim: To help the children understand the meaning of being a Christian. In the Gospel, John the Baptist bears witness that Jesus is God's chosen one. We are invited to open our eyes and recognise Jesus, so that we can be his witnesses and show him to the world.

Leader's reflection: "The Christian is a witness to Christ." Let us consider how the readings are selected. The first reading is normally taken from the Old Testament and harmonises with the Gospel. The Old Testament reading enriches our understanding of the Gospel. The second reading is usually from one of the letters of the apostles. In Paul's letter today and in John's Gospel we read how they both recognise Jesus as ranking before them: the "Chosen One of God". In our daily Christian living it is our task to allow the genius of Christ to shine through our lives by the power of the Spirit that lives within us. We discover God's Spirit and his will for us in prayer. We are enabled to become a witness "that he is the Chosen One of God".

2. We arrive
We sit in a circle ready to listen to the Gospel. Has anyone anything they would like to tell us about last week's Family Sheet?

Focus
Green materials: the colour of hope and life. The Holy Spirit (a dove), a candle to spread light on the Gospel.

Gospel: John 1:29-34 (Catholic)
John 1:29-42 (Anglican)
Read from the Lectionary or Children's Lectionary.

3. We respond
What is the Gospel asking of us?
Work in age groups if appropriate, then come together as a group to end the session.

Young ones

Crowds of people were around John the Baptist as he told them all about the Saviour that God had promised to send. He was baptising them in the River Jordan.
When John saw Jesus, he said, "Look, here is the special one, sent by God. He is the one you must follow now."

Mime or act out this Gospel passage.

How did John the Baptist get everybody ready to see Jesus?
What sign did God send so that John would know that Jesus was the chosen one?
How can we follow Jesus?

Story: A favourite tale

A story linking up with the theme; being like Jesus: kind, caring, compassionate, e.g. *Can't you sleep, little bear?* by Martin Waddell.

Juniors

John said, "Look, here is the Lamb of God who takes away the sin of the world. I saw the Spirit coming down on him from heaven like a dove and resting on him.
I came to baptise you with water so that you would recognise God's chosen one. You must follow him for he will baptise you not just with water, but with the Spirit of God also."

John called Jesus the "Lamb of God". What does this mean?
Where else do you hear the words "Lamb of God"?
How did John prepare the way for Jesus?
When did we first receive the Spirit of God?
Can you remember another time when the Spirit appeared, not as a dove but in another way?

Story: How to live like Jesus

Real-life story or news article of how to live like a Christian and show Jesus to the world. Use articles from CAFOD or Christian Aid, World Vision etc.
Discuss events in their own lives, famous people, saints.

4. Activity
Young ones
Have the small doves cut out from the template.

Colour the doves. Use tissue paper for wings, sequins for eyes. Attach a wooden stick or plastic straw with tape so that the children can take their Holy Spirit doves to places where they choose. In turn, allow them to talk about the Holy Spirit.

"I am taking the Holy Spirit to …"

"The Holy Spirit will give power and strength to …"

Juniors
Using the template of the large dove, write a prayer on the dove about how you want the Holy Spirit to work in your life. Add wings by slotting a piece of paper folded into a fan, through a slit in the body. Join the "wings" at the top and thread cotton through to hang the dove.

Tips for learning difficulties
A dove makes us think of peace and gentleness. Play some relaxing music. The dove makes us look forward to good things – it brings hope. Decorate the template of a large dove, sticking with white feathers, soft white materials and bright sequin eyes.

5. We come together
Parents can be invited to join in at this stage.

Focus
Green materials for Ordinary Time, a dove, a candle to light.

Gospel
Jesus is the chosen one.

When John saw him coming he said, "Look, here is the Lamb of God who takes away the sins of the world. He is the special one that I have told you about. I came to baptise you with water so that you would recognise God's chosen one. You must follow him for he will baptise you not just with water, but with the Spirit of God also."

Prayer
Lord Jesus, may these doves remind us of your Holy Spirit.

We pray that we may be filled with your Spirit to spread your Gospel message of truth, love and understanding. Amen.

Share
The work from the activities: the decorated doves; some prayers from the older ones may be read.

Sing
"Spirit of the living God"

"Peace, perfect peace"

3rd Sunday in Ordinary Time

The 3rd Sunday of Epiphany

1. Introduction to the theme of the day

"Turn back to God"

Aim: To learn how to follow Jesus. Jesus begins his public ministry. His invitation is to listen to what he has to say so that we can enjoy the happiness of the kingdom of God. This involves a change of mind and heart. In the Gospel, Jesus calls his first disciples to leave their nets and follow him.

Leader's reflection: "The Christian's true values".

In the second reading, Paul tries to bring a divided Christian community to its senses by describing Jesus' work as "Good News". In today's Gospel, Matthew describes it in the same words: "Jesus proclaimed the Good News of the kingdom." Our word "Gospel" comes from the Anglo-Saxon form of "Good News", namely, "God spell". In the beginning the story of Jesus' three years of public ministry was passed on by word of mouth. Then the apostles, with the help of the Holy Spirit, discussed among themselves, and deepened their understanding of the great events they had shared in. It was clearly desirable to preserve the teaching, miracles and parables of Jesus. The four Gospels we have today were written by Mark, then Matthew or Luke, and St John's Gospel was the last. To receive the Good News, the light of Christ, we need to see who we are in relation to God; to see where we are going; to see what God is calling us to be. The light that is Christ enables us to do this. The light illuminates gradually; the more familiar we become with the Gospel, the brighter the light will shine.

2. We arrive

We sit in a circle ready to listen to the Gospel. Has anyone anything they would like to tell us about last week's Family Sheet?

Focus

Green materials, vestments, a candle, fishing boat, fishing net.

Gospel: Matthew 4:12-23

Read from the Lectionary or Children's Lectionary.

3. We respond
What is the Gospel asking of us?

Work in age groups if appropriate, then come together as a group to end the session.

Young ones

Story: Retelling the Gospel

One day Jesus was walking by himself along the shore of the Sea of Galilee. He saw some fishermen who were working very hard. They were getting ready to take their boats out onto the lake and they had lots of jobs to do. Jesus stopped them and asked them to leave their fishing boats and help him instead. He had an important job to do. He wanted to tell everyone how much God loved them and he needed some friends to help him.

Straight away they followed Jesus. They listened to everything Jesus wanted to tell them.

What important jobs were Peter, Andrew, James and John doing?

What did Jesus say to them?

What did they do?

How can we follow Jesus?

We can follow Jesus by
.... (each child add their own idea).
Help us to listen when you ask us to follow you.
Help us to show others by how we act that Jesus came to be everyone's friend.
Help us to make good choices and turn away from sin.
Thank you, Jesus, for being my leader.

Juniors

Jesus said to them, "Come with me! I will teach you how to bring in people instead of fish." Right there, the two brothers dropped their nets and went with him. Jesus walked on until he saw James and John, the sons of Zebedee. They were in a boat with their father, mending nets. Jesus asked them to come with him too.

Right away they left the boat and their father and went with Jesus.

Why did Jesus need friends to help him?

Where did he find them?

Did they take long to make up their minds?

What do you think Zebedee thought?

Story: Retold through mime

Use simple "props", e.g. blue sheet for the lake, cushions for boats, paper fish, net curtains for fishing nets.

4. Activity

Young ones

Using the template, colour and decorate the fish. Use glitter glue or metallic pens for the shiny scales and paste on a sequin eye and green tissue for the weed. Write the name of someone you can follow, like Jesus, on the body of the fish.

Juniors

Decorate the fish and write a "thank you" prayer for the friends and family who first told you about Jesus.

Tips for learning difficulties

Have the fish ready for decoration. Play the magnetic fishing game. Talk about Jesus wanting us to be like good fishermen helping him to bring everybody to hear his Good News.

5. We come together

Parents can be invited to join in at this stage.
Invite those gathered to become still.

Focus

Green materials for Ordinary Time, vestments, fishing boat, fishing net, candle to light.

Gospel

Jesus calls Andrew, Simon, James and John to follow him. They are to move away from their work as fishermen and become "fishers of men", gathering people into the kingdom of God. They could not have imagined just how far the new spiritual nets that Jesus was giving them would spread... even as far as N... *(name of the place where you are meeting)*.

Prayer

Jesus, you ask us to be your friends. We can follow you by ...
(children add their own ideas).
Help us to listen when you ask us to follow you.
Help us to show others, by how we act, that Jesus came to be everyone's friend.
Help us to make good choices and turn away from sin.
Thank you, Jesus, for being my leader. Amen.

Share

Talk about what happened in the session and what the children have learnt. Talk about the fact that we are gathered because the apostles did as Jesus asked: we are the fish that Jesus said they would catch.

Sing

"Follow me, follow me"
"I want to build my life"

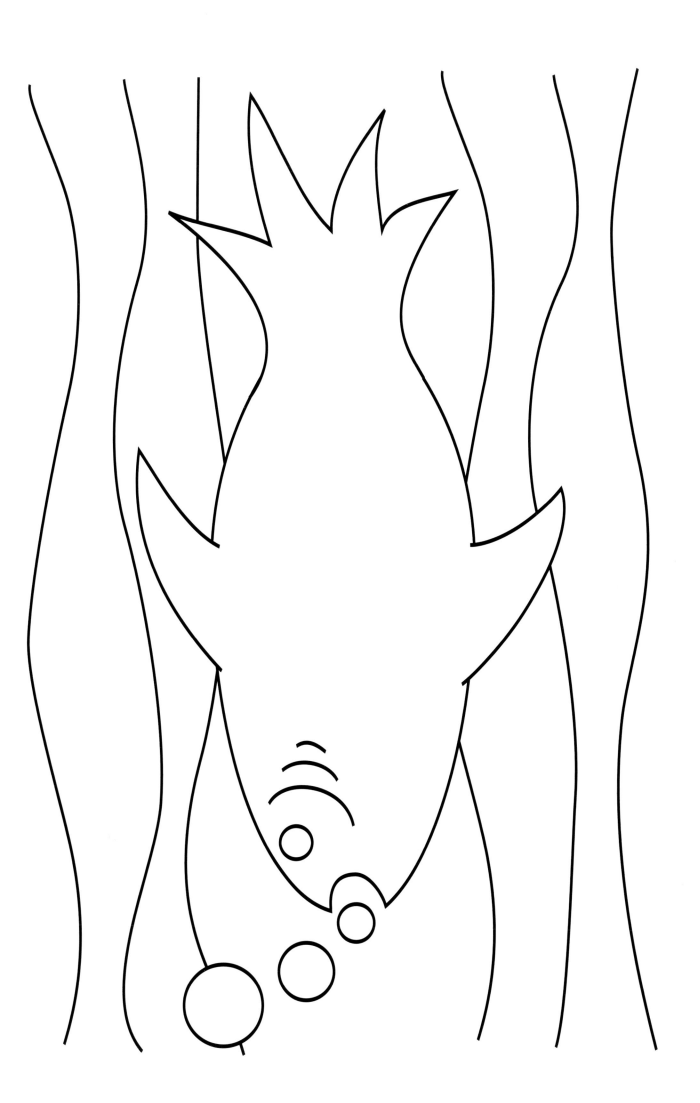

4th Sunday in Ordinary Time

1. Introduction to the theme of the day

"Happy are those who follow my way"

Aim: To understand God. God our Father made us all to be happy. In the Gospel Jesus shows us how to be happy. When we follow his way, we will discover that it is how we treat other people that will lead us to happiness.

Leader's reflection: Today's Gospel, the introduction to Jesus' greatest sermon, presents the blueprint for happiness, or blessedness. The latter is a better word as "hap" means chance as in haphazard, as though happiness is dependent upon the chances and alterations of this life. True bliss, however, is far deeper and more secure than this: it is the joy that comes with the kingdom of heaven. "How happy are the poor in spirit: theirs is the kingdom of heaven." Those who are subjects in the kingdom of heaven are those who allow God to reign in their lives; who place God above all other values. We cannot set boundaries to God's kingdom, nor can we judge who is within the kingdom or outside it.

2. We arrive
We sit in a circle ready to listen to the Gospel.
Has anyone anything they would like to tell us about last week's Family Sheet?

Focus
Our candle to light, green fabric during Ordinary Time, other green items.

Gospel: Matthew 5:1-12
Read from the Lectionary or Children's Lectionary.

3. We respond
What is the Gospel asking of us?
Work in age groups if appropriate, then come together as a group to end the session.

Young ones

Story: Grumble, grumble, grumble

God made us to be happy. Jesus tells us that if we listen to him, then he will show us how to be happy. Today we will think about all the people we know. We will think about the times they are happy and the times they are sad. What is it that makes them happy or sad?
Encourage the children to talk about their families and friends. What sorts of things make them happy? What sorts of things make them sad? When do they feel happiest themselves?

Brian was a very bad-tempered badger. He grumbled about everything. He grumbled about the dark nights, and he grumbled about the wet ground, and he grumbled about the scratchy grass, and he grumbled about the skinny worms. He grumbled about everything. One night as he was wandering around, Brian came across Owen the owl who was hooting merrily.
"Why are you so happy?" asked Brian.
"The night is dark and the stars are bright and the moon is so-o-o beautiful," hooted Owen.
Brian looked at the moon. It was beautiful.
"But the ground is wet," he grumbled to himself, "and the grass is scratchy, and the worms are skinny." Grumble, grumble, grumble.
Next he came across Daphne the duck splashing about and paddling in a puddle on the wet ground,
"Why are you so happy?" he asked Daphne.
"The water is wet and the puddle is deep and I can splash, splash, splash!" quacked Daphne. Brian tried it.

Splashing was fun!
"But," he muttered, "the grass is still scratchy, and the worms are still skinny." Grumble, grumble, grumble. Next he came across Camilla the cow. Camilla was munching the grass greedily.
"Why are you so happy?" he asked Camilla.
"The grass is green and the cud is sweet and I can chew, chew, chew," mooed Camilla. Brian tried it. The grass was very good. "But the worms are still skinny," he grumbled.
Then he came across Wendy the worm. Wendy was his friend. And Wendy was very skinny.
Suddenly he realised that he liked skinny worms!
"How silly I have been," he said to himself. "The moon is beautiful, and splashing is fun, and the grass is delicious and I like skinny worms. I am a very happy badger and I will never grumble again."

Juniors

Story: The life of St Francis

God made us to be happy, and most people spend their lives trying to do the things that they think will make them happy and to get the things which they think will make them happy. But Jesus tells us a different way to be really happy.
Talk about yourself, your family and your friends. What makes them happy or sad? Encourage them to look deeper, beyond the obvious quick fix of pleasure. Have they ever experienced unexpected happiness, through an unselfish action?

St Francis is often described as the "happy saint". He started life as the son of a rich merchant. He grew up to be very popular amongst his friends, and was even considered to be a bit of a catch by the girls. When he was old enough he joined the army and went away to fight. He was injured and became very ill. While he was slowly recovering, he heard the Gospel of the Beatitudes and began to see his life differently. He still wanted to be happy, but in a different way, in the way set out by Jesus. He told his parents that he did not want to be tied down by the family's riches, he wanted to follow Jesus and to

live as a poor man instead, and he left home. It took his parents quite a long time to come to terms with this. St Francis lived in poverty, and happiness, for the rest of his life.
Many men and women saw the way he was living and went to join him. They still do. St Francis started the order of the Franciscans. There are Franciscan friars and nuns all over the world. They still choose to live their lives by following Jesus in poverty. If you meet any of them, you will find they are usually very happy people.

Encourage comments relating the story to the Gospel.
(The story of the Happy Prince by Oscar Wilde would also be suitable here.)

4. Activity

Young ones

Using the picture-frame template, the children can draw a picture of their family or friends doing something which made everyone happy. Try to encourage them to draw something which involves sharing with other people. Put a caption on the picture, e.g. "We are happy when we play together"; "We are happy when we share a meal."

Juniors

Using magazines etc. ask the children to find advertisements and articles which give us examples of how some people think we can be made happy, and (maybe more difficult) articles which give examples of living happily in the way which Jesus taught us. A selection may be brought to the session if time is limited. Put together two collages from these and discuss them with the children.

Tips for learning difficulties

The collage pictures can be selected beforehand so that the children can sort them into the two groups and stick them onto the paper. Alternatively, if there is a large group of children with learning difficulties, they can be given the task of sorting though a pile of (previously selected) pictures which show happy people (e.g. groups of friends) and sad people (e.g. pictures of a war zone). They could make collages of these and try to describe the things which make the people happy and sad.

5. We come together

Parents can be invited to join in at this stage.

Focus

Our candle is lit, green fabric during Ordinary Time, other green items, the collages and the pictures.

Gospel

Jesus was being followed by a large crowd. He climbed a hill and he spoke to them as they were seated around him. He told them how they could be really happy. God's blessing is on:

> Those who are kind
> Those who are forgiving
> Those who are poor in spirit
> Those who are sad and lonely
> Those who are fair.

Even when you feel very alone, God is with you; and that is the kingdom of heaven.

Prayer

We thank God for all the ways in which he makes us happy: children can be invited to contribute.
Suitable responses might be:
— Thank you, God, for making us happy.
— Thank you, God, for showing us the way to be happy.

Share

Share the work from the activities.

Sing

"If you're happy and you know it"

We are happy when we

....

5th Sunday in Ordinary Time

Proper 1

1. Introduction to the theme of the day

> **"You are the salt of the earth. You are the light of the world"**

Aim: To explore the meaning of Christ being the light of the world. When we were baptised we received the light of Christ. In the Gospel Jesus tells us that we are like lamps with the brightness of God's love and goodness shining out to the world. When we help other people to "see" more clearly, our world will be a better place to live in.

Leader's reflection: William Booth founded the Salvation Army in 1865. He took the message of Christ to the poor people by means of open-air services with bands and banners. He was heard and seen. He reinforced his preaching with good works. He fed the poor people and sheltered the homeless people. Effective preaching needs the support of good works. Jesus Christ combined his words and actions, providing an effective sign of God's power. Our words and actions will demonstrate the power of God in our lives. Some people may doubt what we say but they will always believe what we do: actions speak louder than words. However, we must not neglect words: perhaps someone only needs one word of encouragement from us to build up the courage to follow the Gospel more closely. When we are close to Christ we will be able to shed light on the problems of our world.

2. We arrive

We sit in a circle ready to listen to the Gospel.
Has anyone anything they would like to tell us about last week's Family Sheet?

Focus

Use a lamp if possible. Light it and put it on a prominent stand in the middle of the room.

Gospel: Matthew 5:13-16

Read from the Lectionary or Children's Lectionary.

3. We respond

What is the Gospel asking of us?

Work in age groups if appropriate, then come together as a group to end the session.

Young ones

God made us the way that we are, and we are all very special. God wants us to be sparkly people and happy people, so that when other people see us they will know that we are made by God and that God loves us. Discuss with the children the different ways in which they sparkle: what things do they do which make them feel sparkly? (e.g. what are they good at? what do they enjoy doing?) How do other people make them feel sparkly? (e.g. when they help other people, when they are told they are good.)

Story: Teresa the tortoise learns to share

There was once a tortoise called Teresa. She was a very selfish tortoise who did not like to share any of her things. Because of this she did not have many friends. One day when she was digging in the garden, she came across an old lamp. It was a very dirty, old lamp, but Teresa was curious to see what it was like underneath, and so she took it into her house-shell and polished it with some old rags until it was shiny and bright and as good as new. Then she lit it. The light from the lamp lit up the whole garden. Teresa did not want to share the light from the lamp with anybody, and so she put the lamp back into her house-shell where nobody else could see it, and began to wander around the garden in the darkness again, but humming quietly to herself.

After a while she bumped into Brian the badger. He looked very surprised. "Hello," said Brian, "what has happened to you? There is a strange light coming out of your shell. Has something nice happened?" Teresa stretched out her neck and looked over her shoulder at her house-shell. To her surprise she saw that some of the light from the lamp was escaping through a tiny chink in her shell. She was very cross because she did not want to share the light from her new lamp with anybody.

"That's my new lamp," said Teresa, crossly.

"Can I see it, please?" Brian asked.

Teresa did not want to show Brian the lamp, but Brian had asked her very nicely, so she decided to show it to him.

Brian liked the lamp. "That is a very shiny lamp," he said, "and very useful for lighting up the garden at night."

As he began to admire the lamp and to chat with her, Teresa found that she was enjoying herself. Maybe sharing things was not so bad after all.

"Come and show your lamp to my friends," said Brian, and off they went together to find all of Brian's friends. They found Camilla the cow.

"What a beau-ooo-tiful lamp," she mooed. "All the better to chew to."

They found Daphne the duck.

"What a da-da-dazzling lamp!" she quacked. "All the better to splash-splash-splash to."

They found Wendy the worm.

"What a wonderful lamp," she whispered. "All the better to wriggle to."

Soon the garden was full of animals, admiring the lamp and enjoying themselves. And so was Teresa. And the lamp lit up the whole of the garden all night long.

Juniors

Sit in a circle around the lamp. Spend some time quietly and encourage the children to think of the people that they know who make their lives more flavoursome (enjoyable, exciting, meaningful). Go around the group, giving each child an opportunity to thank God for one of the people who gives his/her own life more flavour.

I thank God for... She/he gives my life more flavour by...

Story: The life of St Thomas More

St Thomas More was by all accounts a man of great wit and intelligence. He was successful in the court of King Henry VIII, rising to the post of Lord Chancellor, while maintaining his faithfulness to his Christian principles. When the king asked him to sign a document saying that he, the king, was now the head of the Church in England,

Thomas refused, and for this he was ultimately beheaded. Thomas died a man of integrity. He understood that his life would have no meaning if he agreed to sign up to something he believed was wrong. He would no longer be "salt" to those around him.

For older juniors, in the book *The Amber Spyglass* by Philip Pullman (from the "Dark Materials" trilogy), Lyra opens a way through the land of the dead by telling true stories about her own life. The vultures in the land only want to hear real stories, no matter how simple. They are not interested in the exciting and heroic stories which she makes up at first, trying to impress them.

Encourage comments relating the story to the Gospel.
(The story of the Happy Prince by Oscar Wilde would also be suitable here.)

4. Activity

Young ones

Using the template, paste in pieces of shiny fabric, foil, paper, but leaving one square to draw a picture of themselves doing something good for someone.

Juniors

Have some groceries on display. Note how many contain salt (sometimes potassium chloride or sodium chloride).
Using the template, fill the squares with good works and actions. Write the names of people they know whose example they would like to follow.
Decorate the borders of the squares brightly.

Tips for learning difficulties

The bright people activity can be simplified/exaggerated by acting out being a sparkly person (cheerful, bright, helpful) or a dull person (bad-tempered, cross, grumpy).

5. We come together

Parents can be invited to join in at this stage.

Focus

Place a lamp/candle in a prominent position on a table. Have a cover (e.g. a clay flower pot) ready to "hide" it.

Gospel

Jesus said: "You are like light for the whole world. A city built on top of a hill cannot be hidden, and no one would light a lamp and put it under a clay pot.
A lamp is placed on a lamp stand, where it will give light to everyone in the house.
Make your light shine, so that others will see the good that you do and will praise your Father in heaven."

Older children can demonstrate the words of the Gospel as it is read, using the items from the "Focus" above.

Prayer

Sit in a circle around the lamp. Go around the group, encouraging each child to thank God for one of the ways in which they sparkle. Some may need help.

I feel shiny and bright when I... Thank you, God, for...

Share

Share the work from the activities.

Sing

"This little light of mine"

6th Sunday in Ordinary Time

Proper 2

1. Introduction to the theme of the day

> ## "I do not come to abolish the law, but to fulfil it."

Aim: Over the next two weeks the juniors will think about the difference between the letter of the law and the spirit of the law. The young ones will focus on how rules help us to be good.

Leader's reflection: One of the problems that the early church had to face was its relationship with Judaism. Jesus was a Jew and his early followers were all Jews: they upheld the Law of Moses and they honoured the traditions of their own people. In his Gospel, Matthew shows the continuity with ancient tradition. Jesus does not come to abolish the law and the prophets, rather, he is their completion. The law of Christ contains the hidden wisdom of God. It is a law given by love, and can only be fulfilled by genuine love and concern for others.

2. We arrive

We sit in a circle ready to listen to the Gospel.
Has anyone anything they would like to tell us about last week's Family Sheet?

Focus

A lighted candle, green fabric for Ordinary Time, a book of law or rules (the catechism, or the Bible open at Leviticus), or a picture of Moses with the tablets of law.

Gospel: Matthew 5:17-37

Read from the Lectionary or Children's Lectionary.

3. We respond
What is the Gospel asking of us?

Jesus tells us he did not come to abolish the law. What is a law? Which laws was he talking about?
Work in age groups if appropriate, then come together as a community to end the session.

Young ones

Story: Moses is given the law

Moses was in the desert with the people of Israel. Moses was the leader, and he was fed up because he didn't really want to be leader, and all the people were fed up because there was nothing to do in the desert and they were bored.

One day everyone woke up in a bad mood. It was just that sort of a day. No sooner were they out of their tents in the morning, than they were fed up. By lunchtime they were all squabbling with each other, and by teatime they were so bad-tempered that they started fighting. Moses didn't like it when the people were fed up and squabbling and fighting. So he found a big rock, and sat on it, and asked the people to come to him so that he could sort out all the things they were fighting over. By the end of the day, he was very tired.

The next day Moses went to see God. God had been watching everything. He saw that the people were fed up, and he saw when they started squabbling and he saw when they started fighting, and he saw Moses sitting on his big rock, trying to be the leader and sorting everything out. God wanted Moses to be a good leader, and he wanted the people to be happy and not to squabble or fight, so he gave Moses some rules written on tablets of stone. They were good rules. They would help the people to be happy, and if the people liked the rules and lived peacefully, then the God of Moses would be their God also.

Moses showed the rules to the people. The people saw that they were good rules. They said, "We will keep the rules because they will help us to be happy and we will keep the rules because they will help us to stop squabbling and fighting, but most of all we will keep the rules because they are God's rules, and we want him to be our God."

What do you think the rules were? Do you think they were good rules?

Juniors

Story: The life of St Thomas More

St Thomas More was a very clever man and he was a lawyer.

In 1529 King Henry VIII made him Lord Chancellor of England: the most important job in the kingdom.

Sometime later, King Henry wanted to get married to a lady called Anne Boleyn. There was only one problem, he already had a wife. Even if he divorced his first wife (called Katherine), the Church (whose head was the Pope in Rome) would not let him marry again. King Henry was not happy about being told what to do by other people, so he passed a new law, which said that as he was king, and the head of all England, he was also the head of the Church in England. That way, he could decide for himself who he was allowed to marry.

He tried to get Thomas More to say that this was a good law, but Thomas refused to say anything. He did not think that it was right, but he knew that if he said so, he would be accused of treason and be beheaded. As long as he kept quiet, although everybody knew what he was thinking, he was keeping the law and so he was safe.

In the end, the king persuaded one of Thomas' friends to say that he had heard Thomas say that the new law was wrong. This made Thomas guilty of treason, and so he was beheaded. Thomas More's last words to the crowd were, "I die the king's good servant, but God's first."

Did Thomas try to keep the law? How did he do this? Should we try to keep the law? When might it be right not to keep it?

4. Activity

Young ones

What does it mean to be good or to be bad? You might like to give demonstrations of good behaviour (sitting quietly, sharing, helping) and bad behaviour (stomping around, tantrums, fighting). Ask the children to identify the good and bad elements in your behaviour. How do we feel when we are being good? How do we make other people feel? How about when we are being bad? Do we know any rules which help us to be good? Ask each child to give an example of their own good behaviour in the last week. Draw and write it on the card provided.

Using the card made from the template page, write a rule on the stone tablet and draw inside the card a picture of yourself obeying the rule.

Juniors

What laws or rules do you know? You might have a rule at school which says you must put your hand up before speaking in class.

Why do you have this rule? Can you think of a time when you might not keep it? Choose three or four rules. Try and work out why we have the rules; how do they help people to live and work together? Prepare a short presentation to make to the rest of the group.

Juniors will need Bibles for this week's activities when looking up the Ten Commandments (Exodus 20:1-17; Deuteronomy 5:1-21).

Tips for learning difficulties

Children could have special symbols for "allowed" and "not allowed" – if not, use a tick/cross, or a red/green card. While you are talking about good and bad behaviour, with the young ones, the children can contribute by showing the appropriate card.

5. We come together

Parents can be invited to join in at this stage.

Focus

Gather around the candle and the book of law, the young ones can include their cards in the display.

Gospel

Jesus said: "I am not a rebel. I have not come to break all the rules, but to show you what they really mean, and how best to live them."

Prayer

Jesus, we have rules to help us to live together peacefully. Help us to understand them and to keep them in a way which is helpful to each other. Amen.

Share

The juniors can present the conclusion of their work on rules; young ones can be presented with their cards from the display.

Sing

"Moses, I know you're the man" (the verses could be read in turn, if the tune is unfamiliar)

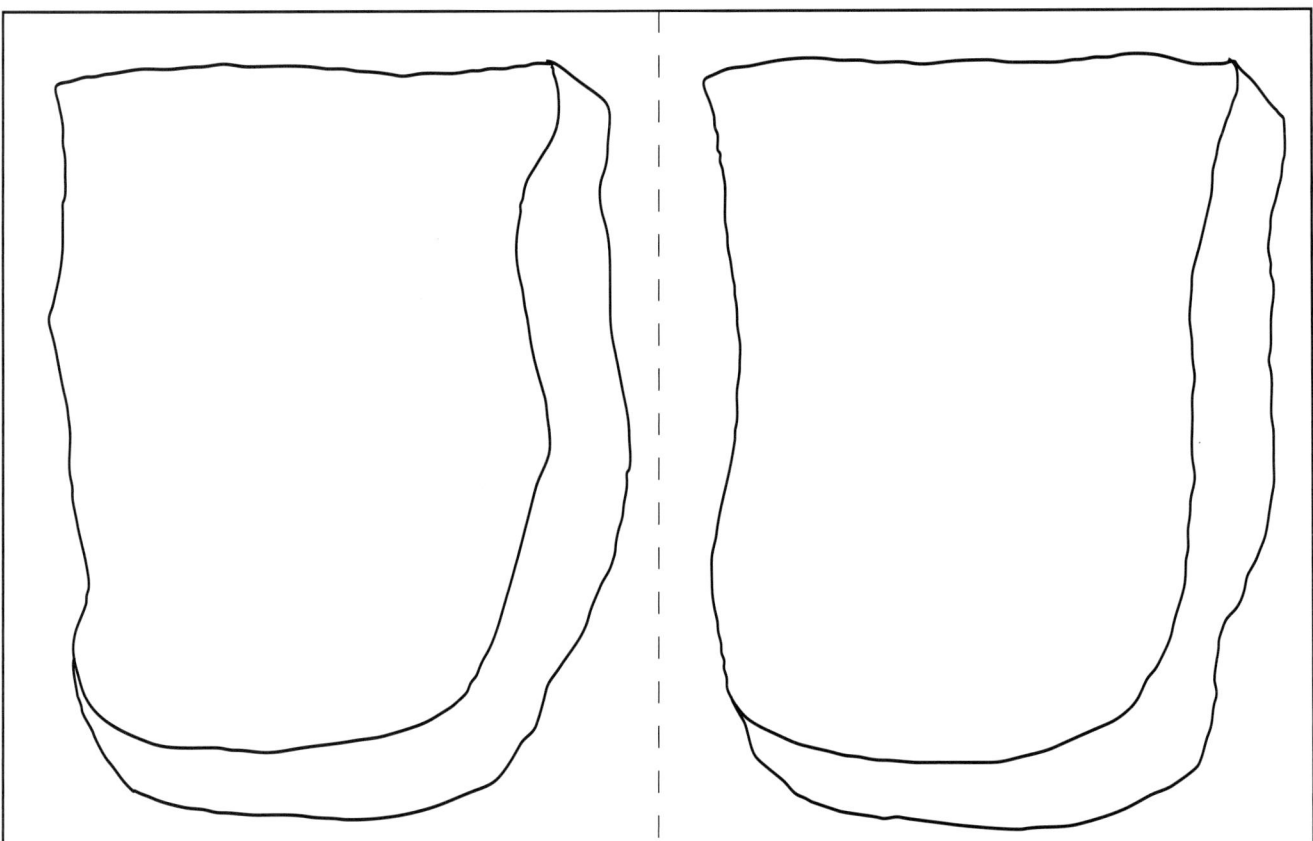

This is
me doing
something
good

7th Sunday in Ordinary Time

Proper 3

1. Introduction to the theme of the day

" Do something extra "

Aim: We think about how Jesus' love for us goes way beyond anything the law might demand.

Leader's reflection: The law of love can be a terrifying proposition: without the benchmark of virtue, which a set of rules and regulations affords us, how can we ever be confident that we have done enough, that we are good enough? This is a fundamental point of difference between the Old Testament teachings and the Gospels. In the Old Testament, a person could stand before God and other people, "justified" by his or her own good deeds as defined by law-keeping. In the Gospels, that notion of self-justification is shattered by the demands of love. When can we say that we have loved enough? We are justified only in God's love for us: God has loved us and sent his only Son.

2. We arrive

We sit in a circle ready to listen to the Gospel.
Has anyone anything they would like to tell us about last week's Family Sheet?
Did you make anyone happy last week?

Focus

A lighted candle; green fabric for Ordinary Time; "Do Something Extra" on a poster, or something similar.

Gospel: Matthew 5:38-48

Read from the Lectionary or Children's Lectionary.

3. We respond
What is the Gospel asking of us?

Last week we talked about laws helping us to be good. What new thing is Jesus saying today? What did Jesus do extra for us? What extra things can we do? Work in age groups if appropriate, then come together as a community to end the session.

Young ones
Story: God does something extra

Moses was feeling a bit better. He was in the desert with the people of Israel. He was the leader, and it was difficult at first sorting out all the people, but then God had given them some laws, and now everyone was happy. Tonight they were having a party. It was a special party called a Passover party. It was God's party.

Suddenly there was a scratching at the entrance to his tent. Moses pulled the flap back. There stood two little boys. They looked a bit scruffy and dirty, and very upset. "You're not ready for the party!" said Moses. "You know what it says in the law; you can only come to the party if you are clean and ready."

"We know," said the boys. "That is why we came to see you. Our Aunty Ruth was poorly, and we were helping, and then she died, and we were helping some more. We have only just finished helping, so we haven't been able to get ready for the party, but it is God's special party, and we really do want to come. We wondered if you could ask God for us. Please!"

Moses looked at the boys: the law said you had to be clean and ready for the party, and the boys certainly weren't clean, and they certainly weren't ready. However, as they had been such good boys doing all that helping, maybe God would let them come after all. He went to speak to God.

He explained everything to God, very carefully. And God listened, very carefully. At the end he smiled at Moses. He was very pleased with the two boys for being helpful, and he was thrilled that they wanted to come to his party. "I'll tell you what," said God. "The law is supposed to help people be happy, not make them sad. Tell the boys to go and get clean and ready. They won't be in time for the big party, but they can have their own party for me instead. Two parties! I am a very happy God!"

Do you think the boys had a good reason to be late for the Passover party? What was it?
Did Moses act fairly? What do you think of the answer that God gave to Moses?
We all wear different clothes for different occasions. Can you think of some?
When do you wear casual clothes and when do you wear smart clothes and why?

Juniors
Story: Love your enemies

It was Christmas Eve, 1993. The Christian monks living in the monastery at Tibhirine in Algeria were preparing the chapel for Christmas, when they were interrupted by several men carrying machine guns.

Two months earlier, the monks had been warned to leave Algeria, by a rebel group which was fighting the government. The monks refused to leave, because the local people still needed their help. They also refused to take sides in the conflict: they said they were a sign of peace and reconciliation; they would give medical help to anyone who was hurt and came to the monastery unarmed, but they would not take sides. The armed men left, politely wishing them a happy Christmas.

It was a dangerous decision to make; already many foreigners had been killed, but the monks knew the risk they were taking. The Abbot, Dom Christian de Chergé, wrote in his diary: "If it should happen one day – and it could be today – that I become a victim of terrorism ... I would like my community, my Church, my family, to remember that my life was given to God and to this country."

For the next two years the monks continued as before, living simply and quietly with their Islamic neighbours, offering them hospitality and sharing their sorrows and hardships. The monks tried to live the Gospel message of love and peace, and they recognised that all their Muslim neighbours were trying to do the same. Dom Christian wrote: "My life has no more value than any other; nor any less value."

In 1996, just before Easter, the monks were kidnapped by another extremist group and taken away. Two months later, the group announced that all seven monks had been beheaded. Dom Christian had written in his diary: "I should like, when the time comes, to ... beg forgiveness of God and of my fellow human beings, and at the same time to forgive with all my heart the one who would strike me down ... may we find each other, happy good thieves, in Paradise, if it pleases God, the Father of us both. Amen. In sha 'Allah."

How did the monks live out today's Gospel message? What effect do you think this had on the people around them?

4. Activity

Young ones

God wants his laws to make us happy, not sad. Colour in the boys looking scruffy and dirty and sad because the law says they cannot come to the party. Then colour them in wearing their party clothes, all ready and clean and happy because God has given them an extra party.

Juniors

You are going to play a game called "The law says". Sit in a circle with a ball. The person holding the ball says, "The law says …" and throws the ball to someone else in the circle. The person who catches it answers, "but Jesus says …" (e.g. "The law says you can fight your enemies, but Jesus says love your enemies").
Compile a list together before the game begins.

Tips for learning difficulties

Play the above game, by sitting on the floor and rolling the ball to each other. The leader says, "Jesus says that he wants us to … to each other." The child is helped to suggest an answer.

5. We come together

Parents can be invited to join in at this stage.

Focus

Gather around the cross and candle, and a display of the young ones' work.

Gospel

Jesus said: "Following the law will help you to be good, but if you really want to be happy you must be more generous than the law. Share what you have, and love your enemies: that way you will be perfect just as God is perfect."

Prayer

Jesus, we want to be perfect like you, but sometimes it is very hard. Help us to love each other so much that it is easy to be perfect. Amen.

Share

Young ones can present their pictures; juniors can demonstrate their game again, maybe including the adults this time. Favourite responses could be drawn up on posters to decorate the meeting room.

Sing

"Love is his word"
"A new commandment I give unto you"

The 2nd Sunday before Lent

1. Introduction to the theme of the day

> ## "That is why I am telling you not to worry"

Aim: To think about Jesus' words on the subject of worries and concerns. Worrying causes us enormous amounts of stress, even to the youngest. We use the serenity prayer as a means of sorting through our anxieties.

Leader's reflection: In today's Gospel Jesus is encouraging us to let go of our worries because they are a barrier to our relationship with God. It might be tempting to think he is advocating a sort of hippy, no ties, freedom which expects little from the world, but contributes even less: "look at the lilies of the field ...", but he makes it clear that he doesn't want us to have no purpose, no priorities, but that we should make God our priority, his kingdom our purpose. The serenity prayer is a familiar expression of Jesus' message which bears frequent revisiting and is the primary vehicle for today's work, especially with the older children.

It would be helpful to have at least the first part of the serenity prayer written out for display as it plays a significant role in this week's activities. You will need a dictionary for the juniors' activity.

2. We arrive

We sit in a circle ready to listen to the Gospel.
Has anyone anything they would like to tell us about last week's Family Sheet?

Focus

A lighted candle, green fabric for Ordinary Time, pictures of an anxious face and a relaxed one.

Gospel: Matthew 6:24-34

Read from the Lectionary or Children's Lectionary.

3. We respond

What is the Gospel asking of us?

Talk about how we feel when we are worried. Jesus tells us not to worry. Why?
Work in age groups if appropriate, then come together as a community to end the session.

Young ones
Story: Don't worry, God will look after you

Moses was still in the desert with the people of Israel. God had given them a law, and that had helped the people to be happy, but they still worried a lot. They worried about their tents being blown away; they worried about their sheep getting sick; they worried about their clothes wearing out; they worried about the cows not giving them enough milk, but most of all they worried about food.

Moses went to see God. "The people are very worried about food," said Moses.

"I know," said God.

"They worry about running out of water to drink," said Moses.

"I know," said God.

"They worry that they have no food for their children," said Moses.

"I know," said God.

"And they worry that they will run out of bread," said Moses.

"I know," said God. Moses waited.

God said, "Go back to the people and do what I tell you." Moses went back to the people. God said, "Hit the rock with your stick." Moses hit the rock with his stick, and out came a stream of water. God said, "Look up into the sky." Moses looked up, and there were lots of quails flying down into the camp. God said, "Go into your tents, and in the morning there will be bread." And the next morning, all over the ground was special bread called manna.

Moses said to the people, "You worry too much; God has given you everything you need."

And the people said, "Amen."

How did the people of Israel get over their worries? Who was there to help them? How did Moses help them? Who was a good example to them? Who helps you get over your worries?

Juniors
Story: The serenity prayer

"God grant me the serenity to accept the things I cannot change, the courage to change the things I can, and the wisdom to know the difference."

This is generally known as the beginning of the serenity prayer. Who actually wrote it is something of a mystery. One possibility is that a man called Dr Reinhold Niebuhr used it at the end of a sermon in the middle of the twentieth century, but even he acknowledges that it might have existed before then: some people claim it goes back to the time of the Greeks.

What we do know, is that shortly after it was used by Dr Niebuhr it was spotted by a member of Alcoholics Anonymous. When people are worried or anxious about something, it can change the way they behave. Some people get very bad-tempered, some people turn on the television, or play music very loudly, and escape from their worries that way. If you are an alcoholic, the first thing you will probably want to do is to have a drink. Alcoholics Anonymous (AA) is a self-help group for people who are addicted to alcohol. They meet regularly to support each other, and to encourage each other to stay away from alcohol even when they are upset or worried, the hardest time.

When the people in Alcoholics Anonymous read the prayer, they thought it was so good that they decided to have it printed out so that everyone could have a copy.

Why do you think this prayer was useful to the people in Alcoholics Anonymous? What do you do when you are worried or anxious about something? Do you think the prayer could help you?

4. Activity

Young ones

What do we mean if we say someone is worried? How do they feel? (Frightened, anxious, upset ...)   What do they look like? (Worried face.) Who do we know who is worried? What are they worried about? (The children might not know, you could give some of your own examples.)

How can we help someone who is worried? (Be kind to them, give them a cuddle, and show them that we love them.)

Make a card or poster for someone who is worried, someone who needs cheering up. This could be a group effort. On the front write, "Don't worry" and decorate it.   Inside write, "God loves you", or "We love you" and sign it with your names.

Juniors

What am I worried about? Use the template to make a list of all the things that worry you. Go through the list, and for each one use the serenity prayer to help you decide if there is something you can do about it: maybe you could talk to someone, or change the way you are doing something. Some of the things which worry you will be completely out of your control and you will not be able to change them, but you can still pray about them. Look up serenity in the dictionary and ask God to help you to live with these things without worrying so much.

Tips for learning difficulties

If the child uses sign language (e.g. Makaton) or symbols, find the ones for worried/anxious/frightened and happy/relaxed before the session. Worried might be too complex an emotion for some children, in which case substitute frightened or scared in the activities. Play act worried or frightened and let the child respond/comfort you. Reverse these roles as appropriate. Use the symbol or sign for God to show that God comforts us when we are worried.

5. We come together

Parents can be invited to join in at this stage.

Focus

Seat yourselves around the table; some with anxious faces on one side, and some with relaxed faces on the other side. Listen to the Gospel below, and then spend some time leaving your worries behind and putting on relaxed faces, joining those on the relaxed side.

Gospel

Jesus said: "You do not need to worry so much. Many of the things that you worry about are not important, but worrying about them stops you from enjoying what you have. Set your heart on God."

Prayer

Jesus, when I am worried, I sometimes get very sad and think that I am all on my own. Help me to remember that you are there looking after me; help me to ask my family and my friends for help if I need it; and help me not to worry so much. Amen.

Share

Allow the younger ones to talk about their poster/card.

Sing

"Be still and know that I am God"
"Do not be afraid"

PROBLEM SOLVING

My worries	What I can do	I need to pray!
		☐
		☐
		☐
		☐
		☐

9th Sunday in Ordinary Time

Proper 4

1. Introduction to the theme of the day

"Build your life on Jesus"

Aim: To understand that Jesus says that if we build our lives the way he teaches us, then together we will be strong.

Leader's reflection: In Mark 1:22 we are told that Jesus taught with authority. Throughout the Gospels there is a growing awareness that Jesus is not just another prophet trying to tell us about God, but that he himself has a unique relationship with God, that he is in fact the Messiah, the Son of God. Because of this, we can be confident of his words and build directly upon his teachings.

2. We arrive

We sit in a circle ready to listen to the Gospel.
Has anyone anything they would like to tell us about last week's Family Sheet?

Focus

Green fabric; a house brick or toy bricks; light a candle.

Gospel: Matthew 7:21-27

Read from the Lectionary or Children's Lectionary.

3. We respond

What is the Gospel asking of us?

Work in age groups if appropriate, and come together as a community to end the session.

Young ones
Story: The three little pigs

The children are likely to know this story already. Allow them to tell the story, with shared input. Compare it to the Gospel of today.

What makes a strong house?
What makes a strong person?
What makes us strong Christians?

Juniors
Story: St Francis of Assisi, builder

We have already heard some stories about St Francis of Assisi. Although he was a very rich young man, he gave everything away so that he could live in poverty and spend his life trying to live according to the Gospel of Jesus.

When he first decided to do this, he lived in a pit for a while, and then he heard the voice of God telling him, "Francis, rebuild my church." St Francis took this instruction very literally, and went straight to the nearby church of San Damiano. This was an ancient church which now lay in ruins. Slowly Francis gathered together the stones and rocks which were lying about, and carefully he began rebuilding the church, praying and listening to God all the time for his instructions. This work took him a few years, and the church of San Damiano can still be seen in Italy, near Assisi.

As a result of his prayer, it became apparent to Francis that God also meant him to build up the people of God. This work took him and his Franciscan brothers the rest of their lives, and is still ongoing today.

We are the Church of God. Together we can build a strong Church, but we need to be sure of our foundations. Foundations are the things that we build on. If they are not secure, then our building will just fall over. Jesus tells us that if we build on him, then we will be strong. We can be sure of this because we know that Jesus is not just somebody who tells us about God: he is God.

What makes us strong in our faith?
Who has helped us so far to make strong foundations?
Whose example can we follow to make sure we stay strong?
How does belonging to a church help us?

4. Activity

Young ones

Give the children a brick template each. Use a wax crayon and make a rubbing over a rough surface to give the paper a brick texture. Choose a word to fill the gap in the sentence "I will be _____ like Jesus" and sign the brick. Paste the brick onto a cardboard box standing on its side – to form a wall collage.

Juniors

Have ready a number of pictures of houses made in different ways, e.g. igloos, tents, houseboats, wooden houses, brick houses etc. Examine them carefully together. How is each adapted to the place that it comes from? What foundations are they built on? Why are foundations important? Some pictures which show the foundations of a house being built would be particularly helpful. You might be able to have access to the foundations of the church or church hall, or pictures of a crypt from a famous old church or cathedral.

Use the blank brick template to write a sentence on what you will try to do to make your faith stronger. Make a wax rubbing as for the young ones, taking care not to obscure your words. These bricks can then be built into a wall as above.

Tips for learning difficulties

Follow instructions for the young ones and talk about being kind, helpful and friendly like Jesus. Offer help with the writing if necessary.

5. We come together

Parents can be invited to join in at this stage.

Focus

Brick wall built during the activity.
Light the candle.
Green fabric for Ordinary Time.

Gospel

Jesus tells his disciples that if they listen to what he says, and try to follow his way, then they can be confident that they are building his kingdom on strong foundations.

Prayer

Let us thank God for the strength which each person gives to the brick wall (the Church).
Thank you, Lord, for (allow a child to read a name from one of the bricks).
Thank you for the way he/she gives us strength by (read what the child will do).
With the help of Jesus, together we will build a strong church community. Amen.

Share

Talk about what you have learnt from the building activity.

Sing

"I want to build my life"
"The wise man built his house upon the rock"

I will be _____ like Jesus

My name is _____

10th Sunday in Ordinary Time

Proper 5

1. Introduction to the theme of the day

> ❝I did not come to call the virtuous but sinners❞

Aim: To understand that Jesus wants to be friends with us all the time. We do not have to be good first.

Leader's reflection: The people around him see Jesus' actions in today's Gospel as scandalous. He calls a tax collector to be one of his close friends, and eats with him and his companions – a banquet quite likely to have been paid for by corrupt means. His message is clear: "I came to call sinners, not the righteous." We are all called by Jesus as we are. We do not have to make ourselves acceptable first.

2. We arrive
We sit in a circle ready to listen to the Gospel.

Focus
Have a large table ready with chairs around it, and decorated in some way. As the children arrive, have ready a bowl of water and towels so you can wash and dry their hands. Welcome them individually and invite them to sit down at the table. Once everybody is seated, light a candle. The leader, or one of the children who is prepared, should then stand up and proclaim the Gospel.
Alternatively, adapt this idea with a smaller table.

Gospel: Matthew 9:9-13 (Catholic)
Matthew 9:9-13, 18-26 (Anglican)
Read from the Lectionary or Children's Lectionary.

3. We respond
What is the Gospel asking of us?
Work in age groups if appropriate, and come together as a community to end the session.

Young ones

Story: Who will be invited to the party?

Daphne the duck decided that she was going to have a party. She went out and bought some bread to make sandwiches, and some sausages on sticks, and some crisps, and some jelly and some iced biscuits, and some currant buns, and a big cake all decorated with pink icing and cherries. Then she sat down and thought of some games to play, and made party hats for all the other animals that were coming. Everything was ready. Then Daphne remembered. She hadn't invited anyone! So she got out a pencil and paper and began to make a list. Who did she want to invite to her party? First she thought of Brian the badger. Brian was her special friend. But Brian was sometimes very bad-tempered, and she didn't want bad-tempered people at her party, so she crossed Brian's name off the list.

Next she thought of Camilla the cow. She liked Camilla. But Camilla was a very greedy cow, and if she came to the party, there might not be enough food for everyone, so she crossed Camilla's name off the list.

Then she thought of Owen the owl. Owen was always very nice to her. But the party was during the day, and Owen might be feeling sleepy. Daphne didn't want people falling asleep at her party. So she crossed his name off the list.

"Oh dear," thought poor Daphne, "there is nobody to invite to the party." Just then Henry the honeybee buzzed by. "Oh Henry," Daphne called sadly, "what shall I do? I want to have a party, but when I looked through a list of my friends, there is something wrong with all of them. Brian the badger is bad-tempered, and Camilla the cow is greedy, and Owen the owl is sleepy. I can't invite any of them. What shall I do?"

"Well," buzzed Henry happily, "you can't have a party without guests, so why don't you invite them all anyway? It is a shame to waste all those sandwiches, and sausages on sticks, and crisps, and jelly, and iced biscuits, and currant buns, and that great big pink cake."

Henry was right, of course, so Daphne invited everyone. Brian the badger was in a good mood for once, and Camilla the cow brought her own share of grass, so there was plenty of food for everyone, and although Owen the owl did fall asleep once, he woke up again with a surprised hoot, when one of the balloons popped, and made everybody laugh. Henry the honeybee came too, and brought with him a pot of his own special honey. It was a very good party, and Daphne was very happy. What did it matter if there was something wrong with each one of her friends? She still liked them all!

Jesus invites all of us to sit down with him and to eat with him. He waits for us to invite him into our homes and our lives. He does not wait until we are good. He wants to come and be with us now.
Imagine Jesus is coming to your house for dinner. Who would you invite? Why? How do you think they would react? What do you think they will say to Jesus? What will Jesus say to them? What will you say to Jesus? What do you think Jesus will say to you?

Juniors

Story: Food to share

The story is told of a man who died and went to heaven. He met St Peter at the gates, and waited to be shown around. St Peter took him by the hand. First he took the man down to hell. In hell all the people were sitting around an enormous table, laden with good food and good wine of all different sorts, but the people who were sitting around were starving and groaning in agony. The man looked puzzled, and asked St Peter why this was: why didn't they eat the food on the table in front of them? St Peter explained to him that all the people in hell were free to eat as much food as they wanted, but they had to eat it using chopsticks nine feet long. When they picked up the food and tried to get it to their mouths, it always missed, so they ended up hungry.

Very subdued now, the man asked if he could see heaven. St Peter led him there, and the man was surprised to see exactly the same scene, an enormous table, spread with many good things, fine food and fine wine, but here the people were sitting around cheerfully, laughing and joking, and very well fed. Clearly the rules were different here, the man protested. But St Peter assured him that the rules were exactly the same. Each person was given chopsticks nine feet long with which to feed themselves. The man was very confused: how then did these people manage to get the food into their mouths using nine-foot-long chopsticks? "Ah," St Peter explained, "these people don't feed themselves, they feed each other instead."

In *The Voyage of the Dawn Treader* by C.S. Lewis, Eustace is a lazy and bad-tempered boy. Although he dislikes everybody, they do not reject him, even when something terrible happens to him. In the end he is the hero of the story.

Encourage comments relating the story to the Gospel.
Explain the different attitudes of those in heaven and those in hell.
How does this encourage you to behave at mealtimes?

4. Activity

Young ones and Juniors

Write out a fun invitation to Jesus, using the loaf-of-bread template, inviting him to a party at your house. Write in the details on the loaf and colour it.

Juniors could write or act out a conversation with themselves and Jesus.

What do you think you will talk about? What would you like to ask Jesus?

Tips for learning difficulties

To heighten the sense of occasion at the beginning or the end, it might be appropriate to pass around a small treat at the table – e.g. a plate of biscuits.

The invitation template can be magnified if appropriate.

5. We come together

Parents can be invited to join in at this stage.

Focus

Sit around the table again, and relight the candle.

Gospel

Jesus was walking through town when he saw a tax collector called Matthew sitting outside one of the offices. In those days, tax collectors were often greedy men, and cheats. They did not have many friends. Jesus invited himself to Matthew's house to have dinner with him. Everybody was very surprised, because they thought Matthew was a bad man. Jesus said that he was friends with everybody. It did not matter if they were good or bad.

Prayer

Dear Jesus, you invite us to be with you today. You want to be friends with all of us, all of the time, even when we are not as good as we want to be. Thank you. Amen.

Share

Share the work from the activities.

Sing

"We have come into his house"
"On this house your blessing, Lord"

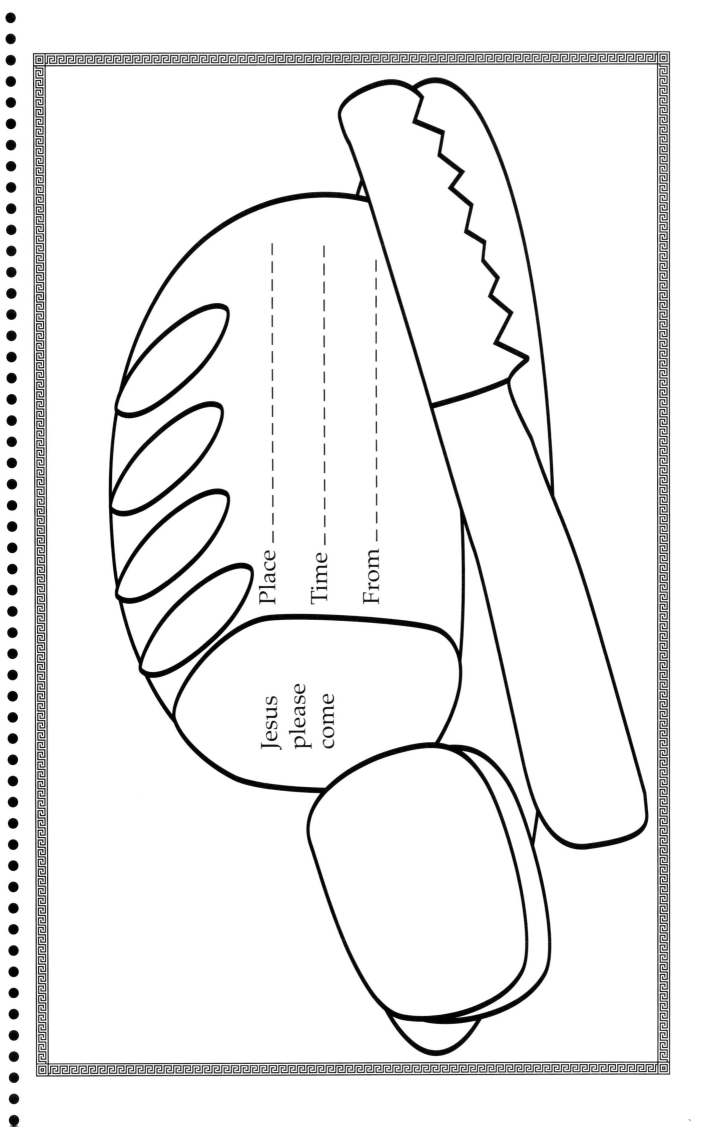

Jesus
please
come

Place - - - - - - -

Time - - - - - - -

From - - - - - - -

11th Sunday in Ordinary Time

Proper 6

1. Introduction to the theme of the day

> "Freely you have received, freely give"

Aim: To understand that the best things in life, including our faith, are free. God has given us so many gifts, and we need to thank him for them all.

Leader's reflection: Our faith is the greatest gift we are given. Amongst other things, it enables us to see beyond the materialistic here and now. It is offered to us freely, and Jesus exhorts us to offer it freely to those around us. To do this, we need also to appreciate the many gifts we are given freely, by God, to sustain us and to enable us to grow towards him, and towards each other.

2. We arrive

We sit in a circle, ready to listen to the Gospel.
Has anyone anything they would like to tell us about last week's Family Sheet?

Focus

Light a candle in the middle of the room. Green fabric during Ordinary Time. Sing together the hymn, "Freely, freely you have received".

Gospel: Matthew 9:36 – 10:8

Read from the Lectionary or Children's Lectionary.

3. We respond

What is the Gospel asking of us?

Work in age groups if appropriate, then come together as a community at the end of the session.

Young ones

Story: Rupert learns a very important lesson

Maggie was a tiny brown mouse. She lived in a little nest under the roots of the old oak tree at the bottom of the field. Maggie was very poor.

One day, Maggie was expecting a visit from her cousin, Rupert the rat. Rupert was very rich. He lived in the roof of one of the houses in town. He liked to dress well and to eat well. He was very smart and very fat!

Rupert drove everywhere in his little red car. He set off from his attic home good and early to get to Maggie's nest in time for lunch, but by lunchtime he had not arrived, and by teatime he had still not arrived. Maggie was beginning to get worried, and, pulling on her wellington boots, she went out to find out what had happened. As she came close to the lane at the top of the field, she began to hear bad-tempered shouting, and the sound of a car engine being revved loudly. It was Rupert. He was stuck in the mud near the gate. "Oh dear," said Maggie, "you will have to walk," and, handing Rupert a spare pair of wellington boots, she began to walk back down the field towards her nest. Rupert stomped along grumpily behind.

"I am too poor to own a car," she explained to Rupert when they got back to her nest, "so I walk everywhere. Walking is free, and I like it."

Rupert slumped down in the nearest armchair, whilst Maggie ran around fetching firewood and lighting up a fire for him. Soon it was blazing merrily and Rupert began to cheer up a bit.

"I am too poor to have central heating," she chuckled to Rupert, "and so I collect firewood from the forest to burn. It is free, and very warm, and I like it." Rupert had to agree that the fire was very warm and cheerful.

They ate their tea happily together and talked about the other mice and rats, and the other animals who lived in the field. After they had finished the washing-up, Rupert looked around for the television. "Oh no," smiled Maggie, "I am too poor to have a television, so I sit on the doorstep and watch the sunset instead. It is very beautiful, and it is free, and I like it."

So they sat on the doorstep and watched the sunset together. It was very beautiful. "You are right, you know," murmured Rupert comfortably. "Some of the best things in life are free."

We are continually being offered "freebies" these days, yet very little of it is really given freely. There is nearly always a catch. But the gifts which God gives us are free. Today we will think of all these things, and thank God for them.

Can you name some other gifts from God?
Does God make us pay for anything?
How can we show God that we are grateful for his free gifts?

Juniors

Story: St Elizabeth of Hungary

St Elizabeth of Hungary was born in the year 1207, the daughter of King Andrew of Hungary. She married young and had three children, but her husband Ludwig of Thuringia died while she was still young and left her a very rich woman. Elizabeth did not keep all these riches for herself; instead she gave them away to the poor people living near the palace. She built a hospice just outside the castle walls, and went there each day to look after the sick, diseased and crippled men and women. She gave her time freely, feeding and cleaning the most poorly herself. The story is told that, at a time of great famine in the town, Elizabeth used to take all the food from the palace to give to the poor people outside the walls. Her family were not very happy about this because they were afraid of starving themselves, but Elizabeth continued to give the food away secretly. One night, as she was creeping through the gardens of the palace with a basket of bread to give away, she bumped into one of the guards, who demanded to see what was in her basket. Trembling, Elizabeth drew back the cloth, and in the basket saw that all the bread had turned into beautiful roses. The guard fell on his knees in wonder at the miracle and was converted to Christianity that night.

The Borrowers by Mary Norton is a popular children's book. It describes the life of some "little people" who live behind the wainscot of a large house, surviving on the cast-offs of the people who live in the house.

Encourage comments relating the story to the Gospel.
How can we share our possessions?
Does anybody use charity shops to buy from or give goods to?
Is there a group in your church that works for people in need?

4. Activity

Young ones

Make a list of all the things mums, dads and carers have to pay for.

Juniors

Have ready a pile of junk mail or advertisements from magazines, making free offers. Help the children to sort it through into those things which are really free, and those which have a hidden price to pay.

Young ones and Juniors

Now make a list of all the things which God gives to us freely. Encourage them in particular to think of skills which they have learnt – talking, writing, cooking etc. Using the "gift" template, colour it and complete the label. Think about the gifts that God has freely given you and thank him for them. You might write a list of gifts given freely to you on the outside of the package.

Tips for learning difficulties

Talk about things that cost money and can be bought in shops. Have magazine pictures cut out ready to paste on one half of a poster. On the other half, paste pictures of things that cost nothing, e.g. countryside, flowers, smiles, hugs etc.

5. We come together

Parents can be invited to join in at this stage.

Focus

Sit around the candle; a green cloth for Ordinary Time with a display of the gift boxes from the activity.

Gospel

Jesus called together his closest friends. These were his twelve apostles. He had spent a long time teaching them, and now he told them to go out and to teach other people. If you want to learn something new, you often have to pay for lessons. But Jesus had taught his apostles for free. He told them that they were to teach other people for free as well.

Prayer

Lord Jesus, thank you for your gifts of nature ... (children to suggest exactly what). Thank you for your gifts of insects, birds and animals ... (suggestions from children). Thank you for our family and friends, their smiles and hugs. Thank you for giving us so many things to love. Amen.

Share

Share the work from the activities.

Sing

"Freely, freely you have received"

To - - - - - - - - - -

From - - - - - - - -

12th Sunday in Ordinary Time

Proper 7

1. Introduction to the theme of the day

> ## "Do not be afraid"

Aim: Jesus tells us not to be afraid. We are worth more than a hundred sparrows.

Leader's reflection: "Do not be afraid." These were the first words that the angel Gabriel said to Mary when he told her that Jesus was to be born. They were the first words of the angels to Joseph and to the shepherds on the hillside near Bethlehem. Throughout his life, and after the resurrection, Jesus was constantly saying to his apostles, "Do not be afraid." These were the first words spoken by Pope John Paul II in St Peter's Square immediately after his election, and in his book *Crossing the Threshold of Hope*, he told us that in these words lies the message of hope offered by the Church today.

2. We arrive

We sit in a circle, ready to hear the Gospel.
Has anyone anything they would like to tell us about last week's Family Sheet?

Focus

Light a candle and place it in the middle of the room. Green fabric during Ordinary Time.

Gospel: Matthew 10:26-33 (Catholic)
Matthew 10:24-39 (Anglican)

Read from the Lectionary or the Children's Lectionary.

3. We respond
What is the Gospel asking of us?

Work in age groups if appropriate, then come together as a community at the end of the session.

Young ones

Sparrows are the most common and the smallest birds in our gardens. Jesus says in the Gospel today that God loves and cares about every tiny little sparrow, and that, as we are worth more than hundreds of sparrows, we can be sure he will be looking after us all the time as well.

But most of us are still afraid, of something, some of the time. Today we are going to think about these things, and ask Jesus to be with us and to help us when we feel afraid.

Story: Being friends

Michael was a mole. There was one problem. Moles like to burrow deep down in the soil, where it is very dark, to find their food, and Michael was afraid of the dark.

There was another problem. Michael was too scared to tell anyone. He thought that if he told the other animals, they would all laugh at him. So he just went on being a very frightened, very hungry, very unhappy little mole.

One day, when he was scratching about at the foot of the old oak tree, trying to find some beetles which had escaped from underground, Wendy the worm came up. "What are you doing, Michael?" she asked. "Shouldn't you be down underground looking for food?" By now Michael was so hungry, that he began to cry. "Oh Wendy," he wept, "do you promise you won't tell anybody?"

"Well," said Wendy, "we might need to ask for help, but tell me first, and then we shall decide what to do about it."

Michael told Wendy everything; how he was a mole, and moles are supposed to burrow deep down into the ground, and how it was very dark underground, and how he was scared of the dark. "Oh dear," said Wendy, "No wonder you are so upset. I have a plan, but first we must ask Owen the owl for his help. Can I talk to him about it?" Michael wasn't sure, but he agreed, so Wendy went to talk to Owen the owl.

Soon Michael heard a hooting behind him, and Owen landed near him carrying Wendy gently in his beak. "Wendy has told me all about your problem. We have a plan, but we will need the help of Camilla the cow." Owen explained his idea to Michael, and he agreed that they could talk to Camilla as well, but nobody else. So off they went to fetch Camilla. Soon Michael heard a mooing behind him, and there was Camilla with Owen and Wendy on her back. "Okay," said Owen, "the plan is this. Wendy will go underground in front of you, Michael. If you get scared then she will be able to wriggle in next to you, and make you feel better. I will stay near the entrance burrow, and keep on hooting, so that if you get scared, you can find your way back to the entrance easily; and Camilla will stamp on the ground above the burrow, so that you will feel the ground shaking, and know that you are not on your own."

What a good plan! Soon Michael was burrowing about happily underground. He could smell Wendy wriggling just ahead of him, and he could hear Owen hooting at the entrance, and he could feel Camilla stamping on the ground above, and he didn't feel scared any more.

"What a silly mole I have been," he thought. "If we ask our friends for help, then we do not need to be afraid any more."

Juniors

Story: St Cuthbert of Lindisfarne and his love of birds

Many of the saints of God are reputed to have had a special relationship with birds and animals. One such, St Cuthbert of Lindisfarne, used to preach to the birds near his monastery, and be fed by them.

On one occasion, he had recently built a thatched shelter to receive guests to the monastery. As he was standing watching the crows building a nest nearby, he noticed that one of them was pulling the thatch from his roof to use as building materials for his nest. He walked over towards it, lifted up his hands and called, "In the name of Jesus, do not harm my roof!" The crow flew away quickly, only to return the next day in a posture of abject sorrow, spreading out its wings in a pitiable manner, and bending its head down before Cuthbert's feet. In a tone of humility it asked pardon by the most expressive signs it could, and asked Cuthbert if it could return to the monastery. Cuthbert gave it permission, and the crow returned with a large piece of fat in its beak, as a present for Cuthbert. The story ends by saying that the crow lived in the monastery for many years after that, and did not once disobey Cuthbert again.

On another occasion, he was travelling with another monk. They were tired and hungry and the monk was complaining. St Cuthbert looked up to heaven and saw an eagle. "Do you see that eagle?" he asked. "In this way God will feed us." And he sent the other monk to where the eagle had landed. The eagle had a fish in its beak which the monk brought quickly back to Cuthbert. "What have you done?" asked Cuthbert. "Why did you take it all? Go back and give her half, because she has done us good service."

These stories were written down by one of the earliest writers in the English language, St Bede, in his book *The Life of St Cuthbert*. St Cuthbert had lots of adventures, and you can read about them all in this book. You can get a copy through your library, or directly off the Internet Medieval Sourcebook at http://fordham.edu/halsall/sbook.html

4. Activity

Young ones and Juniors

Give each child a "sparrow-sheet". Use the blank side for the children to write in, or draw their fears. When it is folded closed, the front cover should show a picture of a sparrow. Give the children some private time and encourage them to fill in the inside of the sheet. Nobody will see this unless they choose to show it. Offer the children sticky tape or a paper clip so that they can seal their sheet ready to offer during the prayer session. They should put their name on the back of the notelet so they can collect it again at the end.

Sharing our worries and fears encourages discussion and the opportunity within the friendship group to find solutions.

Alternatively, talk for a while in more general terms about the sort of things that people might be afraid of, and make a single large "fear sheet", as a group.

Tips for learning difficulties

If there are children who have real difficulty communicating, it is important on this occasion that they are able to work individually with an adult who knows them well.

5. We come together

Parents can be invited to join in at this stage.

Focus

Gather in a circle around the candle, each person should be holding his or her sparrow notelet. Gentle music can be playing in the background.

Gospel

Some people did not like Jesus and threatened to kill him. Jesus knew that his apostles were afraid. He said to them, "Do not be afraid. Look at the tiny sparrows. They are worth nothing, but God still cares and looks after them. You are worth much more than hundreds of sparrows, so you can be sure that God is looking after you all the time."

Prayer

Jesus, you tell us that God cares for each tiny sparrow, and that we are worth more than hundreds of sparrows. Today we want to trust you, by sharing with you the things we are afraid of. Amen.

Share

Children should be encouraged to come forward and to place their sparrow notelet in front of the candle. If they wish to, they could share a few words about what is on the sheet.

Sing

"Do not be afraid"

You are worth more than hundreds of sparrows.
Matthew 10:31

Proper 8

1. Introduction to the theme of the day

> ❝Take up your cross and follow me!❞

Aim: Jesus will not make our lives easy, but he will be with us particularly during the difficult times.

Leader's reflection: The words of Jesus in today's Gospel are difficult. He tells us, "Anyone who does not take his cross and follow in my footsteps is not worthy of me." Jesus is facing the reality that our lives can be difficult. Our faith in him is not a panacea for all ills, and we cannot use it to hide behind. Rather, if we are prepared to face up to the truth and reality of who we are, and especially the truth of who we are in the face of God's perfect love, then we are worthy followers of him.

2. We arrive

We sit in a circle, ready to hear the Gospel.
Has anyone anything they would like to tell us about last week's Family Sheet?

Focus

Place a large cross in the middle of the room and stand a lighted candle by it. Green fabric during Ordinary Time.

Gospel: Matthew 10:37-42

Read from the Lectionary or Children's Lectionary.

3. We respond

What is the Gospel asking of us?

Work in age groups if appropriate, then come together as a community at the end of the session.

Young ones

Story: Friends to the rescue!

Henry the honeybee was very sad. The day had started well. He had been buzzing around the garden, enjoying the sunshine and looking for pollen to make honey. It had been so pleasant that Henry had shut his eyes for an instant to take a deep breath of the wonderful flowery smells, then, BONK! Henry had flown into a tree and hit his head really hard.

Now his head hurt, his eyesight was all wonky, and, worst of all, he had an enormous lump on his head. His head was so big; he would never be able to get into the flowers to collect his pollen now. Oh how sad he was.

"What's up?" hooted Owen the owl from the tree above him. Henry explained miserably, "My head hurts, and I can't see straight, and this bump on my head is so big, I can't get into any of the flowers to collect the pollen."

"Oh dear," said Owen, "let's see what we can do." Owen thought for a while and then he flew off to his nest in the tree. A minute later he was back. "I don't know if these will help," he said, "they are a bit big, but they might help you to see better." Owen held out a pair of the most enormous spectacles Henry had ever seen. They were a bit big, but they did help him to see better. "Thank you, Owen," said Henry.

Just then Wendy the worm poked up from the soil under the tree. "That's a fine pair of spectacles you have there," she squeaked, "but you do look fed up. What's up?" Henry explained again. "I bumped my head and couldn't see straight, so Owen found me these spectacles; but my head still hurts, and this bump on my head is so big, I can't get into any of the flowers to collect the pollen." "Oh dear," said Wendy, "let's see what we can do." Wendy thought for a while, and then she had an idea. She slithered over to where Henry was, and wrapped herself around his head. She was so lovely and smooth and cool that Henry's head soon stopped hurting. "Thank you, Wendy," he said. "Hello, Henry! Hello, Wendy!" came a quack from above. They both looked up. There was Daphne the duck flying over. "You look fed up. What's up?" she quacked. Henry explained again. "I bumped my head and I couldn't see straight, so Owen gave me these spectacles; and my head hurt, so Wendy is making it better; but this bump on my head is so big, I still can't get into any of the flowers to collect the pollen."

"Oh dear," said Daphne, "let's see what we can do." Daphne thought for a while, and then she had an idea. She waddled over to where Henry was. "Get up on my back, Henry," she said. "I can take you to where the flowers are much bigger, so you will easily get your head into them."

"Thank you, Daphne," buzzed Henry, and, wearing Owen's spectacles and with Wendy wound round his head like a hat, he climbed aboard. He was a very happy honeybee again.

Who among us here would say they were a friend of Jesus? Jesus was very sad when he was on the cross. Most of his friends had left him and he felt very alone. Ask the children the ways in which they show each other that they are friends. What do they do if one of their friends is sad? How do they try to make them happy again? We are all sad sometimes. Our mums and dads and the people who look after us are sometimes sad as well. Ask the children what sort of things make the adults in their life sad. How can they help them to be happy again?

Juniors

Last week we looked at the times when we were afraid, but sometimes we find our lives hard in other different ways. Jesus knows that life is not always easy, but he says that although he is with us all the time, he looks after us particularly when things are most difficult. He knows what it is like to be hurting, or afraid, or sad, or to be feeling let down, because he experienced all of these things when he was on the cross. So when we feel like this, we know that he understands us, and is particularly close to us at these times. Everybody has things in their lives which are difficult, and, with Jesus, we can sometimes help each other to carry our "little crosses".

Story: Footprints in the sand

One night a man had a dream. He dreamed he was walking along the beach with the Lord. Across the sky flashed scenes from his life. For each scene, he noticed two sets of footprints in the sand: one belonging to him, and the other to the Lord.

When the last scene of his life flashed before him he looked back at the footprints in the sand. He noticed that many times along the path of his life there was only one set of footprints. He also noticed that it happened at the very lowest and saddest times of his life.

This really bothered him and he questioned the Lord about it:

"Lord, you said that once I decided to follow you, you'd walk with me all the way. But I have noticed that during the most troublesome times in my life there is only one set of footprints. I don't understand why when I needed you most you would leave me."

The Lord replied: "My son, my precious child, I love you and I would never leave you. During your times of trial and suffering, when you see only one set of footprints, it was then that I carried you." (Author unknown)

For older Juniors, in the book _The Amber Spyglass_ by Philip Pullman (from the "Dark Materials" trilogy), Lyra realises that the only way she will be able to help the people in the land of the dead is to go there herself. This causes her a lot of suffering, but in the end she finds a way to release all the people who are trapped there. Encourage comments relating the story to the Gospel. What are the "little crosses" we are asked to carry? Who carried a large heavy cross? Why?

4. Activity

Young ones

Use the template of the footprints as for the Juniors. Draw your face on the middle footprint. On the other footprints draw the faces of people you know who are sad.

Juniors

Use the template of the footprints. On the middle one, the child should write their own name and write one of the things which they sometimes find difficult about their own life. On the other footprints, write the names of people they care for and the things which are difficult in their lives.

Tips for learning difficulties

The idea of things which make us sad, rather than difficulties in our lives, is simpler, and might be more appropriate for children with learning difficulties of any age. Children could use smiley and sad faces to show the things which make them happy, and the things which make them sad. Have some magazine pictures ready to talk about and label.

5. We come together

Parents can be invited to join in at this stage.

Focus

Use a Taizé chant or some quiet music. A large cross, candle and some night lights; green fabric.

Gospel

Jesus knows that some of the things he tells the apostles are difficult for them. He tells them that he cannot make their lives easy, and that following him may even make things more difficult for them. But anyone who is still prepared to "take up their cross", and to try to follow him, is a very special friend of his.

Prayer

Jesus, we know you were sad on the cross. Sometimes we are sad as well. Sometimes the people we love are sad. Help us to make them happy again.

Jesus, we bring you all the little things which we find difficult in our lives. We know that your own life was not easy at times, and that when you died you suffered a lot. Be with us when things get more difficult. Help us to carry our crosses. Help our friends and family to carry their crosses. Help us to help them. Amen.

Share

The work from the activity.

Sing

"We have come into his house"

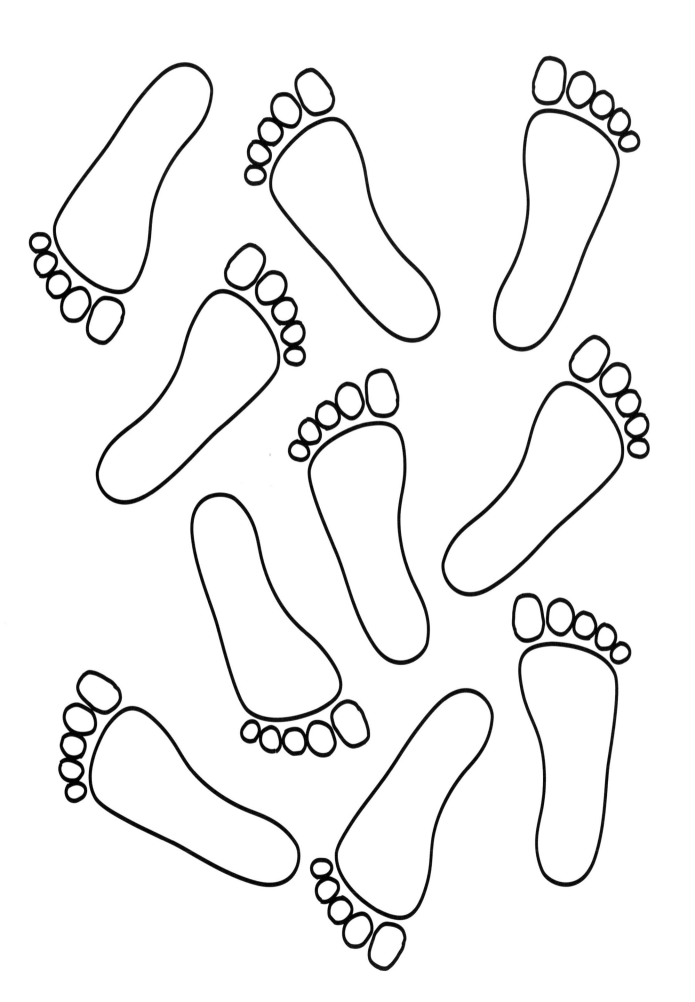

14th Sunday in Ordinary Time

Proper 9

1. Introduction to the theme of the day

"Come to me and we will find rest"

Aim: To understand that God wants to help us with the difficult things in life. Jesus tells us that if we trust in God and follow his ways, he will help us with all our problems.

Leader's reflection: It's easy to forget that even very young children today have a multitude of fears and anxieties, that they live in a world full of competition and effort, of criticism and misguided "values". Their world is a faster, busier, less tranquil world than ever before. Today's Gospel is Jesus' invitation to live God's values, to be gentle and compassionate and find peace and happiness in trusting in God, who shares our burdens with us.

2. We arrive

We sit in a circle ready to listen to the Gospel.
Has anyone anything they would like to tell us about last week's Family Sheet?

Focus

Our candle to light and green fabric for Ordinary Time.

Gospel: Matthew 11:25-30 (Catholic)
Matthew 11:16-19. 25-30 (Anglican)

Read from the Lectionary or Children's Lectionary.

3. We respond
What is the Gospel asking of us?

Work in age groups if appropriate then come together as a community to end the session.

Young ones

God wants us to feel safe, and not to be worried or afraid. Sometimes everything goes wrong, and we are sad or scared. Jesus tells us that we can trust God to be with us and share our troubles, like a friend holding our hand. Jesus tells us the secret of making life happier: if we live the way God wants us to live, and are good and kind, we will make the world a better place for ourselves and for everyone else.

What makes us feel afraid or worried? What makes us feel safe and peaceful? How does what we do affect how other people feel? Encourage the children to notice that kindness and sharing as God wants us to do make everyone feel safe and happy; cruelty and selfishness make us afraid and unhappy. When we behave the way God wants us to, we make ourselves and everyone else feel safer and happier.

Story: No-friends Jane

Jane was a very bossy little girl. She always told everyone what to do. Jane always had to choose what game to play, and she always had to make up all the rules. If the other children wouldn't do just as she said, she got very cross. "You're doing it wrong!" she'd say. "Do it MY way! It's much better!" She would stamp her feet and say horrid things, and sulk.

Well! The other children didn't like Jane very much. She made them sad and miserable. They had good ideas too, and they wanted to have a say in what to do. They didn't like being bossed about. But Jane wouldn't listen to anyone else's ideas. One by one, the other children stopped being friends with Jane, until nobody would play with her at all, and no one would help her with the activities in school.

Jane was very sad and lonely. She liked playing with people. She didn't know how to make friends again. One day Jane was so sad that she cried, right there in the playground, because nobody would play with her. One of the bigger girls came and gave her a hug. "You're too bossy, Jane," she said, "you don't listen to other people, you don't care what they want. Try to listen more and try doing things how someone else wants." Jane thought that would be very difficult: she thought her ideas were the best. But she tried it, and it was easy! The other children let her join in and play, and they even tried her ideas sometimes, because she wasn't bossy any more.

Juniors

Story: A good example to follow

Miss Taylor had a very noisy class. They all talked at once. They all wanted to be first to do something, or to have the best paints or the seat near the window. They pushed and shoved to be first. They never shared their sweets or crayons. They didn't help each other. It was a horrid class, and no one was really happy. Miss Taylor shouted and got angry, and ticked people off all the time. One day, a new boy came to the class, from a different school. His name was Joe. Joe was amazed at what he saw. He didn't know what to do. He told his mother about it. He hated all the noise and jostling and the meanness in Miss Taylor's class. His mother said there was no other school to go to: he had to stay with Miss Taylor. She said that the best thing was not to join in all the noise and meanness. He should just try to do what he knew was right.

So Joe shared his crayons, he never pushed or shoved, he wasn't mean, and he helped people. He was a good, kind boy, and he liked to be helpful: it made him feel good and strong. It made being in that noisy class easier. In fact, Joe's goodness made the class quieter and kinder too. The children he helped and shared his things with were surprised, and they started to like him and want to be his friend. They started to help him and share things too. Bit by bit everyone started helping and sharing. Miss Taylor's class turned out to be the happiest class in the school.

God wants us to feel safe and happy, and not to be worried or afraid or angry. But the world can be a scary place. There are lots of things that could go wrong or harm us. There are people who are mean and unkind. Sometimes everything seems too difficult to manage. Jesus tells us that we can trust God to be with us and share our troubles, like a friend holding our hand.

Jesus doesn't mean that we should forget about the scary and difficult things, or pretend that they aren't there: he wants us to be sensible. He wants us to look after ourselves. But he wants us to understand what really matters, and to face our troubles in the right way.

What makes us feel worried or afraid or angry? Why do those things upset us? What makes us feel safe and happy? Boasting and bullying and meanness and unkindness make the world bad. Kindness and sharing make the world much nicer. Jesus tells us that if we live the way God wants us to live, we will make ourselves and everyone else feel safer and happier. We will make the world a better place.

4. Activity

Young ones

Is there something sad, or something that worries you? Is there someone bossy or horrid at school, or something scary and difficult for you? Shut your eyes and think about it quietly.

Let's ask Jesus for help. Hold your hands up in front of you – pretend you are putting all your problems in a big white bowl, and hold it up to Jesus. Does it feel heavy, with all those worries in it?

Come to us, Lord Jesus, and make our burdens light!

Let God take the weight of your worry bowl away. Let God's hands hold yours. Can you feel God loving you?

If we try to do as Jesus tells us, God will always be there, helping us to know what to do.

How can we say thank you to God for holding our hands and helping us?

Using the "hands" template, colour it then write on the words "God is helping me". Draw pictures around the page showing how we can say thank you to God.

Juniors

Think of something that worries or upsets you. Perhaps some schoolwork is difficult, or perhaps you had a quarrel with a friend, or there's someone mean in school.

Let's share that problem with Jesus. Shut your eyes and imagine a big white bowl. Put all your troubles in the bowl, and hold it up to Jesus.

Come, Lord Jesus, and share our troubles, help us sort them out.

Can you feel God holding your hands and making your worry bowl lighter?

Jesus said: Don't let the worries of the world be your focus. Focus instead on doing God's will, and you will be happier.

Using the "hands" template, write on one thing you can do for someone else. Cut out the "hands" and place them in a basket.

Tips for learning difficulties

The idea that we can influence how good or bad the world is, by our behaviour or our perspective, is hard for young children or for those with learning disabilities to understand. So much of their lives may be controlled by others. They need concrete examples to show how they can change the way things seem. Encourage them to think about some specific occasion which went well because they were loving or affectionate, and how an act of kindness can touch another heart.

5. We come together

Parents can be invited to join in at this stage.

Focus

The candle is lit, the children sitting quietly for a moment in preparation. The basket containing the juniors' work. The pictures displayed by the young ones.

Gospel

Jesus said: "If you are tired from carrying heavy burdens, come to me and I will give you rest... I am gentle and humble, and you will find rest."

Prayer

Leader: I wake up in the morning, I say "Hello" to Jesus.
I work at school.
I play at break time.
I have food to eat.
I share my life with my family at home.
I go to bed and say my prayers.
Response to the leader's prayer: Lord Jesus, be with us always. Amen.

Share

Share the work and ideas from the activities.

Sing

"Be not afraid" or a similar song

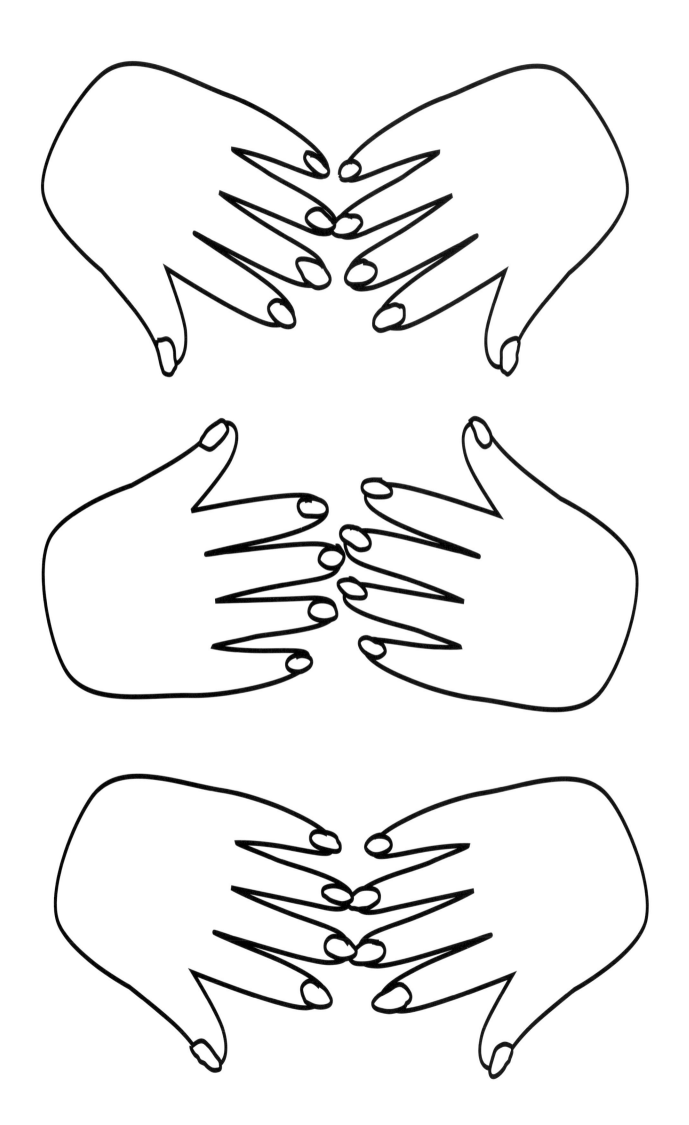

15th Sunday in Ordinary Time

Proper 10

1. Introduction to the theme of the day

> "God sows the seeds of his kingdom in our hearts"

Aim: To understand that God wants us to know him and to live good lives. Jesus came to tell us how God would like us to live. We must listen carefully to understand what Jesus is telling us.

Leader's reflection: Today's Gospel tells of the need to focus on God's message, and of the risk of not understanding, or of forgetting what we have understood, or of being distracted from it. But if we listen to Jesus' words, if we keep coming back to those words, we shall understand more and grow closer to God.

2. We arrive

We sit in a circle ready to listen to the Gospel.
Has anyone anything they would like to tell us about last week's Family Sheet?

Focus

Our candle to light, green fabric, seeds and tray with compost.

Gospel: Matthew 13:1-23

Read from the Lectionary or Children's Lectionary.

3. We respond

What is the Gospel asking of us?

Work in age groups if appropriate then come together as a community to end the session.

Young ones

Have you ever planted seeds in a flowerpot? Perhaps you wanted some pretty flowers. Or perhaps you helped Mummy or Daddy to plant seeds. There are hundreds of tiny seeds in the packet, but only a few flowers grow. First, a few tiny shoots come up, with tiny leaves. If you water them and look after them, they grow into fine strong flowers. But if you forget about them and leave them, they shrivel up and die.

Jesus says that God plants a special kind of seed in our hearts: a seed that won't grow into a flower. It grows in our hearts and leads us to God. Everybody has that special seed, the seed of love. Jesus tells us to look after the special seed of love God has given us, and help it to grow good and strong.

What can we do to make our love grow strong?

Story: The seed of love

Jemima was a very silly mouse. She lived in a church, under an old floorboard. One day, she heard the priest say that God had planted a special seed in everyone, a seed that could grow in our hearts and lead us to God. Jemima listened very carefully. She wanted to find God. The priest said you had to look after the special seed and help it to grow, or it would die.

Jemima was so excited. She wanted the seed to grow. She knew about seeds: you had to put them in the ground and water them to make them grow. Was that what God wanted her to do to make his special seed grow in her heart?

So Jemima decided to go and live in a flowerbed. She dug a little hole, and sat in the earth, and when it rained, she got wet. But she couldn't feel God growing in her heart. "Where are you, God?" she said. "I'm bored, sitting here in the flowerbed!"

By and by, an old rabbit came past, struggling with a huge carrot. "Would you mind, God, if I got out of the flowerbed and helped that poor old rabbit?" said Jemima. She helped him carry the carrot home. "God bless you!" said the rabbit. Jemima was so happy. She felt very special. She went back to her flowerbed and waited for God again.

A hedgehog with a thorn in his foot came by. "Would you mind, God, if I went and helped that hedgehog?" said Jemima. She took the thorn out of his foot and bandaged him up with leaves. "God bless you!" said the hedgehog. Jemima felt very happy. She felt special again. She felt God growing in her heart. "Hello God!" she said. And she rushed back to the flowerbed to wait for God.

Do you think Jemima found God in the flowerbed? What do you think she should do, to make her special seed from God grow good and strong?

Juniors

Have you ever planted seeds in a flowerpot or a seedtray? Or perhaps you have tried growing cress on a flannel, or growing beans in a jam jar at school. You probably sowed lots of seeds, but not all of them grew. Only a few of the seeds produced tiny plants. If you looked after them, gave them water and sunlight, they grew into fine strong plants. But if you forgot to water them, or left them in the dark, the plants grew very badly or they died.

In today's Gospel Jesus tells us that God has given each of us a special kind of seed: a tiny seed that can grow into goodness and strength, and into a proper understanding and love of God. But this special seed needs to be looked after, or it won't grow. If we forget to feed it and take care of it, it will shrivel and die. We must look after it and help it to grow good and strong.

Story: The search for happiness

There's a film called *As Good as it Gets*. It's about a very sad, grumpy man who is all alone in the world. Well, he's a real grouch. He doesn't like anyone else, so no one likes him. He never does a thing for anyone else. He does everything exactly the same way, every day. He goes to the same cafe for lunch, and he eats the same thing every day. He always gets the same waitress, and he's always very rude to her.

One day, this grumpy man goes to the cafe for lunch, and the waitress isn't there. It makes him angry. Next day, when he sees her, he is still angry, but she is kind and patient. Maybe she is the first person who has ever been kind to him and patient with his bad temper. Bit by bit he begins to do kind things for her, too. Bit by bit, he learns to be a much better person. Discovering that someone cares for him helps this grumpy man to learn to be loving, and to be happy.

There are lots of stories like this, where someone learns to be good through finding someone who loves them as they are. The most famous version of the story is *Beauty and the Beast*. But not every beast can be loved better, or changed into a charming prince. No one grows stronger or better without making an effort. You have to pay attention to notice that someone loves you. You have to think about what someone else needs, to learn how to be kind to them. Growing nearer to God is just the same.

4. Activity

Young ones

Complete the picture on the template page with all the plant needs to grow good and strong.

What makes love grow? Think of all the things that make love grow in us.

What makes us grow closer to God?

Sow some herb or lettuce seeds in a pot. Take it home and look after it.

Juniors

What makes love grow, when someone is grumpy and unloving?

Think of the things that make you feel especially loving towards someone else, your parents, a relation, your carer, or a friend.

What makes us grow closer to God?

What can stand in our way and stop us from growing closer to God?

Think of the ways we can pay attention to God, to learn his ways and grow in his love.

Sow some herb or lettuce seeds in a pot. Take it home and give it everything it needs to grow healthy and strong. Alternatively, colour the template picture and write in the words that will make the plant grow good and strong.

Tips for learning difficulties

Metaphors and analogies can be very tricky for young children and for those with learning difficulties. But even very young children can understand parables where the analogy relates to something very concrete and very familiar. You might use pictures of seeds, seedlings and plants in bloom.

5. We come together

Parents can be invited to join in at this stage.

Focus

The candle is lit, the children sitting quietly for a moment in preparation. Pot of seedlings; green fabric; seed packets; sunflower seeds.

Gospel

Jesus said: "A farmer went out to scatter some seed in a field. While he was scattering the seed, some of it fell along the road and was eaten by birds. Other seed fell on thin, rocky ground and quickly started growing because the soil was not very deep. But when the sun came up, the plants were scorched and dried up, because they did not have enough roots. Some seed fell where thorn bushes grew up and choked the plants. But a few seeds did fall on good ground where the plants produced a hundred or sixty or thirty times as much as was scattered."

Prayer

Leader: Lord, we read your words in the Holy Bible;

Lord, we hear your words at Mass;

Lord, we listen to your words when someone tells us about Jesus' life;

Lord, we love your words because you are talking to us.

Response: Lord Jesus, help us to hear and understand what you tell us. Amen.

Share

Share the work and ideas from the activities.

Sing

"We plough the fields and scatter" or a similar song

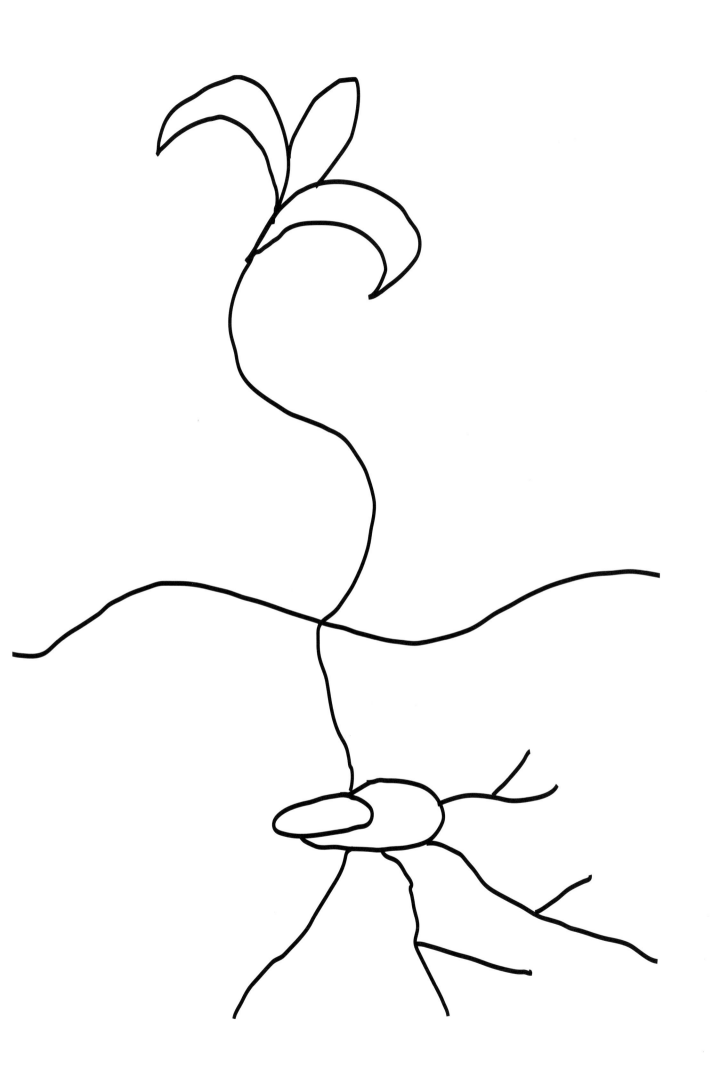

16th Sunday in Ordinary Time

Proper 11

1. Introduction to the theme of the day

"**Let them all grow until the harvest**"

Aim: To understand that God gives every one of us the chance to be part of his team, and make the world into the special place that he made it to be. We can choose to be on God's team and grow good and strong.

Leader's reflection: Today's Gospel parable reminds us that God gives each of us the chance to grow and to bear the fruit of our natures. Unlike the wheat and the weeds, we can choose whether or not to follow God's will and be part of his kingdom.

2. We arrive

We sit in a circle ready to listen to the Gospel. Has anyone anything they would like to tell us about last week's Family Sheet?

Focus

A lighted candle, green fabric for Ordinary Time; pots and pans, wooden spoons etc.

Gospel: Matthew 13:24-43

Read from the Lectionary or Children's Lectionary.

3. We respond

What is the Gospel asking of us?

Work in age groups if appropriate then come together as a community to end the session.

Young ones

Have you ever helped in the garden? Perhaps you have helped to do the weeding, taking out all the bad plants to let the good plants grow properly. Weeding can be tricky. Sometimes you can't tell if a plant is a weed, or if it is really going to turn into a beautiful flower. Sometimes it's best to leave all the plants in the garden, in case you pull up a beautiful flower by mistake.

Jesus tells us that people are like plants in a garden. Some of us will grow up to be beautiful flowers, and some will turn out to be weeds. We can choose to grow into beautiful flowers. God wants us all to be beautiful, and he will help all of us to grow good and strong.

Story: The ugly duckling

Do you know the story of the "Ugly Duckling"? Once there was a duck who laid lots of eggs. But somehow, an extra egg got into her nest. She didn't notice. She thought it was just another one of her eggs. All the eggs hatched out. They were all beautiful little ducklings, except for one. He was too big, and his neck was too long, and he was the ugliest duckling you ever saw. All the others laughed at him. He was so sad. He wanted so much to be beautiful, and for everyone to love him. He was so ashamed of being ugly that he ran away and hid. But he never gave up hoping to grow beautiful. Time passed, and he grew up. One day, he looked at his reflection in the lake, and got a real surprise: he wasn't an ugly duckling at all. He was a beautiful, perfect swan! He was far more beautiful than the ducklings from his nest.

So you never can tell how things will turn out, and who will be beautiful or ugly. Jesus helps everyone to grow into the best person they can be. How can we grow beautiful for Jesus?

Juniors

See discussion points under "Young ones" above. God reaches out and offers us his love and his help to grow good and strong and beautiful.

Story: A life full of choices

Have you ever seen a film called *Bugsy Malone*? There is a very interesting song in that film. It starts off: "We could have been anything that we wanted to be... but we chose to be bad." Imagine choosing to be bad. But some people do just that. And how we turn out is always a choice.

I know a man who behaves very badly. He does just what he wants to do, and never mind how anyone else feels, never mind who gets hurt. He can be lovely, if it suits him. But he can be very spiteful if you make him angry. This man is very clever: he has an important job, and he does it very well. But he is also very silly. He wants to be loved, but his bad behaviour drives everyone away. He doesn't understand that he can change. He thinks he has no choice. He thinks that everyone tries to hurt anyone who hurts them. He thinks everyone is as selfish as he is. He thinks that that is human nature. He thinks God doesn't exist.

Encourage comments relating the story to the Gospel.

We can be anything that we want to be. And who wants to be bad? If you look around you, you'll soon see that people who choose to be bad are seldom happy. People who choose to follow Jesus choose to be good. And you'll see that they are often very happy. It's never too late to choose to be good. God will wait till the very end to see how we turn out. With God's help we will grow good and strong.

4. Activity
Young ones
Using the template of a flower, colour each part then label each part. What did the seed need in order to grow into a beautiful flower? Add these to the picture.

Juniors
Jesus lets us choose to grow good and strong, or to grow bad.

Every day, we get lots of chances to choose a good action. Can you think of situations where we make those choices?

Take a 20cm square of paper. Make a "fortune-teller" by folding the points into the centre. Turn it over and turn the points to the centre again. Fold the square in half, open it out and fold in half the other way. Put your forefinger and thumb in the quarters and activate the fortune-teller. Write in good and bad choices.

Tips for learning difficulties
Young children and those with learning difficulties have problems in recognising that they can take control of their lives, that the things that happen, or the way they behave, are under their control. Have pictures of good and bad situations to discuss.

5. We come together
Parents can be invited to join in at this stage.

Focus
The candle is lit, the children sitting quietly for a moment in preparation. Pot of weeds, pot of flowers or edible plants.

Gospel
Jesus told his disciples this story: "The kingdom of heaven may be compared to a farmer scattering good seed in a field. While everyone was sleeping, an enemy came and scattered weed seeds in the field and then left. When the plants came up and began to ripen, the farmer's servants could see the weeds. The servants came and asked: 'Sir, didn't you scatter good seed in your field? Where did these weeds come from?'

'An enemy did this,' he replied.

His servants then asked, 'Do you want us to go out and pull up the weeds?'

'No!' he answered. 'You might also pull up the wheat. Leave the weeds alone until harvest time. Then I'll tell my workers to gather the weeds and tie them up and burn them. But I'll have them store the wheat in my barn.'"

Prayer
Lord Jesus, help us to grow good and strong in your love. Help us to make the right choices. Be with us throughout the day to be our guiding light. Amen.

Share
Share the work and ideas from the activities.

Sing
"Give me joy in my heart, keep me praising"

17th Sunday in Ordinary Time

Proper 12

1. Introduction to the theme of the day

> ## "The love of God is a treasure beyond price"

Aim: To understand that God's love is a treasure better than anything else in the world. God wants us to have that treasure, but we must be ready to find it.

Leader's reflection: In today's Gospel Jesus tells us that God's love is the only treasure worth having, that it is worth giving up everything else to have that treasure. We find God's treasure, God's love, in the people we share our lives with and in the opportunities we face every day to exercise the values of Jesus. It is in the heart of the ordinary that we discover the presence of Jesus.

2. We arrive

We sit in a circle ready to listen to the Gospel.
Has anyone anything they would like to tell us about last week's Family Sheet?

Focus

Our candle to light; green fabric; treasure box of jewels.

Gospel: Matthew 13:44-52 (Catholic)
Matthew 13:31-33, 44-52 (Anglican)

Read from the Lectionary or Children's Lectionary.

3. We respond
What is the Gospel asking of us?

Work in age groups if appropriate then come together as a community to end the session.

Young ones

Have you ever had a present on your birthday or at Christmas that was so special that you just wanted to play with it all the time? Think of the best present you ever had: what was it? How lovely that present was – how happy and excited it made you feel. But I bet you got bored with it after a while. It didn't seem so special any more.
Jesus tells us that God has a very special present for us that will always make us happy and excited. It is the present of his love. Jesus wants us to feel that love, and be warmed by it.

Story: The best things in life are free

In our village there were two little boys, Ben and Alex. Alex's family were very rich. His mum and dad bought him everything he wanted. He had a whole roomful of toys. Ben's family were very poor. Ben had hardly any toys at all.

Alex often got very cross and bored. He played with the toys, but after a while he didn't want them any more. When he got cross and bored he used to climb a tree in the garden and sulk.

One day, Alex was up his tree, and he noticed Ben playing in a field nearby. Ben was happy and busy all that day. And he was there the next day, too. And the next, and the next, playing in the field, or in the stream that ran through the field, or in the woods at the edge of the field.

Alex couldn't understand it. There were no toys in the field! How could Ben be so happy, when he was so cross and bored? He climbed down the tree and ran over to where Ben was playing. "Why are you so happy?" he said. "My parents have given me a room full of toys, and I'm bored. You have no toys, how can you be happy?" Ben laughed. "Who needs toys," he said, "when God has given us the whole beautiful world to play with?"

Juniors

What would you really, really like to have for your birthday? Perhaps there was something special that you wanted last birthday, so special that you thought about it all the time, hoping and hoping someone would give it to you. How lovely that present was, when you unwrapped it on your birthday. How happy and excited it made you feel. How long was it before you got bored and it didn't seem so special any more?

In today's Gospel, Jesus tells us that God's love for us is so very special that it can always make us happy and excited. It is the best present that anyone could ever have, better than anything else in the world. Better than everything else in the world put together.

Story: The secret of real happiness

Have you seen the film *Harry Potter and the Philosopher's Stone*? Harry Potter grows up in a horrible family where his cousin gets all the presents and all the treats, and Harry gets nothing, and lives in a cupboard under the stairs. But Harry is happy, and his cousin isn't. Things, toys and treats don't really make us happy. The secret of real happiness is quite different.

The Bible is full of stories of people who gave up ordinary things because they suddenly saw the glory of God, and realised what a treasure God's love is.

Take St Paul, for example: his whole life was completely changed in a moment, when God called out to him.

St Paul suddenly understood that the kingdom of God is so special that it is worth giving up everything to have. From that moment on, St Paul gave up his old life and did everything he could do to work to build God's kingdom on earth.

Encourage comments relating the story to the Gospel.

4. Activity
Young ones
What is God's special treasure for us?

Let's make a list of all the things God gives us that are special and good.

Using the template, colour the picture of the friends. You may like to write in speech bubbles of what they are saying.

Juniors
What is God's special treasure for us? What would the world be like, without those gifts from God?

Find a "treasure chest" or make one covered in gold paper.

Think of all the treasures God gives us; write them on bright card and place in the box.

Tips for learning difficulties
The notion of something so abstract as God's love as a more desirable gift than – say – the latest computer game or cult item is a difficult one for young children or those with learning difficulties. It eludes most of the adult population, too. The way into this idea is through exploring feelings: we feel best when we feel loved and appreciated, worst when no one seems to care, or we are criticised or blamed. Every child understands this. God loves and appreciates us all the time.

5. We come together
Parents can be invited to join in at this stage.

Focus
The candle is lit, the children sitting quietly for a moment in preparation; green fabric; the treasure box.

Gospel
Jesus said to his disciples: "The kingdom of heaven is like treasure hidden in a field which someone has found; he hides it again, goes off happy, sells everything he owns and buys it."

Prayer
Lord Jesus, thank you for giving us the best treasure in the world; thank you for giving us your love. Thank you for inviting us into the kingdom of heaven. Amen.

Share
Share the work and ideas from the activities.

Sing
A favourite version of the "Our Father"
"Seek ye first the kingdom of God"

1. Introduction to the theme of the day

"Feeding of the 5,000"

Aim: To understand that Jesus took the little food which was available and shared it amongst all the people. By a miracle there was enough for everybody.

Leader's reflection: One of the interpretations of this miracle is that it was a miracle of sharing. The people had food with them, but nobody wanted to take out the little they had, for fear they would have to share it with others who had nothing, and so go hungry themselves. By encouraging the disciples to share, Jesus broke the chain of selfishness and fear and so everyone was fed. This foreshadowed the Last Supper when Jesus offered himself to be broken and shared for all.

2. We arrive
We sit in a circle ready to listen to the Gospel.
Has anyone anything they would like to tell us about last week's Family Sheet?

Focus
Gather around a lighted candle, a loaf of bread and a fish (real, or drawn on paper); green fabric for Ordinary Time.

Gospel: Matthew 14:13-21
Read from the Lectionary or Children's Lectionary.

3. We respond
What is the Gospel asking of us?
Work in age groups if appropriate then come together as a community to end the session.

Young ones

Story: The problem with sharing!

Henry the honeybee, Camilla the cow, Daphne the duck and Owen the owl had decided to go on a picnic to the Big Field. They were all very excited. The night before, each of them had packed up their knapsack so that it would be ready the next day.

Owen put in his knapsack a kite to play with, and four mouse sandwiches for his lunch. Daphne put in her knapsack a ball to play with and four little fishes for her lunch. Henry put in his knapsack a whistle to play with and four slices of honey cake for his lunch. Camilla put in her knapsack a big rug to sit on and four bunches of grass for her lunch.

The next day all the friends got together under the tree at the bottom of the garden. Owen was there first, and then Henry arrived, buzzing happily to himself. "Where's your knapsack?" Owen asked Henry.

"Here it is," called Henry. It was very small.

"Oh dear," thought Owen. "I hope he hasn't forgotten his lunch. I can't share mine, I haven't got enough for both of us!"

Next Daphne arrived, quacking merrily. "Where's your knapsack?" Owen and Henry asked together.

"Here it is," called Daphne. It was very small.

"Oh dear," they both thought. "I hope she hasn't forgotten her lunch. I can't share mine, I haven't got enough for three of us!"

Finally Camilla arrived, mooing with excitement. "Where's your knapsack?" Owen and Henry and Daphne asked.

"Here it is," called Camilla. It was very small.

"Oh dear," they all thought. "I hope she hasn't forgotten her lunch. I can't share mine. I haven't got enough for all four of us!"

All the friends climbed onto Camilla's back and set off for the Big Field. As they rode, they tied Owen's kite to Camilla's tail, and flew it as they went, and Henry played them all a little tune on his whistle. When they got to the Big Field, Camilla put down the rug and they all sat on it, then they all played with Daphne's ball.

Soon everyone was hungry and it was time for lunch. But nobody said anything. Everybody thought that the others had forgotten their lunch, and nobody wanted to share what they had brought for themselves. So they all sat around, and looked at the sky, and the grass, and the trees, and got hungrier and hungrier and hungrier.

Finally Camilla gave a great moo. She looked around her, there was plenty of grass in the field, and she could always pick some more. "I have brought some grass for my lunch," she said. "There isn't very much, but you can all have some if you like."

Daphne liked grass. "If Camilla can share, then so can I," she thought and gave a great quack. "I have brought some little fish," she said. "There isn't very much, but you can all have some if you like."

Owen liked fish. "If Daphne and Camilla can share, then so can I," he thought, and gave a great hoot. "I have brought some mouse sandwiches," he said. "There isn't very much, but you can all have some if you like."

Henry liked sandwiches. "If Owen and Daphne and Camilla can share, then so can I," he thought, and gave a little buzz. "And I have brought some honey cake," he said. "There isn't very much, but you can all have some if you like."

Everyone liked honey cake. And everybody had a fine lunch. They each had one bunch of grass, and one fish, and one mouse sandwich, and some honey cake to finish with. What a feast!

We are usually happy to share our food with each other when we have more than enough ourselves. It is more difficult if we are anxious that by giving our food to other people, there will be none left for us.
Think of occasions when you have been very happy to share your food, your toys and games, your schoolwork etc. How did this make you feel? What do you not like to share?

Juniors

Story: "Live Aid"

In 1984, the British public were shocked by stark images of millions of people starving to death in Ethiopia. Michael Buerk, the BBC news reporter in Ethiopia, relayed harrowing details of this terrible famine. The response from the British public was generous, but insufficient to prevent the deaths of thousands of people.

Bob Geldof, a pop star from the band The Boomtown Rats, saw the reports on television, and decided he could not sit back and just watch the people suffering and dying. He wrote a song, "Do they know it's Christmas?", and persuaded nearly 40 of the world's most famous pop stars to sing it with him for free, all the proceeds going to Ethiopia. The single was released on 7 December, became the Christmas Number One, and raised £8 million in just three weeks.

Bob then turned his sights to greater things, and decided he was going to organise the world's biggest pop concert, all proceeds going to Ethiopia. He travelled the world, arguing, persuading and demanding that other pop stars give their services free as well. Bands said that he was impossible to refuse.

The concert, called Live Aid, took place on 13 July 1985 and was held simultaneously in Wembley Stadium, London, and JFK Stadium, Philadelphia in the United States, with huge screens broadcasting alternate acts from each of the venues. At its peak, over 24.5 million people in Britain had tuned in to watch the show. The event raised about £40 million for famine relief.

Because Bob was willing to give of his time and his talents, he could ask others to do the same. His work for famine relief still continues. Encourage comments relating the story to the Gospel.

4. Activity
Young ones and Juniors
Bring to the session jigsaw puzzles suitable for the two age groups. (The number of puzzles is dependent on the number of children in the group.) Before the session, divide each one up into two or three bags. Give these to the children; they will soon find they are unable to complete their jigsaw without sharing.

Alternatively, use the suggestion on the template page.

Tips for learning difficulties
Play a matching game. Remove shoes then mix them up. Place an unmatched pair of shoes in front of each child. In turn, let them ask another for their correct shoe. Exchange in a friendly helpful manner.

5. We come together
Parents can be invited to join in at this stage.

Focus
Gather round the loaf, fish and candle; green fabric in Ordinary Time.

Gospel
Jesus was teaching many people on a hillside. There were more than five thousand people there. It was getting late, and the disciples were anxious because there was nowhere for the people to go to get food. Jesus asked his disciples what they had to eat. They found two loaves of bread and five fishes. Jesus prayed over the loaves and the fishes, and told his disciples to share them with all the people. When they did this, they found there was enough for everyone to eat.

Prayer
Jesus, we know that there is plenty of food in the world, if only we could learn to share it all out fairly. Help our government and the people who make important decisions not to be frightened of sharing our riches with the poor countries in the world. Help us to share what we have with the people around us. Amen.

Encourage the children to add their own prayers.

Share
All that has been learnt from the activity.

Sing
"Feed us now, O Son of God"

WORDS I USE WHEN
I AM TRYING TO SHARE

19th Sunday in Ordinary Time

Proper 14

1. Introduction to the theme of the day

> ## "Peter walks on water"

Aim: Jesus asks Peter to trust him. It is not always easy to trust, as Peter found out. Even if we do not trust God, if we ask for help, God will still be there to save us.

Leader's reflection: There are many facets to this story. The most reassuring is, when Peter starts sinking because he takes fright and no longer trusts Jesus, Jesus' response is to hold out a hand and rescue him. Our experience of "trusting" God is often like this. We would like to trust God fully, but deep down we feel that we are really more adept at dealing with our own little problems. No matter; God still reaches out to save us when we call to him.

2. We arrive

We sit in a circle ready to listen to the Gospel.
Has anyone anything they would like to tell us about last week's Family Sheet?

Focus

A candle, a bowl of water with a toy boat on it; green fabric for Ordinary Time.

Gospel: Matthew 14:22-33

Read from the Lectionary or Children's Lectionary.

3. We respond

What is the Gospel asking of us?

Work in age groups if appropriate then come together as a community to end the session.

Young ones
Story: Dabbling ducklings

Daphne the duck was very happy. She had been sitting on her eggs for weeks now, and finally they were beginning to hatch. She could feel the tapping and scratching under her tummy, and, when she looked down, there were three tiny little yellow ducklings all wet and bedraggled, peering up at her.

Daphne took very good care of her little family. She cuddled them in her feathers to keep them warm, and she collected tiny little worms for them and fed them, and she prodded and stroked and groomed them to keep them really clean. She called them David, Debbie and Dickie.

The ducklings quickly learnt how to walk, and started to waddle around the nest by themselves, finding beetles and other little creatures to eat. Then, one day, Daphne decided that it was time for them to learn how to swim.

She took the ducklings down to the pond, and jumped in herself, then called to the little ducklings to follow her.

David was very brave. He took a deep breath, gave a great jump, and plop. There he was in the pond, swimming next to his mummy. Hoorah!

Debbie was not so sure. She put in one toe, then another. The water felt quite nice really. She tiptoed in until it was up to her knees. It was all warm and wet. And then plop. She sat down in it. Suddenly she found that she was swimming. Hoorah!

Dickie did not like it at all. He looked at the water. It was big, and deep and wouldn't keep still. He looked at his mummy and his brother and sister swimming away from him. He felt very scared, and very lonely.

Daphne carefully counted her ducklings. One, two ... but where was Dickie? She looked over to the edge of the pond and saw him standing there all by himself.

"Oh, dear," she quacked as she swam back over to him. "What's wrong?"

"I don't like it," wept Dickie, "and I'm scared."

'Don't you worry about that," whispered Daphne, giving him a big cuddle. "You just climb onto my back and I will carry you instead. You don't have to learn to swim today, we can try again tomorrow. You just hold tight to me, and I will keep you safe."

And so he did.

Who did Dickie put his trust in?
How did he feel when he put his trust in his mother?
Jesus asks us to trust him. Who are the people in our lives that we can really trust? Who are the people who will look after us and keep us safe, and make sure that nothing will happen to us?
Jesus says that he wants to look after us in the same way.

Juniors
Story: Riding the waves

George Freeth was the son of an Irish man and a Hawaiian princess. He was born in 1883, and was brought up in Hawaii. As a child his mother told him many stories about his Hawaiian ancestors, and he saw pictures of them; in particular an old Polynesian painting that showed young chiefs and princes, standing on boards and riding them across the waves. The art of board riding had by then died out, but, as a young adult, George became fascinated by the possibilities and decided to try it out for himself.

His first attempts were disastrous; he made boards which were sixteen feet long, far too big and unwieldy. He risked his life several times trying to ride on them. Eventually, in frustration, he decided to try cutting them in half. Surprisingly, the new shorter boards worked exceedingly well, and soon George and his "long board" became the talk of the islands. Between 1907 and 1915, George's boards developed and became increasingly popular with the visitors to the islands. George meanwhile turned his attention to other matters, developing his swimming and diving skills, and becoming the first lifeguard in southern California. He risked his life several times undertaking many acts of bravery and was awarded medals for saving the lives of stranded fishermen in the Santa Monica Bay.

He died at the age of 36 years, from influenza. He is honoured in the Hawaiian Islands for his life of service, and for risking everything, in order to fulfil his dream of walking on water.

It has been suggested that the film of *Superman* (Clark Kent) is in some ways a reflection on the life of Jesus. In particular, at one point he takes Lois Lane out for a flight, and encourages her to fly on her own. Everything is fine until she stops trusting him...
Compare this story with Peter's trust in Jesus in the Gospel.
Who are the people in our lives that we can really trust?
Who are the people who trust in you?

4. Activity

Young ones and Juniors

Use the template of a boat to colour and write on, or make a paper boat using these instructions. It should float, but if you want to make it last a bit longer you can colour it with wax crayons, or use glossed paper. Make one boat for the people that you can trust, and put their names on it. Younger children may have the boats already made ready to decorate.

* You will need a rectangular piece of paper. A4 size is fine. Have it in front of you with the short side closest.

* Fold it in half so the top corners touch the bottom.

* With the crease at the top, fold each of the top two corners down so that they meet in the middle and you have a sharp point at the top.

* At the bottom are two rectangular flaps. Fold them upward, one in front, and one behind. You now have a triangle which could be a simple hat.

* Open up the inside of the hat, and bend the two outside corners to meet each other. Holding them together, pull out the sides so that you end up with a square. Flatten it.

* Now fold those two same corners upwards to meet the top corner, one in front and one behind. You should have a triangle again.

* Again, open up the inside of the triangle, bend the two outside corners to meet each other to make a square and flatten it.

* This is the clever bit. At the top of the square are two points. Hold them and gently pull them away from each other to make your boat. The sail will be left in the middle.

Tips for learning difficulties

Using larger sheets of card which have been pre-scored or folded is helpful. Or have the boats ready made, and let the children decorate them instead.

5. We come together

Parents can be invited to join in at this stage.

Focus

Light the candle, saying, "May the light of Jesus warm our hearts and shine in our lives." Children can lay their boats before the candle, and have a bowl of water beside the paper boats.

Gospel

The disciples were all in a boat together. It was night time, and Jesus had finished praying in the hills, and came down to meet the disciples. They were still out at sea, so, instead of waiting, Jesus walked over the water towards them. Peter was in the boat and was astonished to see Jesus walking on the water. Jesus called to Peter to join him so Peter jumped out of the boat, and started to run towards Jesus. But he quickly got scared, and started to sink. Jesus reached out a hand and saved him, and held him tight until they got back to the boat.

Prayer

Jesus, these are the people we trust and who care for us. We want to say thank you for all the ways they look after us. Amen.

Share

Each child says a name then places their boat on the bowl of water.

Sing

"Michael, row the boat ashore"

20th Sunday in Ordinary Time

Proper 15

1. Introduction to the theme of the day

"Faith keeps asking!"

Aim: To remind ourselves that sometimes we need to persevere in prayer.

Leader's reflection: One of the first kinds of prayer we learn and which we pass on to the children in our care is the prayer of asking, or intercession. It is natural to turn to God to ask for what we need and a sign of our confidence in him that we place our needs and concerns in his hands.

Experience tells us that God will not always respond to our prayer immediately or in ways that we ourselves would have chosen. These are important lessons, even if they are not easy. Quite often, we need time in which to mature, to find strength that we may not have known we had, or patience, or the love of others sustaining us through dark times.

God's time and greater understanding of our situation may bring a far better solution than the one we envisaged.

Perseverance and prayer are both gifts that help us to grow in confidence in a God who loves us and desires the best for us.

2. We arrive

We sit in a circle ready to listen to the Gospel.

Does everyone know everyone else? Are there any visitors with us this week? Has anyone come back from holiday? Did they have a good time?

Focus

Green cloth, candle, Bible open at today's Gospel.

Gospel: Matthew 15:21-28

Read from the Lectionary or Children's Lectionary.

3. We respond

What is the Gospel asking of us?

Work in age groups if appropriate. Alternatively, choose the discussion ideas, story and activity most suitable for your group. Come together as a community to end the session.

Young ones
Story: Lois' longing

Lois wanted a pet more than anything else in the world. She asked her mum and dad for one at least three times a week but every time their answer was the same: the flat is too small. It would be cruel to have an animal here. They had suggested a goldfish, but Lois had said that was boring. She wanted something she could really look after, something she could cuddle and talk to. But her mum and dad remained firm and said that there was no way they could get a pet for Lois; she would have to wait.

A few months later, Dad came home and said that he had a new job and that they would be moving to a new town. It would mean moving to a new home and, Dad said, because he would earn more money, they should be able to afford a house. Lois was very excited and immediately asked, "Does that mean I can have a pet?"

"We'll see," said Mum, "there are lots of things to think about before that!"

First they had to find a house; then they had to find a new school for Lois; then they had to do some decorating; then they had to do some gardening; and every so often, Lois would just remind her mum and dad that she really wanted a pet more than anything in the world.

Then, one day, the family were sitting at the table and Mum and Dad smiled at Lois. "Well," they said, "we know that you really want a pet and you have been very patient. We think you're old enough now, and we have the space, so let's think about what kind of pet we would all like to have living in our home."

What kind of pet might the family choose? What things will they have to think about now they're getting a pet? Have the children ever really wanted something and had to wait for it? Do they sometimes pester their mums and dads for things they don't really need?

Juniors
Discussion story: St Paul's pain

In St Paul's second letter to the people at Corinth, he tells them that he has been given something like a thorn in the flesh. We don't know what it was, but he suggests that it was something that God had allowed to happen. He doesn't tell us what the problem was, but it was obviously something that was painful, or uncomfortable, or embarrassing, because he says that he had appealed to the Lord three times for it to leave him. And, three times, God had not allowed it to be taken away.

St Paul has thought about this: why would God not answer his prayer?

Surely God knows that he would be an even better apostle without the problem?

Gradually, St Paul begins to realise that God has a very good reason for not answering Paul's prayer as he thinks he should. Paul is doing very great things and might be tempted to think that it was all down to him. Because he has a weakness, he knows that, in fact, it all depends on God, and so what seems like weakness actually makes him strong.

Paul realises that God has heard his prayer but has done what is best for Paul, as he writes that the Lord has said to him: "My grace is sufficient for you, for my power is made perfect in weakness." Once he has learnt this, Paul is proud, not of himself, but boasts of his weakness because it shows that the power of Jesus is working through him.

Look again at the Gospel for today and compare the woman with the sick daughter, who was praying in desperation to Jesus, and St Paul's prayer to God in the discussion story above. How does each answer teach us about faith in God?

4. Activity

Young ones

Children can work individually or in a group. If individually, the children colour in the picture of Lois and then add the pet they think her parents will let her have. Think about what she will need to look after it properly. We have a responsibility for the things we have asked for.

Juniors

When God said "yes" through Jesus.

On a large sheet of paper, or on individual sheets, the children think about some of the Gospel stories, particularly the miracles. What examples can the children think of when Jesus responded to prayer, as people had hoped? (The woman in today's Gospel, the blind man, the lepers.)

Can they think of examples where Jesus did not respond as expected? (The rich young man; waiting before going to see Lazarus; not calling on an army to defend him at his trial.)

They may wish to include St Paul and offer examples of prayers (their own or others) that have seemed to go unanswered, but which they can now see were answered, but differently from the way they had expected.

Tips for learning difficulties

Have some pictures of different pets cut out for the children to suggest which pet Lois would have chosen. Paste it onto the template page.

5. We come together

Parents can be invited to join in at this stage.

Focus

Light the candle. Invite those gathered to become still.

Gospel

In the Gospel, Jesus has moved into an area where he meets people from other backgrounds and cultures, that is, not Jewish people or people from the House of Israel as they were sometimes called.

A woman comes and asks him to heal her daughter as he has done for so many people. At first, Jesus seems reluctant, which seems rather unkind at first sight. But his hesitation gives the woman, a native of Canaan, the opportunity to show that, although she is not of the House of Israel, she is a woman of great faith.

Jesus is pleased to witness such faith and responds by granting her desire and her daughter is made well.

Prayer

Lord Jesus, we thank you for always hearing our prayer.

Help us to be grateful when the answer comes easily and as we hope,

and to trust you when the answer seems slow in coming, or is different from what we expect. Amen.

Share

We have been thinking about how God answers our prayers. The younger children heard a story about Lois who really wanted a pet. (Invite the children to talk about the story... You may wish to draw from them that Lois did not get the pet because she pestered her parents enough, but because her parents waited until the time was right for her to have one!)

The older children have been hearing how St Paul had to learn to live with something that seems to have caused him some pain and discomfort. He thought at first that his prayers were not being answered but eventually realised that God had a greater understanding of what was needed. Invite the children to comment and to talk about the work they have done on Jesus answering prayer, or waiting for the right time.

Sing

"Give me joy in my heart"
"Holy, holy, holy is the Lord"

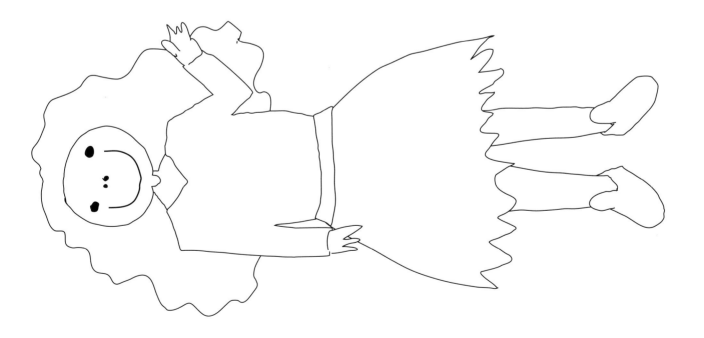

21st Sunday in Ordinary Time

Proper 16

1. Introduction to the theme of the day

"Who do you say I am?"

Aim: To discover who Jesus is to us.

Leader's reflection: At what point did Jesus begin to understand who he was, and when did this begin to crystallise into a certainty? Jesus asks the question of Peter, "Who do people say I am?" and then more searchingly, "And who do you say I am?" This is towards the end of his ministry, and shortly afterwards Jesus sets off towards Jerusalem for his final Passover. It is as if the words of Peter, "You are the Christ, the Son of the living God", were the confirmation Jesus needed in order to face the growing inevitability of his Passion and death.

2. We arrive

We sit in a circle ready to listen to the Gospel.
Has anyone anything they would like to tell us about last week's Family Sheet?

Focus

A lighted candle, several different images of Jesus: icons, Bible pictures, a crucifix etc.; green fabric for Ordinary Time.

Gospel: Matthew 16:13-20

Read from the Lectionary or Children's Lectionary.

3. We respond

What is the Gospel asking of us?

Work in age groups if appropriate then come together as a community to end the session.

Young ones
Story: Who am I?

Henry the honeybee had lost his memory. A few weeks ago, he had been out flying and enjoying the sunshine, when BONK! He had hit his head on a tree. His head was much better, but now he could not remember anything. He could not remember his name, and he could not remember the things he liked doing, and he could not remember the things he was good at. He was very confused. "Who am I?" he asked himself time and again, and he did not know the answer.

"Hello, Henry," came a moo from behind him. Henry looked round.

"Am I Henry?" he asked.

"Of course you are, silly," said the cow who had called to him.

"Oh, that is useful to know," said Henry. "Thank you." But he could not remember the cow's name.

"Hello, Henry," came a quack from behind him. "Thank you for coming to my party." Henry looked round.

"Did I come to your party?" he asked.

"Of course you did, silly," quacked the duck who had called to him. "And you brought me some honey. It was very nice."

"Oh, that is useful to know," said Henry. "I am good at making honey. Thank you ..." but he could not remember the duck's name!

"Hello, Henry," came a tiny little squelch from underneath him. "How is the bump on your head?" Henry looked round.

"Did I bump my head?" he asked.

"Of course you did, silly," squelched the little worm. "And it looks like you have lost your memory now. Would you like some help finding it again?"

"Oh, that would be useful," buzzed Henry happily. "Thank you," he giggled, "but first of all, you will have to tell me what your name is. I've forgotten!"

Talk about who Jesus is. What do the children know about him? Let them look really closely at the images from the focal point. What do they tell us about Jesus? You might have some contrasting music: the Hallelujah Chorus from Handel's *Messiah* contrasted with a hymn like "Were you there when they crucified my Lord?"
How were the creatures in the story helpful to Henry?

Juniors
Story: "You will be known by your actions"

There are very many stories of people who try to disguise themselves, but who are eventually recognised by what they do, rather than the way they look. Robin Hood is a very good example of this. He was an outlaw of Nottingham, and lived in the forest with his friends. Little is known of him, although many tales are told. He is reputed to have stolen from the rich people of the town, and to have given all the money away again to the poor people. One thing that is known about him is that he had a reputation as an excellent archer.

One day the people of Nottingham decided to hold an archery contest. Robin Hood wanted to go because he knew he could win, but he also knew that if he went into the town, he would be arrested and imprisoned. So he decided to go in disguise.

All was well until the competition started. Nobody recognised Robin, they thought he was a stranger, and he felt quite safe in his disguise. However, once the competition started, the people were amazed at how well the stranger could shoot. There was only one person that they knew of who could shoot so well – Robin Hood! They realised that the person who was shooting was Robin Hood. He had to escape very quickly.

***Robin Hood, Prince of Thieves* is a great film of the legend.**
You should be able to order it through your local video/DVD rental shop.
Encourage comments relating the story to the Gospel.
What were some of the descriptive names given to Jesus?

Sometimes people are known by what they do, rather than an actual name. In the catacombs in Rome, where the early Christians were interred, the bodies were wrapped in cloth and placed on a type of shelf in the rock. This shelf was closed across the front with stone. Scratched into the stone was a picture of the trade of the deceased, e.g. a loaf of bread for a baker, as the family were unlikely to have learnt how to write.

4. Activity
Young ones
What do you think Jesus was like? What do you think he liked doing? Draw a picture of him showing these things.

Juniors
When you apply for a job, you often have to send a curriculum vitae (CV). This tells people who you are, and what you can do. Write a CV for Jesus using the form on the template page. Use everything that you know about him to fill it in. Where do you think he went to school? What qualifications did he have? What do you think his interests and hobbies were?

Tips for learning difficulties
Talk about Jesus using the pictures from a children's Bible.

If there are children with profound or severe learning difficulties, try to find some images of Jesus which are more tactile in nature: statues, dressed dolls, a Bible, water etc.

5. We come together
Parents can be invited to join in at this stage.

Focus
Gather together all the images of Jesus; include the children's work in the display.
Light a candle and put it in the display.

Gospel
Jesus said to his disciples, "Who am I?" At first the disciples didn't answer, then Peter said to Jesus, "You are the Christ, the Son of the living God."

Prayer
Jesus, we know many things about you. But the two most important are that you are God, and that you love us. Thank you, Jesus. Amen.

Share
The work from the activities.

Sing
"Jesus, you are Lord"

Curriculum Vitae

Name: Jesus Christ
Age:
Place of birth:
Family home town:
Education:

Qualifications:

Interests and hobbies:

Special friends:

Describe in a few sentences your mission, or your particular work, in life.

Write in the space below anything else you would like to tell us about yourself.

22nd Sunday in Ordinary Time

Proper 17

1. Introduction to the theme of the day

"Take up your cross"

Aim: Living God's way might sometimes seem strange or difficult, but it is really what we most want to do.

Leader's reflection: We are finite, limited creatures. Learning to live in relationship with infinite, uncreated love, to engage fully with life itself, challenges us beyond our imagination, but that is what we are called to do. In fact it is achievable only by the transforming power of God's grace, and that process of transformation can seem to us to be very difficult, alien to our natural instincts for safety and familiarity and comfort. Ultimately, though, it is the only thing that can satisfy us.

2. We arrive

We sit in a circle ready to listen to the Gospel.
Has anyone anything they would like to tell us about last week's Family Sheet?

Focus

A lighted candle, green fabric for Ordinary Time, packet of balloons.

Gospel: Matthew 16:21-27

Read from the Lectionary or Children's Lectionary.

3. We respond
What is the Gospel asking of us?

Work in age groups if appropriate then come together as a community to end the session.

Young ones

This week the main message is contained within the story for the young ones and everybody should read this together. If the juniors would enjoy something more substantial in addition, use the story about St Margaret Ward.

Story: Billy, the blown-up, grown-up balloon!

Billy was a balloon. He was a bright red balloon and he lived in a plastic bag with lots of other balloons. Most of the time Billy was quite happy in the bag with his friends, it was cosy and safe and he liked it there. But some of the time he wondered if life couldn't be a bit more exciting, he felt a bit unfinished, as if he could be something bigger and better and brighter if only he was given the chance.

One day a girl came along and pulled Billy out of the bag. Billy was very excited. At last! This might be the chance he had been waiting for. To his surprise, the girl put Billy in her mouth. "Oh, stop!" shouted Billy. "Please don't eat me." But the girl didn't eat him. She did something very strange instead.

She started to blow air into him; blow, blow. At first Billy quite liked it; it was like feeling full up after a good meal. Blow, blow, then he began to feel a bit giggly and dizzy.

Blow, blow; as the girl kept on blowing he began to feel his sides stretching out; it wasn't quite so comfortable now. Blow, blow, "Ouch!" squeaked Billy. "You're blowing too hard!" Blow, blow, but the girl kept on blowing: now it really hurt quite a lot, Billy was stretched so much he thought he might pop! Then at last the girl stopped. She tied him up so the air could not escape and put him on the table.

Billy was left feeling very strange and very stretched. He did not know if he liked what had happened at all. Then he heard lots of whispers close by. "Wow, look at Billy!" It was his balloon friends who were watching from the bag. "Look at how big and bright he is now!" Suddenly Billy was very happy. He forgot that he was hurting all over, and that he felt strange and stretched. Now he was a proper blown-up balloon. This was the best thing that had ever happened to him.

How did Billy the balloon change?
Did he want to change at the beginning, when he was in a bag with other balloons?
How did he feel at the end of the story?

Juniors

Story: St Margaret Ward

There are some people that God chooses to stretch so full of his Spirit, that there is no room left for anything else. For Margaret Ward the most important thing in her life was being full of God's Spirit, even though that meant that her life might sometimes be uncomfortable or even dangerous. Without God's Spirit she knew that she would never really be fully alive, and so she was prepared to die rather than give up her faith.

Margaret Ward was a Catholic Englishwoman who lived during a period called the Reformation, when it was dangerous to be a Catholic. She worked as a housekeeper in London, close to Bridewell prison where Catholic priests and the people who supported them were locked up. There was a prisoner at that time called Fr William Watson. It seems likely that he was a little bit crazy – he was always getting into mad scrapes and escapades. He had been arrested before and agreed not to be a Catholic any more, and then, when he was released, he had gone straight back to the Church. Now he was in prison again, and was trying again to prove

that he didn't want to be a Catholic, but this time nobody believed him and he was treated very badly. Even the Catholics were unkind to him because they thought he was a traitor, but Margaret heard about him and felt sorry for him, so she brought him gifts of food and clothing and helped him to plan his escape. Next time Margaret visited him she brought a rope, just long enough to reach from his window to the river below. She arranged for a friend to be ready in a boat on the river the following night. All went well, until Fr Watson decided that the rope was too good to be left behind, and tried to take it with him. He slipped and fell, breaking an arm and a leg and making a lot of noise! Somehow he managed to escape, but Margaret and her friend were captured and arrested. Margaret was tortured and brought to trial, but she refused to say where Fr Watson was hiding, and she refused to stop being a Catholic. She was condemned to die because she refused to give up her faith, and was hanged at Tyburn on 30 August 1588.

Discussion ideas:
Think how the balloon changed. How do you think you will change between now and being a teenager, being an adult?
How does God want us to develop?
What help will he give us?
What challenges or difficulties may we have to face?

4. Activity

Young ones and Juniors

When God created us, he wanted us to be like him, so all during our lives he fills us with his Spirit. Sometimes that feels good and we enjoy growing with God. Other times it isn't so comfortable and we feel a bit stretched. But in the end we grow into bigger, better, brighter people – the way we really want to be.

Draw faces on balloons using markers. Blow God's Spirit into them.
Alternatively, colour the balloons on the template page. Draw a smile on both and see how big your smile can be when you are full of God's Spirit!
Describe the difference between the two balloons in words on the template page.

Tips for learning difficulties

Some children might need help with painting faces, or with blowing up balloons: avoid using a balloon pump as it spoils the analogy with God's Spirit.

5. We come together

Parents can be invited to join in at this stage.

Focus

Gather around the table. Billy the red balloon could be put on the table.

Gospel

Jesus said, "If you want to be like God, you will have to be filled with his Spirit and let yourself be stretched. Sometimes that might hurt a bit, but in the end it is worth it."

Prayer

Dear Jesus, when you were stretched on the cross it hurt you a lot, but it was worth it in the end because now you are alive for ever. We want to grow into bigger and better and brighter people, and we want to live with you for ever. Help us not to mind being stretched a bit but please don't stretch us too much until we are ready. Amen.

Share

Show off the balloons, you might like to try and match them to their owners.

Sing

"Abba, Father, send your Spirit"
maybe substitute a couple of new verses, e.g.
Blow your Spirit deep into us …
Fill us up with Jesus' Spirit …
Let him stretch us, let him fill us …

23rd Sunday in Ordinary Time

Proper 18

1. Introduction to the theme of the day

"Forgive one another"

Aim: Where appropriate, to welcome the children to a new academic year; to help new children to settle in and to remind ourselves and the children that these gatherings are to help us to learn more about God and Jesus, and that, when we are gathered, Jesus is here among us. To think about the importance of forgiveness in loving relationships.

Leader's reflection: Your group may have been meeting over the summer, but it is likely that this will be the first large gathering after the break. This time of year has a feeling of newness about it, as children start in new classes and sometimes new schools. There is a mixture of excitement and apprehension as they meet new people and start new books and work. We can share that enthusiasm and encourage the children to see these sessions as something to look forward to:

• times to hear God's word saying something special for them,
• times to be creative and reflective, times of companionship and learning how to get on with each other,
• times to remember that when you come together, Jesus has promised to be there with you.

2. We arrive

We sit in a circle ready to listen to the Gospel. Has anyone anything they would like to tell us about last week's Family Sheet?

Introduce any new people. A fun way to do this is to ask the children to find out the names of the people on either side of them in the circle. Then, going round the circle, they say the name of the person on one side, their own name, and the name of the person on the other side. In this way each person hears everyone's name three times.

Focus
Green cloth, candle, Bible open at today's Gospel.

Gospel: Matthew 18:15-20
Read from the Lectionary or Children's Lectionary.

3. We respond
What is the Gospel asking of us?
Work in age groups if appropriate. Alternatively, choose the discussion ideas, story and activity most suitable for your group. Come together as a community to end the session.

Young ones

Story: A new start; a new school

Jess was starting a new school. I wonder how she was feeling...?

(Invite the children to think about how she might feel.)

What was worse was that she had had a big argument with her big brother... I wonder what that could have been about?

(Invite the children to speculate.)

He had promised to stay with her until it was time to go into her new class so Mum could get off to work. But what if he changed his mind?

Jess got up and got washed and dressed. She could hear Ben, her brother, getting ready next door. He seemed to be making more noise than usual. She could hear the radio in the kitchen and Mum singing along to it. But she just sat on the bed ...

(How is Jess feeling? What could she do to help herself to feel better?)

In the end, Jess took a big breath and opened her bedroom door. At the same time, Ben opened his bedroom door... I wonder what's going to happen?

Ben looked at Jess and said, "Nervous?" Jess nodded. "I remember feeling like that too," said Ben. "Look, I'm sorry about ..." (whatever you and the children decided the argument was about).

"Me too," said Jess.

"Can't have you miserable on your first day, can we?" said Ben. "Come on, little sis, let's go and get some breakfast." And he put his arm round her shoulders and they went down to the kitchen where Mum was waiting for them.

(How is Jess feeling now? Why is she feeling like that?)

Help the children to understand the importance of forgiveness in loving relationships.

Juniors

Story: Joseph and his brothers

Tell the story of Joseph and his brothers (Genesis chapters 37-47).

Explain how Joseph was the son of Jacob's favourite wife, Rachel; his other wife was her sister Leah. Jacob and Leah had six sons, he and Rachel had two and, sadly, Rachel died when her baby Benjamin was born.

Joseph was a dreamer and saw in his dreams that he would become greater than his brothers. Of course, they were very jealous and planned to kill him. In the end, they sold him into slavery. After time in prison, Joseph

was called to interpret the dreams of Pharaoh. He was so accurate that Pharaoh made him second in command.

When famine hit the land, Joseph's brothers came to Egypt in search of food. Joseph gave them food but when the brothers brought Benjamin, his youngest brother, back, Joseph accused him of stealing. When the brothers pleaded for Benjamin, Joseph saw that they had changed and gave them his forgiveness.

Invite the children to explore the feelings of the people in the story and how forgiveness reunited the family.

4. Activity

Young ones

Use the templates of Jess and Ben having an argument. Invite the children to think about what they might be saying as they colour them in.

Next, use the picture of Ben putting his arm round Jess and going into the kitchen. What expressions are on their faces? What will they be saying?

Juniors

Invite the children to role-play the Joseph story, many may know it from the musical. If you have a recording of it listen to some of the songs as the children act out the various parts. If time and circumstances permit, make a few props to add to the role-play, for example: simple palm trees; sun, moon and stars; sheaves of wheat; sacks; goblet.

Alternatively, write the story around Jess and Ben's argument on the template page.

Tips for learning difficulties

Use the activity most suited to the children. Talk to them about love and putting things right. Have they been upset by people? How did they feel? How can we put things right? Think about hugs and saying "sorry", and how we should react if someone asks us to forgive them.

5. We come together

Parents can be invited to join in at this stage.

Focus

Light the candle. Invite those gathered to become still, to look at the candle and think about the time of year.

Gospel

In the Gospel, Jesus teaches us about forgiveness:
that if we have a quarrel we must try to put things right.
He also reassures us that when two or three of us are
gathered together he is with us.

Prayer

Jesus, you promise that you are with us
and we trust your promise.
Help us to be loving people,
always ready to say sorry when we need to,
and to forgive others when they ask us. Amen.

Share

The children have heard stories about people loving and forgiving: Jess and Ben, and Joseph and his brothers. We have thought about the importance of putting things right so we can start again. Invite the children to tell their families about what they have been doing.

Sing

"God forgave my sin" or
"Amazing grace"

24th Sunday in Ordinary Time

Proper 19

1. Introduction to the theme of the day

"Be fair!"

Aim: To explore further the importance of forgiveness in the Christian life, linking this with the need to work for racial justice.

Leader's reflection: One of the greatest gifts we have is the gift of forgiveness. Imagine for a moment a life without forgiveness. Life would be utterly impossible if during the course of a lifetime we became increasingly crushed by the weight of the guilt of past sins, offences, slights. It would be even harder, perhaps, to live in a state of unforgiving. Imagine never being able to forgive anyone who had ever hurt you, having a memory of every injury, and that memory coming between you and those around you, never to be laid to rest. Human relationships depend on mutual forgiveness, on releasing and being released from things that could otherwise hold us bound.

2. We arrive

We sit in a circle ready to listen to the Gospel. Is there anything to share from last week's Family Sheet?
Can everyone remember each other's name?

Focus

Green cloth, candle, a globe, Bible open at the reading for today. If you are reflecting on Racial Justice Sunday, have photographs of children of different races.

Gospel: Matthew 18:21-35

Read from the Lectionary or Children's Lectionary.

3. We respond
What is the Gospel asking of us?

Work in age groups if appropriate. Alternatively, choose the discussion ideas, story and activity most suitable for your group. Come together as a community to end the session.

Young ones
Story: Damien cares about Constance

Constance had come to school but she wasn't very happy.

Why might she be unhappy?

(Invite the children to think of reasons.)

The thing that really made Constance unhappy was that, although she had best friends, there was a group of children who kept calling her names.

(Why might children do that?)

The fact was that Constance came from … (choose a different part of the world, e.g. the Caribbean/ Philippines/Africa/India…). It meant that her skin was a different colour and some people thought it was fun to be rude about it.

Constance wasn't sure what to do. Her friends told her to tell Mrs Arthur, but Constance was embarrassed. She didn't want to make a fuss. She was proud of who she was but still got upset. In the end Damien said that it had to stop and if Constance wasn't going to tell Mrs Arthur, he was!

(What do the children think about Damien's decision?)

At the end of the morning, Damien said, "Are you coming with me, Constance, to see Mrs Arthur?"

Mrs Arthur listened hard to what Damien was saying and then she turned to Constance,

"How does this make you feel?"

Constance said she felt miserable but didn't want to make a fuss.

"Do you think it is fair?" asked Mrs Arthur. "Would you call people names?"

Constance hadn't thought of it like that.

"No," said Mrs Arthur, "it isn't fair. We need to help these children understand that; leave it with me."

When they came back from lunch, Mrs Arthur was talking to the group. They looked a bit ashamed of themselves.

"Constance," said Mrs Arthur, "can you tell these children how their teasing makes you feel?"

(Invite the children to fill in the words…)

"We were only joking!" exclaimed one of the group.

"No, you weren't," said Mrs Arthur. "You were trying to upset Constance. I know you didn't know how much, but now you do. So what are you going to do?"

The group looked embarrassed and then Carl came forward: "Sorry," he said. And then the others muttered sorry too.

Constance could see they meant it and said, "That's OK. Shake on it?" She reached out her hand and Carl shook it.

"Excellent," said Mrs Arthur, "now we can go and get on with our painting. Come on, everyone."

Juniors
Story: A lesson on forgiveness

José Burgos was born in Vigan, Ilocos Sur, in the Philippines on 9 February 1837. From his earliest years he wanted to become a priest. He was a brilliant student and graduated at the top of the class.

He became a priest and was determined to show that Filipinos were as good as the white people who looked down on them. He fought for reforms in the country and human rights. When a mutiny broke out, the Spanish authorities saw this as a very good opportunity to get rid of him. He was arrested and charged with conspiring against the state and organising the mutiny.

He did not receive a fair trial. Even his defence lawyer said that José had confessed that he was guilty. José stood up in the court and said that he was not guilty, but the court had already made its decision. He and two other priests were to be executed.

José was the last to die and before doing his work, the executioner approached him.

"Father," said he, "forgive me for what I am about to do."

"I forgive you, my son," was the quiet reply. "Do what is your duty."

Then he turned to the people who were present and blessed them.

He is honoured as a martyr for the cause of the Filipinos.

Look on the globe to find the Philippines. Talk about the Spanish settlers, the ruling class and the native Filipinos. What do the children think of José and his cause?
(Look up wikipedia.org to learn more about the history of the Philippines.)

4. Activity

Young ones

Forgiving makes things better! On the template sheet and under the speech bubbles containing Carl's' "Sorry" and Constance's "That's OK. Let's shake on it", invite the children to draw in the characters and colour them in.

Juniors

Talk about people who have fought for the cause of equality and human rights: Fr José, Mahatma Gandhi, Martin Luther King, Nelson Mandela etc. How are people like these helping to build God's kingdom on earth? How can we build God's kingdom? Are there people of different races among us? Perhaps our parents or grandparents came from another country?

The Bible says that God made human beings in his own image and likeness, so God is present in all races and colours. What does that tell us about how we should treat other people, especially those who seem different from us?

If your parish is a diverse community, children could draw themselves and paste the pictures onto a poster inside a large circle called "Our parish/community family".

Alternatively, invite the children to draw children from different races, colour them in and decorate bubble-writing letters spelling out "All God's Family!"

Tips for learning difficulties

Choose the activity most suited to the child. Talk about making friends again after a quarrel. Gently find out if they have experienced teasing for being different and explore how to deal with it.

5. We come together

Parents can be invited to join in at this stage.

Focus

Use the focal point from the beginning of the session. Light the candle. Invite those gathered to become still, to look at the candle and think about our world, made up of people from different countries and racial origins.

Gospel

In the Gospel we heard how a master freed one of his servants from a huge debt that he couldn't pay. That servant then went to another servant, who owed him a little money, and had him thrown in prison.
When the master heard how unfair this man had been, he sent him to prison.

Prayer

Lord Jesus,
you remind us of how much God loves us and how he forgives us.
Help us to remember that great love and treat other people with love and forgiveness. Amen.

Share

We have been thinking about Jesus' story about being fair. We thought about a girl called Constance. Invite the children to retell the story and what they thought it meant. The older ones were thinking about people who fought for fairness and justice between people of different races. Invite the children to talk about what they have discussed.

Sing

"When I needed a neighbour", or
"Make me a channel of your peace"

25th Sunday in Ordinary Time

Proper 20

1. Introduction to the theme of the day

"Our generous God"

Aim: To reflect on God's generosity and on how, with God, things may not always be as they seem.

Leader's reflection: At first sight, the parable seems to speak of unfairness on the part of the landowner, paying the people who came at the eleventh hour the same as those who had worked all day. A denarius was, however, a fair day's pay and had been agreed between the landowner and workers at the start of the day. In giving the same amount to everyone, the landowner was doing more than he need have done, but through his generosity in giving to the latecomers more than they deserved, he ensured that they would be able to provide a meal for their families.

2. We arrive

We sit in a circle ready to listen to the Gospel. Is there anything anyone wants to share from last week's Family Sheet?

Focus

Green cloth, candle, Bible open at today's Gospel.

Gospel: Matthew 20:1-16

Read from the Lectionary or Children's Lectionary.

3. We respond

What is the Gospel asking of us?

Work in age groups if appropriate. Alternatively, choose the discussion ideas, story and activity most suitable for your group. Come together as a community to end the session.

Young ones

Story: Life is so exciting!

Ciara and Christopher loved going to Gran and Grandad's house. Gran made lovely cakes and Grandad would take them into the woods at the end of their road.

This time, they had come to sleep round at Gran and Grandad's because their mum was going to have twins.

The children had come to stay with Gran and Grandad for a few days until the babies were born.

Ciara was used to staying round there, but this was Christopher's very first time.

Ciara could remember him being born two years before and remembered how tiny he was. He was a bit boring too, she thought.

Christopher was not boring now! "That child never stops," said Gran, smiling. "George, take the children to the woods and let him run off some energy."

Grandad did as he was told and soon the children were in among the trees. It was autumn and Ciara noticed acorns on the ground. Christopher looked as if he thought he might try and eat one, but Grandad pulled out a carrier bag and told him to put it in there. "See if you can find any more," he suggested. Soon, the children had a carrier bag full, not just of acorns, but of conkers and "helicopters" too.

"Grandad, why do the trees produce so many acorns and things?" asked Ciara. "They only need one or two to grow into new trees."

"It's a mystery," said Grandad. "It's the way God works. He never does things by halves; he just loves creating things!"

When they got back to the house, Christopher had great fun with the things they had collected, sorting them out and building little piles of them. He was still busy when the phone rang. Gran went to answer it and came back a few minutes later beaming.

"You have a new baby sister and a new baby brother," she exclaimed. Ciara clapped her hands. "Oh, when can we go and see them?" she asked.

"Your dad said to let Mum have a good night's sleep and we can go in tomorrow."

"Did you hear that, Christopher?" Ciara said. "We can go and see our new babies tomorrow!"

Christopher looked at her and smiled. "Nice," he said, and then went back to playing with his hundreds of acorns, conkers and "helicopters".

What does the story tell us about how generous God is? Talk about God's gifts all around us in our families, our friends, the parks, woods and countryside, the animals, birds and insects.
Does everyone receive the same gifts from God?
What gift do *you* get excited about?

Juniors

Story: Learning from each other, across the world

Emma and Josh's school had twinned with a school in Cameroon. Their diocese was twinned with a diocese called Bamenda and some of the schools had the idea of finding out more about life in Africa and becoming "partners" with them.

At first it had been done by letters and drawings being sent in the post, but one day the great news came that a computer had been donated to the school in Cameroon, and they had received a grant to allow them to use the internet. The children in Africa put pictures of their school online and Emma and Josh's school did the same.

They felt a bit embarrassed about doing this as their school had lots of computers, not just one; in fact, their school was amazingly well equipped compared to the school in Africa. But the African children were very enthusiastic and in their emails talked about how much they enjoyed school and how education was the way to make their country more prosperous. They said that the internet was brilliant because it meant that they could find all sorts of information without having to buy expensive books.

The class discussed this in circle time…

Use a globe to show the position of Cameroon.
Invite the children to be the class in circle time: thinking about the differences in wealth, attitudes to learning, possible ways to share resources more fairly.
How could Emma and Josh's school help their twin school? What could they learn from the schoolchildren in Africa?

4. Activity

Young ones

Under the banner "God is generous", have the children colour in a picture of Ciara and Christopher with their acorns, conkers and "helicopters" on one side, and a picture of Mum with her two babies on the other. As they colour in talk about how generous God is, providing thousands of acorns, and two babies to love.

How else is God generous to us?

Juniors

Find out some facts and figures about the distribution of wealth in the world.

Try these websites: www.cafod.org.uk or www.christianaid.org.uk

On a map of the world use piles of coins to show the respective wealth of various countries. What do the children think? Can they think of any solutions? What do they think is God's will for the world?

Emphasise God's generosity in providing abundant resources for the earth. You may like to look at Genesis 1 where (depending on the translation) the writer uses words like "teems", "of every kind", "swarms" and "I have given you every plant..." How can we help to bring about that vision for humanity so that, like the people in the Gospel, everyone has enough to feed themselves and their families?

Tips for learning difficulties

Use the story and activity for younger ones or invite the children to count out the coins on the map.

5. We come together

Parents can be invited to join in at this stage.

Focus

Light the candle. Invite those gathered to become still, to look at the candle and think about the time of year.

Gospel

In the Gospel, Jesus talks about a landowner who agrees in the morning to pay his workers one denarius each: that's enough to feed a family. The problem arises when he pays the same amount to people who have only done one hour's work. The people who worked all day complain, but the landowner says that if he wants to be generous then that is his right.

Prayer

Lord Jesus,

you remind us of God's generosity and his desire to make sure everyone has enough to live on.

Help us to be generous too. Amen.

Share

In our session, the younger children thought about how generous God is. Invite the children to tell the story and how God was generous in providing acorns, etc. and babies! The older children thought about how God's resources are not always fairly spread. They thought about how education and access to information is one way to help poorer countries, and made a map to show how wealth is distributed in the world.

Sing

"O Lord, all the world belongs to you" or
"You are salt for the earth, O people" or
"Sent by the Lord am I"

God is generous

26th Sunday in Ordinary Time

Proper 21

1. Introduction to the theme of the day

"Doing God's will"

Aim: To help the children to realise that talking about doing God's will and actually doing it are two different things.

Leader's reflection: We have all met people who, in the popular phrase, "can talk the talk but cannot walk the walk". They are the people with plans and ideas but not the focus or energy to put them into practice. In religious terms it is quite easy to say, "I'm a Christian but I don't need to go to church", or do anything that might mark them out as one. As catechists, we are "walking the walk" – as well as talking the talk, of course!

We are doing God's will by giving our time to share the love of our faith and of the word of God with the children and their families. Your example, of choosing to do something for God, is as much part of your ministry as leading the sessions themselves.

2. We arrive

We sit in a circle ready to listen to the Gospel. Does anyone want to share anything from last week's Family Sheet?

Focus

Green cloth, candle, Bible open at today's Gospel.

Gospel: Matthew 21:28-32 (Catholic)
Matthew 21:23-32 (Anglican)

Read from the Lectionary or Children's Lectionary.

3. We respond
What is the Gospel asking of us?

Work in age groups if appropriate. Alternatively, choose the discussion ideas, story and activity most suitable for your group. Come together as a community to end the session.

Young ones
Story: In a minute

Todd's nickname was "in-a-minute-boy" for the very good reason that whenever he was asked to do something he always said, "Yes", but always added, "in a minute".

And sometimes, the minute became two minutes, or five minutes, or sometime, or never!

So when his mum said, "Todd, can you feed your hamster now?" Todd said,

All: Yes ... in a minute.

And when his dad said, "Todd, can you bring me the screwdriver from the shelf?" Todd said,

All: Yes ... in a minute.

And when his sister said, "Todd, can you give me back the felt tips you borrowed?" Todd said,

All: Yes ... in a minute.

And when his teacher said, "Todd, will you clean the board, please?" Todd said,

All: Yes ... in a minute.

At the parents' evening, Todd's mum and dad mentioned this problem to the teacher.

"Is he the same in school?" they asked.

Mr Green raised his eyes. "Oh yes!"

They decided to try something to help Todd to learn an important lesson.

So when Todd said, "Mum, can you get me my clean socks?" Mum said,

All: Yes ... in a minute.

And when Todd said, "Dad, can we go and play football?"

All: Yes ... in a minute.

And when Todd said, "Meg, can we change channel to watch (name of children's programme)?"

All: Yes ... in a minute.

And when Todd said, "Could I have a go on the computer?" Mr Green said,

All: Yes ... in a minute.

Todd got fed up of waiting for a minute, or two minutes, or sometime, or never and said so when the family were sitting down to dinner.

"It's not fair that you keep saying 'in a minute' and then don't do it," he moaned.

Everyone looked at each other and smiled.

"That's just what we thought, in-a-minute-boy!" said Dad.

"Even Mr Green said the same, you always say 'in a minute', and then you don't do it," said Mum. "We thought if you knew how it felt you might think twice about saying it in future."

Todd got the point and said, "OK, see what you mean. I'll try."

After the meal, Mum asked Todd to take the dishes into the kitchen and Todd said,

All: Yes ... in a minute.

And everyone looked at him and said, "Todd!" And Todd said ... "Only joking!"

Can the children give any examples of situations where people have said they wouldn't do something, and then thought better of it? And vice versa?

Juniors
Story: St Augustine of Hippo

St Augustine is one of the great saints in the Church but his early life was less than perfect. He spent years travelling, trying different religions, and keeping bad company. His mother, St Monica, prayed for him and eventually Augustine did come to see Christianity as true, but didn't become a Christian because he didn't think he was good enough!

One day, he heard about two men who had suddenly been converted after reading the *Life of St Antony*, and he felt terribly ashamed of himself. "What are we doing?" he cried to his friend Alipius. "Other people are taking heaven by force, while we, with all our knowledge, are so cowardly that we keep rolling around in the mud of our sins!"

He heard a child singing a song: "Take up and read!"

Thinking that the words came from God, he picked up the book of the letters of St Paul, and read the first passage his gaze fell upon. It was just what Augustine needed. In it, St Paul said, "Put away all impurity and live in imitation of Jesus." That did it! From then on, Augustine began a new life.

He was baptised, became a priest, a bishop and a famous Christian writer.

How can we do God's will?
How can we find out what God wants us to do?
Who can help us?
What can help us?
"Actions speak louder than words." What does this saying mean?

4. Activity

Young ones

I'll do it now! Decorate and colour the template design.

Under the speech bubble, invite the children to choose one of the things Todd used to take his time to do and to draw it.

Juniors

Create two lists: Things we like to do straight away and things we put off doing! Write ideas on a large piece of paper or a flipchart.

Invite the children to contribute ideas to both lists. Then discuss with the children why they put things off – why don't they want to do them? Then ask them to suggest ways in which they could get themselves started.

Tips for learning difficulties

Choose the activity best suited to your children. Do they find it hard to start things off? Some children with learning difficulties might be put off if they think something is going to be too hard; how can they make little starts to get going?

5. We come together

Parents can be invited to join in at this stage.

Focus

Light the candle. Invite those gathered to become still – to look at the candle and think about the time of year.

Gospel

In the Gospel, Jesus tells us about two sons, one who said he wouldn't do something his father asked but then thought better of it and went to do the task, and the other, who first of all said that he would do it, but didn't. Jesus asks, "Which one was doing what the father wanted?"

Prayer

Jesus, help us to be like the person who did the will of the father.
Teach us always to put what God wants first.
Amen.

Share

The children have thought about the Gospel in different ways.
The younger children have heard about "in-a-minute-boy"!
Invite the children to tell their families about the story and what they did during the activity.

The older children heard about St Augustine. Who can tell us about his life? We then looked at the things we did, and didn't like doing, straight away. Show the list and invite the children to share their thoughts.

Sing

"Sent by the Lord am I" or
"Take the word of God with you"

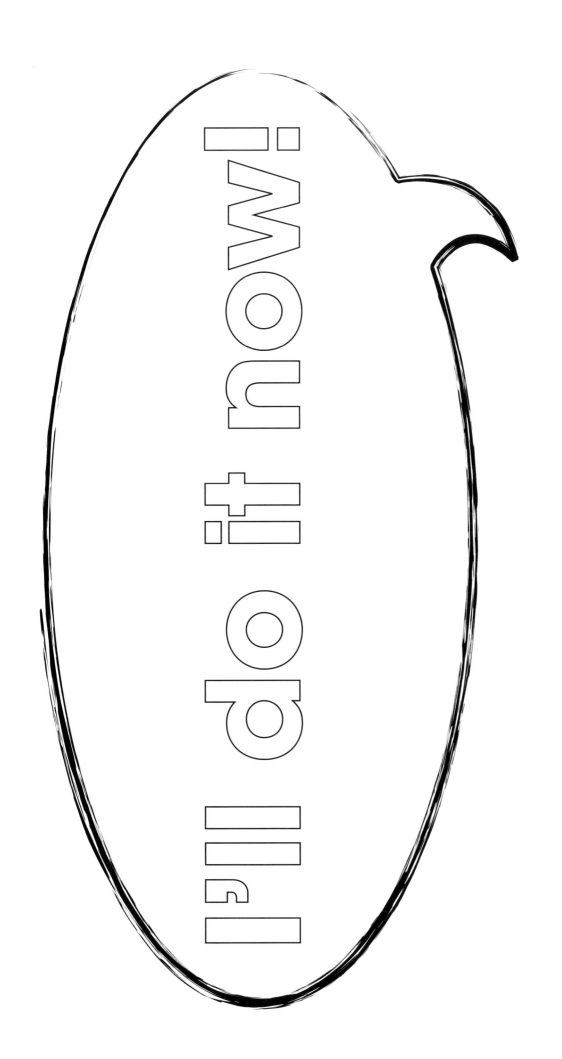

1. Introduction to the theme of the day

> "The stone rejected by the builders has become the keystone"

Aim: To find out about keystones. How is Jesus like a keystone?

Leader's reflection: Foundation, corner- and keystones are used interchangeably in different versions of today's Gospel. They are all quite distinct, although they serve the same general purpose – that of keeping a building upright. Foundation stones are large flat stones on which the building rests; these may be visible but are often buried underground. Cornerstones are wedge-shaped stones forming the angle between wall and roof. Keystones are blunt wedges at the centre of an arch, stopping it from falling inwards; they are the last stone to be put in place. Take away any of these and the building collapses. Although many aspects of our faith and lives are as essential as the stone for the walls and the slates for the roof, the building can still survive (albeit in a somewhat weakened state) without any particular one of them. Only Christ is described as a keystone; without him there is no building.

2. We arrive

We sit in a circle ready to listen to the Gospel.
Has anyone anything they would like to tell us about last week's Family Sheet?

Focus

A lighted candle, green fabric for Ordinary Time. A large, flat or wedge-shaped stone.

Gospel: Matthew 21:33-43 (Catholic)
Matthew 21:33-46 (Anglican)

Read from the Lectionary or Children's Lectionary.

3. We respond

What is the Gospel asking of us?

Work in age groups if appropriate. Alternatively, choose the discussion ideas, story and activity most suitable for your group. Come together as a community to end the session.

Young ones
Story: The very odd-shaped stone

He was a very odd-shaped stone, "chip off the old block", his dad always said. And he was right. Not a chip like something you eat, with sausages and tomato sauce. Not *that* sort of chip at all; but a chip like something which is a bit broken, not quite right. A chip off the old block.

All the other stones, which were square and smooth and regular, used to ignore him. He didn't fit into any of their patterns. He left gaps and holes in the brickwork when he tried to join in – holes where the wind and rain could get through. No good for a wall. All in all, he was a pretty useless stone.

Until one day. One day the men were building a church. Up and up they built it, very grand it was. The odd-shaped stone watched enviously while all the other smooth, square, regular stones were put in their places: "Eeeh! Aiee!" they squealed, as they squeezed into the pattern; then "Uuugh", a grunt of satisfaction as they settled into the cement. Oh how the odd-shaped stone wished he could be a part of the building! Best to be high up in the wall so he could see a long way off, but he wouldn't even mind being one of the bottom stones, holding up all the others. If only he could be of some use. If only he wasn't such an odd shape.

Then he heard one of the workmen. "Almost there," he called to his mate. "We only need the keystone to hold it all together. Strange shape, that one will have to be," and he showed the shape with his hands. "None of these is any good, they're all too square."

The odd-shaped stone jumped with excitement. The shape that the man had shown was *his* shape! The man must have heard his little squeak of delight because he looked over towards him.

"Hang on a second," he called to his mate, "might have something over here."

Up and up went the odd-shaped stone. Up and up in the bucket of the crane. Up and up past the bottom stones holding the building up. Up and up, past all the smooth, square, regular stones in the walls. Up and up. Right to the top of the building. And then he saw it: right in the middle of the archway, a space which was exactly his shape. With a yelp and a squeal just like all the other stones, he slotted into place. A perfect fit. He looked out from his new home right at the top of the church with a big smile on his face. He was the keystone, right at the top, holding everything together. How happy he was.

Have a look at the drawings on the activity sheet. Keystones and cornerstones are strange shapes – it is no surprise that the builders threw them away, they would be useless for putting into the wall of a building, although they are essential for keeping the building upright.
If possible, look at the brickwork or stonework of your church or the building you are meeting in.
Look at the importance of the keystone and explain how Jesus was called the keystone.

Juniors
Story: St Francis of Assisi

The Church celebrates the feast day of St Francis of Assisi on 4 October. St Francis is a very well-known and popular saint, renowned particularly for his poverty and his joyfulness. He was born into a wealthy family in 1182, and became a soldier, but was captured after a battle and imprisoned. He was released a year later but soon became sick, and spent another year lying ill in his bed. Lots of time for thinking and praying! He planned to join the army again, but changed his mind at the last minute, and started spending his time helping poor people and visiting sick people. His father, Pietro, was very upset about this, and they had a very famous quarrel in front of everybody in the local town square. Pietro threatened to

disown his son, so Francis gave back everything which his father had given him, including the clothes he was wearing at the time. Somebody lent Francis a workman's smock to wear, and he went off to live by himself, praying, preaching and helping poor people.

Other men and women soon joined him, and there are some wonderful stories written about their adventures. You can read about them in a book called *The Little Flowers of St Francis*. *(If there is time you could read one here.)* These were the first Franciscan friars and Poor Clare nuns, communities which still attract people to join them, even today.

What made St Francis change his mind about rejoining the army all those years ago? He heard a voice in a dream saying, "Follow the master, not the man." He realised the master was Jesus, and he decided to make him the keystone of his life, the person on whom everything else was built. Take Jesus away, and the whole of St Francis' life would have fallen apart.
How can we make Jesus the keystone of our lives?
What would our lives be like if Jesus was the keystone of our lives?

4. Activity
Young ones and Juniors

Use children's building bricks to try and build arches and buildings which rely upon foundation/corner-/keystones. Foundation stones are easiest! Or have a game of Jenga: the foundation stone is the brick which makes the tower collapse when it is removed.

Which of the designs on the template page would make a good foundation, corner- or keystone. Have you seen designs like these on buildings? Draw in the keystone in the arched shape.

Tips for learning difficulties

Use larger blocks for children with manipulative difficulties, or let them be the "inspector": the person who pulls away the important stone.

5. We come together

Parents can be invited to join in at this stage.

Focus

Gather around the candle and stone.

Gospel

Jesus said to the people: "You don't understand what I say to you because I teach you in a new and different way. But be careful, because I am the keystone which holds together all the stories about God which you already know. The Bible doesn't make any sense without me."

Prayer

Jesus, you are the keystone in our lives, you make sense of everything we have. Thank you, Jesus.

Sometimes the world does not seem to make any sense at all: people fight although they want to live in peace, and people starve although there is plenty of food for everybody, and people are sick although there are medicines which could cure them. At this time of the year we celebrate the harvest and try to live in a way which makes more sense by sharing what we have been given. Thank you, Jesus, for everything you have given us. Help us to share it. Amen.

Share

The children can show off any successful buildings.

Sing

"We have come into his house"

28th Sunday in Ordinary Time

Proper 23

1. Introduction to the theme of the day

> " Come to the wedding "

Aim: To remind the children of the many things they have received and encourage a sense of gratitude.

Leader's reflection: It is easy to assume, as God seems to us to be so extraordinary, that we can only find him in extraordinary experiences. St Teresa's message to us is that God is to be found in the ordinary. She was very strict in counselling her sisters to be wary of the extraordinary, and was forever instructing them to return to their regular duties and daily routines, rather than cultivating experiences of God which removed them from these things. So today too, the ordinary people, not blinded by their self-importance, end up at the wedding feast of God.

2. We arrive

We sit in a circle ready to listen to the Gospel.
Has anyone anything they would like to tell us about last week's Family Sheet?

Focus

A lighted candle, green fabric for Ordinary Time, a pan.

Gospel: Matthew 22:1-14

Read from the Lectionary or Children's Lectionary.

3. We respond
What is the Gospel asking of us?

Sometimes we wonder if we are special enough for God. Both of today's stories tell us that God likes ordinary people and ordinary things. That is why he made so many of them.
Work in age groups if appropriate, then come together as a community to end the session.

Young ones
Story: The very-ordinary-people

God was having a party. He thought about it for a long time, and then he decided, for a change, to invite all the Very-Important-People.

Who do you think they were?

He invited all the People-in-Charge *(suggestions)*, and all the Very-Rich-People *(suggestions)*, and all the Very-Good-People *(suggestions)*.

Everybody in heaven was very busy cooking and cleaning and putting up decorations. At last everything was ready and the day for the party arrived. God put on his most sparkly clothes and his most shiny crown, and then he went and sat and waited for all the Very-Important-People to arrive.

… And he waited … and he waited. After waiting for a very long time, he called one of his angels to him. "Go and find all the Very-Important-People," he said, "and ask them why they are late for my party."

So the angel went. The first Very-Important-Person he found was a Person-in-Charge. "Why are you late for God's party?" he asked.

"Oh," said the Person-in-Charge, "can't you see? I am in charge of all these people down here. If I leave them they won't do what they're supposed to do. I can't go to a party!"

So the angel went and found the next Very-Important-Person who was a Very-Rich-Person. "Why are you late for God's party?" he asked.

"Oh," said the Very-Rich-Person, "can't you see all this money? If I go to a party, somebody might take it. I can't go to a party!"

So the angel went and found the last Very-Important-Person who was a Very-Good-Person. "Why are you late for God's party?" he asked.

"Oh," said the Very-Good-Person, "can't you see all the good things I have to do today? I am far too busy. I can't go to a party!"

So the angel went back and told God what had happened. God was thoughtful, and then he said to the angel, "Is there anybody else who could come to my party? Did you see anybody else?"

"Well," said the angel, "I suppose there are all the Very-Ordinary-People. They don't seem to be so busy, I suppose you could always invite them."

"The Very-Ordinary-People! Of course! Great idea!" cried God happily. "They are very good at parties! Get them all up here, and we will have a wonderful time!" And do you know what? They did!

Did you feel sorry for anyone in this story?
What was their problem?
What sort of person are you?

Juniors
Story: St Teresa of Avila

On 15 October we celebrate another monastic feast day. St Teresa of Avila was a Spanish woman born in 1515. Teresa was intelligent, attractive and very popular. In those days women had two choices: they could get married, or they could become a nun. Teresa felt that marriage had too many drawbacks: it involved obeying a man, and ran the risk of death through childbirth. So although she didn't really want to be a nun either, she joined the Carmelite convent in Avila where her best friend already lived. Teresa tells us herself that she was not a very good nun. She lived very comfortably, had lots of visitors, and spent her prayer time listening for the clock to strike the end of it! But Teresa did not like to fail at what she was trying to do, and so she kept going, and slowly made progress.

After 15 years of struggling in this way, Teresa recognised that the life in her convent was too luxurious and easy-going to really be helpful in her spiritual life, so she started to set up smaller, poorer monasteries all around Spain. The other Carmelites were not very pleased about this and she had many battles to face, but she was brave, wise and astute, and the authorities found it very difficult to stand up against her.

Teresa began to have profound mystical experiences, visions and suchlike, during her prayer time, and sometimes when she was trying to get on with her work as well. She generally found these to be a great nuisance, and would have avoided them if she possibly could, teaching her nuns that "God is to be found amongst the pots and pans." She always emphasised that God was closest to us in the ordinary and everyday.

The nuns and friars from the reformed convents asked her to write about her experiences, and the books she wrote for them are considered to be so wise and profound that she has been made a Doctor of the Church. One of her most enjoyable books is *The Book of Foundations* which is a great adventure story about her travels throughout Spain.

"God is to be found among the pots and pans"; what did Teresa mean by this phrase?
How did Teresa get closer to God?
How can anyone find God?
What top tips would you give to someone who wanted to get closer to God?

4. Activity

Young ones

What things do you use every day? Draw one of them or cut it out of a magazine and stick it on the front of the card from the template page. Inside write "Thank you, God, for …"

Juniors

Choose something ordinary, e.g. chair, spoon. Look at it carefully then draw it on the front of the card. Inside, write down the ways in which it is designed to do its job really well.

Tips for learning difficulties

Talk about routine jobs done in the home. The washing up of dishes is often a boring, everyday task, but how important is it?

5. We come together

Parents can be invited to join in at this stage.

Focus

Gather around the candle and the pan.

Gospel

Jesus said, "God held a great feast in heaven, and he invited all the important people, but they were too busy to come. So he sent out his angels to invite all the ordinary people instead."

Prayer

Dear Jesus, sometimes we ignore the ordinary things you have given us and take them for granted. When you were on earth, you did very ordinary things, and you thought they were great. You met lots of ordinary people and thought they were fantastic. Help us to enjoy all the ordinary things as well. Amen.

Share

The children can celebrate their "ordinary things" – maybe the juniors can give a short talk about their chosen object.

Sing

"Let us with a gladsome mind" or
"If I were a butterfly"

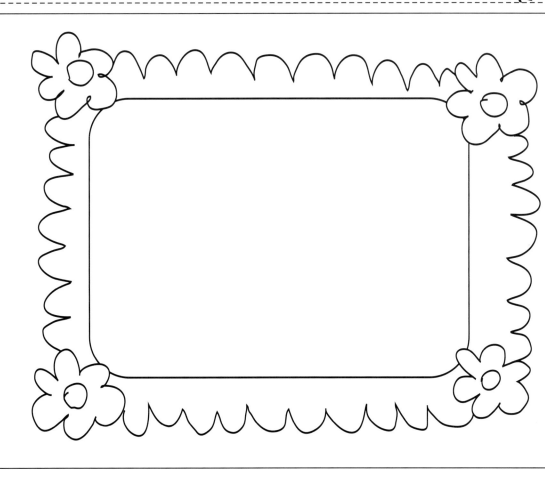

29th Sunday in Ordinary Time

Proper 24

1. Introduction to the theme of the day

> ## "Give to Caesar"

Aim: Jesus was a Jew. We think about how this is reflected in his way of teaching.

Leader's reflection: Jesus was born into a very particular culture – one which had a very strong tradition of oral discourse and riddle telling, so we should not be surprised at his ready answer to the Pharisees. In fact his answer is more closely allied to the tradition than is their rather direct and mercurial question. Maybe this was an indication of their growing frustration and impatience, and of Jesus' supreme confidence even as the reality of his Passion looms closer.

2. We arrive

We sit in a circle ready to listen to the Gospel.
Has anyone anything they would like to tell us about last week's Family Sheet?

Focus

A lighted candle, green fabric for Ordinary Time, a pile of coins.

Gospel: Matthew 22:15-21

Read from the Lectionary or Children's Lectionary.

3. We respond

What is the Gospel asking of us?

We think about the way the Pharisees tried to trick Jesus by asking him riddles. Work in age groups if appropriate. Come together as a community to end the session.

Young ones

Story: Caesar has a problem

Caesar was a very important man. He was also a very rich man. He was rich because lots of people gave him lots of money. Caesar liked being rich.

One day, Caesar heard about a man called Jesus. He knew that Jesus was important because lots of people listened to what he said, and tried to be good like he was. One of the ways they tried to be good was by sharing all their money with the poor. Caesar didn't like that at all. If the people shared their money with the poor, there would be little left for him. He sent some of his friends to find out more.

Caesar was a very important man, and he was also a very impatient man. By the time his friends came back to see him, two whole weeks later, he was in a very bad mood. "Well," he snapped, "what did you find out?" His friends looked a bit worried. They didn't like it when Caesar was in a bad mood. Sometimes he chopped off people's heads when he was in a bad mood. "It's like this," they began, "we asked Jesus about people giving money to you."

"Yes, yes, get on with it!" Caesar interrupted impatiently.

"Well," said his friends, "well, there's good news and there's bad news." Caesar groaned and looked very fierce. His friends hurried on, "Well, the good news first then: Jesus said, 'Give to Caesar what belongs to Caesar.'"

"Mmm," grunted Caesar, almost smiling, "that sounds about right. Give me what belongs to me. Lots of lovely money, just for me. That Jesus man has some sense after all."

"Yes, but ..." his friends looked very scared and began to back away a bit, "but Jesus said something else as well." Caesar began to frown again, and look very cross. "He said ... he said, 'and give to God what belongs to God'." Caesar looked at them, very puzzled. "Give to God what belongs to God?"

"That's right," said his friends, sliding towards the door.

"Give to God what belongs to God?" repeated Caesar. "What belongs to God?

"But ... everything belongs to God!"

"That's right," yelped his friends as they disappeared down the corridor, running for their lives. Poor old Caesar!

Why was Caesar cross?
What was Jesus trying to teach his followers?
How did Jesus solve the problem?

Juniors

Story: The book of Proverbs holds the answers

In today's Gospel, Jesus was set a riddle by the Pharisees to try to catch him out. Jesus does not seem surprised by this; the Jewish people love telling each other riddles and puzzles and such things, it is one of their great traditions that still exists today. So Jesus probably had a lot of practice at answering them, and had a very good answer ready. The Pharisees were very cross and went away to think up something even more difficult to ask him next time.

Some Hebrew riddles are written down in the Bible. Probably the most famous one is in the story of Samson (Judges 14).

Out of the eater came something to eat, Out of the strong came something sweet. Samson's wife gave away the answer to that one, and it cost him thirty pieces of fine linen and thirty party frocks.

Sometimes the Jews made wagers on the answers to riddles, like with Samson. At other times they used them to show off how clever they were, or to test how wise their wise men were, or even just used them as entertainment at feasts and festivals.

King Solomon is supposed to have used them a lot. He was not only a very clever king, but he was also very wise. Most of his riddles had some sort of moral lesson in them, teaching people how to behave. In fact there is a whole book called the book of Proverbs which is full of them. See if you can guess the answers to these:

What is worse than meeting an angry bear? (Proverbs 17:12)
What is sweet at first and then tastes like grit? (Proverbs 20:17)
Which four tiny creatures are the wisest of the wise? (Proverbs 30:24-28)

Have a look in a Bible to find out the answers!
In today's Gospel, Jesus answered the Pharisees' question with another riddle. What was clever about the way he answered?
Do *your* teachers answer your questions in such a way that they lead you to the answer without actually telling you?

4. Activity

Young ones

Cut out the templates and make two coins – a Caesar coin and a Jesus coin. You will need to draw the head of Jesus on the front of the Jesus coin. The Caesar coin is for you to keep. The Jesus coin is to go in the collection plate in church. If you explain what you are doing, your mum or dad or carer might give you an ordinary coin to put inside it.

Juniors

Try to write your own riddle about something in the Bible, or something to do with your church community. Here are a couple of examples to get you going.

Who was the holiest woman in the Bible and a great sinner?   (Mary – mother of Jesus & Magdalene)
Where did the Pharaoh's daughter meet Eminem?   (in the rushes – Moses & Miriam)

Tips for learning difficulties

Children could illustrate the riddles instead: the riddle of the "little creatures" would be the most suitable.

5. We come together

Parents can be invited to join in at this stage.

Focus

Gather around the candle and the pile of coins.

Gospel

The Jews asked Jesus if they should give Caesar any money for taxes. Jesus said, "Give to Caesar what belongs to Caesar, and to God what belongs to God."

Prayer

Jesus, sometimes we find it difficult to understand what you are saying. Help us to understand. Amen.

Share

Juniors can share their riddles, young ones can get their coins ready for the collection plate.

Sing

"Open your ears, O Christian people" or
"Where would we be without Christ our Lord?"

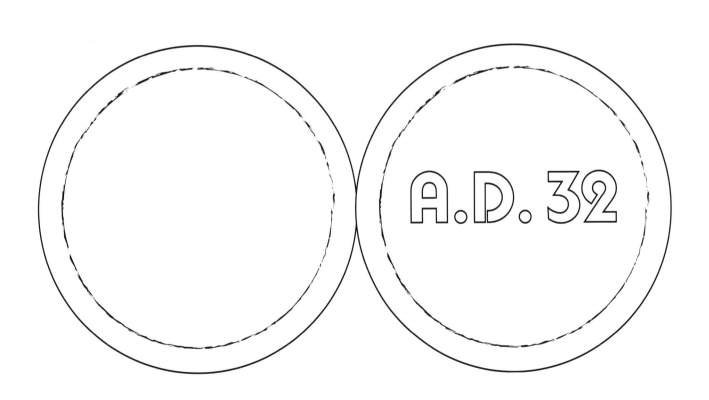

30th Sunday in Ordinary Time

Proper 25

1. Introduction to the theme of the day

> ❝The greatest commandment❞

Aim: We have a mission to the whole world – to love our neighbour as ourselves.

Leader's reflection: We think of the Church throughout the world serving humanity by spreading the Good News of Christ through word, through action and through prayer. We celebrate today the greatest commandment, "You must love the Lord your God and your neighbour as yourself."

2. We arrive

We sit in a circle ready to listen to the Gospel.
Has anyone anything they would like to tell us about last week's Family Sheet?

Focus

A lighted candle, green fabric for Ordinary Time, big pink heart (balloon, or cut out of paper or card).

Gospel: Matthew 22:34-40 (Catholic)
Matthew 22:34-46 (Anglican)

Read from the Lectionary or Children's Lectionary.

3. We respond
What is the Gospel asking of us?

Work in age groups if appropriate then come together as a community to end the session.

Young ones
Story: The "Most-Important-Lesson"

Aelred was back at angel school. Usually he was down on earth with Jesus, because he was Jesus' guardian angel, but sometimes he had to go back to school to learn more about God.

Today, there were lots and lots of angels in the classroom, all coming to learn more about God. They had been told that today was the "Most-Important-Lesson" ever, so everybody was very excited. Lots and lots of angels, but no teacher. The only thing at the front of the classroom was a great big blackboard on which somebody had drawn an enormous pink heart. At first, everybody giggled and chattered when there was no teacher, but then everybody began to get a bit worried, and a bit hot and bothered. How could they learn anything if there was no teacher? They looked at each other, and they looked at the pink heart on the blackboard. Then one of the angels sitting near the front piped up in a squeaky voice. "Maybe," she said, "maybe that is the lesson we have to learn," and she pointed at the big pink heart. The angels looked very puzzled, and they looked at each other. A big pink heart?! What sort of lesson could that be?

Children can make suggestions.

"Well," said another angel, a bit older than the first, who had sat down again very quickly when she had said her bit, "we know that the lesson is about God, and we know that it is the 'Most-Important-Lesson' we have to learn. Can anybody think how a great big pink heart might be the Most-Important-Lesson ever about God?"

Children's suggestions again.

Aelred was very scared. He lived with Jesus most of the time, so he thought he knew what the 'Most-Important-Lesson' about God might be, but he didn't really want to say it in front of all these angels. He stood up very slowly. "Ahem," he said. "Ahem, I think I might know." All the other angels turned round in their seats and stared at him. He could feel himself going bright red. "I think," he started, flustered by everybody staring, "I think it might be that God loves us." There was silence. "And he wants us to love him, and to love each other as well." He sat down with a bump! Silence still, as the angels looked at him, and then they looked at each other, and then they started nodding ... and smiling ... and clapping ... and cheering!

"Thank you, God," thought Aelred. Thank God he always listened to what Jesus said. "Love God and love each other." He was always saying it. Now Aelred knew it was the "Most-Important-Lesson" ever.

How do we love ourselves?
How can we love God?
How can we love each other?

Juniors
Story: Servant to the Church and to humanity

Pope John Paul II served the Church and all humanity right up to his death on 2 April 2005.

Just eight weeks before, he was in hospital following a difficult breathing attack. He was 84 years old and already very poorly, he could hardly speak and he was confined to a wheelchair. It had been announced that John Paul was going to appear at the window of his hospital room, and give a blessing, so big crowds gathered underneath it. He appeared as promised, and blessed the people who were standing there, and then he made an announcement: "In this hospital, in the middle of other sick people, I can continue to serve the Church and all humanity."

Like the leaders of all Christian churches, it is our mission or job to serve each other (the Church), and the whole of humanity, everybody in the world. That includes people who need our help in countries far away, but it also includes the people that we see every day. We do not need to be strong, powerful, important people in order to do that. We can do it wherever we are, even if we are sick and in hospital.

How do you think Pope John Paul could do that?
Can you think of other leaders of faith communities that set us a good example?

Discuss together the different ways we can serve each other: refer to today's Gospel.
What does Jesus ask us to do?
How can we love God?
How can we love our neighbour?

4. Activity

Young ones

Colour in the heart on the front of the card. Pink would be a good colour. Write on the heart, "God loves … (your name)". Inside the card write, "So I love … (the name of someone you love)".

Juniors

You will need a local and national newspaper and maps or a globe for this activity. Select events which the children might be interested in. Help the children to locate their homes and neighbourhoods on the local map (you can use Monopoly houses as markers), and then locate some events that are happening. Ask the children what else is happening around them and locate this on the map as well. Discuss how they can be missionaries in their own neighbourhood. Locate the town, country etc. on the larger maps, and the events selected from the national papers. Locate any friends and family they have in other countries. How can they be missionaries to the whole world through our example of living life as Jesus has taught us?

Tips for learning difficulties

Use the activity suggested for the young ones and colour the card. Draw or write on the card.

5. We come together

Parents can be invited to join in at this stage.

Focus

Gather around the candle and the heart.

Gospel

Jesus said: "This is the most important thing I will tell you. You must love God with all your heart, and you must love other people as much as you love yourself."

Prayer

Jesus, thank you for loving us. Teach us how to love you, and how to love each other. Sometimes it is not easy to love each other; help us when we find it hard. Amen.

Share

The juniors can share the work they have been doing, the young ones can give out their cards if the people are present.

Sing

"Jesus is King, let the whole world rejoice"

31st Sunday in Ordinary Time

1. Introduction to the theme of the day

"Practise what you preach"

Aim: What really makes us good? Words, or deeds?

Leader's reflection: One of the essential criteria for canonisation as a saint, according to current regulations, is to have lived a life of "heroic virtue". Thus, irrespective of visions or wisdom or profound writings, the emphasis is placed very firmly on how the individual has coped with the ordinary everyday challenges of living with oneself and with one's neighbour. Today Jesus addresses the Pharisee in each of us: it is not what you say, or what people think of you that counts, but whether you are truly prepared to follow his example and to serve each other.

2. We arrive
We sit in a circle ready to listen to the Gospel.
Has anyone anything they would like to tell us about last week's Family Sheet?

Focus
A lighted candle, green fabric for Ordinary Time, a pile of haloes (made of tinsel or silver foil).

Gospel: Matthew 23:1-12
Read from the Lectionary or Children's Lectionary.

3. We respond
What is the Gospel asking of us?
Work in age groups if appropriate, and come together as a community to end the session.

Young ones

Story: Aelred, the "learner" guardian angel

Aelred was worried. The angel-inspector was coming. Aelred was Jesus' guardian angel, but he had spent most of the last couple of weeks studying and trying to learn stuff about God so that he could answer all the inspector's questions. He sighed. He couldn't seem to remember much of it at all.

The day arrived. The angel-inspector was an old angel. He wore glasses hooked on to the edge of his halo, and his wings were turning silver at the edges.

"Good morning," he said to Aelred sternly.

"Morning," mumbled Aelred nervously.

"First," said the inspector, "some questions, then you can show me the things you have been doing." Aelred swallowed nervously; oh dear.

"Tell me about God," said the inspector.

"Well," began Aelred, then a voice came from the distance: "Aeaeaelred!"

"Excuse me," said Aelred, "that's Jesus calling. I won't be a minute." And he flew off to see what Jesus wanted. Jesus just pointed to a little boy who was crying, so Aelred flew over and put his wings around the boy. Soon he was happy again and Aelred flew back to the inspector.

"Ahem!" said the inspector. "You were telling me about God."

"Yes," Aelred began again. "Well ..." then Jesus' voice came again, "Aeaeaelred!"

"Sorry!" whispered Aelred. "But I always go when he calls me," and off he flew again. This time Jesus pointed to an old lady who had fallen over and dropped all her shopping. So Aelred flew over and picked it all up and carried it home for her. By now it was getting late. He hurried back to the inspector.

"Harumph!" said the inspector looking at his watch. "Now, about God."

Aelred looked despondent: oh dear, the inspector was in a bad mood. "Aeaeaelred!" Jesus' voice again. This time Aelred didn't say anything; he just smiled weakly at the inspector and flew away again to help. When he came back the inspector had gone. Aelred sat on the grass and started to cry. When Jesus saw him, he came and sat down beside him. "What's wrong?" he asked gently. Aelred explained about the inspector, and how he hadn't answered the question, and how he must have failed and would be sent away and never see Jesus again. Jesus smiled broadly. "Don't worry," he said, "I spoke to the inspector while you were doing jobs for me. I asked him how you were doing and he said you didn't seem to know much about God, but that you always did what God asked, which is what really counts! You passed with flying colours. Of course you did!"

How much did Aelred *really* know about God?
Why was he too busy to answer the inspector's questions?
Can you think of any times when you have done what God wants?
Do you think you would make a good guardian angel?

Juniors

Story: Unsaintly business!

1st November is the feast of All Saints. These days, to be canonised as a saint you need to pass certain tests. People must think you were holy, the Church must agree with everything you said about God, you must have lived with "heroic virtue", and, once you have died, you must cause a miracle to happen, not once, but twice.

In the olden days, there were different tests and saints were canonised for all sorts of reasons: because they had visions, or worked miracles or just because people thought they were good. St Ethelnoth was an eleventh-century English saint. His story is not well known, but it is fascinating for all the old English names it involves. He was the son of man called Ethelmaer, and lived at Cerne Abbas in Dorset where he was taught by a man called Aelfric. The archbishop at the time was called Lyfing, and when he died, the king (called Cnut) asked Ethelnoth to take over. He was well respected, and went to Rome to meet the Pope, who was impressed by him, but he also did some things which would seem very dubious today. Relics of the saints were very fashionable in those days: the more relics you had, the more important you were. A saint called Aelfheah had just been buried in St Paul's Cathedral in London. Ethelnoth and the king decided to give the body to a monastery in Glastonbury as a relic, so in 1023 a monk (called Godric) broke into the tomb to get it out. The people of London were very angry that their new saint was being stolen, and stormed the church. The king was taking a bath at the time, but still he rushed down to the church without any clothes on, to take charge of the proceedings! An armed guard had to escort the king, Ethelnoth and the relics of St Aelfheah all the way to Glastonbury to make sure they got there safely.

Ethelnoth was a fairly dubious saint, but it is right that we celebrate his life. Not all saints are perfect, but they can still tell us about God even so.

Do you know any saints?
Do you know anyone who *is* a saint, but hasn't actually been recognised as one?
What sort of actions could you describe as being saintly?
Look at the passage from today's Gospel again. What does Jesus tell us about our thoughts and actions?

4. Activity

Young ones

Saints are people who really love God, and they show this by loving other people. Who do you know who could be a saint? Draw a picture of them in the frame and put their name at the top.

Juniors

We all hope to be saints, even if we aren't canonised. Write down, on the template frame, times when you have experienced saintly actions from a friend or family member; and the times when *you* have acted as a saint!

Tips for learning difficulties

Children could use photos or pictures from magazines to build up a collage of the ways they are a saint.

5. We come together

Parents can be invited to join in at this stage.

Focus

Around the candle and the pile of haloes.

Gospel

Jesus said: "Saints are not people who say the right thing, and then do something different. People might admire what you say, but they will love you for what you do."

Prayer

Jesus, when we read about the saints, it is very difficult for us to imagine being that good. We say we want to be good, but it is not very easy when we try. Help us this week to do the things we say we want to do. Amen.

Share

Each child can sit in turn on a "throne" and suggestions can be made as to why they might be considered for sainthood (keep these as concrete and specific as possible). If appropriate, they can be given a halo!

Sing

"Lord, for tomorrow and its needs" or
"This is what Yahweh asks of you"

32nd Sunday in Ordinary Time
The 3rd Sunday before Advent

1. Introduction to the theme of the day

"Stay awake, be ready!"

Aim: To help the children to be aware of Our Lord's constant presence and to be ready to find opportunities of service.

Leader's reflection: We look for the Lord's presence in church, in our daily prayer – but how ready are we to recognise him in the ordinary, commonplace activities of life? Are we "awake" to him, looking for opportunities to welcome him and serve him in our everyday lives?

2. We arrive

We sit in a circle ready to listen to the Gospel.
Has anyone anything they would like to tell us about last week's Family Sheet?

Focus

Photographs/pictures of people involved in various activities, surrounding the open Bible, placed on green material.

Gospel: Matthew 25:1-13
Read from the Lectionary or Children's Lectionary.

3. We respond
What is the Gospel asking of us?

Work in age groups if appropriate then come together as a community to end the session.

Young ones

Use the photographs of various tasks as a starting point. Ask the children if they can tell you what all the people are doing. Pick out a photograph of someone with children around her.

Story: I'm ready!

This photograph is a picture of Mrs Lenton. She is always busy. She has three children of her own and seven grandchildren. Mrs Lenton loves being with her family, but she has a job too. She is a dinner lady.

She is the sort of dinner lady who always has time to spend with children who have no one to play with, or the ones who are upset because they've had a bad morning, or children who have fallen over. She has a basket of toys, balls, skipping ropes, hula hoops, and she will always have a go herself when there is a new game or a new dance craze. When she has to sit down (because her knees are not so good these days), she always has a crowd of children who want her to tell them a story or sing a song with them. Mrs Lenton is good at sorting out arguments, and doesn't stand any nonsense from children who won't let the other person tell their side of the story.

Mrs Lenton always says the same thing:
"Come on, I'm ready for you."

She said it when she took the new children out to the playground at lunchtime on their first day. She said it when Ali fell over, and she took him in to wash his cut knee. She said it when Year 1 wanted to play "What's the time, Mr Wolf?"

She said it to the Year 2 children who wanted to have a hula-hoop competition. She said it when the whistle went and dinner play was over. She said it when Year 3 boys had an argument about the offside rule in their football game and it needed sorting out. She said it to Grace when she was crying because her mum and dad were unhappy.

"It's important to keep your eyes open and be ready for people when they need you," Mrs Lenton would say. "It makes *you* happy."

Mrs Lenton was the sort of person who did what Jesus wanted. He wants us to be ready for him – ready to be kind and helpful just as if we were doing things for him.

We know what *we* need and what we want to do. How can *we* work out what other people need?

How can you be ready to help someone?

Mrs Lenton kept an eye open for children and loved helping them.

Juniors

Story: Be prepared!

"Dad, were you a scout when you were young?" said Danny one day. He was out for a run with his dad. Dad was trying hard to get fitter but Danny knew he couldn't talk *and* run. They stopped. Dad collapsed onto a park bench.

"Yes," he said, "and I wouldn't be half so out of breath if we did scout's pace rather than trying to run all the way."

"What's scout's pace?" asked Danny.

"Well, you run twenty strides then you walk twenty strides then you run again… you can keep going a lot longer and not get so breathless."

"What else did you do with the scouts?" Danny asked.

"Well, I learned to tie knots; I learned about codes; I went away to camp and did some cooking and sailing; it's surprising I'm still alive really, looking back. Half the food was burned and half raw and I spent more time in the water than in the boat. It was good fun and I learned some useful things about being prepared."

"Like having a piece of string, some money and a clean handkerchief," laughed Danny.

It was one of Mum's jokes about Dad.

"Yes, we were always expected to be ready for things that might happen. The money was for a phone call; we didn't have mobiles. The handkerchief was to be a bandage and you can use string for loads of things. What started this conversation anyway?"

"Peter has joined the Cubs. They become scouts later, you know."

"Yes," said Dad. "Do you want to give it a go too?"

"I'm just thinking about it. Come on, we could do scout's pace for a bit."

They set off running twenty paces, but, on pace fourteen, Danny stumbled and fell. There was broken glass on the path, the vandals had been out again last night. Blood poured from a cut on Danny's leg. Out came the handkerchief.

"You see," said Dad. "Be prepared."

Jesus told a story about being ready. Can you remember it? How do we stay ready for Jesus? How shall we recognise him and serve him? Remember the photos, all the different jobs people do, how can all these people serve Jesus? How do we know we are doing what he wants, ready for him?

4. Activity

Young ones
What can you do to be ready for Jesus? Draw yourself and make a list of things you could do to please him.

We are ready for Jesus when we do the sorts of things he likes us to do: when we look for chances to help other people and do the best we can in our work.

Juniors
Use the template and decide how the various people can be ready for Jesus.
Write next to the pictures.

Tips for learning difficulties
Draw a picture of themselves ready to help someone. Give what help is needed and talk through the child's day, emphasising the joy they bring to others, while the activity is ongoing.

5. We come together
Parents can be invited to join in at this stage.

Focus
The children and parents may gather together around the children's pictures of themselves and a lighted candle.

Gospel
(read by one of the children)
The sensible bridesmaids were ready to meet the bridegroom when he came to the wedding. They had enough oil to keep their lamps alight.
Jesus said, "Stay awake, because you do not know when I shall be coming."

Be quiet for a few moments. Remember Jesus is with us now.

Prayer
Thank you for being with us always even when we are not ready to notice you or work for you. Help us to keep our eyes open and look for you every day. Amen.

Share
Share some of the work from the activities.

Sing
"Give me oil in my lamp, keep me burning"

33rd Sunday in Ordinary Time

The 2nd Sunday before Advent

1. Introduction to the theme of the day

> ❝ **Remember,**
> **use it or lose it!** ❞

Aim: To help the children to recognise their own talents and delight in the gifts of others.

Leader's reflection: No one made by our God is without some special gift. On Remembrance Sunday, which is celebrated around this time of the year, we take the time to remember not only those who gave the gift of their lives in wartime but those who share their own unique gifts with us all. A talent which is not shared, or used, is a sadness to the whole community.

2. We arrive

We sit in a circle ready to listen to the Gospel.
Has anyone anything they would like to tell us about last week's Family Sheet?

Focus

Green background material and items which bring a special memory to mind, e.g. photograph, baptismal candle, birthday card, a poppy (if Remembrance Sunday falls on this day).

Gospel: Matthew 25:14-30

Read from the Lectionary or Children's Lectionary.

3. We respond

What is the Gospel asking of us?

Work in age groups if appropriate then come together as a community to end the session.

Young ones
Story: You are special

"Everyone is special, no one else is just like you, and can be the person you are," said Fr Jones to the children in church.

"What special talents have you got; what are you good at?"

All the children started to shout out answers,

"I'm brilliant at football."

"I'm good at ballet."

"I know all my tables."

"My mum says I'm really good at cooking."

"I can make my granddad laugh."

There were lots more answers. Fr Jones smiled. "And," he said, "is there anyone here who is good at all those things: anyone who can play football, do ballet, sing, cook, is good at maths with a granddad who needs cheering up?"

The children shook their heads. They knew they couldn't be good at everything.

"It doesn't matter," said Father. "God wants us to share what we can do with everyone else so we all enjoy the things each of us can do."

"I'm not really good at anything," whispered Sean.

Everyone stopped and looked at him, he went bright red.

"I'm no good at sports, I'm not much use in school, I haven't got a granddad."

Fr Jones looked worried.

Then Josh said, "I can think of lots of things you are good at. You cheer everyone on when they play matches for the school; you never make anyone unhappy by fighting and arguing; you enjoy parties and you always say thank you. My mum says you are very polite and a pleasure to have round to play, and..."

"Yes," Fr Jones said, "and you make your mum and dad very happy, just being you. That's a very special gift."

What are your special gifts to share with everyone? What will remind you of them?
What difference do you make to the people around you?

Juniors
Story: I remember how special I am

Using the "reminders" from the opening focus, begin a discussion.

We use special ways to remind ourselves of events in the past, of things that make us happy or sad. Each of those events involves a special gift or talent from God.

Let's see if we can work out what gifts these "memory joggers" celebrate.

Today lots of us are wearing poppies: why? What special gift does this remind us of?

We have got some certificates for First Communion, and a candle for a baptism. What gift does God give us, what gifts do we give him?

Birthday card: your parents and friends are celebrating the gift of you.

Holiday photographs: we are remembering happy times together, the talent for sharing things we enjoy.

Shopping list: a reminder of the things our family needs so we can share the gift of caring for each other.

School tie: a reminder of the school community, the things we share and belong to. It reminds us of the talent we have for friendship and for work.

Can you think of some other reminders? What talents/gifts do they bring to mind?
Jesus told a story in today's Gospel about talents. (Recap the story.) He was talking about money and using it but he was really telling us to be sure to use the special gifts God gives us. When we do, God always says, "Well done," just as the master did in the story. Of course the story has a warning too. If you don't use your talents and gifts you will lose them. If you don't do the training exercises properly you won't be able to dance or play football; if you don't learn your tables or how to spell, maths and literacy will always be hard; if you don't exercise your talent for friendship you won't have friends.

4. Activity

Young ones

An elephant never forgets! Using the template of the elephant, draw pictures of all the reminders you can of your talents and gifts. You might draw yourself painting if you are good at art, or doing karate, or helping at home. Don't forget to draw yourself, just yourself – you are a gift to everyone just by being you.

Juniors

You can choose to write on the elephant, or draw, as you wish.

Tips for learning difficulties

Talk about one thing the child is good at doing or being – draw or write this and colour in the elephant.

5. We come together

Parents can be invited to join in at this stage.

Focus

Some of the children's work added to the earlier "reminders".

Gospel

(Read by one of the children.)

Jesus says,

"Well done, good and faithful servant. You have shown that you can be trusted to use your talents wisely. Come and share my happiness in what you have done."

Prayer

Help us to share ourselves and our gifts with everyone and to enjoy the people and gifts which are shared with us. Amen.

Share

The work from the activities. Some children may like to read out another's list of gifts, and pictures could be displayed.

Sing

"Father, I place into your hands"
"One more step along the world I go"

Our Lord Jesus Christ, Universal King

Christ the King

1. Introduction to the theme of the day

> ## "You did it for me"

Aim: To encourage the children to recognise Jesus as the king who longs for our love and service.

Leader's reflection: Over the past two weeks we have been helping our children to recognise the presence of Jesus each day and find opportunities to serve him. This feast puts Our Lord in his proper place. He is our king, an absolute monarch. If we intend to serve him, we must serve his people. There is no ambiguity about the Gospel, no shades of grey, our faith demands our service.

2. We arrive
We sit in a circle ready to listen to the Gospel.
Has anyone anything they would like to tell us about their Family Sheet last week?

Focus
Lighted candle, a crown.

Gospel: Matthew 25:31-46
Read from the Lectionary or Children's Lectionary.

3. We respond
What is the Gospel asking of us?
Work in age-related groups if appropriate then come together as a community to end the session.

Young ones and Juniors

Recap the Gospel story with all the children. Then re-enact the story as a play.
Here is a possible script.
Characters:
Jesus (the king),
Angels (the escort to his throne),
Five children to be "sheep", the rest to be goats. Expand the angels, sheep and goats groups as necessary.

A play: Who is Jesus?

(Jesus comes to his throne escorted by angels. He calls to the people assembled in front of him.)

Jesus: *(to 1st person),*
You are welcome in my kingdom. I was hungry and thirsty and you had a Family Fast Day to send money to CAFOD/Christian Aid.

1st Person:
I didn't know I had fed you and given you a drink. We always send money to CAFOD/Christian Aid.

Jesus: What you did to one of my friends in the middle of Sudan you did to me.

(pointing to the 2nd person)
You are my friend too, you gave me new clothes when I needed them.

2nd Person:
I knew I had sent money to "Shelter" at Christmas, but I never gave you new clothes.

Jesus: When you gave money for new clothes you did that for me.

(pointing to the 3rd person)
Come to me, well done.
When I came to live near you and didn't speak your language, you smiled at me and made me welcome.

3rd Person:
I don't remember seeing you before, my Lord.

Jesus: When you smiled at that refugee you made me happy and welcome.

(pointing to the 4th person)
You are the person who came to see me when I was ill. You did my shopping, you sent me a get-well card. Come and sit with me.

4th Person:
I know I helped my neighbour out but I never helped you.

Jesus: What you did for your next-door neighbour, you did for me.

(calling to the 5th person.)
I was in prison when you came to see me.

5th Person:
No, Lord, I did not see you in prison. Those people were criminals.

Jesus: When you took time to come and visit and thought the criminals were still important you gave me time too.

You are all very dear to me. Whenever you served my people you served me, your king.

"Goats": We never saw you needing anything, Lord. If we had, we would have helped you.

Jesus: You didn't bother to help my friends, so you didn't bother to help me. Off you go.

(The goats go out looking sorry for themselves.)

What does Jesus look like?
Where can we find Jesus?
How do we serve Jesus, our king?

4. Activity
Young ones

Today's Gospel told us some of the sorts of things that the king rewards his servants for doing. Can you draw pictures in the middle of the template page of some different things we can do for others which our king would think we were doing for him?

Colour in your friends and family around the edge of the page.

Juniors

As for the young ones, but you may like to describe some of the actions Jesus talked about in the Gospel. Decorate and colour the page.

Tips for learning difficulties

Come prepared with a number of pictures of people doing kindly acts: nurses, firefighters, street cleaners, mother and child. Stick these on the paper and talk through how these people are doing what the king wants.

5. We come together

Parents can be invited to join here if the drama presentations have not been made to the whole of the congregation.

Focus

Put some samples of the children's work around the candle.

Gospel

Read by one of the children.

Jesus says, "You are welcome in my kingdom. You are my good servants. Whenever you did a kindly act to one of my people you did it for me."

Prayer

Dear Lord, our king, we are your servants. Help us to find ways to serve other people, so that we are serving you. Amen.

Share

Children act out the dramas.

Sing

"Seek ye first the kingdom of God" or
"Make me a channel of your peace" or
"Sing we the king who is coming to reign"

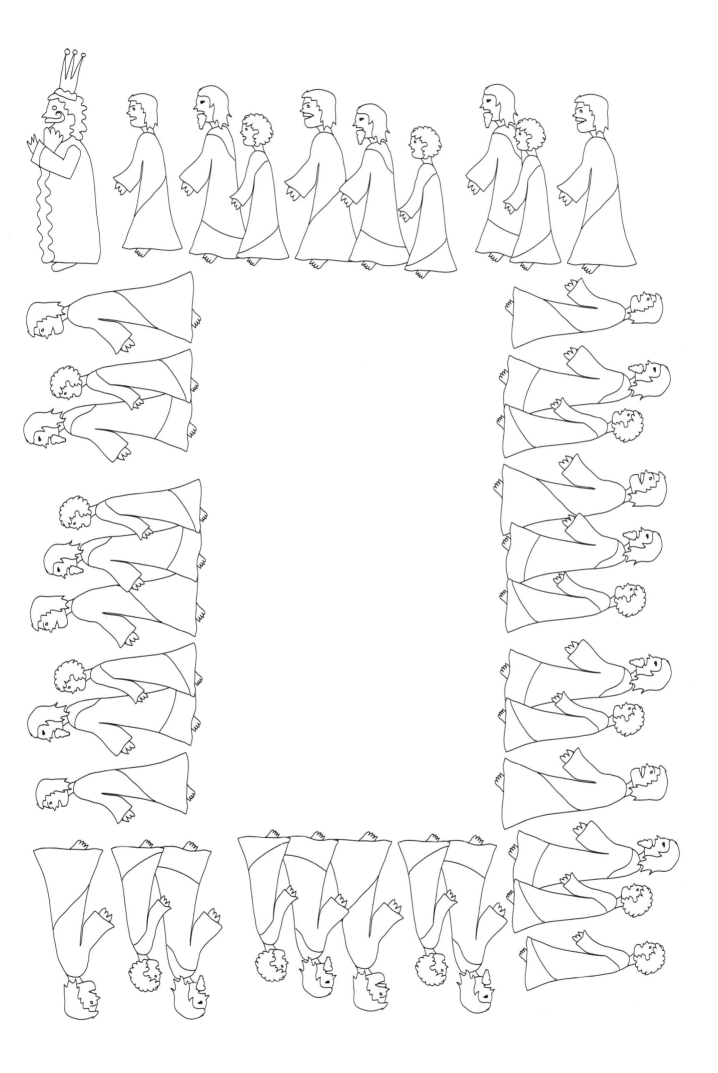

The Most Holy Trinity

1. Introduction to the theme of the day

"Jesus, our brother"

Aim: To understand that Jesus is the Son of God who lived on earth so that all people might come to know God and be saved. Jesus, by living on earth, made us his brothers and sisters so we can now say that we are all children of God, children of the Father, who have been given life through the Holy Spirit.

Leader's reflection: The writer of the Gospel is here meditating or reflecting on the unique place of Jesus in the plan of salvation. Jesus is the only Son of the Father yet the Father sent his Son into the world, which means the Father allowed his only Son to die as all people die. This supreme sacrifice saves the world. It is through the giving of the Son that eternal life becomes possible. Through the Holy Spirit, as was shown at Pentecost, we can finally understand God's plan for salvation.

2. We arrive
We sit in a circle, ready to listen to the Gospel.
Has anyone anything they would like to tell us about last week's Family Sheet?
The Lectionary is placed where the children can see it but is not decorated in any way.

Focus
Trinity symbols: triangle/shamrock/three interlocked circles/dove.

Gospel: John 3:16-18
Read from the Lectionary or the Children's Lectionary.

3. We respond
What is the Gospel asking of us?
Work in age groups if appropriate, then come together as a community to end the session.

Young ones

Jesus is the Son of the Father but he was born, like us, and grew up like us. Jesus is the greatest gift God ever gave to the world, he is our brother now and for ever.
Who has a brother or a sister? How do you feel about your brother or sister?
How do people show their love for each other in a family?
Why is it important for people in a family to love one another?

Story: Let's all play

Saturdays were great in the Roberts family. No school and the whole day to play. Lizzie was the eldest, at eight, then there was Harry who was six and Jack came last at five. Most of the time Lizzie organised the games and had good ideas. This particular Saturday she decided she was too old to join in with her brothers' "baby" games. Harry and his brother went to the dressing-up box for some inspiration. It wasn't long before King Harry emerged wearing a curtain hooked round his shoulders like a cloak, and a golden cardboard crown on his head. In his hand he held a broomstick with a flag tied on the top. Prince Jack followed close behind, dressed in an old fleece dressing gown. He looked rich in the deep red gown but had difficulty in walking as the hem covered his feet. On his head he wore a pull-on hat with one of Mum's brooches clipped on.

Mum, Dad and Lizzie watched the two boys parading around the living room. They were having such fun. King Harry trying to look serious while Prince Jack shuffled along in his gown, holding on tightly to the bottom of the cloak. Mum smiled, Dad joined in and rushed for the camera. Lizzie felt sad and so "left out". It wasn't any fun being old. She ran upstairs to have a good cry on her bed. "Families should be happy places," she sobbed, "I still love my brothers and want to play with them."

While she lay there she saw her nightdress peeping out from under the pillow. That was enough to give her an idea. A little while later, Lizzie was walking like a princess, carefully down the stairs in her long nightdress with a sparkly headband in her hair. She went into the living room and perched up high on the back of the chair. King Harry and Prince Jack stopped giggling and looked up. "Please rescue me, I'm a princess in distress," cried Lizzie. The king with his prince soon had the princess down into their land of happiness and safety, surrounded by cushions to guard them from dragons. Dad came in with some crisps and drink and left them at the cushion door. The Roberts family chatted happily together, and no one was left out and alone any more.

In the story, who had a problem? How did she feel? How did she solve the problem?

Juniors
Story: The two brothers

Stanislaus and his brother Paul lived in Poland. Their father paid for a private teacher until Paul was sixteen and Stanislaus fourteen. Then their father sent them to attend a school in Vienna, Austria. Paul was high-spirited and just wanted to have a good time, but Stanislaus was serious and studious and wanted to become a priest.

Paul teased and made fun of Stanislaus for two years. Stanislaus couldn't ask his father for help because his father didn't want him to become a priest either. Finally, Stanislaus decided that he would walk the 350 miles to Rome to train in the Jesuit seminary there. Paul set out to find his brother, so sorry now that he had not understood how bad his brother had felt. He couldn't find him.

Stanislaus had been accepted by the Jesuits in Rome and was very happy there. However, the summer heat of Rome made him ill. His father sent his son Paul to bring him home.

By the time Paul arrived in Rome, angry and ready to tease his brother again and demand that he return with him, he was too late. His brother had died. Paul never got over the shock. He spent the rest of his life wishing he had been nicer to his little brother. When Paul was 60 years old he decided to join the Jesuits, just as his little brother had done many years before.

Encourage comments relating the story to the Gospel.
Who do you think is the most important member of a family?
Why are birthdays so special in families?
When brothers and sisters argue and fight does that mean they don't love each other any more?
Do people in a family stop loving each other when they grow up?
Do you think that the way you show your love for your family changes as you get older?
How important is love in a family?

4. Activity

Young ones

Using the template of the shamrock, colour it green and add the words Father, Son, Holy Spirit in the three petal shapes. Practise making the sign of the cross.

Juniors

On the shamrock template write the words Father, Son and Holy Spirit on the petals. Write the word LOVE on the stalk.

Write a short prayer underneath beginning with L (Lord, Let us, Loving ...). Do the same with the other letters: O (Our brother Jesus, On this day ...); V (Very special Jesus, Very many thanks, Voices raised in ...); E (Each one, Every time, Everyone ...). Decorate the prayers with coloured pencils.

Tips for learning difficulties

Have a number of models to show the three persons in one God. A triangle, a large trefoil or shamrock or a large cross. Practise making the sign of the cross.

5. We come together

Parents can be invited to join in at this stage.

Focus

Light the candle.
Shamrock/triangle.

Gospel

"God loved the world so much that he gave his only Son, so that everyone who believes in him may not be lost but may have eternal life."

Jesus, by living on earth, made us his brothers and sisters, so we can now say that we are all children of God, children of the Father who have been given life through the Holy Spirit.

Prayer

Encourage children to think of practical ways of sharing the Gospel.

We take this Gospel message:

To our families: "Dear Lord, I can share my - - - - with - - - - - -"

To our friends: "Dear Lord, I can share my - - - - with - - - - - -"

To the people we meet: "Dear Lord, I can show I care by saying please and thank you."

To people we don't know: "Dear Lord, I can support charities in the work they do." Amen.

Share

The work on the shamrocks. Make the sign of the cross together.

Sing

"Glory to God, glory to God" or
"Father, in my life I see"

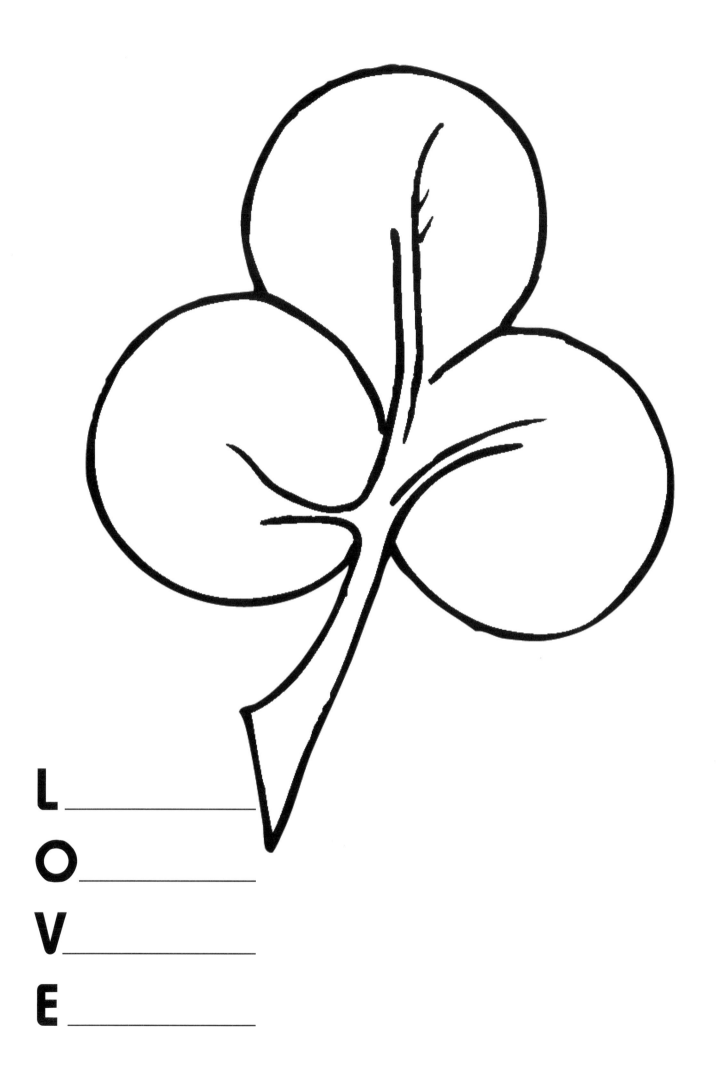

L_____

O_____

V_____

E_____

The Body and Blood of Christ (Corpus Christi)

1. Introduction to the theme of the day

"The bread of eternal life"

Aim: To reflect on Jesus' promise that he offers us food that leads us to everlasting life.

Leader's reflection: Today's Gospel is part of a long section of John's Gospel in which Jesus moves from the sharing of bread among five thousand people to explaining that this miracle is as nothing compared to the gift that he is to offer the world: his own body. This is a rich and complex theology and one that has been explored by some of the greatest minds and hearts in history. It is one that, in our keenness to explain, we risk making simplistic, putting something that is awe-inspiring mystery into human words that cannot hope to convey the majesty of what we believe.

Our task as catechists is to take children to a threshold of faith, to open the door to the wonder of faith. We give them words and symbols to express something of what we understand of the mystery, but also a silence in the face of what, in so many ways, goes beyond anything the human mind, heart and imagination could express.

2. We arrive

We sit in a circle, ready to listen to the Gospel.
Has anyone anything they would like to tell us about last week's Family Sheet?

Focus
White cloth, candle, Bible open at today's Gospel, a small loaf and cup of wine.

Gospel: John 6:51-58
Read from the Lectionary or the Children's Lectionary.

3. We respond
What is the Gospel asking of us?
Work in age groups if appropriate. Alternatively, choose the discussion ideas, story and activity most suitable for your group. Come together as a community to end the session.

Young ones

Story: Mateo and Maria's First Communion Day

Does anyone remember Mateo and Maria? We heard about them a few weeks ago. (If no one remembers, they were two children whose baptism provided our story for Ascension Day.)

When Mateo and Maria were baptised, their mum and dad were baptised too. Because they were adults, their mum and dad had made their First Communion and had been confirmed at the same time.

Fr Joe had said that it might be better for the children to wait a little while and make their First Communion with the friends they had made during the children's sessions.

At the last session, Fr Joe and the catechists talked to all the children and helped them to practise for their First Communion Day. They were allowed to taste the altar bread and to hold the chalice.

"But", said Fr Joe, "this is only a practice; when you receive Communion at Mass what will be different?"

Maria put up her hand. "Well, it will look and taste the same, but it will be Jesus coming to us in a special way... like he promised."

The great day came and the family was very busy putting on their special clothes. They wore the same things that they had worn for their baptisms and everyone thought everyone else looked really special.

When they arrived at the church they found all the other families were also very excited as they found their places and got ready for Mass.

Mateo and Maria helped with the "Presentation of the Gifts" and at last joined their mum and dad for Communion. They stood very still and took the host very reverently and ate it. As they did, they reminded themselves that this was Jesus' special way of giving himself to be with them always.

They had a wonderful time at the party afterwards but, as Mum and Dad tucked them into bed after their night prayers, they all agreed, the food was fantastic, but the greatest food they had all had that day was Jesus.

Have any of the children been to a First Communion celebration?

What do they think it feels like to have Jesus living with them?

Juniors

Discussion story: Pope Benedict talks about Communion

Soon after he became Pope, Benedict XVI had a meeting with children who had recently made their First Communion. He invited them to ask him questions and one of them called Anna asked what the Pope thought Jesus had meant when he said, "I am the bread of life."

Note to catechists: depending on your group you may wish to adapt some of the words and phrases. The full text of the meeting can be found here: www.vatican.va/holy_father/benedict_xvi/speeches/2005/october/documents/hf_ben_xvi_spe_20051015_meeting-children_en.html

Here is what Pope Benedict said,

"First of all, perhaps we should explain clearly what bread is. Today, we have a refined cuisine, rich in very different foods, but in simpler situations bread is the basic source of nourishment; and when Jesus called himself the bread of life, the bread is, shall we say, the initial, an abbreviation that stands for all nourishment. And as we need to nourish our bodies in order to live, so we also need to nourish our spirits, our souls and our wills. As human persons, we do not only have bodies but also souls; we are thinking beings with minds and wills. We must also nourish our spirits and our souls, so that they can develop and truly attain their fulfilment.

And therefore, if Jesus says: 'I am the bread of life', it means that Jesus himself is the nourishment we need for our soul, for our inner self, because the soul also needs food. And technical things do not suffice, although they are so important. We really need God's friendship, which helps us to make the right decisions. We need to mature as human beings. In other words: Jesus nourishes us so that we can truly become mature people and our lives become good."

What do the children think of Pope Benedict's answer? Explain any words they did not understand. Help them to see that the Pope is emphasising that, just as we need good food all our lives to make us strong, so we need to receive Jesus in Communion frequently, so that he can feed us and make our souls, our inner selves, strong too.

4. Activity

Young ones

Invite the children to colour in the picture of themselves and then to draw or write different things that make them strong. For "inside things", help them to think of things such as hugs, kind words, playing and so on.

Juniors

As with the young ones, but explore more spiritual, perhaps less tangible things:

seeing something in nature; doing something for someone else; some times of prayer; Jesus coming to them in Holy Communion; reading or watching stories where good proves stronger than evil, and so on.

Tips for learning difficulties

Ask the children to bring in a photograph of themselves. Talk about their gifts and how they love others. Paste the photograph onto a piece of card and, around the picture, draw some of the good things that they do for others.

5. We come together

Parents can be invited to join in at this stage.

Focus

Light the candle. Invite those gathered to become still; to look at the candle and the setting of bread and wine.

Gospel

Today's Gospel was very hard for the people who followed Jesus to understand, and it can be hard for us too. Jesus tells us that he is living bread and that anyone who eats this bread will live for ever. He tells us that his flesh is real food and that he will raise anyone who eats it to eternal life.

Prayer

Loving Lord, you give us yourself in Holy Communion to help us to grow strong in faith, hope and love.
Thank you for such a great gift. May we always welcome you into our hearts and live good, holy and happy lives. Amen.

Share

During our session, we heard a story about children making their First Communion and the older ones have been hearing about some of the things Pope Benedict said to children who had recently made their First Communion.

We have thought about how we need good food to feed our bodies, and how this helps us to understand that we need good spiritual food to make our souls strong too, and this is the food Jesus promises to be for us.

Sing

"Eat this bread" (Taizé)
"I am the bread of life"

Things that make my body strong

Things that make me feel strong inside

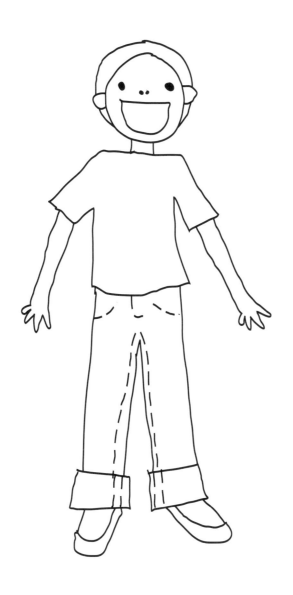

The Presentation of the Lord

The Presentation of Christ in the Temple

1. Introduction to the theme of the day

"My eyes have seen it"

Aim: To encourage the children to a trust in God based on experience.

Leader's reflection: Our children have the benefit of being brought up in the faith. They take their beliefs and celebrations of our faith on the word of parents, teachers, catechists, priests and others. Our task must be to lead them to a faith based on their own experience.

"Now you can let your servant depart in peace because *my eyes have seen...*"

2. We arrive

We sit in a circle, ready to listen to the Gospel.
Has anyone anything they would like to tell us about last week's Family Sheet?

Focus
A lighted candle.

Gospel: Luke 2:22-40
Read from the Lectionary or the Children's Lectionary.

3. We respond
What is the Gospel asking of us?
Work in age groups if appropriate, then come together as a community to end the session.

Young ones
Story: Fruit and vegetables

Year 1 had been looking at ways of keeping healthy. Miss Carter had brought in a whole basket full of different vegetables and fruits.

"Eating some of these different sorts of fruit and vegetables can be a good way of staying healthy," she said. "Who knows what they all are?"

The children took turns to name the things in the basket. Some things were easy, like potatoes and carrots, apples and oranges. Other things were not so well known.

"Now, let's ask some harder questions. Who knows where these things come from and how they grow?"

Again lots of the children tried to work out where things came from and sort out the things which grew in this country. Some children had lived in other countries and they had seen oranges growing on trees and olives pressed to make olive oil.

"My mum and dad came from Ghana and we grew cocoa there," said Ibrahim. "You use it to make chocolate."

Luis, whose parents came from Brazil, said,

"We had coffee growing in my country. You have to grind up the beans to make coffee to drink."

"That's interesting," said Miss Carter. "Now let's sort out the things which grow well in our country here."

The children sorted out the potatoes and carrots, the beans and peas, apples, pears and lots of the other fruits and vegetables. There were still some left. Then Grace said,

"My granddad grows lots of these things on his allotment. I help him."

She picked up some brightly coloured stems with leaves on.

"Those are chard, and these are Jerusalem artichokes; this is asparagus, granddad takes great care of that."

"You do know a lot of these," Miss Carter was surprised. "I thought I should catch you out with lots of these things."

"It's not so hard when you have seen things grow with your own eyes," said Grace.

In today's Gospel two of the people who saw Jesus when he was taken to the Temple had been longing and praying to see this special child. What were their names? When they saw Jesus what did they say and do? They had trusted God and now they believed because they saw Jesus "with their own eyes".

Juniors
Story: The dark of winter

Today is the feast of the "presentation" of Jesus. It has another name, do you know it? We call it Candlemas. We carry candles in church and bless them because they symbolise Jesus who is the light and glory of his people. Can you remember what Simeon said about him? Why is light important? Listen to this story:

Saeed took his bike around the side of the house, it was time to go to school and he was late.

"Bye, Mum!" he shouted, as he set off down the street. As he pedalled he realised that it was dark and raining. That was the trouble with winter mornings, he thought. Now why did that car hoot at him? He was at the side of the road, not in anyone's way. He pedalled on furiously, trying to get to the shelter of the school before he was soaked.

Another car hooted and the driver wound down his window and shouted something. Saeed didn't hear him, his words were lost in the wind and rain. Nearly there, thought Saeed.

He signalled carefully and pulled to the centre of the road ready to turn right. He remembered how he had passed his cycling proficiency test. He was pleased that he was a careful good rider.

Then there was a sudden shock: Saeed found himself on the ground, his bike clattered away. There was a voice, "Are you all right? I'm sorry I didn't see you, your lights aren't working and it's dark."

Then Saeed knew what the car drivers had been trying to tell him. He struggled to his feet.

"I'm sorry," he said. "I was riding carefully but I was late and I forgot to check my lights were switched on and working before I set off."

"Well if you are OK and the bike is," said the driver of the car, "I'll be on my way."

Saeed pushed his bike to the side of the road and this time he switched on his lights, they were working. He remounted and hurried on to school.

We call Jesus the Light of the World.

What do you need to do to see his light in your life with your own eyes?

4. Activity

Young ones

Light helps us to see with our own eyes.

Have some household white candles available, one for each child. You will need some coloured paint, powder paint works well, or ready-mixed paint and PVA glue. Mix the glue with the paint and use the paint mix to decorate the candle with patterns or pictures.

Alternatively, decorate the candle from the template page and add some coloured foil for the flame.

Juniors

As for the young ones, but in addition they may like to copy some of the words from the Gospel reading onto their candle.

Tips for learning difficulties

Choose either of the options above that is most suitable for the children. Coloured foil, stickers or pictures could be glued to the candle picture.

5. We come together

Parents can be invited to join in at this stage. Take a few moments to be quiet.

Focus

The lighted candle surrounded by the children's own lighted candles from the activity.

Gospel

Simeon said:

"Now, Master, you can let your servant go in peace, just as you promised; because my eyes have seen the salvation which you have prepared for all nations to see, a light to enlighten the pagans and the glory of your people Israel."

Prayer

Master, thank you for showing us yourself, the light; help us to trust you and try to be a light for other people. Amen.

Share

Talk about the candles and the designs that have been created.

Sing

"This little light of mine"
"The light of Christ has come into the world"

The Birth of St John the Baptist

1. Introduction to the theme of the day

Aim: Today we are going to celebrate the birthday of John the Baptist and think a little about his childhood.

Leader's reflection: Any new baby is a cause for celebration, but the birth of John the Baptist was always going to be special, even before he was conceived. Luke's is the only Gospel which tells the story. In fact, John's birth could equally well have been included in the Old Testament rather than the New. He prepares the way for Jesus in the same way as all the Old Testament prophets. He is, however, the only one of them to witness the fulfilment of his own prophecy.

If at all possible, celebrate today as a birthday, with a cake and party.

It would be helpful if there were some props around the place to help the children prepare for John's birth and Zechariah's party: maybe brushes, dusters etc. to make the room clean, a box for a cot, coats as blankets etc.

2. We arrive

We sit in a circle ready to listen to the Gospel.

Has anyone anything they would like to tell us about last week's Family Sheet?

Focus

A lighted candle, white for today's feast, a birthday cake, or a birthday card.

Gospel: Luke 1:57-66. 80

Read from the Lectionary or Children's Lectionary.

3. We respond
What is the Gospel asking of us?

Why is John the Baptist so special? Why do we celebrate his birthday?

Work in age groups if appropriate, then come together as a community to end the session.

Young ones

Story: A new baby!

Elizabeth and Zechariah were going to have a baby. They were very excited, but a little bit worried because they were both very old, too old really to have a baby. They were worried as well because Zechariah had lost his voice: he couldn't speak at all, not one word!

The way it happened was this: one day, an angel had arrived and told Zechariah that Elizabeth was going to have a baby. Zechariah didn't believe him, because Elizabeth was so old. He asked the angel to prove it. Now babies take a long time to grow inside their mummy, so the angel couldn't prove it straight away, so instead he took away Zechariah's voice. That way he couldn't ask any more questions until the baby was born. It made life very difficult for Zechariah.

At last the day arrived for their special baby to be born. Everybody from around about came to the house when they heard the news. It was a boy! They waited to find out what the new baby would be called. Zechariah came out of the house. He couldn't speak to them, so he wrote on a big board:

HIS NAME IS JOHN!

Suddenly he could speak again, and he told the people all about the angel and his new baby boy. Everybody was very happy. That night they had a big party to celebrate.

Have you any cousins? John the Baptist was Jesus' cousin. Why was John called the "Baptist"? When is Jesus' birthday? Why do we make a great celebration of John the Baptist's birthday?

Juniors

Story: John the Baptist grows up

The Gospel accounts tell us very little about John the Baptist, and nothing at all about his childhood. However, there are some traditions which tell us a few stories about him.

One story tells that Zechariah's family (John's father) had a house at a place called Torine, probably in the desert. When Zechariah died, Elizabeth, his wife, went to live there with her son, John. Mary came to visit her there, and Elizabeth seemed surprised that Mary managed to find the place. "I wonder how you knew where to find me, and who showed you the house of Zechariah!" she said, when Mary turned up on the doorstep.

When John was only seven years old, Elizabeth died, and Mary visited again, this time bringing Jesus with her. The story says that they stayed with him for a while, teaching him how to live in the desert. It is quite likely that the Holy Family were desert dwellers themselves for a while, when they were refugees from the threat of Herod and his soldiers, so they would have had a lot of experience to share with John.

Shortly after this, Herod died and it was safe at last for Mary and Jesus to return to Nazareth where Joseph's family lived. Mary was naturally very anxious about leaving John on his own (he would have been about eight years old), but Jesus is supposed to have reassured her with the news that John would not be alone, but would live in a community of prophets and angels!

This does not seem entirely likely, in the way we think of prophets and angels these days, but we do know that there were large communities of pious Jews who lived in religious communities in the desert, and it is quite possible that John spent much of his time with them. Maybe these were the "prophets and angels" Jesus was referring to.

There are many pieces of writing from about the time these stories were written, giving different versions about what happened in Jesus' life, and why it happened. The books which we know as the Gospels have been studied hard and accepted into the "Canon" (the authorised books) of the Church. The other writings are not necessarily true, but we can still use them to get a picture of how life might have been for Jesus and John when they were growing up.

What is a prophet? John was a prophet. What news did he foretell? Do you know how he survived in the desert: what he wore; what he ate?

4. Activity
Young ones and Juniors
Elizabeth and Zechariah are having a baby ... and then they are having a party! They need to get ready. You are going to help Zechariah get everything ready – cleaning, tidying, making a cot, making a drink for Elizabeth etc.
Mime the actions of Zechariah, but speak Elizabeth's part.

Juniors
Imagine going into the desert (or into the countryside) to live by yourself. Using the template page, make a list of all the things you would want to take with you so you could survive. Most of these things (mobile phone, camping stove, waterproof tent) did not exist when John was living in the desert. Discuss what he would have taken instead.

Tips for learning difficulties
Juniors could use cut and stick for their list of things to take with them. It might be helpful to bring along a camping catalogue so they can find the things they want.

5. We come together
Parents can be invited to join in at this stage.

Focus
Gather around the table for a birthday celebration with the items used for the start of the session.

Gospel
Elizabeth and Zechariah were having a baby. They were very old, so everybody was surprised. When the baby was born they called him John, which means "God is gracious", because they knew he was a gift from God. When he grew up he went to live out in the wilderness to help prepare the way for Jesus.

Prayer
Dear Jesus, when you were a boy, John the Baptist was your special friend. Help us to be friends with each other. Thank you for our special friends. Thank you especially for ... (take it in turns to name the child sitting beside them in the room, so that no one is left out). Amen.

Share
Share the cake, if you have one. The young ones will enjoy giving a guided tour of the room showing all their work.

Sing
Happy Birthday to John the Baptist

What I would use in the desert	What John the Baptist used
 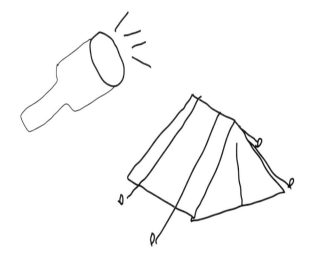	

Ss Peter and Paul, Apostles

1. Introduction to the theme of the day

> **"On this rock I will build my Church"**

Aim: To help the children to see that they belong to a worldwide family of Christians past and present.

Leader's reflection: The apostles were responsible for the first spread of the Gospel. We have benefited from their work, teaching and sacrifice and have our own responsibility to pass on the message of the truth as members of the same great family of believers.

2. We arrive
We sit in a circle ready to listen to the Gospel.
Has anyone anything they would like to tell us about last week's Family Sheet?

Focus
Red cloth; a candle; a Bible open at today's Gospel (symbol of St Paul's preaching of the new Law); a pair of keys, crossed (symbol of St Peter's authority) or a map of Paul's missionary journeys.

Gospel: Matthew 16:13-19
Read from the Lectionary or Children's Lectionary.

3. We respond
What is the Gospel asking of us?
Work in age groups if appropriate, then come together as a whole community to end the session.

Young ones

Story: Offertory

Marco, Li, Emma and Jo had been chosen by their teacher to take part in the offertory procession at church on the feast day of Ss Peter and Paul.

Marco and Li were to carry up the bread and wine and Emma and Jo were going to collect the money from the congregation.

"This is a very special day," said their teacher, "so I want to be sure there will be no mistakes. Mrs Patel is going to take you into the hall to practise."

In the hall the children went to the end to pick up the hosts and the wine and water, and Emma and Jo collected the baskets for the money.

"Now," said Mrs Patel, "show me what you have to do; I'm not a Christian and I don't know what happens in your church on this special day."

The children were surprised. It was true they had never seen Mrs Patel in church on Sundays, they'd just never thought about it before. So they explained what they had to do.

"Well, show me how it happens and do it very carefully and slowly so that I have time to think about it," said Mrs Patel.

The children formed up into a procession as they always did.

"We follow the altar servers to take up the gifts," said Marco. "You'll have to imagine they are at the front. Then we hand the gifts to Father Tony ready for the next part of the celebration."

He and Li fitted the actions to their words and Mrs Patel pretended to be Father.

"Then we bow and turn round to go back to our places," Li went on, "and Emma and Jo take up the money brought by the people in church and bring that to the front."

"The altar servers take the baskets from us and carry them up to the front of the altar and we bow and go back to our seats," said Jo.

"That's very clear," said Mrs Patel, "but why do you bring the gifts; what are they for?"

Emma explained about the bread and wine and what Father did next.

"And the money?" asked Mrs Patel.

"Well," said Emma, "my dad says there are a lot of things to pay for in the church. Some are ordinary like the lights and the gas bill and dinner for Father Tony."

Mrs Patel had met Father Tony. She really liked him.

"I can see he would want his dinner," she said.

"I think the money that we're going to collect will go somewhere else," Jo put in. "We could check, but I think it goes to our bishop or archbishop."

"They have even more bills to pay," said Emma, "and some of those are for poor people all over the world, because Father Tony says we belong to a very special family of people and in families we all have to help each other."

"Quite right too! Now let's have another practice to make perfect," said Mrs Patel.

Sometimes it helps us to understand what we are doing when we have to explain it to other people who don't know the things we do. Today is a special day when we remember Ss Peter and Paul.

What could you tell Mrs Patel about them? The children are likely to know more about St Peter, you may have to help them over St Paul. These saints tried to tell everyone they met about Jesus. We think of St Peter as our first pope and bishop.

Who is our pope or bishop today, where does he live?

St Paul travelled all over the Roman world to tell people the Good News. He was a missionary. There are still people today who spread the Good News about Jesus in lands that are not their own. Mention a few saints and missionaries: St Francis Xavier travelling to Goa, St Columba to Scotland, Mother Teresa to India, David Livingstone to Africa, William Carey (Baptist Missionary Society), Edith Cavell. Christians live in every part of the world, one great family.

Juniors

Story discussion on the lives of Ss Peter and Paul

Try to draw on the children's present knowledge of the lives of these two saints; encourage them to find out more. If you were to write a biography of the saints of today's celebration, what could you write? Let's start with St Peter. When do we first hear about him? What was his job? Who introduced him to Jesus? Which relative of Peter's was healed by Jesus? In which of the stories about Jesus does he get a mention? What happened when Jesus died, and after the resurrection and at Pentecost? What do we think finally happened to Peter? Today's Gospel reading is about the time when Peter recognised who Jesus really was. What did he say, and what did Jesus answer?

We actually know much more about St Paul because of the letters he wrote and the stories written in the book Acts of the Apostles. What do you know? When he is first mentioned, was he a Christian? How did he become a follower of Jesus? Where did he travel? The routes of his journeys are often drawn on a map to show us how far he went. (Give the children an idea of mission, of spreading the Gospel and spreading it outside their own familiar circle.)

What finally happened to St Paul? These men were two of our most important leaders but there are many other leaders in our worldwide Christian family. Which ones do you know by name?

4. Activity

Young ones

Use the picture of the world in space from the template page. Colour in the sea with blue and the land in green, brown or white. You might like to surround the world with stars and the moon. Mark the country you live in.

Fill in the missing words in the sentences. There could be a number of answers.

Juniors

You will need to bring an atlas to help the children, and a map of Paul's missionary journeys as a comparison.

Show them a map of Eastern Europe and the Middle East. Mark on it these places which are a part of the story of these two great leaders of our Church:

Sea of Galilee, Jerusalem, Damascus, Crete, Cyprus, Athens, Rome.

Note the area that the two apostles travelled to spread the Good News of Jesus Christ.

Tips for learning difficulties

Use the work for the young ones with these children. Talk to them about their place in the wider family. They may stick their photo near where they live. Use coloured paper and glue, sticky stars... to complete the world picture.

5. We come together

Parents can be invited to join in at this stage.

Focus

As for the start of the session and add samples of the children's work and a lighted candle.

Gospel

Jesus said,
"Who do people say I am?"
The disciples gave many different answers, then Peter said,
"You are the Christ, the Son of the living God."
Jesus said,
"You are Peter and on this rock I will build my Church; I will give you the keys of the kingdom of heaven."

Prayer

Father, thank you for inviting me into your worldwide family. Thank you for the people who lead our Church. Help them to be sure of your love and care for them. Help us to spread your Gospel of love to everyone we meet. Amen.

Share

Talk about the spread of faith in God throughout the world, while sharing the products from the activities.

Sing

"All over the world, the Spirit is moving"
"I sing a song of the saints of God"
"Bind us together, Lord"

All over our world people have learned about _____

God's _____ cares for everyone.

The Transfiguration of the Lord

1. Introduction to the theme of the day

> ## "Come, let us go up to the Lord"

Aim: We think about sacred places, and in particular the place Jesus chose to reveal himself.

Leader's reflection: High places have long been experienced as sacred places. In the thin air of the mountain top, our sense of God can be more acute, enhanced no doubt by the sense of exposure, isolation and revelation as all is laid out before us. It is in such an exposed, rarefied space that Jesus chooses to reveal himself.

Such places are not available to us on an everyday basis: Jesus was born a man, not an angel. This was the briefest and most secret of glimpses into his transcendence and the Gospel makes the point that "they came down from the mountain". Although we may not find it quite so thrilling, the experience of God in the mundane and ordinary is just as authentic.

2. We arrive

We sit in a circle ready to listen to the Gospel.
Has anyone anything they would like to tell us about last week's Family Sheet?

Focus

A lighted candle; white fabric for the feast day; picture of a snow-capped mountain.

Gospel: Matthew 17:1-9 (Catholic)
Luke 9:28-36 (Anglican)

Read from the Lectionary or Children's Lectionary.

3. We respond
What is the Gospel asking of us?

Young ones are introduced to the story of the transfiguration; juniors explore the idea of sacred places.
Work in age groups if appropriate, then come together as a community to end the session.

Young ones

Story: Henry sees Jesus

Henry the honey bee was on holiday. He was staying with some friends in a hive near the top of a mountain. He was having a lovely time.

One day, when he was buzzing out around the flowers, he heard some voices.

"Are we nearly there yet?" He buzzed himself around the back of a very pretty pink flower and waited to see who was coming.

First around the corner came a tall man with a beard and wearing a long garment and sandals, then three more men appeared. They looked tired and fed up.

"This is such a high mountain," they complained, "why have you brought us all the way up here?"

Henry looked around him, it was very high, but it was very beautiful as well.

"Nearly there," said the tall man, "just round this next bit …"

Henry followed them, visiting a few flowers on the way. By the time he got to the top, the men were already there, sitting on the grass.

"Actually, Jesus, this isn't bad at all," said one of the men admiring the view, "though it is a long way to come just to say our prayers."

"Let me show you," said Jesus, and he stood up and started praying. Henry knew about praying, so he shut his eyes and joined in. Suddenly he noticed it had all gone quiet; he opened his eyes just a little bit to take a peek, and nearly fell off his flower in surprise! Jesus was still standing there, but his face was shining, like the sun; and his clothes had turned whiter than white, like snow. The other men were standing there, staring at him with their mouths wide open. Suddenly a loud voice came down from heaven: "This is Jesus, my Son. I love him. Listen to him." The three men nodded their heads, unable to say a word. Henry was so surprised, he just shut his eyes again and pretended he wasn't there.

When he looked again, Jesus was back to normal and the three men were asking him lots of questions. Henry had lots of questions as well. What do you think they were?

Spend some time answering Henry's questions about the story before moving on to the activity.

Juniors

Story: The lure of the mountains

George Mallory was a mountaineer, and possibly the first man to climb to the top of Mount Everest. He started climbing when he was still at school, and, when he was a teacher himself, he went on longer expeditions to the Alps and the Himalayas. In 1921 he joined the first British expedition to Everest. This was a reconnaissance expedition to find out if it might be possible to climb the mountain. A year later he was back to lead the first serious attempt on the summit. This failed through bad weather and ended tragically: seven of the sherpas who were supporting the climbers were swept off the mountain in the storm. In 1924 George Mallory tried again. On 8 June 1924 he was seen climbing the last few hundred metres towards the summit. He was not seen again until his body was discovered, frozen by the snow, in 1999. We shall never know if he made it to the top or not.

Another climber, Todd Burleson, who has been team leader for Everest expeditions since then, writes this about his experience on the mountain: "We crawl into our tents and secure oxygen masks in a futile attempt to get a night's sleep. The team climbed from 23,500ft to almost 27,000ft with air so thin it's like breathing through a paper straw. I certainly wonder why I would put myself through this again and again, the winds are howling at 75mph, we're exhausted and the only thought is the excruciating and dangerous climb that awaits us after a few hours of sleep. Yet in the middle of the night I walk out of my tent, the winds have died down a bit and as a full moon sits on Lhotse (the 4th highest peak in the world) it is so awesome and stunning that I cannot imagine never returning."

Mountain tops are very special places; here we read about some of the people who gave their lives to the mountains.

What was special about the mountain top which Jesus took his friends to?

What happened there? How do you think Jesus felt, being there?

4. Activity
Young ones and Juniors

We are all in Jesus' family. God says to each of us, "This is my son (daughter), I love him (her)." Draw a picture of yourself in the frame on the template, and decorate the words. Alternatively, children can draw each other if this can be assigned fairly, and present their pictures to each other during the sharing session.

Juniors

When asked why he wanted to climb Mount Everest, George Mallory replied, "Because it is there." Getting to know God can be very similar: we pray, because God is there. Some places can help us feel closer to God: maybe the top of a mountain or in a church; maybe in our bedroom or in the garden. Think about a prayer space for yourself. Where would you like it to be, what would you like to put in it? Draw or write about your space. Put yourself in it.

Tips for learning difficulties

Young ones can use a photo of themselves. Juniors can find/draw a picture of a mountain and paste/draw themselves on the top of it.

5. We come together

Parents can be invited to join in at this stage.

Focus

Gather quietly around the focus used at the start of the session. Encourage the children to close their eyes and imagine they are talking to God on the top of a mountain. The juniors can imagine themselves into their prayer space. Spend a few moments just sitting there quietly enjoying God in this special place.

Gospel

Jesus went up the mountain with Peter, James and John. When he was there, he was transfigured: his face shone like the sun and his clothes became as white as light. A voice came from heaven: "This is my Son, the loved one. Listen to him."

Prayer

Jesus, you are here in this place with us. We love you, Jesus. Amen.

Share

Young ones can present their pictures, to each other if appropriate. Juniors can share their ideas about praying places.

Sing

"Be still for the presence of the Lord"
"We are gathered together unto him"

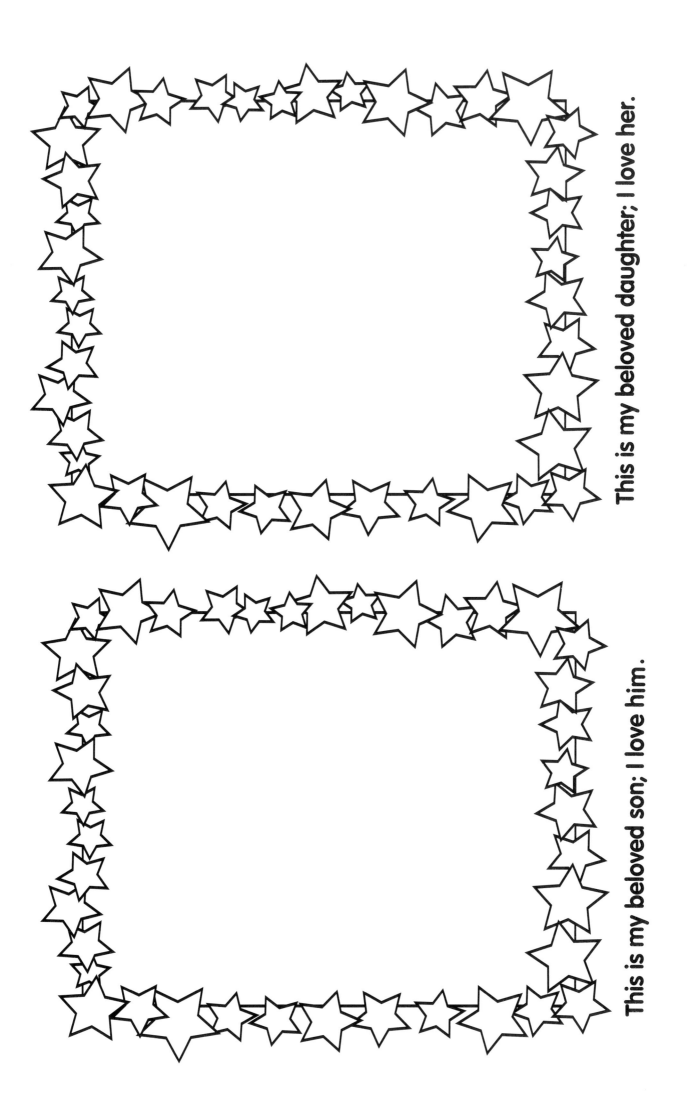

This is my beloved daughter; I love her.

This is my beloved son; I love him.

The Assumption of the Blessed Virgin Mary

1. Introduction to the theme of the day

> ## "My soul proclaims the greatness of the Lord"

Aim: To encourage the children to see something of God's greatness and Mary's joy in it.

Leader's reflection: The Gospels tell us very little about Mary: she seems always to be pointing away from herself, to her son. Today we celebrate her joy, the joy expressed in her song of exultation on her visit to Elizabeth. We tend to be wrapped up in ourselves; Mary's example of joy in God's work, and pointing from herself to Jesus, is one we can encourage the children to follow.

2. We arrive

We sit in a circle ready to listen to the Gospel.
Has anyone anything they would like to tell us about last week's Family Sheet?

Focus
A statue or picture of Mary, lighted candle.

Gospel: Luke 1:39-56
Read from the Lectionary or Children's Lectionary.

3. We respond
What is the Gospel asking of us?
Work in age groups if appropriate then come together as a community at the end of the session.

Young ones

Story: The visit

Mum was taking the twins John and Grace to visit an old friend of hers. Mum usually went when the twins were at school. Mrs Keighly was old, Mum said she was nearly 90, but she lived in her own bungalow and looked after herself. Mum helped her by doing some shopping, posting letters and spending time with her.

"When you are as old as Mrs Keighly, it can be hard to get out and do everything for yourself. Her legs are not as strong as they used to be, she has bad arthritis," Mum said, "but mostly it can be very lonely, living by yourself without your family nearby, unless people call in to see you."

The twins had never thought about being at home on your own all day, every day.

"What does she do all the time?" asked Grace.

"Ask her," said Mum.

So after they had all settled down and Mrs Keighly had given the children one of her home-made chocolate muffins each, Grace did just that.

Mrs Keighly laughed; she often did.

"I make cakes for my visitors, and I make them for your mum to sell at church when there's a cake stall. I write letters to all my friends who can't come to see me, your mum posts them. I talk to people on the telephone. I read books, watch TV, oh yes, and I'm getting to grips with the internet."

"Don't you ever get bored?" asked John, who was often bored.

"No, never bored. Sometimes I get lonely and wish I had someone to talk to about what I've seen, or found out, but then people like your mum and you drop in to see me and we keep up to date on all the local gossip. God has been very good to me. I enjoy the things in his world, not just the things in the garden, but the people he made and the life I've lived. It makes me happy just to think about it all."

Mum chatted for a while and the children went out into the garden to play.

"It makes you think," said Grace.

"Think what?" asked her brother.

"Think about all the times we are fed up because there's nothing we want to do, or we can't have something we want, and people like Mrs Keighly are happy stuck at home on her own."

Do you ever feel bored and miserable? What makes you really happy? Do you think how good God is and thank him for the things that make you happy? Mary was happy to do what God wanted, and when she'd had time to think about it on her visit to Elizabeth she was ready to praise God in the song in today's Gospel.

Juniors

Story: Discussion on the life of Mary

What do you know about Mary?
The annunciation; visitation; presentation; the visit to the Temple; the wedding at Cana; coming to Jesus on his travels because of the things she had heard about him; at the crucifixion and the resurrection.

After Jesus' ascension on the day of Pentecost, Mary was with his friends in the upper room in Jerusalem where they had been waiting together. Before he went back to his Father in heaven, Jesus had told them to wait for the Holy Spirit to come.

None of the disciples had understood what he had meant, but their leader was alive again and they had all seen him, talked to him, and had meals with him. They trusted him and did as he asked.

Mary was with them. She had remembered all the times she had been with her son and thought them over. After the misery of seeing him killed, seeing him alive again must have brought her amazing joy. Now she was waiting as they all were for the coming of God's Holy Spirit.

And then it happened: the disciples could only explain it as a sound like a wind rushing through the room, and fire above them. However they described it, the coming of the Spirit changed their lives for ever. It set them free to speak openly about Jesus, it set them free to spread the Good News. It gave them the power to exult in God's power and praise him for the gift of his Son.

We can only imagine what this was like for Mary, perhaps beyond words. Perhaps she remembered that first song of praise, her reply to Elizabeth more than 30 years ago.

Read the Magnificat again with the children from Luke 1:46-55. It is also included in section 5.

4. Activity
Young ones and Juniors
Use the template to make a poster to celebrate God's greatness: the things for which you can praise and thank him.
What pictures would you draw on this poster to illustrate God's greatness and gifts to you? What did Mary praise him for in her song?
Alternatively, children could work on a large poster together.

Tips for learning difficulties
Have pictures available: God's creation, family, friends, Jesus, Mary, which could be stuck on the poster.

5. We come together
Parents can be invited to join in at this stage.

Focus
The children's work, the statue or picture of Mary.

Gospel
Mary said,
"My soul proclaims the greatness of the Lord and my spirit exults in God my Saviour, because he has looked upon his lowly handmaid.
Yes, from this day forward all generations will call me blessed, for the Almighty has done great things for me.
Holy is his name, and his mercy reaches from age to age for those who fear him.
He has shown the power of his arm, he has routed the proud of heart.
He has pulled down princes from their thrones and exalted the lowly.
The hungry he has filled with good things, the rich sent empty away.
He has come to the help of Israel his servant, mindful of his mercy, according to the promise he made to our ancestors, of his mercy to Abraham and his descendants
for ever."

Prayer
Let's say the Hail Mary together and remember that together with Mary we praise our God.

Share
The work done by the children, their reasons for recognising God's greatness and praising him.

Sing
"My God is so great, so strong and so mighty"
"Jubilate everybody"
"I've got that joy, joy, joy, joy down in my heart"

The Triumph of the Cross

Holy Cross Day

1. Introduction to the theme of the day

> " We adore thee, O Christ, and we praise thee, because by thy Holy Cross thou hast redeemed the world "

Aim: We honour the cross of Jesus, lifted up for our healing.

Leader's reflection: There are two days in the year when we really focus on the cross; the first is Good Friday. This is a day of sorrow when we recall the Passion and death of Jesus. Today's feast is the converse of that: it celebrates the "lifting up" of Jesus on the cross, as a moment of revelation and triumph.

"When you lift up the Son of Man, then you will realise that I am he, and that I do nothing on my own, but I say only what the Father taught me" (John 8:28).

In today's Gospel, Jesus likens himself to the serpent in the desert that was lifted up to heal the stricken Israelites. Jewish tradition understood that the healing came about, not directly through looking at the serpent, but through the act of looking upwards, shifting their gaze from themselves to God. It was their renewed focus on God that healed them.

2. We arrive

We sit in a circle ready to listen to the Gospel.
Has anyone anything they would like to tell us about last week's Family Sheet?

Focus
A lighted candle, red fabric for the feast day; a decorated cross.

Gospel: John 3:13-17
Read from the Lectionary or Children's Lectionary.

3. We respond
What is the Gospel asking of us?
Why is the cross so important to us? Point out the cross in the church and in the meeting room. The cross was used to kill Jesus, but today is a day of honour and triumph. Why do we celebrate the cross in this way?
Work in age groups if appropriate, then come together as a community to end the session.

Young ones

Story: A story of the "true cross"

When Jesus died, everyone was so sad that they left the cross where it was on the hill near Jerusalem; and when Jesus rose from the dead, they were so happy that they forgot all about it, so it stayed on the top of the hill for a long time until at last it fell down and was buried by all the weeds.

Years later, a lady called Helena came along. She wanted to find Jesus' cross, so she dug around on the top of the hill. What do you think she found? She didn't find one cross; she found three! Who did the other two belong to? Helena couldn't tell which cross was Jesus' cross, so she thought up a plan. This is what she decided to do. She found a man who was very poorly, and she asked him to lie on the first cross. Nothing happened. She asked him to lie on the second cross. Nothing happened. She asked him to lie on the third cross. Suddenly the man was better. He was not poorly any more. He stood up and started dancing around. Now Helena knew which cross was Jesus' cross. Which one was it?

Once the cross had been found, everyone wanted some of it, and part of it was taken away to another country. A king called Heraclius (we will call him King Herry) decided to bring it back. He went and found the piece of the cross and brought it back to Jerusalem. Because the cross was so important, before he came into Jerusalem, he dressed himself in his best clothes with lots of jewels and finery, and then he picked up the cross and set off for the city. But a strange thing happened. As he got closer and closer to the city gates, King Herry found it more and more difficult to move. In fact it was so difficult that he stopped moving altogether. He was stuck! Now King Herry was a good king, and so he decided to pray. He asked God why he was stuck, and God gave him an idea. King Herry took off all his fine garments and his jewels, and he put them on the cross instead. Now he could move again. It was the cross that was important, not him!

Who did the three crosses belong to? What did Helena believe would happen? Was she surprised at the curing of the sick man? Why not?
King Herry was taught a lesson; what was it?

Juniors

Story: Prefiguring the cross in the Old Testament

The events of our redemption: the birth, Passion, death and resurrection of Jesus, are all predicted in some way in the stories in the Old Testament. Sometimes this is through prophecy, for example, it says in Isaiah,
"A virgin will conceive and bring forth a child …" (what does this predict?); other times it is through prefiguring: the event is predicted through a symbol or something that happens. These are not so easy to recognise; it is only looking back at the Old Testament once we know about the events of the New Testament, that we can spot them.

One of these is when Moses lifts up the serpent in the desert: this prefigures Jesus being lifted up on the cross. A serpent might not seem to be a very good symbol to prefigure Jesus, but, if we know the rest of the story, we begin to understand it a bit better.

The way it happened was this: as usual, Moses was having a hard time with the people of Israel; they were always grumbling about something or other. On this occasion they were fed up with eating manna. They complained to Moses and to God. We don't read about Moses' reaction, but God lost patience! He sent fiery serpents into the camp, which bit and frightened the people. They soon repented, and went back to Moses, asking him to plead with God to save them from the snakes. God told Moses to make a fiery serpent. Moses made one out of bronze, a fairly lengthy process. You can imagine all the people standing around impatiently, while Moses painstakingly put in the last few details: the eyes, the scales, that flicking tongue. Then God told Moses to set the serpent at the top of a standard or tall pole, and to put it where the people could see it. Anyone who had been bitten by a serpent could look at the bronze serpent, and they would live.

How does this prefigure Jesus on the cross?
Can you think of any other events in the Old Testament which prefigure events in the New?
(Abraham – willing to sacrifice his only son; Joseph, the rejected one saving the Israelites; the Exodus, from death to the promised land; Jonah, three days in the "tomb" of the whale; David, shepherd and king of Israel; Samson, self-sacrifice to save the people.)

4. Activity
Young ones
Stick the template onto cardboard, cut out the cross and decorate it using paints, colours, foil paper, jewels and fabric, whatever is available.

Juniors
Juniors can use the template given, or they can draw and cut out their own cross to decorate.

Tips for learning difficulties
Have the cross shape ready to decorate.

5. We come together
Parents can be invited to join in at this stage.

Focus
Gather around the table and the focal point from the start of the session. Display the decorated crosses.

Gospel
Jesus said: "None of you has ever been to heaven, but I have been to heaven; and when you lift me up on the cross, I will be showing you the way to heaven, so that you can believe in me and follow me and live there with me."

Prayer
Concentrate on praying the sign of the cross really well this week.

Share
The children can share their work; a procession with the decorated crosses would be a good way of doing this, either around the meeting room or back into church.

Sing
"Were you there when they crucified my Lord?"
"Sing Alleluia to the Lord"
"We are walking in the light of Christ"

All Saints

1. Introduction to the theme of the day

> ## "Seeking saints"

Aim: To seek the saints of everyday life and to see how saints are those who seek God and his will for their lives.

Leader's reflection: We have all met people whose lives seem to be distinguished by a quality of goodness, kindness, generosity or desire for justice that seems to go beyond the ordinary. Their lives are not striking or startling, but somehow the world is better for having them there. They often seem to have a deep relationship with God, apparently living with an awareness of the presence of God and a desire to live in accordance with his will for them.

We may say, "he/she's a saint" and, when they die, there is a feeling that their journey to God will be short as the desire of their lives to be with him eternally is at last brought to its fulfilment.

These are the saints whose feast we celebrate today.

2. We arrive

We sit in a circle ready to listen to the Gospel.
Has anyone anything they would like to tell us about last week's Family Sheet?

Focus

White cloth, candle, Bible open at today's Gospel.

Gospel: Matthew 5:1-12

Read from the Lectionary or Children's Lectionary.

3. We respond
What is the Gospel asking of us?

Work in age groups if appropriate. Alternatively, choose the discussion ideas, story and activity most suitable for your group. Come together as a community to end the session.

Young ones

Story: A very ordinary saint

Mr Tomlinson had been away from school for over a month. Mrs Jones, the head teacher, had told the children at assembly that Mr Tomlinson's mother was very ill and that he had gone to be with her. Then, a few days later, she had told them that Mrs Tomlinson had died and that Mr Tomlinson was sorting things out and would be back at school in a week or so.

When Mr Tomlinson came back, he looked tired and his class tried hard to be helpful. Billy brought the register and Teresa nudged Tom who always went into a daydream when it was time to say he was present. Molly made sure the books were in tidy piles and David checked that all the coats were hung up. **(What other things might children do to help Mr Tomlinson?)**

At the end of October, Mrs Jones said that the school would be looking for saints to celebrate on All Saints' Day. She told the children to talk to their families to see if they could find saints in their family or friends, or think about what an everyday saint might be like.

On All Saints' Day, Fr Mark talked to the children and asked if anyone could say who their saints were. Fr Mark asked them to say who their saint was and why they thought they were saints. Mr Tomlinson was the last to speak.

"Well," said Mr Tomlinson, "my mother was someone who always went to Mass and said her prayers: two very good reasons for her being a saint. And she was very brave when she was so ill... And..." But Mr Tomlinson stopped. He had loved his mother a lot and was a bit upset, so Tom put his hand up.

"She always nudged Mr Tomlinson when he went into daydreams and forgot things, like Teresa nudges me!" Teresa smiled and winked at Mr Tomlinson, who smiled back.

Molly put her hand up, "And she always made sure Mr Tomlinson kept his books tidy." And David said, "She put his clothes in his wardrobe when he was too busy studying to remember, and only told him off when his exams were over."

And Billy said, "She kept the registers in the parish so people had records of when they had been baptised."

Mr Tomlinson beamed at them all. He had told them about these things and was so proud that they had remembered.

Fr Mark smiled thoughtfully, "Well," he said, "it sounds to me like Mrs Tomlinson was a very good and holy woman, perfect saint material."

Mr Tomlinson's class all sat up a bit straighter and looked at him. They were very pleased to think that *their* teacher had a mother who was a saint and was with God for ever.

What good things can the children remember about Mrs Tomlinson? How might the children be learning from her example? Think about doing the simple things in an especially kind way.

Juniors

Discussion story: Mrs Tomlinson and the Beatitudes

You may wish to use the story used for the younger children with a little more interaction. Invite the children to think of other things about Mrs Tomlinson that might have marked her out as a saint in the making. Encourage them to think beyond what she did: look at the Beatitudes and think about how she might have put those into practice. How might she have been "poor in spirit" (think of humble/not seeking attention)?

Who might she have been gentle with, and how? Who might she have comforted? And so on... How might her doing good have made some people hostile to her? (Speaking up for the poor/asylum seekers/unborn children or other vulnerable people.)
Can the children think of people they know who might be saints?

4. Activity
Young ones

Using the template page, colour in Mrs Tomlinson and draw in some of the things that Mrs Tomlinson did in the story, or their own ideas about what made her life that of "a saint in the making".

Juniors

Using the template page, the children either draw some of the events from the story in the picture frames, or write a short description of them and how they show Mrs Tomlinson's good qualities. They could surround her with bubble-writing words from the Beatitudes, for example: gentle, merciful, peacemaker, pure in heart, comforter, wanting what is right, and decorate them.

Tips for learning difficulties

Bring some pictures cut from magazines/newspapers of people portraying the Beatitudes: showing care, kindness, sympathy, helping others and so on. Use these to paste onto the template picture, while talking about someone that they know well.

5. We come together

Parents can be invited to join in at this stage.

Focus

Light the candle. Invite those gathered to become still.

Gospel

In the Gospel today, we hear about some of the qualities that saints seek to build their lives on. They are often called the Beatitudes because Jesus used a word that can be translated as "blessed" or "happy". Some seem strange: how can we be happy when we mourn, or when people are against us because of our faith?

But these are the things that Jesus knows are the foundations of a saintly life.

Prayer

Lord Jesus, you have taught us the way to happiness in this life
and how to prepare ourselves for eternal life with you.
Help us to grow in love and faithfulness to the Beatitudes. Amen.

Share

We have been thinking about a story of a lady who had died but whose goodness was remembered by her son and the children he taught. (Invite the children to talk about some of the things Mrs Tomlinson did and, for the older ones, how they illustrate a life lived according to the Beatitudes.)

We all know people like this, and All Saints is a good day to think about them and give thanks for their lives.

Sing

"Oh when the saints go marching in"
"For all the saints who showed your love"

This is Your Life

The Commemoration of All the Faithful Departed (All Souls)

1. Introduction to the theme of the day

> ❝Thank you, Father, for revealing these things to the children❞

Aim: We explore the idea of the souls in purgatory and their need for our prayers.

Leader's reflection: We often reassure youngsters that those we love go straight to heaven when they die. Today we explore a little further the idea of purgatory and our role in praying for those who have died. In the catechism it is written that all who die in God's grace and friendship, but still imperfectly purified, are indeed assured of their eternal salvation; but after death they undergo purification, so as to achieve the holiness necessary to enter the joy of heaven. From the beginning the Church has honoured the memory of the dead and offered prayers for them ... so that thus purified, they may meet God face to face.

2. We arrive

We sit in a circle ready to listen to the Gospel.
Has anyone anything they would like to tell us about last week's Family Sheet?

Focus

A lighted candle, purple fabric for the feast day.

Gospel: Matthew 11:25-30

Read from the Lectionary or Children's Lectionary.

3. We respond
What is the Gospel asking of us?

What happens when we die? What is heaven like? Does everyone go straight there? Why not? How can we help the people who are waiting to get into heaven?
The remembrance of All Souls will often fall on a weekday, and attendance is likely to be lower than a Sunday Mass. For that reason, and in order to explore the idea of praying for the souls in purgatory in more depth, one longer story is offered today, exploring the power of a child's prayer, which is suitable for both age groups.

Young ones and Juniors
Story: The bad man goes to heaven

One day, a bad man died. The angels came, and he was taken straight up to heaven, and dropped off right outside the pearly gates. He looked through the gates – there were lots of people in there, all clean and bright and all wearing white shining garments. He looked down at himself, all grubby and dirty with the bad things he had done, and he began to cry.

Then he heard a voice behind him: "Hey!" He turned around, afraid that he might be in trouble again. A large stern-looking gentleman was standing there, looking at him.

"I think I'm lost," said the bad man, "I just died, and …"

"No, not at all," said St Peter (for that is who it was), "everyone comes up here first, though …" he looked the bad man up and down, "you do need a bit of sorting out before you go any further." The bad man whispered miserably.

"Sorting out? I thought it was too late for sorting out?"

"Well," said St Peter, "I can't sort you out, but other people can. Come on, let me show you." And he pointed towards a beautiful fountain just by the gate.

The man followed St Peter. "First you must wash yourself in Jesus' fountain," said St Peter, "that will make you clean again." The man pulled off his clothes and splashed and danced around in the fountain. Soon he was all clean and bright. He jumped out and stood in front of St Peter for inspection.

"Good," said St Peter. "Now you need a white shining garment like all the others." He gave the man a long piece of white cloth. "But you cannot make it yourself; other people must make it for you."

The man looked puzzled, "Who is going to make me a garment?"

St Peter pointed down through the clouds, "People who knew you when you were alive will make it for you with their good memories and their happy thoughts and their prayers." And he went away.

The bad man felt a bit lost. He sat down all alone outside the gates of heaven. He tried to think of somebody who might have good memories of him, or happy thoughts; or who might even be praying for him; but he had been so bad when he was alive that he could not think of anybody. And he began to cry again. He cried for a very long time.

At last he couldn't cry any more. He picked up the long white cloth and wiped his tears, and looked through the clouds. He saw lots of people he knew, but they weren't thinking good thoughts about him. Then he spotted someone he used to go to school with. This person had heard that the bad man had died, and, when he heard, he began to smile! He was remembering when he was at school with the bad man, and they had spent one very happy afternoon helping each other to do some cutting out. He was remembering and smiling! The bad man unfolded his white cloth carefully, and already saw that it had been cut into pieces for his garment.

The bad man peered through the clouds more hopefully now; maybe somebody else was having good thoughts about him. He saw a lady he used to work with. She was sewing herself a new dress.

She gave a little sigh and then smiled, "What a shame the bad man died," she was thinking. "I would have liked to show him my new dress." The bad man waved the pieces of his white garment towards the lady, but even as he shook it out he saw it was already sewn together! He shouted "thanks" to the lady, but she could not hear him.

The bad man tried on his new clothes, they fitted him perfectly, but they were very crumpled. He would need to get them properly ironed before he went into heaven. Once more he looked through the clouds. He looked for a very long time, hoping and hoping that somebody else might be thinking nice thoughts about him, but nobody was. He had almost given up when he spotted a little girl, kneeling by her bed.

He didn't know her, but she was praying very hard, "Dear Jesus, when the bad people die, please be kind to them, and help them to be sorry, and let them into heaven." The man knelt down as well, outside heaven, and closed his eyes, and he prayed with the little girl.

"Jesus, I am very, very sorry," he said, "I know I can't get into heaven on my own, and there are no more good thoughts about me, but only this little girl's prayer; it is the only thing I have left." When he had finished praying, the man hardly dared open his eyes but, when he did, there was his beautiful white shining garment all perfectly ironed and ready to put on.

"Thank you, Jesus," he said, "and thank you, little girl."

What can we learn from this story? Is it good for us to pray?
Who do you pray for? How do you pray?
Do you pray for anyone who has died? What do you think heaven is like?

4. Activity

It is possible to use either of the activities for a mixed group, although two are offered as usual.

Young ones

Cut out the template of a white garment. On the back make a list of all the people to include in the prayers when we come together.

Juniors

We pray for friends who have died, but we need to pray for other people as well, especially the people who have no one else to pray for them.
Write two prayers: one for someone you know who has died, and one for somebody you don't know. These may be written on the back of a white garment also.

Tips for learning difficulties

Draw and colour a picture of heaven, full of happy people.

5. We come together

Parents can be invited to join in at this stage.

Focus

Gather around the table and candle: the white cloth represents the white garment of our baptism, the burial cloth of Jesus, and the white garment we will wear in heaven.

Gospel

Jesus said, "Thank you, Father, for hearing the prayers of the children and showing them the way to heaven." Then he said to the people, "Come to me all you who labour and are overburdened and I will give you rest."

Prayer

Use the prayers that the juniors have written.

Share

If you have time, as the children share their work, spend some time talking about the people who have died; maybe parents can contribute little stories about the people they know.

Sing

"Jesus, remember me"
"God is love, his the care"

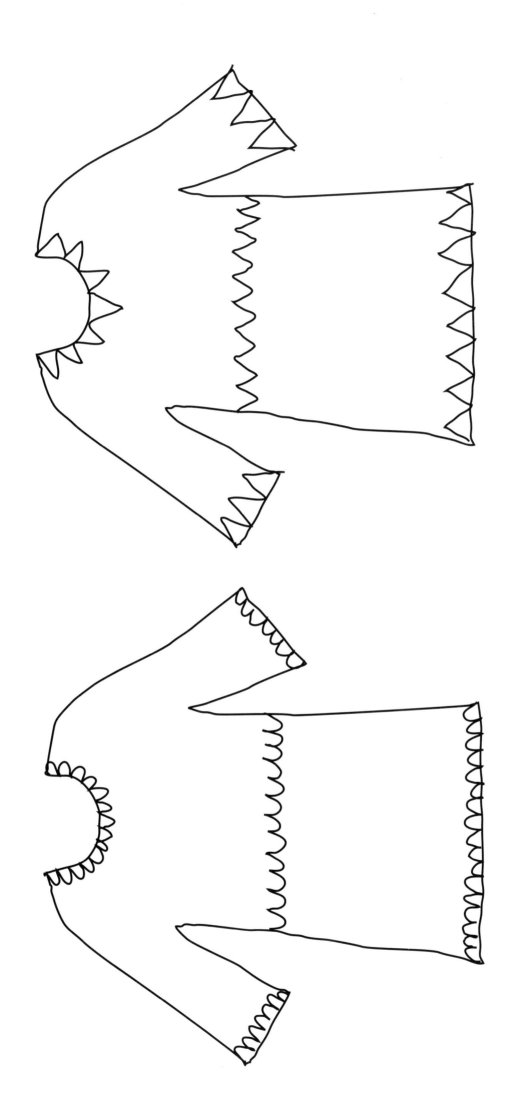

The Dedication of the Lateran Basilica

1. Introduction to the theme of the day

> ## "Stop turning my Father's house into a market"

Aim: To help the children to understand that a church is a holy place, a place for prayer and thanksgiving.

Leader's reflection: Our celebration of this dedication is a celebration of unity within our faith and within Christendom. This is the church of the Bishop of Rome, the mother church of all churches. We celebrate here its dedication to be a holy place, set apart for worship. This is the dedication of all sacred buildings, set apart for worship.

2. We arrive
We sit in a circle ready to listen to the Gospel.
Has anyone anything they would like to tell us about last week's Family Sheet?

Focus
Pictures or models of sacred buildings: churches, chapels, small and large.
If possible, add in buildings from other faiths, temples, mosques etc.
Lighted candle.

Gospel: John 2:13-22
Read from the Lectionary or Children's Lectionary.

3. We respond
What is the Gospel asking of us?
Work in age groups if appropriate, then come together as a community to end the session.

Young ones
Story: Special places

Toni had a special place she went to when she wanted to be by herself. It was behind the shed in the garden and under the apple tree which grew next to the fence. In spring, the tree was covered with pinkish white blossom, in summer it was a green-roofed space, cool and dark. In autumn the leaves on the tree rustled as they started to die and the apples showed among them. Toni didn't come to her place much in winter, but even then it was sheltered from the wind, and she could sit on an old box she had there, and do her thinking.

Sometimes, Toni went there when people in her house were arguing. Sometimes it was because there were too many people around. Sometimes it was because everything seemed to be going wrong: her parents were cross with her or she had fallen out with her friends. Sometimes she went there because she was very happy and felt she would "burst" if she didn't go somewhere she could shout with joy. Sometimes she went there just to play.

Today, Toni was there with her animal hospital toys. The special place had become a sanctuary for animals that needed help, they came by ambulance and went into the special hospital building to be made better.

"Toni, where are you?" It was her mother's voice. "Toni, come on, it's time to go shopping."

"Bother," thought Toni, but in this place she knew she could not hide. It might be her special place, but Mum would know where she was.

"Come on, Toni, hurry up," Mum was getting irritated.

Toni left everything where it was and came out. "Coming!"

"In that dark corner again," said Mum. "Don't know why you keep disappearing down there when there's a whole house and garden to play in."

Toni couldn't have told her mum why it was a special place for her, and she didn't try, she just hurried to find her jacket.

Do you think Mum knew that Toni's place was special even if Toni could not explain? Do you think Toni's mum had a special place? Do you? Why was the Temple a special place? What made Jesus cross about the way it was being used?

Juniors
Story: Chatter, chatter, chatter!

The service/Mass had ended; all over the church people were having conversations. There was not a lot of noise, but more than Mrs Ellis liked to hear. She finished her prayers and stood up to go home. Before she got in her car, she was going to tell Father Paul that things were not like they used to be. It wouldn't be the first time she had told him that, but it was getting to be all too much.

She hurried to the back of church. There was nowhere for Father Paul to say goodbye to everyone except just inside the door which opened directly into the nave. He often stood outside but today it was cold and wet. On her way to the door Mrs Ellis noticed that Mr Patel was being helped to his feet by one of his old friends who was asking how he had got on during the week and if he needed a lift home. The two of them stood talking and she heard Mr Patel thanking his friend for the offer of a lift.

Two of the flower guild ladies were standing in front of a display by one of their members:

"Didn't Moira do this well? I really like the way those scarlet gerberas stand out, it really makes you feel cheerful."

"We must find her and say thank you for all the work that's gone into this."

Mr and Mrs Giardina were putting their new baby into a "grow bag":

"He'll need to be warm outside in this cold weather," said Mr Giardina.

Then Mrs Ellis saw one of her old friends, Mrs Nicholson. Mrs Nicholson was looking very tired and sad. Her husband had died recently and it was strange to see her in church on her own.

"I shall have to go over and say hello," thought Mrs Ellis. She sat down next to her friend.

"How are you?" she asked. "I expect it's all very strange and life's a bit difficult at the moment."

"It is, but I'm so glad I came to church. So many people have come over, like you, to speak to me. I'd quite forgotten just how many people care about me."

"Well," said Mrs Ellis, "that's what we are here for. Do you think you'd like to come round and have a coffee one morning this week?"

"Oh that would be nice, we could have a long chat and it would help me to stop feeling so lonely."

When Mrs Ellis finally said goodbye to Father Paul, she had forgotten about the noise after Mass/the service.

"Quite important things happen in quick conversations in special places," she thought to herself as she drove home.

Why is church a special place? Is it special to you? The Basilica of St John Lateran in Rome is a special church among churches because it is the Pope's Cathedral of Rome. The first church was built here by Constantine about 300 years after the death of Jesus. Have you visited any cathedrals in this country? What do you know about them? Why are they special? What sorts of things do you think should happen in church?

4. Activity
Young ones and Juniors

If possible take the children for a walk around their church: perhaps invite the priest to lead this tour.

If this is not possible, use the diagram of the church on the template page to name and label some of the features.

Make a list to include the nave, sanctuary, choir, sacristy, lady chapel, altar, sanctuary light, font, holy water stoup, pulpit, lectern, tabernacle and any additional special features such as statues or carvings which could be added to the drawing.

Children can be encouraged to label the church as a whole group activity.

Why is the church a special place? Write a sentence that explains this.

Tips for learning difficulties

Talk about what happens in the church. Do the children recognise any parts of the church building in the drawing? Have pictures of the parts of the church. The children may stick these in the correct places.

5. We come together

Parents can be invited to join in at this stage.

Focus

A photo or picture of your church; a lighted candle.

Gospel

Jesus went to the Temple. He found people buying and selling cattle, sheep and pigeons and money changers sitting at their tables. He drove them all out and overturned the tables of money.

"Take all this out of here and stop turning my Father's house into a market," he said.

Prayer

Thank you, Lord, for bringing us together in this special place. Help us to make this a place where we turn to you and always find you here with us. Amen.

Share

Some of the work done by the children and their thoughts about why the church is a special place. Perhaps some of the adults present have things they may share with the children (their weddings, baptisms, Easter vigil, special services).

Sing

"Bind us together, Lord"
"For I'm building a people of power"
"Your hand, O God, has guided"

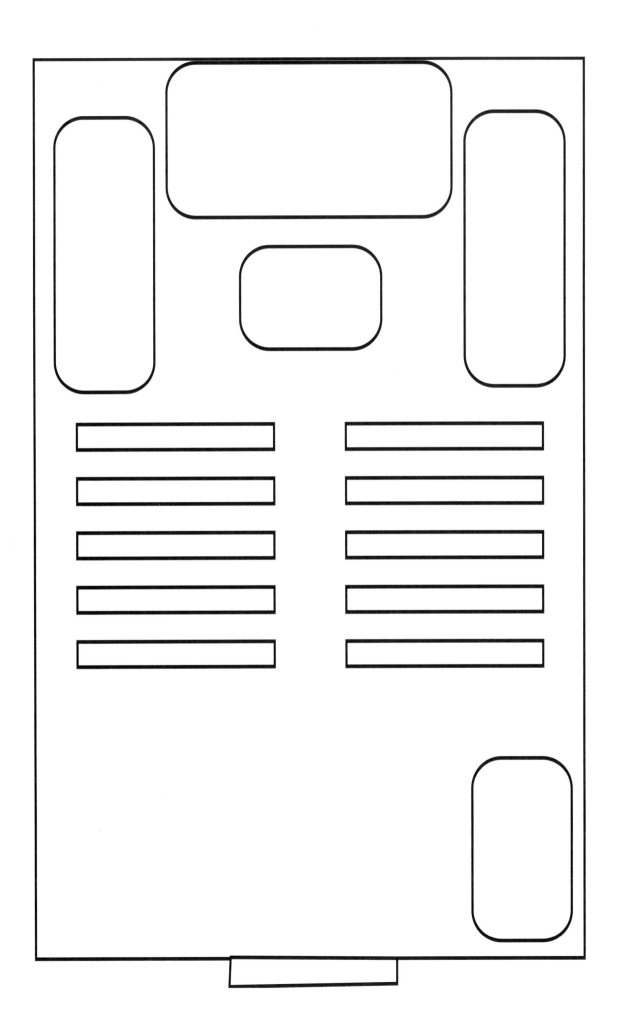

St David, Bishop

1. Introduction to the theme of the day

> ## "Be cheerful!"

Aim: We think about the life of St David and how he can teach us today.

Leader's reflection: St David, patron saint of Wales, was very much a man of his era. His ascetic lifestyle will seem excessive to our modern outlook. In fact, even in his day it was considered to be notable. He was known as the Man of Water, because he is reputed to have drunk only water for the whole of his life. Today we learn a little about him, and think about the principles underlying his way of living. What did he do to ensure that Jesus remained the centre point of his life? How can we apply his wisdom so that it is relevant for us?

2. We arrive

We sit in a circle ready to listen to the Gospel.
Has anyone anything they would like to tell us about last week's Family Sheet?

Focus

A lighted candle, a flag of St David (black cross on a gold background), white or gold fabric for the feast day in Wales or churches where this is the patronal feast.

Gospel: Matthew 5:13-16

Read from the Lectionary or Children's Lectionary.

3. We respond
What is the Gospel asking of us?

If we want to be the salt of the earth and the light of the world then we need to make Jesus the centre of our life. To do that, we have to make the time and space to listen to him, and to develop our friendship with him.
Work in age groups if appropriate, then come together at the end of the session.

Young ones

Story: St David preaches to the people

Today is the feast of St David. He lived in Wales and he was a bishop. *What is a bishop? Have the children met their bishop? What is he called?*

One day, David was talking to the people. He was very good at talking and the people came from far away to listen to him. But today was a special day. Today the people were trying to choose a new archbishop (discuss as appropriate). They didn't know which bishop to choose, so they decided to listen to all of them, and the one who talked the best would be the archbishop. One by one the bishops stood up in front of the crowd and talked to the people about God. Some of them were quite good, and some of them were just all right, and some of them were not very good at all. Then it was David's turn. He stood up in front of the people and started to talk. When they heard David talking, the crowd suddenly got a lot bigger, so big, in fact, that the people at the back couldn't hear him. "Louder!" they called. "We can't hear you!" David looked around to find something to climb on. He asked all the people to put their coats on the ground and to make a great pile of them. When they had done that, David climbed to the top of the pile and began talking again. But by now the crowd was even bigger so they still couldn't hear him. David didn't know what to do. Suddenly, there was a rumble in the ground underneath him, and then another, and then the ground began to rise up to make a little hill. Now David was so high up everybody could hear him!

They thought he was a great talker and the best, and so they chose him as their archbishop straight away.

What did St David do that matches up with the Gospel advice?
What do you think of St David?

Juniors

Story: St David – the ascetic

St David was an ascetic. That is a technical word for someone who likes to live the hard way. David always chose the hard way. If he was given a bed to sleep on, David would sleep on the floor. If he was offered pie for supper, David would stick to bread and water. If he was given warm clothes to wear, David would put on a rough tunic made of animal skins. That was the way ascetics lived. David didn't start off that way. He was the son of a king, the prince of Cardiganshire. But in the sixth century (when David lived), a lot of people believed that the best way to get close to God was to clear away all the nice and comfortable things in their lives, so that the *only* nice thing they had was God.

Imagine you were in a room with your favourite programme on television, a new computer game to play, and an exciting book to read – and your gran was visiting and wanted to sit down and chat with you. Even if you loved your gran very much, it would still be difficult not to be distracted by all the other interesting things. But if you were cold and hungry in an empty room and hadn't seen anybody for days, and your gran came in and gave you a big hug – how pleased would you be to see her then! That is how asceticism works. If God is the only good thing going on around you, you begin to appreciate him a bit more.

Nowadays asceticism is not so fashionable. We can see that making life as tough as possible for ourselves might not always be a good thing – but for David it seems to have worked. Just before he died he said, "Be cheerful, keep the faith, and do the little things you heard and saw in me." Not bad for someone who had so little to be cheerful about!

4. Activity
Young ones

St David is celebrated especially in Wales because he is their patron saint. The Welsh flag is white and green with a red dragon in the middle, but the flag of St David is less well known. It has a black cross on a gold background. Use the template to colour in the Welsh flag, and, on the back, draw and colour in the flag of St David.

Juniors

Asceticism like St David's is not really suitable for us, but we can still learn from him. Imagine your gran came to visit. Make a list of all the things which might distract you from giving her your full attention. Now think about your week, and find ten minutes each day for not doing any of those things, in fact, for doing nothing at all. You can look out of a window, or sit quietly in the garden, but no talking, no music, no games. Write down a promise to yourself for next week, and see what happens.

Tips for learning difficulties

The young ones' activity should be accessible to everyone, with support. The juniors' activity could be encouraged by having a chart available with the days of the week and time slots. Use a sticker to mark their "time to do nothing".

5. We come together

Parents can be invited to join in at this stage.

Focus

Gather around the candle table. Pin to it the flags which the young ones have prepared.

Gospel

Jesus said to his followers, "You are the salt of the earth. You are the light of the world. If you make me the centre of your life, then other people will want to follow me as well."

Prayer

Jesus, thank you for St David and for all the saints who make you the centre of their lives. When we look at them, we can see your light shining through. Help us to be good followers of yours so that people can see your light in us as well. Amen.

Share

The flags made by the young ones are already on display – they could attach them to garden sticks and walk into church waving them if appropriate. To make it a little more binding, the juniors might like to stand up and read aloud their promise to "do nothing" some time each day next week.

Sing

Welsh hymns and folk songs (in Welsh where known)
"All through the night"
"Guide me, O thou great Redeemer"

St Patrick, Bishop

1. Introduction to the theme of the day

> **"Happy St Patrick's Day Beannachtaí lá fhéil Pádhraig duit!"**

Aim: To honour the feast of the patron saint of Ireland and to celebrate some aspects of Irish culture.

Leader's reflection: Although St Patrick lived over 1,500 years ago, his feast is celebrated with great enthusiasm in countries all around the world. The St Patrick's Day parade in New York is a great celebration for Irish Americans and other New Yorkers. There is even a St Patrick's Day parade in Tokyo. One of St Patrick's greatest achievements was to bring the Good News to the Celtic peoples of Ireland in their own language. His captivity as a young man had made him fluent and so, unlike other missionaries sent before him, he knew both the language and druidic customs and was able to communicate directly with people who heard the power and hope of the words he spoke. He also used signs and symbols to help his teaching – the most famous being his use of the shamrock to illustrate the mystery of the Trinity. We continue that work: opening God's word in ways that people can understand and using sign and symbol to deepen people's understanding of it.

2. We arrive

We sit in a circle ready to listen to the Gospel.
Has anyone anything they would like to tell us about last week's Family Sheet?

Focus

White cloth; Bible open at the Gospel reading (or first or second reading if chosen); shamrock if available; Celtic cross.

Gospel: Luke 10:1-12. 17-20

Read from the Lectionary or Children's Lectionary. The first reading (Jeremiah 1:4-9) and second reading (Acts 13:46-49) are also helpful in giving a scriptural context to St Patrick's life.

3. We respond
What is the Gospel asking of us?

Work in age groups if appropriate. This week, a short story is provided for the young ones and detailed discussion ideas are offered for the juniors. Come together as a community to end the session.

Young ones
Story: The life of St Patrick

St Patrick was not born in Ireland, he was born in Wales. When he was sixteen he was kidnapped and taken over the sea to Ireland where he was sold as a slave and lived in what is now Antrim in the north of Ireland. He worked for six years and, during the long hours of loneliness watching his master's sheep, learned to pray, lots of short prayers, so that sometimes he thought he must have said over a thousand in one day!

One day he was lucky enough to escape and went to France where he learned more and more about God and realised he wanted to be a priest.

Years later, he thought he heard a voice calling him to go back to Ireland. He was not happy about this as it had been a hard and unhappy part of his life. But he sensed that God wanted him to go back and so he trusted that God would be with him and would protect him.

St Patrick did have problems – the powerful chiefs and druids (the pagan religious leaders) tried to stop him, but God always came to his help. One example was when a chief had said that all fires had to be put out until his own fire was relit. The problem for St Patrick was that this happened just before the Easter Vigil when he needed to light a fire to prepare to celebrate the resurrection. He went ahead and lit the fire and, though his life was threatened and people tried to put it out, he was kept safe and the fire continued to burn. St Patrick told the crowds that this was a sign from God that the Christian faith would continue to burn in Ireland whatever happened in the future.

For many people, 1,500 years later, his words are still true.

Juniors

Think about the reading you have chosen and invite the children to respond. How is St Patrick like Jeremiah, or Paul and Barnabas, or the people Jesus sent out to the villages?

How do their problems mirror those of St Patrick?

Think about his time in slavery, the opposition he met from Irish chiefs and druids, the miracles he worked and the power of his words changing people's lives.

What does his example encourage us to do?

How can we learn to be strong in faith?

How can we share our Good News with other people and help them to come to know Jesus?

4. Activity

Young ones

Use the template to cut out a shamrock. Invite the children to decorate their shamrock – not necessarily just green! With sticky tape fix a safety pin on the back and put it on the child as a badge.

Juniors

Invite the children to write and decorate part of St Patrick's Breastplate. Explain that he used the idea of putting on spiritual armour to protect him when he was facing the Irish chiefs and druids who opposed him.

> I bind to myself today
> God's Power to guide me,
> God's Might to uphold me,
> God's Wisdom to teach me,
> God's Eye to watch over me,
> God's Ear to hear me,
> God's Word to give me speech,
> God's Hand to guide me,
> God's Way to lie before me,
> God's Shield to protect me,
> Against everyone who would injure me,
> Whether far or near,
> Whether with few or with many.

If you are having a party, older children could prepare a "feast" of traditional Irish food. Use shamrock and Celtic designs to decorate the tables. White cloths with green ribbon/streamers would also look good. Ask one or two children to prepare to read traditional folk tales from Ireland; have them practise in readiness for the party. If paints/felt tips are available, other children might like to do illustrations for the stories. Celebrate the Irish love of poetry and song.

Tips for learning difficulties

Choose the activity which best suits the gifts of the children in the group. Some children will be natural welcomers and hosts, others might prefer a more artistic activity.

5. We come together

Parents can be invited to join in at this stage.

Focus

Light the candle. Invite those gathered to become still. If shamrock is available, people might like to pin some on their clothes.

Gospel

In our reading today, we heard about how God chooses people to take his Good News to the world. Quite often they do not feel very confident, like St Patrick. However, God is on their side and protects them from harm and gives them strength and power to fulfil their mission.

Prayer

Here is another part of St Patrick's Breastplate prayer. He used to imagine that he was putting on spiritual armour when he knew he was facing threats and difficulties. This gave him the courage and strength to carry on with his mission:

Christ with me, Christ before me,
Christ behind me, Christ within me,
Christ beneath me, Christ above me,
Christ at my right, Christ at my left,
Christ in the heart of everyone who thinks of me,
Christ in the mouth of everyone who speaks to me,
Christ in every eye that sees me,
Christ in every ear that hears me. Amen.

Share

We have been thinking about St Patrick and how he brought the Good News to Ireland. It was a difficult job but he spoke to the Celtic people in their own language and many were happy to hear about God's love for them. He used symbols like shamrock to explain difficult ideas like the Trinity. (Invite those who made the shamrock badges to indicate how they show God, Jesus and Spirit as three leaves on one plant.)

We thought it would be good to celebrate the feast day by having a small party. Some of the children have prepared some stories for us as well.

Sing

"Hail glorious St Patrick"
"St Patrick's Breastplate"
Any Irish hymn

Family Sheet

To do at home with your family

For parents: Weekly Thought

Epic adventures depicting the fight between good and evil are current in junior fiction, and are finding their own following amongst "young-at-heart" adults. Apart from some of the Narnia stories, none of these is a direct allegory of the Christian story, but they might still be used to "warm up" the spiritual imagination.

FAMILY PRAYER

Dear Jesus, you have told us that at the "End of Time", you will come again to earth, in glory. That seems to be a very long time to wait, but help us to be ready when it happens. In four weeks' time, we will be celebrating your birthday – the time you come to earth as a baby. Help us to be ready for that as well. Amen.

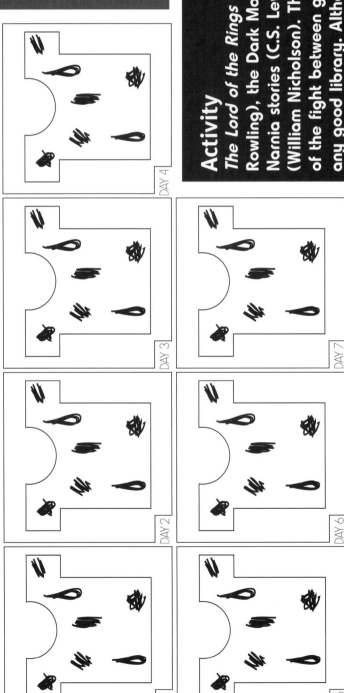

DAY 1

DAY 2

DAY 3

DAY 4

DAY 5

DAY 6

DAY 7

The T-shirts in this week's calendar all have dirty marks on them. Each day, when you have done something good, ask a grown-up to help you use correcting fluid to clean up one of the T-shirts.

This sheet has been completed by ....

Activity

The Lord of the Rings (J.R.R. Tolkien), Harry Potter (J.K. Rowling), the Dark Materials trilogy (Philip Pullman), the Narnia stories (C.S. Lewis), the Wind on Fire trilogy (William Nicholson). These are all books that tell stories of the fight between good and evil. You will find them in any good library. Although they are all fiction, they each have some sort of real-life meaning in them. Can you work out what it is? Is it the same in all of them? How do they compare to the stories Jesus told, and all the things that happened to him?

© Redemptorist Publications, Alphonsus House, Chawton, Hants GU34 3HQ. To be used solely as part of FaithMap Programme.

2nd Sunday of Advent

Family Sheet

To do at home with your family

For parents: Weekly Thought

Think about the preparations you are making for Christmas, involve your children in them, especially those which involve kindness to people outside the family. Let them know that your preparations for Christmas involve service to our king, prayer, reconciliation, gifts to the less fortunate. Especially let the children know that you do not always find the demands of the kingdom easy, let your children encourage you.

FAMILY PRAYER

Lord Jesus, help us to remember what your kingdom of love and kindness is like. May your kingdom come. Amen.

Young ones – Colour in this picture of the queen on her throne.
Older ones – Precious stones (jewels) are often said to stand for a particular quality. The Victorians sent messages using gem stones in jewellery. Can you design a brooch or necklace using rubies (love), sapphires (wisdom) and emeralds (hope)?

DAY 1

DAY 2

DAY 3

DAY 4

DAY 5

DAY 6

DAY 7

Colour in a jewel each day when you keep the promises you made to Jesus while making your crown.

This sheet has been completed by ....

© Redemptorist Publications, Alphonsus House, Chawton, Hants GU34 3HQ. To be used solely as part of FaithMap Programme.

3rd Sunday of Advent

Family Sheet

To do at home with your family

For parents: Weekly Thought

It is important not to give up our preparations for the coming kingdom even when life isn't what we expect and especially when faith seems hard. Jesus always encourages. Keep on through the bad patches – trust him.

FAMILY PRAYER

Keep us close together as we get ready for your birthday. Thank you for the happiness that comes because we trust you. Amen.

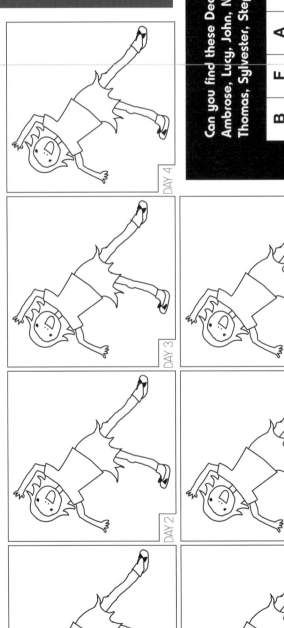

DAY 1 DAY 2 DAY 3 DAY 4
DAY 5 DAY 6 DAY 7

This week colour in the "jump for joy figure" every time you feel happy and remember to thank God for it.

This sheet has been completed by ....

Can you find these December saints in this word search?
Ambrose, Lucy, John, Nicholas, Francis Xavier, Damasus, Peter, Thomas, Sylvester, Stephen

B	F	A	M	B	R	O	S	E
E	R	P	E	T	E	R	Y	T
D	A	M	A	S	U	S	L	H
S	N	L	J	E	L	F	V	O
A	C	U	O	S	O	N	E	M
N	I	C	H	O	L	A	S	A
T	S	Y	N	A	I	L	T	S
A	Y	S	T	E	P	H	E	N
B	O	X	A	V	I	E	R	T

© Redemptorist Publications, Alphonsus House, Chawton, Hants GU34 3HQ. To be used solely as part of FaithMap Programme.

4th Sunday of Advent

Family Sheet

To do at home with your family

For parents: Weekly Thought

With the excitement building we all need to concentrate on the immediate, the things we need to do today. Hang on to the important things – Jesus was born, he changes our lives, he can deal with our worries and fears if we let him. Keep looking forward, but not too far!

FAMILY PRAYER

In the excitement of looking forward and of Christmas itself, help us, Lord, to listen to the messages of peace and hope you send to us. Amen.

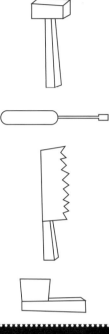

Young ones – Can you follow the lighted Advent candle to reach the stable at Bethlehem?

Older ones – Joseph was a carpenter. Can you name these tools?

DAY 1

DAY 2

DAY 3

DAY 4

DAY 5

DAY 6

DAY 7

Colour an angel each day to remind you how Mary and Joseph did what God wanted.

This sheet has been completed by ....

© Redemptorist Publications, Alphonsus House, Chawton, Hants GU34 3HQ. To be used solely as part of FaithMap Programme.

Family Sheet

To do at home with your family

For parents: Weekly Thought

Relax and find a little time to offer a "Happy Birthday" thought. Enjoy the holiday.

FAMILY PRAYER

Thank you, Jesus, for coming into your world as a child. Help us to welcome you and to think with joy about the astonishing things that happened at Bethlehem. Amen.

Activity

We call Jesus the Light of the World, and we use candles to help us remember it. How many other ways of lighting do you know? Draw them, or write them on the back of this sheet.

Follow the black line and help the shepherds find a way to the stable.

DAY 1

DAY 2

DAY 3

DAY 4

DAY 5

DAY 6

DAY 7

This week draw some candles and decorate the birthday cake each day you remember that Jesus welcomes you just as you welcome his birthday.

This sheet has been completed by ....

© Redemptorist Publications, Alphonsus House, Chawton, Hants GU34 3HQ. To be used solely as part of FaithMap Programme.

The Holy Family of Jesus, Mary and Joseph

Family Sheet

To do at home with your family

For parents: Weekly Thought

We deal each day with the hopes and fears of our children as well as our own. To do it effectively we need a safe pair of hands in which to place those hopes and fears. There is no safer pair of hands than those of our God who loves us beyond reason.

FAMILY PRAYER

Dear Lord, we pray for any of your children who are afraid today. Help us all to trust you to bring freedom from fear. Help us to do what you want. Amen.

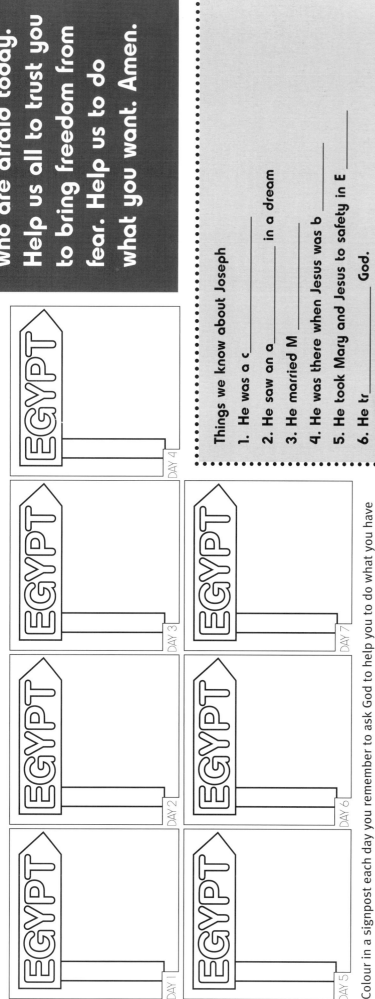

DAY 1

DAY 2

DAY 3

DAY 4

DAY 5

DAY 6

DAY 7

Things we know about Joseph

1. He was a c _____

2. He saw an a _____ in a dream

3. He married M _____

4. He was there when Jesus was b _____

5. He took Mary and Jesus to safety in E _____

6. He tr _____ God.

Can you find out how long it would take to walk from Bethlehem to Egypt (walking at 3 miles an hour for 6 hours each day)?

Colour in a signpost each day you remember to ask God to help you to do what you have said you will do.

This sheet has been completed by ....

© Redemptorist Publications, Alphonsus House, Chawton, Hants GU34 3HQ. To be used solely as part of FaithMap Programme.

Solemnity of Mary, Mother of God

Family Sheet

To do at home with your family

FAMILY PRAYER

There is a beautiful blessing that God gave to Moses to bless the sons and daughters of Israel:
"May the Lord bless you and keep you.
May the Lord let his face shine on you and be gracious to you.
May the Lord uncover his face to you and bring you peace."
You might like to use this as a bedtime or going to school blessing.

For parents: Weekly Thought

Most of us have moments when we are a little overawed by the trust God has placed in us by giving us our children. Day-to-day life is often so busy: the places to get our children to, their numerous activities, thinking about their food fads – all these things can bog us down in the routine and mundane and we can forget that we have acted as co-creators with God in bringing our children into the world. But this is one of the things that God has called us to do. Like Mary, part of our discipleship is to honour these gifts from God, and, through our daily lives and example, help them to grow into the disciples that they are called to be.

DAY 1   DAY 2   DAY 3   DAY 4

DAY 5   DAY 6   DAY 7

Colour in a picture of Mary and baby Jesus each day. Think about how Mary looked after Jesus when he was young and then showed people how to be good disciples when he grew up.

This sheet has been completed by ....

New Year's Resolution

At the start of a New Year, lots of people think about things they would like to learn to do, or try to stop doing things that they feel are bad for them. What New Year's Resolution can you make? Don't make it too difficult! Think of something you can succeed in.
Look forward to the year to come. What do you hope will happen this year?

© Redemptorist Publications, Alphonsus House, Chawton, Hants GU34 3HQ. To be used solely as part of FaithMap Programme.

2nd Sunday after Christmas

Family Sheet

To do at home with your family

For parents: Weekly Thought

As you never withdraw your love from your children so God never withdraws his love from us, his adopted children.

FAMILY PRAYER

Father, thank you for sending your Son Jesus to show us what you are like. Thank you for making our family part of your great family of adopted children. Help us to grow more loving every day. Amen.

Activity

Young ones

Fold a strip of paper into a concertina. Use this template to make a family of children all holding hands.

Older ones

How many "family" words do you know? Make a list to take with you next week to your class. You could start with parents, mother, father etc.

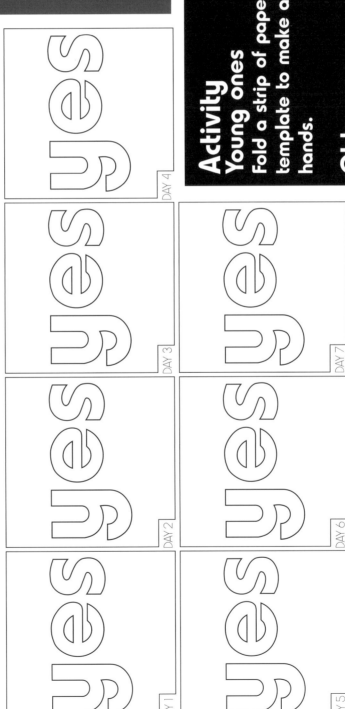

DAY 1

DAY 2

DAY 3

DAY 4

DAY 5

DAY 6

DAY 7

This week colour in a "Yes" on each day you remember to speak to your Father in heaven.

This sheet has been completed by ....

© Redemptorist Publications, Alphonsus House, Chawton, Hants GU34 3HQ. To be used solely as part of FaithMap Programme.

The Epiphany of the Lord

Family Sheet

To do at home with your family

For parents: Weekly Thought

God entered human history in a real place, one that exists to this day. Ours is not a distant God who resides only in heaven but one who entered fully into the life of human creatures. God, in the person of Jesus, breathed the air as we breathe it; ate food as we eat; and drank as we drink. Because Jesus lived on the earth, all that we *could* see as everyday has been sanctified. He did not spurn the things of daily life, but through living with them – and in the case of air, food and water, depending on them – he made them holy.

This offers us a reminder of how we can deal with the everyday things around us. Everything has the potential to speak to us of God – if we allow it.

FAMILY PRAYER

God, our loving Creator, we thank you for giving us each other.

Lord Jesus, we thank you for coming to live in our world.

Gracious Spirit, we thank you for making everyday things holy.

Bless our family and make our home a place where there is love, light and happiness.

Amen.

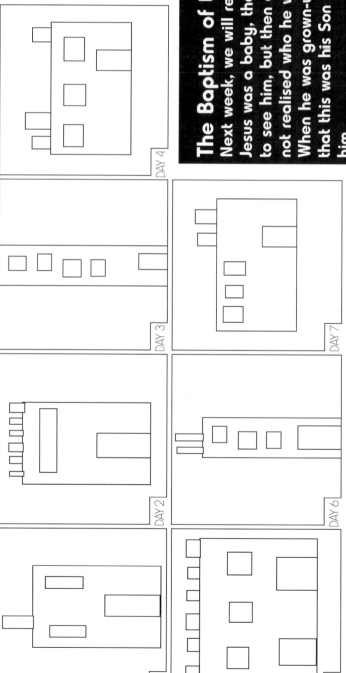

DAY 1 · DAY 2 · DAY 3 · DAY 4 · DAY 5 · DAY 6 · DAY 7

The Baptism of the Lord

Next week, we will remember the baptism of Jesus. When Jesus was a baby, the shepherds and wise men had come to see him, but then a long time passed when people had not realised who he was.

When he was grown-up and baptised, God told the world that this was his Son and that everyone should listen to him.

See if you can find pictures of your baptism. Find a quiet time to think about God choosing you as his son or daughter. Say thank you to God for giving you this special new life in Jesus.

Colour in a house each day to remind yourself that Jesus was born and lived in an ordinary house. As you colour, thank God for the gift of your home and pray for people who do not have a home of their own.

This sheet has been completed by ....

© Redemptorist Publications, Alphonsus House, Chawton, Hants GU34 3HQ. To be used solely as part of FaithMap Programme.

The Baptism of the Lord

Family Sheet

To do at home with your family

For parents: Weekly Thought

Today we listened to the Gospel about Jesus being baptised in the River Jordan by John (the Baptist). Jesus, the Son of God, came to carry out God the Father's work. When we are baptised the Father has similar hopes and expectations of us. God believes in us. He hopes that each one of us will achieve our true purpose in life.

FAMILY PRAYER

The best prayers are those which come from the heart. There are times when we find it difficult to pray and it is then that we need the help of prayers we have learned "by heart".

MORNING PRAYER

O my God, you love me,
you're with me night and day.
I want to love you always
in all I do and say.
I'll try to please you, Father.
Bless me through the day. Amen.

NIGHT PRAYER

God our Father, I come to say
thank you for your love today.
Thank you for my family
and all the friends you give to me.
Guard me in the dark of night
And in the morning send your light.
Amen.

water, white garment, candle, oil

Baptismal Font

We pretended to be at a baptism ceremony. Through role play we learnt about all the symbols of baptism.

TO DO

Take a look at the baptismal font in your church. They come in different shapes and sizes.

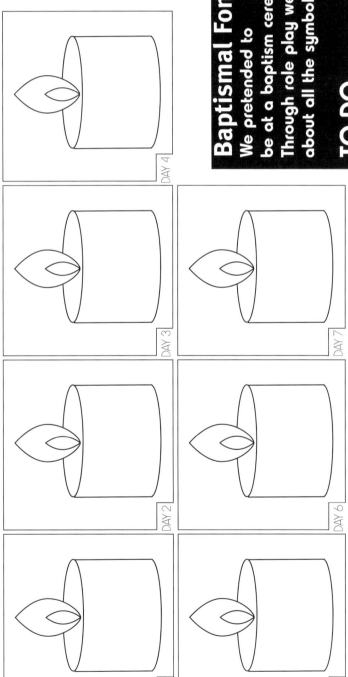

DAY 1

DAY 2

DAY 3

DAY 4

DAY 5

DAY 6

DAY 7

Colour or write in the candle when you have shown yourself to be a Christian this week.

This sheet has been completed by ....

© Redemptorist Publications, Alphonsus House, Chawton, Hants GU34 3HQ. To be used solely as part of FaithMap Programme.

1st Sunday of Lent

Family Sheet
To do at home with your family

For parents: Weekly Thought

The promise of salvation enters the world through one man's obedience: Jesus of Nazareth. Like God in the Garden of Eden, he comes to look for those who have hidden themselves from God. "I have come to seek out and to save the lost." Today we talked about the desert, the wilderness where Jesus went to be alone to listen to God. As the season of Lent begins, we can make time to look where we are in our lives and discover God's presence anew.

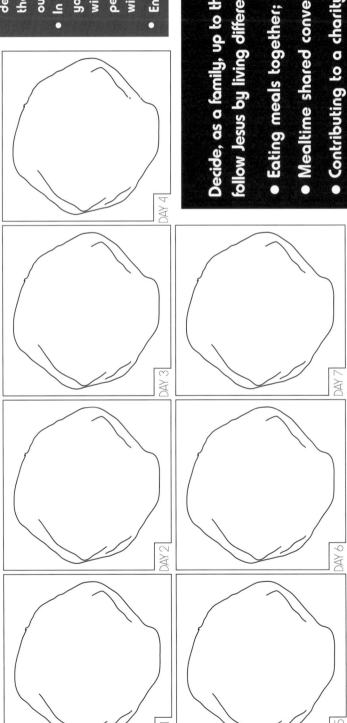

DAY 1

DAY 2

DAY 3

DAY 4

DAY 5

DAY 6

DAY 7

Colour or write in the boulder when you thought about how to help other people each day.

This sheet has been completed by ....

FAMILY PRAYER

- If you are praying with your family, light a candle — Jesus is the light of the world.
- Sit or kneel quietly and listen to the quietness, thinking of the solitude of the desert in today's Gospel. Then listen to the sounds and noises in the room and outside the room.
- In turn, thank God or pray for the sounds you can hear (e.g. thank you, God, for the wind blowing outside. We pray for all the people who are driving today that God will keep them safe on their journeys).
- End with the Lord's Prayer.

Decide, as a family, up to three ways in which you will try to follow Jesus by living differently during Lent, for example:

- Eating meals together;
- Mealtime shared conversations;
- Contributing to a charity;
- Getting in touch with an elderly friend or relation;
- Praying together, at mealtimes, bedtime, morning times.

© Redemptorist Publications, Alphonsus House, Chawton, Hants GU34 3HQ. To be used solely as part of FaithMap Programme.

2nd Sunday of Lent

Family Sheet

To do at home with your family

For parents: Weekly Thought

Jesus changed paths when he left Nazareth to work as a wandering prophet. The story of the transfiguration in today's Gospel tells how Jesus was able to make the journey to Jerusalem in the declared love of the Father. Jesus is the one who is to suffer but he is named and owned by the Father. We are all directed to listen to him. We are helped to make difficult decisions knowing that we are loved and supported.

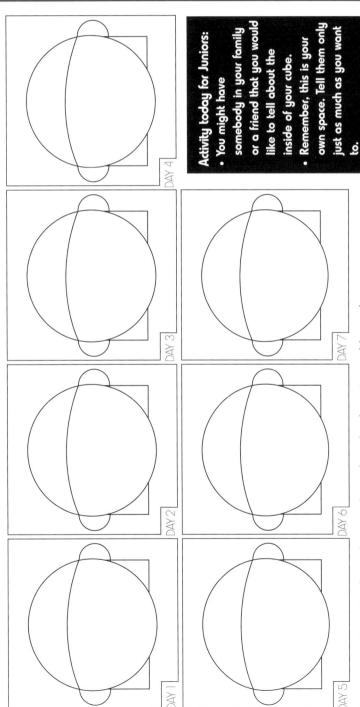

DAY 1

DAY 2

DAY 3

DAY 4

DAY 5

DAY 6

DAY 7

Activity today for Juniors:
- You might have somebody in your family or a friend that you would like to tell about the inside of your cube.
- Remember, this is your own space. Tell them only just as much as you want to.
- Find some time this week to talk to God about the 6 secret faces of your cube.

Colour or write in the face when you have thought about Jesus this week.

This sheet has been completed by ....

© Redemptorist Publications, Alphonsus House, Chawton, Hants GU34 3HQ. To be used solely as part of FaithMap Programme.

FAMILY PRAYER

Psalm 139:1-6
The Hound of Heaven

Lord, you have examined me and you know me.

You know everything I do; from far away you understand all my thoughts.

Response: Lord, you know all that we do.

You see me, whether I am working or resting. You know all my actions. Even before I speak, you already know what I will say.

Response: Lord, you know all that we do.

You are all around me on every side; you protect me with your power.

Your knowledge of me is too deep; it is beyond my understanding.

Response: Lord, you know all that we do. Amen.

Share the praying of this prayer around the family. Light a candle if appropriate.

3rd Sunday of Lent

Family Sheet

To do at home with your family

For parents: Weekly Thought

The woman at the well came to understand Jesus first as a Jew; then as a prophet; then as the Messiah; then as the Saviour of the world. She is one of the first witnesses who leads others to Jesus. Her past does not hinder her from being a messenger of good news. She has a story to tell. Have we?

FAMILY PRAYER

Sometimes it's hard to feel God loving us. But if you sit quietly, if you wait, you'll feel it come. Here are some things you can do this week:

● Ask mummy or daddy to light a candle, and then sit very quietly together for a minute and ask God to fill up your hearts with his love. Can you feel it coming?

● Lie quietly in bed, as still as you possibly can. You could say a simple prayer, like "Come, Lord Jesus," very slowly. Feel your body relax and get all warm and peaceful. Can you feel God there too?

● God's love is there all the time, but we just don't notice it. Practise noticing God loving you every day.
If you start looking for it, you'll be surprised where you feel God's love! Try to spot God loving you every day.

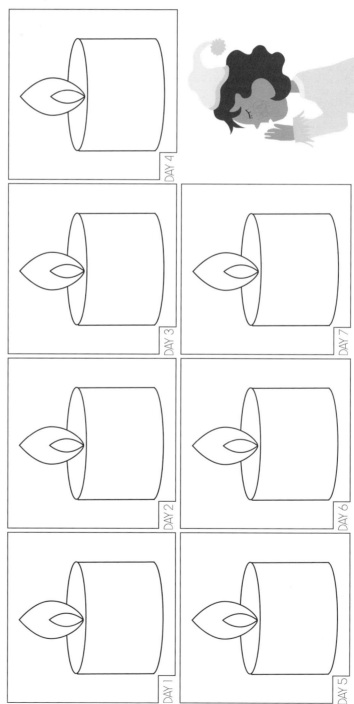

DAY 1

DAY 2

DAY 3

DAY 4

DAY 5

DAY 6

DAY 7

Colour or write in the candle when you have spotted God's love that day.

This sheet has been completed by ....

© Redemptorist Publications, Alphonsus House, Chawton, Hants GU34 3HQ. To be used solely as part of FaithMap Programme.

4th Sunday of Lent

Family Sheet
To do at home with your family

For parents: Weekly Thought

In our baptism we have been chosen to point to Jesus by the witness of our Christian lives. We allow God to work in us. In today's Gospel we hear how a blind man came to see the light, both physically and spiritually. The blind man grows in insight and identifies Jesus as a prophet. He will display the work of God and point to who Jesus really is. Today the children explored the gift of sight and the importance of taking time to look; how others see things differently; and how to look beyond face value.

DAY 1

DAY 2

DAY 3

DAY 4

DAY 5

DAY 6

DAY 7

Colour or write in the flower each day as you see something good or beautiful and when you do something good for someone else.

This sheet has been completed by ....

FAMILY PRAYER

Lord Jesus, help us see your light in the world, and help us to make it burn brighter. Amen.

Look out for God's light and help it burn a bit brighter! Look for things that are beautiful and good and kind. Every time we make something more beautiful, or do something kind, God's light burns a bit brighter.

Word search on "Light". Can you find the following words forwards, backwards, across and down?

D	I	T	L	N	U	S	H
F	S	I	G	H	T	H	C
D	I	S	C	O	V	E	R
H	C	T	A	M	S	R	O
N	B	F	N	M	E	I	T
O	L	I	D	F	E	F	O
O	U	N	L	I	G	H	T
M	B	D	E	P	M	A	L

MATCH,
LIGHT,
CANDLE,
TORCH,
LAMP,
BULB, SEE,
DISCOVER,
FIND, FIRE,
SUN, MOON,
SIGHT.

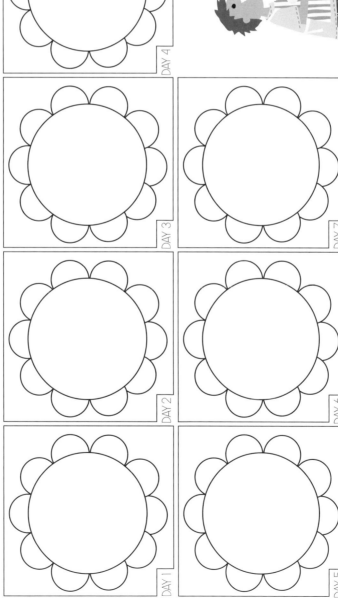

5th Sunday of Lent

Family Sheet

To do at home with your family

For parents: Weekly Thought

Today we talked about being truly alive. We described life and death through a flower: a bud, a full bloom, a dried flower, a dead bloom. The Gospel story of Lazarus shows us that Jesus is very special, sent from God. He trusts God. When we really trust God we become like the flower in bloom, fully alive. We can be "dead" in the midst of life – hoping for a word and a community that will put us together again. The Gospel challenges us to take responsibility for our brothers and sisters, who, like Lazarus, are loved by Jesus.

HEALING

Don't forget to talk to God every day. Think of something to tell God, or something to ask God, or something to say thank you for, every day.

• Tell God the most important thing that happened: was it something good or something bad?

• Ask God to mend the bad things.

• Thank God for the good things.

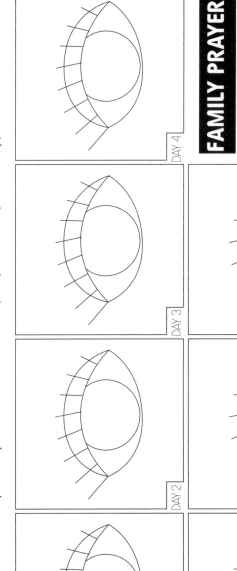

FAMILY PRAYER

Lord Jesus, thank you for my fingers and toes, my eyes and my nose, for making the world a beautiful place! Amen.

DAY 1

DAY 2

DAY 3

DAY 4

DAY 5

DAY 6

DAY 7

Colour in the eye when you have noticed someone that needs your help this week.

This sheet has been completed by...

© Redemptorist Publications, Alphonsus House, Chawton, Hants GU34 3HQ. To be used solely as part of FaithMap Programme.

Passion Sunday (Palm Sunday)

Family Sheet

To do at home with your family

For parents: Weekly Thought

The cross of Jesus stands at the centre of the Christian story as a sign of the lengths love will go to in its passion for others. The love of one who "did not cling to his equality with God but emptied himself" to become as we all are, to show that, in spite of our sins and stupidities, God loves us.

Today we explored the themes of triumph and disaster and the presence and support of God in both.

HEALING

Let's try to do something for God every day. Let's remember what Jesus did for us, dying to save us, and let's say thank you by doing what God wants us to do too.

● Can you find something God would like you to do for other people? Maybe you could help someone at home, or maybe you could be specially kind to someone sad.

● Can you find something God would like you to do for yourself? Maybe you could try to be specially happy: it's sad thinking of Jesus dying. But we know a secret the soldiers didn't know. We can be happy, waiting for Jesus to come back to life.

● Can you find something God wants you to do for himself? Maybe you could give him a special thank you for sending Jesus to save us.

Fill out your calendar every day: did you do something good for God today?

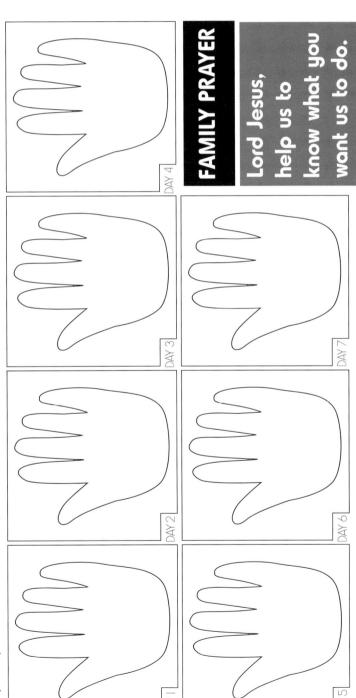

DAY 1

DAY 2

DAY 3

DAY 4

DAY 5

DAY 6

DAY 7

Colour or write in the hand when you have shown yourself to be a Christian, a follower of Jesus, this week.

This sheet has been completed by ....

FAMILY PRAYER

Lord Jesus, help us to know what you want us to do. Help us to be good and kind. Amen.

© Redemptorist Publications, Alphonsus House, Chawton, Hants GU34 3HQ. To be used solely as part of FaithMap Programme.

Easter Sunday

Family Sheet

To do at home with your family

For parents: Weekly Thought

We believe that God's graciousness will be extended to ourselves; that we will participate in Jesus' resurrection on the last day. Today the challenge of Easter is to understand the history of human suffering in the light of Jesus' resurrection. This means that we have to take God's part in protesting against the violence and suffering that are accepted so readily as inevitable.

Today we explored the theme of new life – through Jesus' rising from the dead. We looked at springtime and the symbols of Easter. We planted seeds and talked of eggs as symbols of new life. Jesus' words "I am the resurrection and the life" mean that God's work continues today.

FAMILY PRAYER

Lord Jesus, thank you for keeping your promises, thank you for making the world come alive. Amen.

- Jesus promises to make us feel alive for ever. What makes you feel alive?

- Do you feel alive when you're happy? What makes you feel happy?

- How about when you're sad or scared? What makes you feel sad or scared?

- Fill out your calendar every day: did you feel happy, did you feel really alive today?

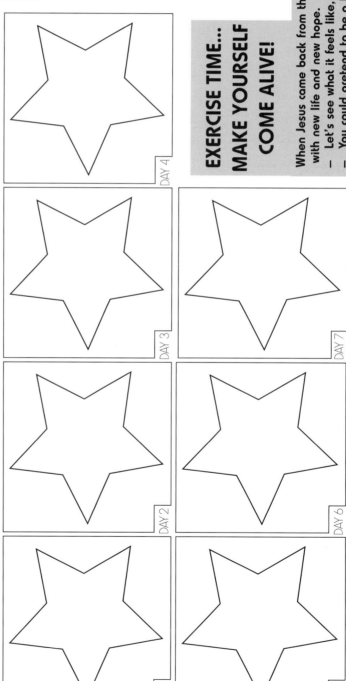

DAY 4

DAY 3

DAY 2

DAY 1

DAY 7

DAY 6

DAY 5

Colour or write in the star each day when you felt really happy and alive.

EXERCISE TIME... MAKE YOURSELF COME ALIVE!

When Jesus came back from the dead, he changed the world for ever, filled it with new life and new hope.

- Let's see what it feels like, coming back to life.
- You could pretend to be a little seed in the ground, waiting in the dark for the winter to end. You could sit very still, being like that seed.
- Now, slowly, slowly, start to grow. First your roots, your legs and your toes stretch and grow. Then the leaves grow, your arms and your fingers stretch up to the sun. Last of all, your face stretches up like a flower.
- Stretch as far as you possibly can. Stand on tiptoe! Try to reach the sky!
- Jump up at the sky.
- Feel how alive you are.

This sheet has been completed by ....

© Redemptorist Publications, Alphonsus House, Chawton, Hants GU34 3HQ. To be used solely as part of FaithMap Programme.

2nd Sunday of Easter

Family Sheet

To do at home with your family

For parents: Weekly Thought

In today's Gospel John builds a bridge between those who saw Jesus and those who do not: "Happy are those who have not seen and yet believe." That blessing is directed at us: we who believe in Jesus without seeing him. Seeing did not necessarily lead to believing; but the apostles saw and believed and shared with us their Christian faith. It is a great chain of faith which is linked to the person of Jesus himself.

FAMILY PRAYER

Dear Jesus, we do not see you, but we know that you are here with us. You are always with us: during meals, when we work, when we watch TV, during playtime, when we sleep and when we go out together. We are glad that you like to be with us. Help us to see you more and more in our home and with our family so that we can be like Jesus' disciples who were always happy to see him. Amen.

LOOK... SEE... UNDERSTAND

2 objectives for the week

1. Look out for unexpected things that happen which are nice surprises for you. When you discover one, say thank you to God for it.

2. The disciples like Thomas were able to see God with their own eyes. During the week, try to find and see God in the world around you.

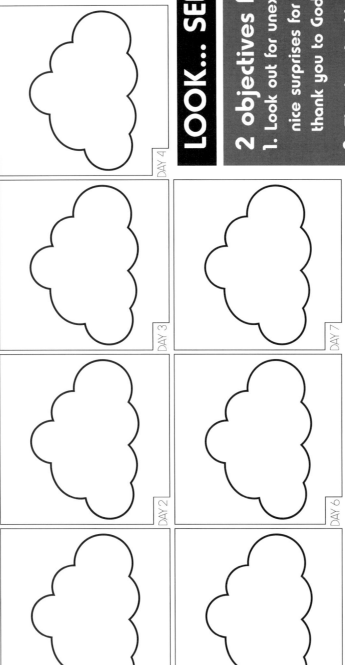

DAY 1

DAY 2

DAY 3

DAY 4

DAY 5

DAY 6

DAY 7

Colour in the clouds when you have thought about God each day.

This sheet has been completed by _____

© Redemptorist Publications, Alphonsus House, Chawton, Hants GU34 3HQ. To be used solely as part of FaithMap Programme.

3rd Sunday of Easter

Family Sheet

To do at home with your family

For parents: Weekly Thought

We gather to celebrate the Eucharist each week, to listen to the word of God and break bread together. As with the disciples in today's Gospel, Jesus comes among us not as a stranger; rather, he comes to give us new hope to face the future with faith in him. Through talking, walking, eating and sharing together, through being generous and unselfish, the disciples start to see Jesus with them and they discover that God never leaves them. May we, too, come to that realisation.

FAMILY PRAYER

Dear Jesus, thank you for being with us all the time, even when we forget that you are there. You are always with us, especially when we talk and play together, when we eat and share together. Help us to remember that you never leave us. Teach us to be generous and unselfish like you were. Amen.

Two objectives for the week

1. Try to share something of yours, e.g. a toy, book or game with someone you find it difficult to be generous with.

2. Stop at times during the week and remember that Jesus is right beside you, even though you cannot see or touch him. Thank him for being always with you.

DAY 1 · *Jesus is beside you*
DAY 2 · *Jesus is beside you*
DAY 3 · *Jesus is beside you*
DAY 4 · *Jesus is beside you*
DAY 5 · *Jesus is beside you*
DAY 6 · *Jesus is beside you*
DAY 7 · *Jesus is beside you*

Colour or write in the book when you feel that Jesus is beside you this week.

This sheet has been completed by ....

© Redemptorist Publications, Alphonsus House, Chawton, Hants GU34 3HQ. To be used solely as part of FaithMap Programme.

4th Sunday of Easter

Family Sheet

To do at home with your family

For parents: Weekly Thought

Today is "Good Shepherd" Sunday. The children learnt of the work of shepherds – feeding and guarding their animals; bringing them in at night so they will sleep safely. The Gospel gives us an image of Jesus as someone who hopes that people will come to recognise his voice. He addresses who they are and where they are; he leads them without disguise and without pretence. His is the voice of the one who loves us with an everlasting love – the shepherd who is willing to die for his sheep.

FAMILY PRAYER

Dear Jesus, thank you for promising to be with us and for saying that you will always look after us like a good shepherd looks after his flock. Please stay always with our family and friends. Help us to follow you and to become more like you every day. Amen.

Jesus is like a good shepherd

Shepherds are people who look after animals like sheep, goats and cows. Early in the morning, the shepherd leads the animals out of the farm and brings them to find grass to eat and water to drink. The shepherd keeps watch too at all times to see that all the animals are safe. If any wander away and get lost, the shepherd looks for them until they are found. And at the end of the day, the shepherd brings all the animals home so that they can sleep safely during the night. Jesus says he looks after us like a good shepherd who cares for his own animals.

DAY 1 · DAY 2 · DAY 3 · DAY 4 · DAY 5 · DAY 6 · DAY 7

Colour or write in the sheep when you thought about how to help other people each day.

This sheet has been completed by ....

© Redemptorist Publications, Alphonsus House, Chawton, Hants GU34 3HQ. To be used solely as part of FaithMap Programme.

5th Sunday of Easter

Family Sheet

To do at home with your family

For parents: Weekly Thought

Today we learnt that Jesus will prepare a place for each one of us in his Father's house. There is room for everyone in God's kingdom, for men, women and children; for people of all colours and nationalities. Jesus trusts his followers down the ages to face the confusion and complexity of the world. Jesus as the Way, the Truth and the Life wants us to put our faith to work.

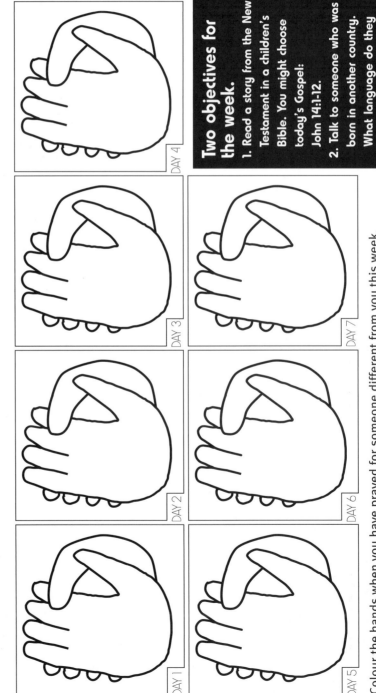

DAY 1

DAY 2

DAY 3

DAY 4

DAY 5

DAY 6

DAY 7

Two objectives for the week.
1. Read a story from the New Testament in a children's Bible. You might choose today's Gospel: John 14:1-12.
2. Talk to someone who was born in another country. What language do they speak at home? What type of food do they eat? Do they dress in a special way?

Colour the hands when you have prayed for someone different from you this week.

This sheet has been completed by ....

© Redemptorist Publications, Alphonsus House, Chawton, Hants GU34 3HQ. To be used solely as part of FaithMap Programme.

FAMILY PRAYER

Dear Jesus, we thank you for making our world so full of people of different colours, ages and cultures. You have invited us all to live together as friends here on earth, so that one day we can be together again in heaven in God's house. Teach us to love everyone, especially those who are different from us. Amen.

Family Sheet

To do at home with your family

For parents: Weekly Thought

You are loved as a child is loved. It goes beyond what you do and is all about who you are, a child of the Father with Jesus as your brother. We have been talking about the Gospel reading in which Jesus was having his last meal with his best friends. He told them not to worry if anything happened to him, he would always be with those he loved. It is easy sometimes to forget that we are loved and forget those who love us. Sometimes we get so busy or worried or upset that we only think about ourselves. But the love of Jesus and the love of the Father have been brought to us by the Holy Spirit and so, whatever happens, we can always hope that this love will eventually bring us to peace and joy. And that's good news, isn't it?

DAY 4

DAY 3

DAY 7

DAY 2

DAY 6

DAY 1

DAY 5

Colour or write in the hand when you have shown yourself to be a Christian this week.

This sheet has been completed by ....

FAMILY PRAYER

Dear Jesus, we have heard how you promised always to be with those you love. Help us to remember this promise especially when things in life make us sad, worried or upset. Amen.

To do at home

Have a large sheet of paper with a coloured circle in the centre.

Each day one of the family draws around their hand, colours in the outline, cuts it out and pastes it around the coloured circle. A FLOWER of HOPE will be created by the end of the week.

© Redemptorist Publications, Alphonsus House, Chawton, Hants GU34 3HQ. To be used solely as part of FaithMap Programme.

The Ascension of the Lord

Family Sheet

To do at home with your family

For parents: Weekly Thought

When your child was born, you gave him/her a name and welcomed him/her into your family. When you asked for baptism, you were asking God for the gift of eternal life for your child and committing yourself to bringing him/her up to know God, to follow Jesus and to grow in faith. He/she was also welcomed into the worldwide family of the Church and joined over a billion people who have also heard the Good News and seek to live as Christians. Whatever their race, colour or culture, they are all our brothers and sisters in Christ. This is an awe-inspiring thought!

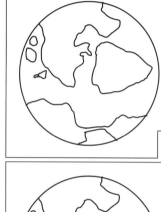

DAY 1

DAY 2

DAY 3

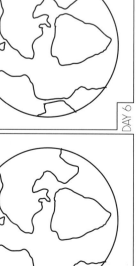

DAY 4

DAY 5

DAY 6

DAY 7

Colour in a picture of the world each day. As you do, think about your brother and sister Christians in a different country each day.

This sheet has been completed by ....

FAMILY PRAYER

Lord God, we thank you for the gift of our baptism and for making us your children. We ask you to bless your daughter N... your son N... (name each person). Keep us faithful to your teaching and keep us close to you. Amen.

**ASCENSION THURSDAY is 40 days after Easter but as it is an important feast we sometimes celebrate it on a Sunday. When the disciples went back to Jerusalem to prepare for their mission, they spent time in prayer, waiting for the coming of the Holy Spirit.
You might like to do the same. Spend a short time each day. Ask your parent or carer to light a candle for you and say a short prayer, perhaps like this traditional one:**

**"Come, Holy Spirit, fill the hearts of your faithful.
Kindle in them the fire of your love.
Send forth your Spirit and we shall be created
And you will renew the face of the earth."**

Family Sheet

To do at home with your family

For parents: Weekly Thought

No life on earth goes on for ever. Have I faced and understood that fact and tried to make sense of it? As we travel towards Pentecost next Sunday we have been thinking about what life is really all about. Life has so many different parts and, to some, life can be so different from what they want or expect. Some people are successful and happy; others seem to suffer very much and some people can make quite a mess of life. But we know that life is about travelling to God's love. We all take different ways to that love, but Jesus has told us that knowing the Father and knowing Jesus is the life that matters and that life will go on happy in God's love for ever.

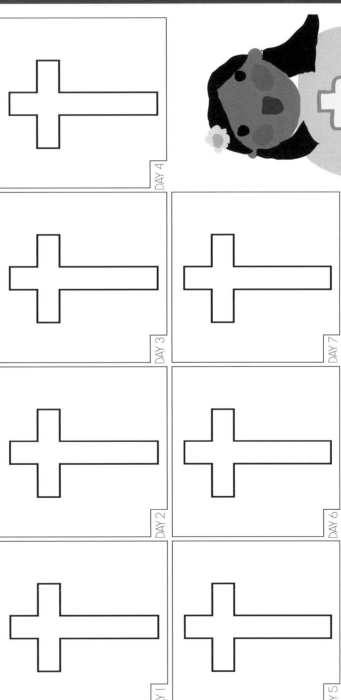

DAY 1

DAY 2

DAY 3

DAY 4

DAY 5

DAY 6

DAY 7

Fill a cross with flowers when you pray for someone you love who has died, and is now with Jesus in heaven. Your family will help you.

This sheet has been completed by ....

© Redemptorist Publications, Alphonsus House, Chawton, Hants GU34 3HQ. To be used solely as part of FaithMap Programme.

FAMILY PRAYER

Dear Jesus, you lived and died and know what life is like. You suffered and were hated so you know life can be difficult. You met and talked to people who were sinners so you know people can go very wrong. But you told your friends to tell everyone that you loved them and you brought them the Father's love. You told us, through your friends, that love waits for us. Help us to remember that future love as we live our lives and grow up and grow old.
Amen.

Pentecost Sunday

Family Sheet
To do at home with your family

For parents: Weekly Thought

Today we heard the Gospel tell of how Jesus kept his promise not to leave his friends. We heard how he rose from the dead to show his friends that death was not the end of everything and that life after death in the love of the Father was possible. We heard that Jesus wanted everyone to know this wonderful news and gave the Holy Spirit to his friends so that they would be brave enough to go out and tell the Good News to all the people they could.

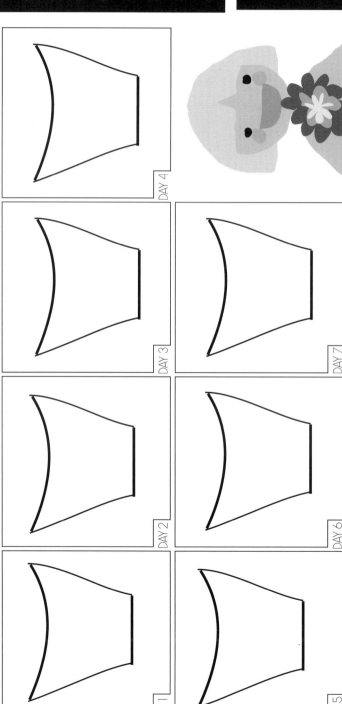

DAY 1

DAY 2

DAY 3

DAY 4

DAY 5

DAY 6

DAY 7

Draw a seed in each pot of compost. When you have shown care for someone each day draw in some droplets of rain over the pot.

This sheet has been completed by..

FAMILY PRAYER

Dear Father in heaven, we all live such different lives here on earth. Help us to remember that although our lives on earth are very important, one day they will end. Then by the power of Jesus and through the Holy Spirit, we can all be happy together in heaven with you. Thank you for such good news to carry through our lives. Amen.

At home

When you plant your seed you can watch it grow if you care for it properly. Remember to water it regularly and keep it warm.

© Redemptorist Publications, Alphonsus House, Chawton, Hants GU34 3HQ. To be used solely as part of FaithMap Programme.

2nd Sunday in Ordinary Time

The 2nd Sunday of Epiphany

Family Sheet

To do at home with your family

For parents: Weekly Thought

In the Gospel, John the Baptist points to Jesus as the Saviour. The gifts of the Holy Spirit have been given to us all at our baptism, signifying hope and love as we live out our Christian lives.

FOR CHRISTIAN UNITY

"May they be one, so that the world will believe that you sent me... and that you love them as you love me." John 17:21-23

FAMILY PRAYER

Dear Jesus, one word can bring encouragement to another. Please help me to make and take every chance to offer that word to others. Thank you for loving me and giving me your strength. Amen.

To do:

Search for words from today's Gospel, up, down, and across

B	O	L	I	F	E	N
A	J	E	S	U	S	W
P	O	D	P	Q	T	A
T	R	D	I	E	G	A
I	D	O	R	P	S	E
S	A	V	I	O	U	R
E	N	E	T	H	J	K

HOPE   JORDAN

DOVE   SPIRIT

WATER   BAPTISE

LIFE   JESUS

SAVIOUR

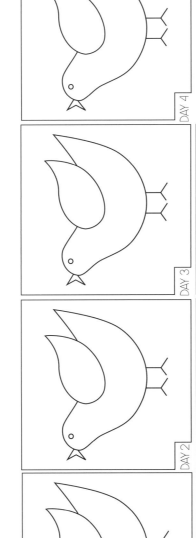

DAY 1   DAY 2   DAY 3   DAY 4

DAY 5   DAY 6   DAY 7

Colour or write in the dove when you have asked the Holy Spirit for help and guidance.

This sheet has been completed by ....

© Redemptorist Publications, Alphonsus House, Chawton, Hants GU34 3HQ. To be used solely as part of FaithMap Programme.

Family Sheet

To do at home with your family

For parents: Weekly Thought

Today we talked about being followers of Jesus. We need to look to the Gospel for the Good News it contains. The light of Christ will come into our lives, the more familiar we become with the message of the Gospel. Then we will see how much God cares for us. We will see where we are going and see what God is calling us to be.

FAMILY PRAYER

Dear Lord, let us pray for our teachers in school. Give them wisdom and enthusiasm to prepare our lessons so that each child will feel good about learning in school.

Let us pray for our priests, deacons and catechists as they teach the message of the Gospel. May we know and love Jesus more and more.

Let us pray for parents: Give them patience and time to talk to their children, to listen to their children and show by their example how to live like Jesus.

Thank you for the gift of knowledge. May we use our education to make our world a better place in which to live. Amen.

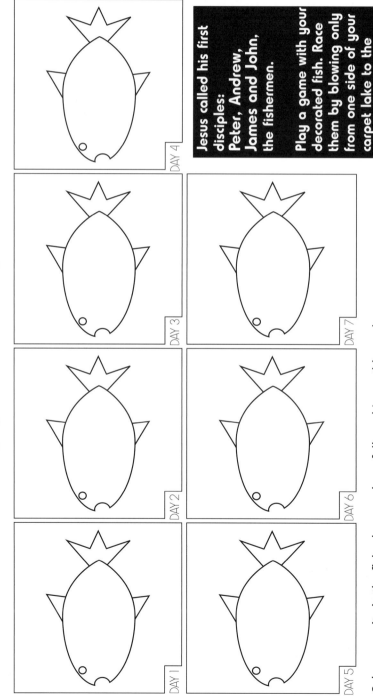

Jesus called his first disciples: Peter, Andrew, James and John, the fishermen.

Play a game with your decorated fish. Race them by blowing only from one side of your carpet lake to the other.

Show a younger brother or sister how to make a fish like yours.

Colour or write in the fish when you have followed Jesus this week.

This sheet has been completed by ....

© Redemptorist Publications, Alphonsus House, Chawton, Hants GU34 3HQ. To be used solely as part of FaithMap Programme.

Family Sheet

To do at home with your family

For parents: Weekly Thought

In today's Gospel from the "Sermon on the Mount", we listened to the heart of Jesus' message. Jesus Christ came to show us how we find true happiness. He promises us the kingdom of heaven if we follow his way and hold on to his values. Those who belong to his kingdom are those who allow God to reign in their lives, those who place the Gospel above all other values.

FAMILY PRAYER

Dear Jesus, you cured sick people; you cared for those who were poor and wept with those who were sad. You forgave sinners and taught them to forgive each other. You loved everyone and showed us how to be kind. You took children into your arms and blessed them. Thank you for all your blessings. Amen.

BEATITUDE

Another word for beatitude is "blessing". The eight points of the Maltese Cross represent the blessings that Jesus tells us about in the Sermon on the Mount.

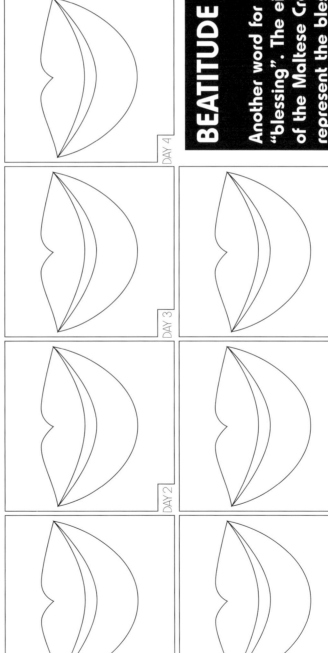

DAY 1

DAY 2

DAY 3

DAY 4

DAY 5

DAY 6

DAY 7

Colour in the smiles when you have made someone smile each day.

This sheet has been completed by ....

© Redemptorist Publications, Alphonsus House, Chawton, Hants GU34 3HQ. To be used solely as part of FaithMap Programme.

Family Sheet

To do at home with your family

For parents: Weekly Thought

In today's Gospel, Jesus says, "You are the salt of the earth. You are the light of the world." We, as baptised Christians, are like lamps with the brightness of God's love and goodness shining out to the world. Our words and actions will demonstrate the power of God in our lives. When we are close to Christ we are better able to shed light on the problems of our world.

DAY 1

DAY 2

DAY 3

DAY 4

DAY 5

DAY 6

DAY 7

Draw in a candle when you have felt shiny this week.

This sheet has been completed by ....

FAMILY PRAYER

Dear Lord, we ask you for the strength and power we need to bring light to the world. Inspire all Christians with the light of your Holy Spirit to preach the Gospel throughout the world. Show us how we can begin, by reading the scriptures in our own home. Let us pray for the men and women of the Salvation Army and all those who work with the homeless and hungry. May their hard work bring comfort. Thank you, Lord, for giving us _____ and _____ as examples of people doing good work. Glory be to the Father and to the Son and to the Holy Spirit. Amen.

TO DO: A coded message

Jesus gives us two special messages today. Break the code by starting with "Y", then use every 2nd letter.

1. "YGOSU BATROE ZTOHGE SLCIDGWHRT POIF FTNHAE MWFOTRYLXD."

2. "YAODU PAZRYE FTUHXE BSCAHLKT ROTF UTWHDE ZEBAGRJTMH."

© Redemptorist Publications, Alphonsus House, Chawton, Hants GU34 3HQ. To be used solely as part of FaithMap Programme.

Family Sheet

To do at home with your family

For parents: Weekly Thought

Jesus did not come to abolish the law, but to reach right into the heart of the law and reveal the truth within it: that our perfect living was to be a reflection of God's love for us, freely given, freely accepted. Jesus showed that the fulfilment of the law lay not in observance, but in love: as St Augustine was to say at a later date, "Love, and do as you will." Over the next two weeks the juniors will think about the difference between the letter of the law and the spirit of the law. The young ones will focus on how rules help us to be good.

FAMILY PRAYER

Jesus, we have rules to help us live together happily. Help us to understand them and to keep them in a way which is helpful to each other. Amen.

(You might like to choose a family rule to discuss each day before saying this prayer together.)

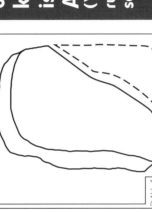

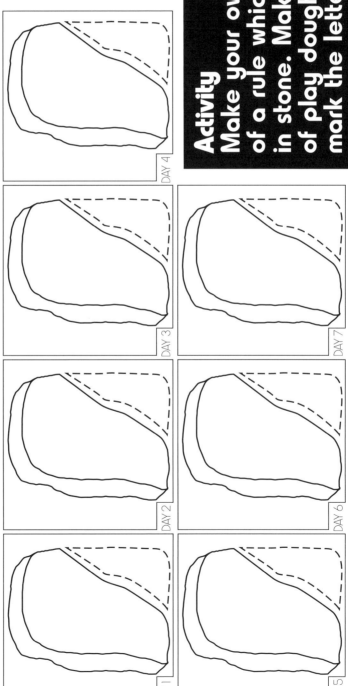

Activity

Make your own tablet of stone. Think of a rule which you would like writing in stone. Make a tablet of stone out of play dough or clay and scratch or mark the letters onto the surface. Leave to harden and dry out, somewhere warm.

The tablets of stone have been broken; you can mend them again by keeping the rules. Each day you keep a rule, mend one of the tablets by joining the dots to make the stone tablet whole again.

This sheet has been completed by ....

© Redemptorist Publications, Alphonsus House, Chawton, Hants GU34 3HQ. To be used solely as part of FaithMap Programme.

Family Sheet

To do at home with your family

For parents: Weekly Thought

The law of love can be a terrifying proposition: without the benchmark of virtue which a set of rules and regulations affords us, how can we ever be confident that we have done enough – that we are good enough. When can we say that we have loved enough? We can only be sure that God loves us unconditionally and sent his Son to lead us on the path of love.

FAMILY PRAYER

Jesus, we want to be perfect like you, but sometimes it is very hard. Help us to love each other so much that it is easy to be perfect. Amen.

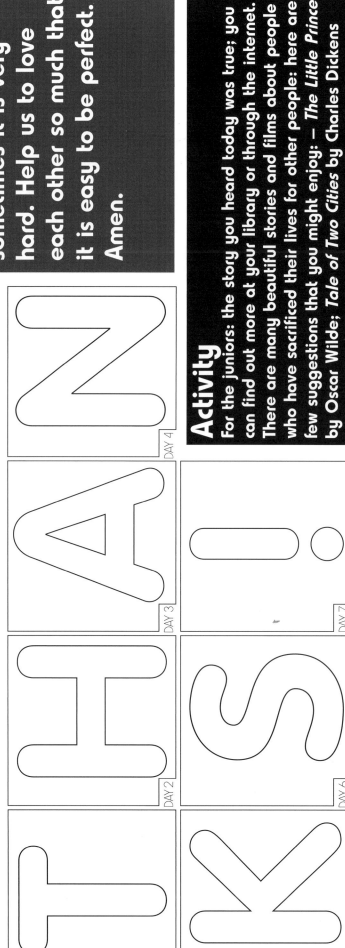

DAY 1 — T
DAY 2 — H
DAY 3 — A
DAY 4 — N
DAY 5 — K
DAY 6 — S
DAY 7 — !

Colour in a letter each day that you do something extra for your mum or dad, or the person who looks after you.

This sheet has been completed by ....

Activity

For the juniors: the story you heard today was true; you can find out more at your library or through the internet. There are many beautiful stories and films about people who have sacrificed their lives for other people: here are a few suggestions that you might enjoy: – *The Little Prince* by Oscar Wilde; *Tale of Two Cities* by Charles Dickens (also a film); *The Return of Martin Guerre* by Natalie Davis (made into a film called *Sommersby*); *Les Miserables* by Victor Hugo (a very long book – but it has been made into a wonderful musical).

© Redemptorist Publications, Alphonsus House, Chawton, Hants GU34 3HQ. To be used solely as part of FaithMap Programme.

Family Sheet

To do at home with your family

For parents: Weekly Thought

This is the full version of the serenity prayer around which many of this week's activities are based:

God, grant me the serenity to accept the things I cannot change, courage to change the things I can, and the wisdom to know the difference: living one day at a time, enjoying one moment at a time, accepting hardship as the pathway to peace: taking, as he did, this sinful world as it is, not as I would have it: trusting that he will make all things right if I surrender to his will; that I may be reasonably happy in this life, and supremely happy with him for ever in the next. Amen.

FAMILY PRAYER

God, grant me the serenity to accept the things I cannot change, the courage to change the things that I can, and the wisdom to know the difference. Amen.

Pack up your troubles in your old kitbag and smile, smile, smile.
While you've got Jesus there's no need to lag,
smile, boys, that's the style.
What's the use of worrying?
It never was worthwhile, so,
pack up your troubles in your old kitbag
and smile, smile, smile.

Activity

This song is based on one which was sung by the soldiers going to war nearly a hundred years ago. The 3rd line has been changed: maybe you can think of something better. Try changing the 5th line: instead of boys, try using girls, mum, dad etc. Enjoy singing!

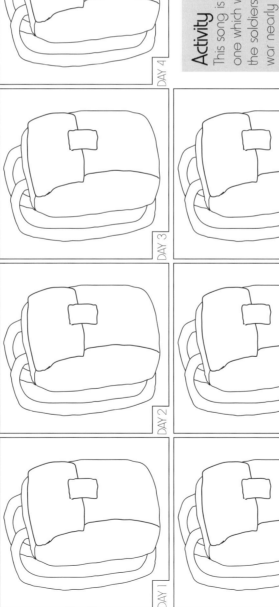

DAY 1 · DAY 2 · DAY 3 · DAY 4 · DAY 5 · DAY 6 · DAY 7

In the kitbag write or draw something each day which is worrying you, or ask your mum or dad to do it for you. Chat about your worry then colour it over, pack it up, and smile!

This sheet has been completed by ....

© Redemptorist Publications, Alphonsus House, Chawton, Hants GU34 3HQ. To be used solely as part of FaithMap Programme.

Family Sheet

To do at home with your family

For parents: Weekly Thought

The teaching of the Sermon on the Mount constitutes the law of the kingdom of heaven. Those who follow this law, who not only listen to Jesus' words but obey them, will build their life on a secure foundation. We might be involved in all sorts of religious activities, but if they are not based on the sure foundation of the word of God we will be fooling ourselves. It is the word that shows us the way to our Father in heaven.

FAMILY PRAYER

Dear Jesus, thank you for showing us the way to love through your words in the Bible. Help us to listen to them and do what they say. Help us to love and forgive our family and friends as you do. Help us all to live in God's love today. Amen.

FOUNDATIONS –

If possible, have a look at the foundations of your own home. If it is easy, ask your parents or carers if you can see under the floorboards, or, if you have one, go down into the cellar to see how the house is built. Ask the caretaker or a teacher if they can show you the foundations at school. Look out for any houses being built nearby and look at the foundations. (Always observe the No Entry signs around a building site.)

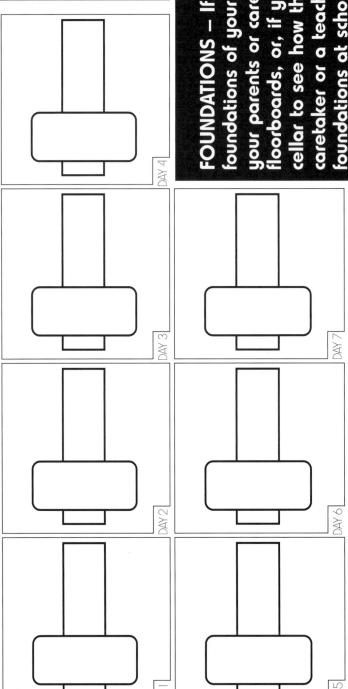

DAY 1 · DAY 2 · DAY 3 · DAY 4 · DAY 5 · DAY 6 · DAY 7

Colour in a mallet when you have helped to build God's kingdom this week.

This sheet has been completed by ....

© Redemptorist Publications, Alphonsus House, Chawton, Hants GU34 3HQ. To be used solely as part of FaithMap Programme.

Family Sheet

To do at home with your family

For parents: Weekly Thought

Compassion is a beautiful quality and one we hope our children will develop. Family life offers many opportunities to show love and compassion towards each other. Spending time listening to our children encourages them to listen to others. Offering reassurance when they are troubled soothes their fears but also gives them the experience of being loved which will, in turn, help them to become more loving.

FAMILY PRAYER

Grace before a meal

Grace before a meal
(This is sung to the tune of "Amazing Grace")

Oh, thank you, Lord
for all our food;
you call, you guide, you feed.
Help us to share your love and care, with
those who are in need. Amen.

A SPECIAL MEAL

Ask the person who cooks the meals in your house if you can help them to prepare a special meal for the family. You could:

- Choose a menu together – you might like to write it out and decorate it.
- Decorate the table in some way to make it a special occasion.
- Write out formal invitations for the family, or even invite a friend.
- At Passover, the Jews always leave a spare seat during the meal for the prophet Elijah.
- Saying a grace before a meal reminds us that Jesus is very near.

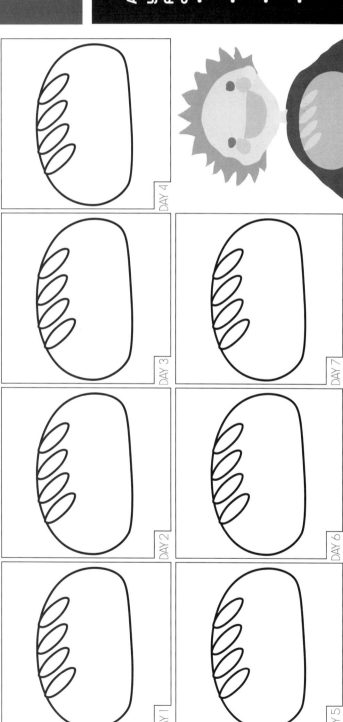

DAY 1 · DAY 2 · DAY 3 · DAY 4 · DAY 5 · DAY 6 · DAY 7

On the loaf of bread each day, write the names of the people that you shared your main meal with, on that particular day.

This sheet has been completed by ....

© Redemptorist Publications, Alphonsus House, Chawton, Hants GU34 3HQ. To be used solely as part of FaithMap Programme.

Family Sheet

To do at home with your family

FAMILY PRAYER

Dear Jesus,
you are with us and help us. Let us pray that your message will continue to spread over the whole world. May we always be children and adults who will tell others about Jesus. May those who do not know Jesus come to find him and be with us. Amen.

WHAT CAN I DO?

Think carefully about all your skills and all the things which you have learnt to do. Choose one which you can use to give away freely by doing a job for somebody else. Be careful not to wait for something in return. Remember, you are giving it freely!

This week in your prayers, thank God each day for something free which he has given you during the day.

For parents: Weekly Thought

We are called to holiness, we are all called to follow Jesus, we are all called to make Jesus known to all peoples. The Church moves on in the life of faith; each community of believers must give birth to its own apostles. The apostles of every age must be as self-effacing as the apostles of the first age: they must point others to the living Lord.

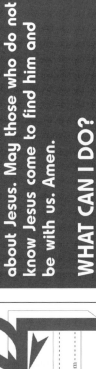

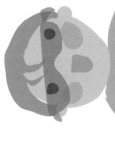

DAY 1

DAY 2

DAY 3

DAY 4

DAY 5

DAY 6

DAY 7

Colour in the gift box and write the label when you share one of your gifts each day.

This sheet has been completed by ....

© Redemptorist Publications, Alphonsus House, Chawton, Hants GU34 3HQ. To be used solely as part of FaithMap Programme.

12th Sunday in Ordinary Time

Family Sheet

To do at home with your family

For parents: Weekly Thought

The challenge to confess the name of Jesus is one that is issued to every generation and every Christian. The intimidation we experience may not be one of terror and persecution, but it can still be felt when we come face to face with those who resent the Gospel. When we believe in our worth before God we can face that intimidation: God's love for each one of us is everlasting.

FAMILY PRAYER

Dear Lord,

you care for each one of us every minute of the day and night. When we are frightened, help us to trust in you and call on your love to give us courage. Thank you, Lord Jesus, for the different people that make up my family. Show us how to listen to one another and how to be generous with our time and talk. Amen.

During your night prayers this week, talk with Jesus about the things you are afraid of. Ask him to comfort you.

Talk to an adult, or a friend you can trust, about your fears and their fears.

You have been writing in a notelet with a picture of a sparrow on the front, and with the words "You are worth more than hundreds of sparrows" (Matthew 10:31). Think about the people who are worth more than hundreds of sparrows to you. Tell them how special they are, or write a letter, send a card or make a phone call.

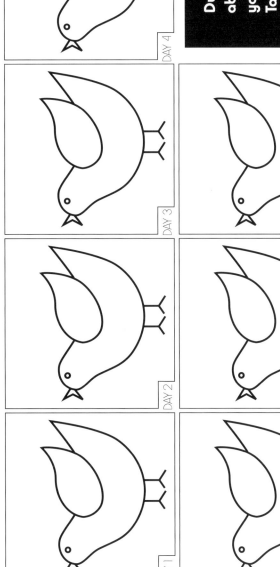

DAY 1

DAY 2

DAY 3

DAY 4

DAY 5

DAY 6

DAY 7

Colour in the sparrow when you have trusted in God's love, or been brave this week.

This sheet has been completed by ....

© Redemptorist Publications, Alphonsus House, Chawton, Hants GU34 3HQ. To be used solely as part of FaithMap Programme.

13th Sunday in Ordinary Time

Family Sheet

To do at home with your family

For parents: Weekly Thought

When Jesus arrives at journey's end and the cross looms large, we see that he prays for the resolve to continue. He too is tempted to give up and return to the quiet security of Galilee. The journey to Jerusalem is seen as a route which all his followers must take. It is an inward journey that is plotted through our experience, our journey to God in the footsteps of Christ.

FAMILY PRAYER

Dear Lord,

we come together to praise and thank you for your goodness.

May we welcome you into our hearts and be changed by your presence. Help us to look out for those who need our help. Glory be to the Father, and to the Son and to the Holy Spirit, as it was in the beginning, is now, and ever shall be, world without end. Amen.

ENCOURAGEMENT

Encourage the children to look out for people in their family who are sad during the week. Encourage them to try and find ways to make them happy again.

Older children: Think of something that you really don't like doing, but you have to do. Maybe a chore around the house, or homework, or just getting up in the morning. Each day this week, just before you have to do this thing, say a short prayer asking Jesus to help you, then do it cheerfully, without grumbling at all.

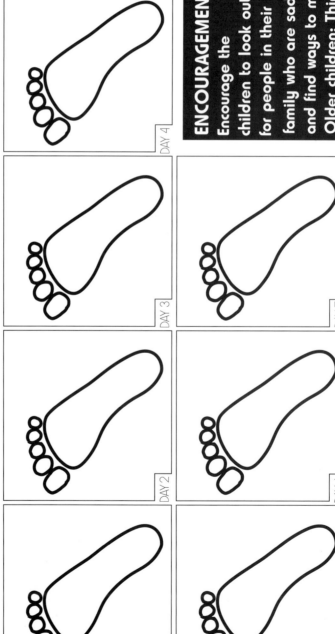

DAY 4

DAY 3

DAY 2

DAY 1

DAY 7

DAY 6

DAY 5

Colour or write in the feet when you have shown yourself to be a Christian this week.

This sheet has been completed by ....

© Redemptorist Publications, Alphonsus House, Chawton, Hants GU34 3HQ. To be used solely as part of FaithMap Programme.

14th Sunday in Ordinary Time

Family Sheet

To do at home with your family

For parents: Weekly Thought

In today's Gospel we heard that Jesus will share our troubles and give us comfort. He asks us to live as God wants us to live, and to find real happiness whatever may happen in our lives. Following Christ gives us a different perspective on the world.

FAMILY PRAYER

Lord Jesus, you are always with us.
Help us to know you.
Help us to trust you.
Help us to understand
that loving you, following you,
matters more than anything else. Amen.

How can we help Jesus to help people in trouble?
* If someone is being teased, and is upset, we can take their side.
* If someone is bullied, we can defend them.
* If someone is sad, we can hug them.
* If someone is afraid, we can help them.
* If someone is tired, we can let them rest.

Come to me and you will find rest
* When things go wrong, do we call on Jesus and share our worries with him?
* When things go wrong, do we mend them with kindness?
* Can we feel God holding our hands, helping and guiding us?
* Do we do God's work and help others, when things go wrong for them?

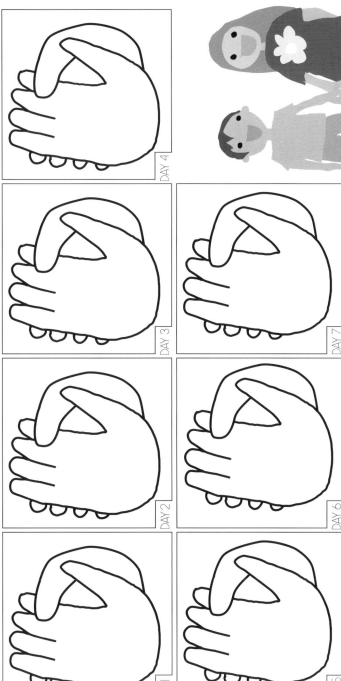

DAY 4

DAY 3

DAY 7

DAY 2

DAY 6

DAY 1

DAY 5

Colour in the "holding hands" symbol each day when you have had no troubles, or when you have helped someone else in trouble, or felt God with you holding your hand.

This sheet has been completed by ....

© Redemptorist Publications, Alphonsus House, Chawton, Hants GU34 3HQ. To be used solely as part of FaithMap Programme.

15th Sunday in Ordinary Time

Family Sheet

To do at home with your family

For parents: Weekly Thought

Like everything else, practising Christian values makes perfect.

In today's Gospel we heard that God has planted the seed of love in our hearts. Jesus asks us to look after it and make it grow.

FAMILY PRAYER

Lord Jesus, you give us the gift of God's love.

Let us always feed that gift, and make it grow.

Let us never forget how precious that gift is. Amen.

For the week ahead:
* What makes love grow?
* What makes us grow closer to God?
* Do we make time every day to feel God with us?
* Do we make time every day to share God's presence with our families?
* Do we do what God wants us to do?

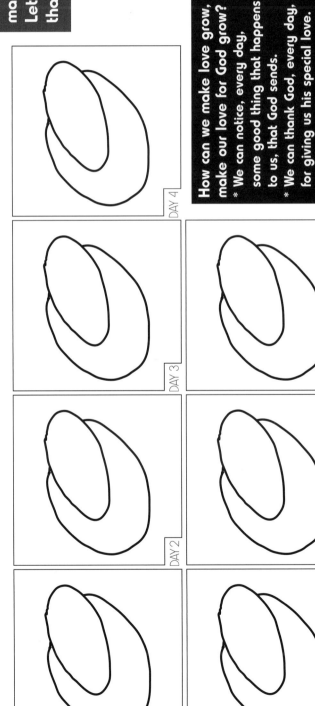

DAY 1

DAY 2

DAY 3

DAY 4

DAY 5

DAY 6

DAY 7

How can we make love grow, make our love for God grow?
* We can notice, every day, some good thing that happens to us, that God sends.
* We can thank God, every day, for giving us his special love.
* We can share God's love with other people: we can be good and kind and gentle.
* We can search, every day, for how God has helped us to be happy.
* We can learn what God wants us to do.

Colour in the seed symbol each day when you have felt the love of God.

This sheet has been completed by ....

© Redemptorist Publications, Alphonsus House, Chawton, Hants GU34 3HQ. To be used solely as part of FaithMap Programme.

Family Sheet

To do at home with your family

For parents: Weekly Thought

We can each choose the future: to be beautiful as God wills, or not.

In today's Gospel we heard that God gives each of us the chance to grow beautiful and strong in his love.

FAMILY PRAYER

Lord Jesus, you call us to be on your team.

Help us to know what you want us to do.

Help us to do what you want us to do.

Help us to grow, every day, closer to you. Amen.

For the week ahead:
* Do we behave as God would want us to behave each day?
* Do we remember to thank God, when things go well?
* Do we ask for God's help, when we are anxious or upset?
* Have we chosen to be in God's kingdom?

How can we choose to be in God's team?
* We can remember always that God is with us.
* We can remember that we are God's hands in this world.
* We can help others as God wants us to.
* We can be happy as God wants us to be.

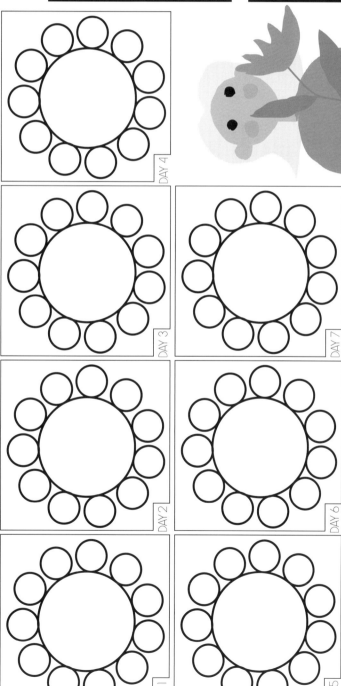

DAY 1

DAY 2

DAY 3

DAY 4

DAY 5

DAY 6

DAY 7

Colour in a flower for each day when you have done something to make someone happy, or done something good or kind.

This sheet has been completed by ....

© Redemptorist Publications, Alphonsus House, Chawton, Hants GU34 3HQ. To be used solely as part of FaithMap Programme.

Proper 12

17th Sunday in Ordinary Time

Family Sheet

To do at home with your family

For parents: Weekly Thought

In today's Gospel we heard that God offers us a present that is worth more than any other thing in the world, a present that will never become boring. It is his gift of love. Accepting God's love is accepting a gift beyond imagination.

FAMILY PRAYER

Lord Jesus, you give us the gift of your love.
We thank you, we praise you.
We ask your help in sharing that special gift with everyone. Amen.

For the week ahead:
* Have we felt God's love, like warm arms hugging us?
* Have you felt special because God loves you?
* Have you behaved the way God would like you to behave?

How can we thank God for the treasure of his love?
* We can thank him every day.
* We can live as he wants us to.
* We can be good and kind and gentle.
* We can be God's helpers on earth.

DAY 1 DAY 2 DAY 3 DAY 4 DAY 5 DAY 6 DAY 7

Colour in a smile each day when you have felt happy because God is with you.

This sheet has been completed by ....

© Redemptorist Publications, Alphonsus House, Chawton, Hants GU34 3HQ. To be used solely as part of FaithMap Programme.

18th Sunday in Ordinary Time

Family Sheet

To do at home with your family

For parents: Weekly Thought

The crowds have sought out Jesus. They have come with hope that he will do something. Jesus takes pity on them and heals their sick. The crowd need feeding. Jesus takes the little that the disciples have, raises his eyes to heaven, blesses it and gives it to the disciples to distribute. The miracle is that the little food Jesus and his disciples have is sufficient for everyone there. We can only give what we can, and the great teaching of today's Gospel is that even the little we give can be more than enough.

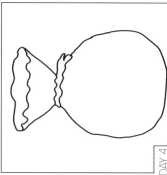

DAY 1

DAY 2

DAY 3

DAY 4

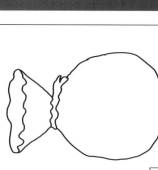

DAY 5

DAY 6

DAY 7

Colour in a sack each day when you have shared something with someone.

This sheet has been completed by ....

FAMILY PRAYER

God, my creator, you provide our world full of beauty and good things.
Help me to share with those who have nothing to make your kingdom come.
Lord, we are all made in your image. Whatever our race or colour, help us to treat one another with love and kindness.
Help us to talk to each other with respect.
Help us to live together in peace.
Amen.

Something to Investigate

Find out about the work of a charity which helps to feed the hungry. It could be a charity working in developing countries, or it might be something more local – a soup kitchen or similar. (You may know an adult who would be able to take you there to see the sort of work they do.)

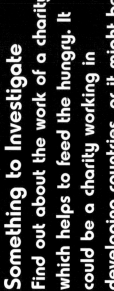

© Redemptorist Publications, Alphonsus House, Chawton, Hants GU34 3HQ. To be used solely as part of FaithMap Programme.

Family Sheet

To do at home with your family

For parents: Weekly Thought

In today's Gospel we read that Peter "felt the force of the wind, took fright and began to sink". Matthew is telling his struggling community that even if their faith falters and they panic when they look at the surrounding danger, Jesus, even though he is with the Father, will come and save them. When we are battling against the odds we have the word of God and the bread of life and the support of each other to keep us afloat.

FAMILY PRAYER

Dear Lord, give us the courage and faith of Peter, whose belief was so strong that he could walk to Jesus across the lake.
When we are weak, reach out your hand to support us and rescue us from our doubts.
May each member of our family, young and old, learn to love and support one another.
May we always share the laughter, peace and security that is founded on your love.
Amen.

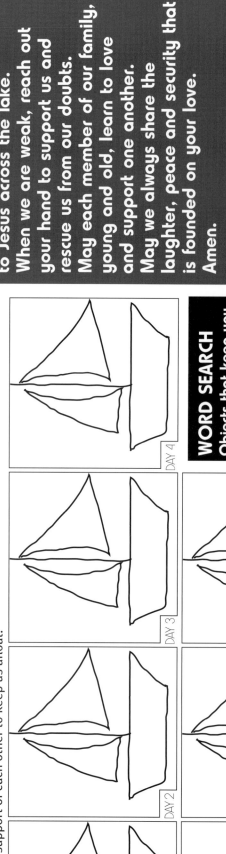

DAY 1 DAY 2 DAY 3 DAY 4

DAY 5 DAY 6 DAY 7

Colour in a boat each day when you have been of help or support to someone.

WORD SEARCH

Objects that keep you afloat:
YACHT, BOAT, FLOAT, DINGHY, TYRE, RAFT, SURFBOARD, ARMBANDS.

S	U	R	F	B	O	A	R	D
X	W	A	Q	Z	O	T	S	I
B	Y	F	L	O	A	T	B	N
O	J	T	Y	R	E	V	K	G
A	R	M	B	A	N	D	S	H
T	G	Z	F	T	H	C	A	Y

This sheet has been completed by ....

© Redemptorist Publications, Alphonsus House, Chawton, Hants GU34 3HQ. To be used solely as part of FaithMap Programme.

Family Sheet

To do at home with your family

For parents: Weekly Thought

"Pester power" is a fairly well-known marketing ploy! Most of us have succumbed to it at one time or another; sometimes for a quiet life, and sometimes because we genuinely don't want our children to be disappointed. There are times, though, when we know that to do something straight away would not be in the best interests of our children or the family. In those cases, children learn that showing our love for them does not depend on what we give them or the speed with which we give it. Rather, it is our concern for them, our knowledge of them as individuals, and our own experience that help us to decide what and when things may be most appropriate for them to receive.

DAY 1

DAY 2

DAY 3

DAY 4

DAY 5

DAY 6

DAY 7

Colour in some sand in the hourglass each day. You might like to start with a lot in the top and a little in the bottom and each day put more in the bottom and less in the top. Use this to remind yourself that sometimes our prayers take a while to be answered.

This sheet has been completed by ....

FAMILY PRAYER

Loving God and Creator, thank you for your great love for us and for giving us the wonderful things in our lives.
(You may like to name some of them at this point.)
Help us to remember these good gifts especially when we need to wait for an answer to our prayers, or when your answer is not what we would choose. Amen.

Tyre and Sidon

In the Gospel, we are told that Jesus went to "the region of Tyre and Sidon". These were two great seaports which were very important to the Phoenician civilisation as they traded goods with the rest of the ancient world for hundreds of years before Jesus was born. They are on the coast of the Mediterranean Sea and still exist today, as modern cities in Lebanon. Look for them on a map of Jesus' time: http://scriptures.lds.org/en/biblemaps/11 and compare the region to a modern map.

© Redemptorist Publications, Alphonsus House, Chawton, Hants GU34 3HQ. To be used solely as part of FaithMap Programme.

21st Sunday in Ordinary Time

Family Sheet

To do at home with your family

For parents: Weekly Thought

"Who am I?" Peter is the one who confesses who Jesus is. He is also the one who denies Jesus; he is the one who falters in that faith. He has to be helped by Jesus in all that he does, but the Gospels indicate that he is Jesus' choice to lead the community in the future.

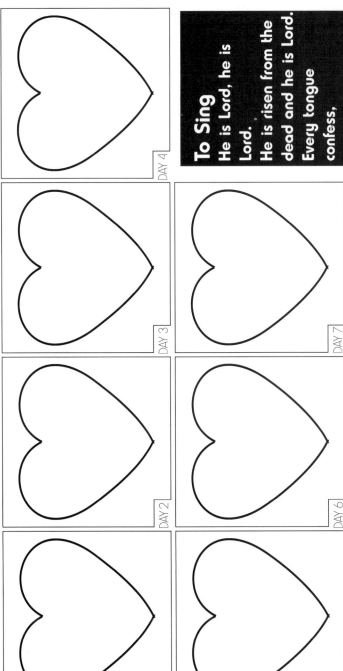

FAMILY PRAYER

The Apostles' Creed

I believe in God, the Father almighty, creator of heaven and earth.
I believe in Jesus Christ, his only Son, our Lord.

He was conceived by the power of the Holy Spirit and born of the Virgin Mary.
He suffered under Pontius Pilate, was crucified, died and was buried.
He descended to the dead.
On the third day he rose again.
He ascended into heaven, and is seated at the right hand of the Father.
He will come again to judge the living and the dead.

I believe in the Holy Spirit, the holy catholic Church, the communion of saints, the forgiveness of sins, the resurrection of the body, and the life everlasting.
Amen.

(Adopted in its present form in the 11th century. In 12 articles it contains the truths taught by the apostles. In early centuries, people were required to learn and recite it before baptism.)

To Sing
He is Lord, he is Lord.
He is risen from the dead and he is Lord.
Every tongue confess,
everyone profess
that Jesus Christ is Lord.

DAY 1

DAY 2

DAY 3

DAY 4

DAY 5

DAY 6

DAY 7

Colour in a heart each day as you show Jesus' love to someone else.

This sheet has been completed by ....

© Redemptorist Publications, Alphonsus House, Chawton, Hants GU34 3HQ. To be used solely as part of FaithMap Programme.

Family Sheet

To do at home with your family

For parents: Weekly Thought

"Take up your cross and follow me" is a difficult message for children and young people. Above all else our faith is about life, not death. So this week we have used the analogy of a balloon to try to explain it – without air, the balloon is limp and useless; without God's Spirit there is no life. But as with a balloon, the process of transformation, of being filled, can leave many of us feeling stretched and more than a little bit hurt. Jesus is not asking us (well, not many of us) to embrace the cross in gargantuan proportions; rather, he is asking us to engage with all the muddle and heartache and joy that is life itself, with compassion and with integrity. This is where Jesus is to be followed, and, for most of us, this will be transformation and "cross" enough.

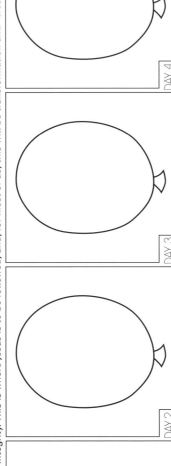

DAY 1

DAY 2

DAY 3

DAY 4

DAY 5

DAY 6

DAY 7

Do something each day which seems to stretch you a bit: something new, or something which you find a bit hard. Colour in a balloon each day to celebrate!

This sheet has been completed by ....

FAMILY PRAYER

Dear Jesus, being a Christian and loving you is always very exciting and stretches us so that we grow to be more like you, but sometimes we don't feel like being excited or stretched. That is when we need each other most. Help us to help each other and to encourage each other so that we can grow into bigger, brighter, better people. Amen.

Activity (with adult supervision)

Buy a packet of balloons, blow them up and decorate them, one for each person that you love in your family or friends. As you pray for them each night, hold each balloon in turn and ask God to fill and stretch your special people with his Spirit.

© Redemptorist Publications, Alphonsus House, Chawton, Hants GU34 3HQ. To be used solely as part of FaithMap Programme.

23rd Sunday in Ordinary Time

Family Sheet

To do at home with your family

For parents: Weekly Thought

Love and forgiveness and the importance of saying "sorry" are crucial lessons for our children. By helping your child not to be afraid of owning up, by offering ready forgiveness, you are offering them a model of the love of God.

In the sacrament of reconciliation, we approach God as our children approach us, willing to say that we are sorry for things we have done, knowing that God is simply waiting to forgive us.

FAMILY PRAYER

Lord Jesus, thank you for our family.

Help us to remember that when we are together, you are with us.

Remind us to say sorry when we need to, and to be quick to forgive. Amen.

Who are the people in your group?

Draw their portraits here and write their names.

As you draw them, say a little prayer asking God to bless them and all the things you will do together over the next few weeks.

MY GROUP

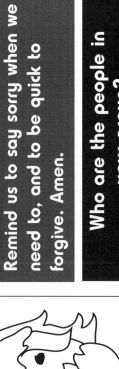

DAY 4

DAY 3

DAY 2

DAY 7

DAY 6

DAY 1

DAY 5

Colour in one of Jesus' faces each day. Think about how Jesus is with you always and especially close when you pray.

This sheet has been completed by ....

© Redemptorist Publications, Alphonsus House, Chawton, Hants GU34 3HQ. To be used solely as part of FaithMap Programme.

24th Sunday in Ordinary Time

Family Sheet

To do at home with your family

For parents: Weekly Thought

The Church is quite clear that every human being, whatever their race or colour, is equal. Sadly our society is often less clear and we can find within ourselves a prejudice against people who are different. Part of our own growth is coming to accept others as brothers and sisters, and helping our children to do the same.

FAMILY PRAYER

**Our Father in heaven,
you have made human beings
wonderfully different.**

**Help us to treat all people as our
brothers and sisters,
and help others
to do the same.
Amen.**

Racial Justice

The Catholic Association for Racial Justice (CARJ) helps to work for justice for people of all races. St Martin de Porres, the first black American saint is its patron. Aged 11, he worked as a servant in a Dominican priory. He learnt how to care for the sick, worked in the priory hospital and cured many people, especially those in the slums. He was the first black person to become a Dominican priest.

The Churches' Commission for Racial Justice coordinates the work of the Christian churches in Britain. It works closely with black and minority ethnic communities to ensure that the Christian voice is heard effectively in support of racial justice. It also encourages Christians to be informed and to take action, where necessary.

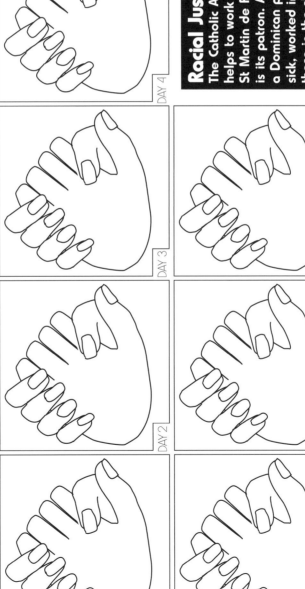

DAY 4

DAY 3

DAY 7

DAY 2

DAY 6

DAY 1

DAY 5

Colour in a handshake each day and think about the importance of being fair and making up if we have hurt someone.

This sheet has been completed by ....

© Redemptorist Publications, Alphonsus House, Chawton, Hants GU34 3HQ. To be used solely as part of FaithMap Programme.

Family Sheet

To do at home with your family

For parents: Weekly Thought

God's generosity far surpasses anything human beings can match, but the seeds of it are sown in everyone. Encourage your child to be generous, something that is not always easy for children. Help them to think about how blessed they are and how little others have. Remind them that God gave the world and its resources for everyone to share and think of small ways in which they can bring that vision about.

FAMILY PRAYER

Heavenly Father, creator of everything, give us a spirit of generosity like your own.

Help us to share what we have in our family with each other and with people in need. Amen.

S	I	T	S	E	M	I	T
T	C	U	D	H	M	Y	O
F	C	L	O	T	H	E	S
I	O	G	O	L	F	N	H
G	I	I	G	A	O	O	A
I	N	V	E	E	O	M	R
P	S	E	B	W	D	O	E
Q	U	A	Y	Y	A	R	P

God is Generous

Word Search

Find the words below, up, down, forwards or backwards.

SHARE, GIVE, GOODS, PRAY, MONEY, GIFTS, COINS, WEALTH, CLOTHES, FOOD, TIME

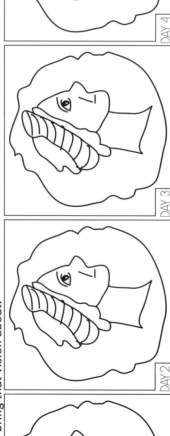

DAY 1 DAY 2 DAY 3 DAY 4
DAY 5 DAY 6 DAY 7

Colour in a denarius (den-ar-ee-us) for each day. Pray for people who do not have enough to live on, and the people with the power to make a difference.

This sheet has been completed by ....

© Redemptorist Publications, Alphonsus House, Chawton, Hants GU34 3HQ. To be used solely as part of FaithMap Programme.

Family Sheet

To do at home with your family

For parents: Weekly Thought

It is a fact of life that there are things that we cannot really get ourselves motivated to start. Part of growing up is learning to do the things that we would rather put off. When you encounter moments when your child doesn't want to do something, try to break it down into manageable bits. Praise them for the little steps to encourage them to go further.

DAY 1

DAY 2

DAY 3

DAY 4

DAY 5

DAY 6

DAY 7

Colour in a tick every day. Try to think of something you did straight away without saying, "In a minute!"

This sheet has been completed by ....

FAMILY PRAYER

Dear Lord, thank you for our family. Help us to love each other and do things for each other without putting them off. Amen.

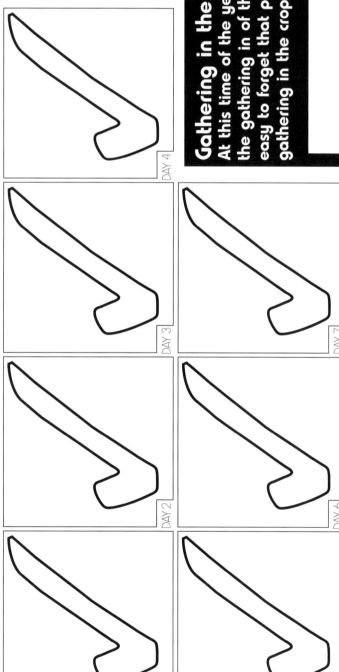

Gathering in the harvest

At this time of the year, many places celebrate the gathering in of the harvest. In cities and towns, it is easy to forget that people are busy out in the fields gathering in the crops ready for the winter. All round the world, people are harvesting and storing God's gifts.

Draw some of your favourite fruits and vegetables and write a short prayer to thank God for all the wonderful food nature provides us with.

© Redemptorist Publications, Alphonsus House, Chawton, Hants GU34 3HQ. To be used solely as part of FaithMap Programme.

27th Sunday in Ordinary Time

Family Sheet
To do at home with your family

For parents: Weekly Thought

Foundation, corner- and keystones are used interchangeably in different versions of today's Gospel. They are all quite distinct, although they serve the same general purpose: that of keeping a building upright. Foundation stones are large flat stones on which the building rests, these may be visible but are often buried underground. Cornerstones are wedge-shaped stones forming the angle between wall and roof; keystones are blunt wedges at the centre of an arch, stopping it from falling inwards: they are the last stone to be put in place. Take away any of these and the whole building collapses. Although many aspects of our faith and lives are as essential as the stone for the walls and the slates for the roof, the building can still survive (albeit in a somewhat weakened state) without any particular one of them. Only Christ is described as a keystone, without him there is no building.

DAY 4 · DAY 3 · DAY 7 · DAY 2 · DAY 6 · DAY 1 · DAY 5

Each day write the name of a person or a thing which is important in your life onto one of the stone symbols. Say a prayer thanking God for them.

This sheet has been completed by ....

FAMILY PRAYER

Dear Jesus, you are the keystone in our lives, you make sense of everything we have. Thank you, Jesus. Help us to make the world a better place to live, by being kind to each other and sharing things more fairly in the way that you taught us. Amen.

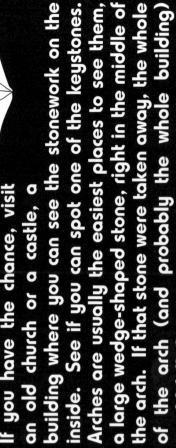

Activity

If you have the chance, visit an old church or a castle, a building where you can see the stonework on the inside. See if you can spot one of the keystones. Arches are usually the easiest places to see them, a large wedge-shaped stone, right in the middle of the arch. If that stone were taken away, the whole of the arch (and probably the whole building) would fall down.

© Redemptorist Publications, Alphonsus House, Chawton, Hants GU34 3HQ. To be used solely as part of FaithMap Programme.

28th Sunday in Ordinary Time

Family Sheet

To do at home with your family

For parents: Weekly Thought

It is easy to assume, as God seems to us to be so extraordinary, that we can only find him in extraordinary experiences. But in today's Gospel we learn that it was the ordinary people, not blinded by their self-importance, who ended up at the wedding feast of God. St Teresa of Avila instructs us very clearly that God is to be found in the ordinary and everyday: the "pots and pans". We may not take kindly to being likened to a pot or a pan, but if we take the time to look, it soon becomes apparent that such objects have only become ordinary because of the sheer elegance, ingenuity and brilliance of their design. We can learn to look at other people, and ourselves, in the same way.

FAMILY PRAYER

Dear Jesus, sometimes we ignore the ordinary things you have given us and take them for granted. When you were on earth, you did very ordinary things, and you thought they were great. You met lots of ordinary people, and you thought they were fantastic. Help us to enjoy ordinary things as well. Amen.

Activity

Choose just one thing which you use every day. Use books, the internet, the library etc. to find out as much as you can about it. Each day when you are using the object, thank God.

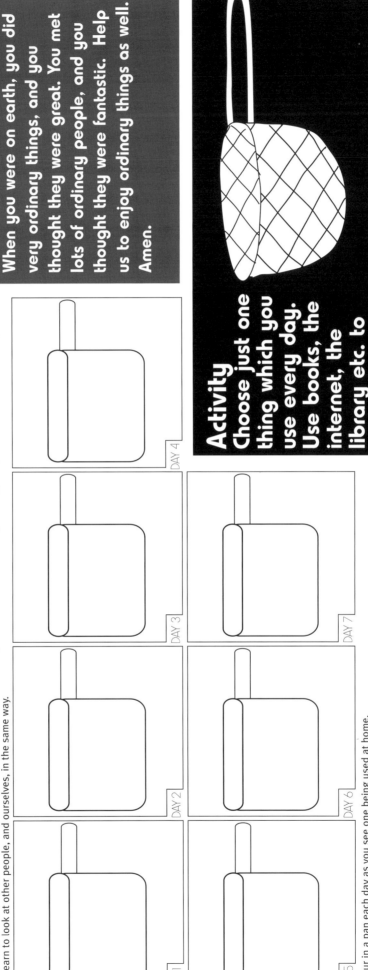

DAY 4

DAY 3

DAY 7

DAY 2

DAY 6

DAY 1

DAY 5

Colour in a pan each day as you see one being used at home.
Ask if you can help by stirring what is in the pan. Ask if you can wash it up. Take a good look at the pan. How many different sorts of pans do you use at home?

This sheet has been completed by ....

© Redemptorist Publications, Alphonsus House, Chawton, Hants GU34 3HQ. To be used solely as part of FaithMap Programme.

Family Sheet

To do at home with your family

For parents: Weekly Thought

"Give to Caesar what belongs to Caesar." Taxes are no more popular today than in first-century Palestine, but we all recognise our responsibility as citizens to pay our fair share. There was a time when some religious orders considered it a virtue to live solely off charitable donations, but most have come to recognise that they too have a duty of self-maintenance, and of contributing towards the general social order. Children aged 7-11 will become aware of taxes and other bills through the media, and by the groans with which payment demands are greeted! Their interest can be encouraged by explaining who they are paid to, and what they pay for.

FAMILY PRAYER

Dear Jesus, we use money just the same as you did. The grown-ups have to work hard to earn it, and then we give it to other people to pay for our food and our clothes. Help us to remember the people who don't have very much money and cannot buy enough food to eat. Amen.

Activity

Ask your mum or dad or carer about the taxes they pay. Who do they pay them to, and what is the money used for? Can they contribute to decisions about how the money is spent? How do they do that?

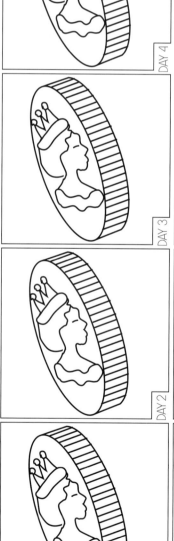

DAY 4

DAY 3

DAY 7

DAY 2

DAY 6

DAY 1

DAY 5

Colour in one of the coins on the chart each day that you find out more about how your family's money is spent.

This sheet has been completed by ....

© Redemptorist Publications, Alphonsus House, Chawton, Hants GU34 3HQ. To be used solely as part of FaithMap Programme.

30th Sunday in Ordinary Time

Family Sheet
To do at home with your family

For parents: Weekly Thought
The Catholic Church celebrates World Mission Day on the penultimate Sunday in October. We think of the Church throughout the world serving humanity by spreading the Good News of Christ. Although there is clearly a place for direct action or words, we often share the Good News most effectively by example, and frequently don't realise we are doing it. Of course, when the pressure is on, it can be much more difficult to present a "Christian" front to the world. At times like these we need to remember that repentance and forgiveness are also signs of God's life within us.

FAMILY PRAYER

Jesus, thank you for loving us. Teach us how to love you, and how to love each other. Sometimes it is not easy to love each other; help us when we find it hard. Amen.

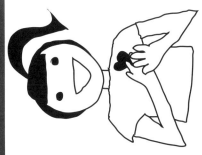

Activity
One of the best ways of sharing the Good News is just by living it, and showing other people that it is possible to live the way Jesus asked us. Help your parents or carers to organise a "family event", something your family or group can do together, but not at home. It should be somewhere more public so that other people might be encouraged by your example.

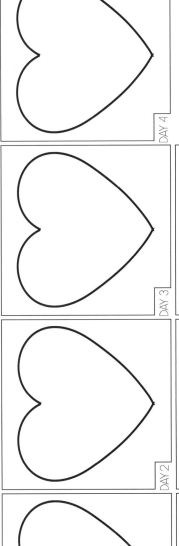

DAY 1, DAY 2, DAY 3, DAY 4, DAY 5, DAY 6, DAY 7

When we love someone, we need to show it to them in some way. Colour in a heart each day to show someone that you love them.

This sheet has been completed by ....

© Redemptorist Publications, Alphonsus House, Chawton, Hants GU34 3HQ. To be used solely as part of FaithMap Programme.

Family Sheet

To do at home with your family

For parents: Weekly Thought

We have been considering the phrase "practise what you preach". Irrespective of any aspirations to sanctity demonstrated through words or writings, the emphasis is placed very firmly on how the individual has coped with the ordinary everyday challenges of living with oneself and with one's neighbour.

As we know from experience, "being good", and "wanting to be good" are two entirely different matters! Encourage the children to name, in advance, one good thing they are going to do during the day.

FAMILY PRAYER

Jesus, when we read about the saints, it is very difficult for us to imagine being that good. We say we want to be good, but it is not so easy when we try. Help us to do one good thing each day (name the good thing for the next day). Amen.

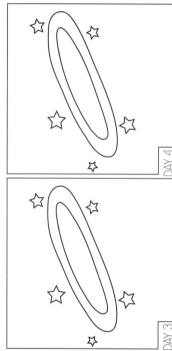
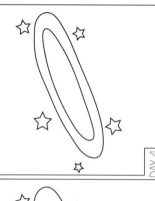

DAY 1 / DAY 2 / DAY 3 / DAY 4 / DAY 5 / DAY 6 / DAY 7

Colour in one of the haloes each day when you do something good, as if you were a saint.

Activity

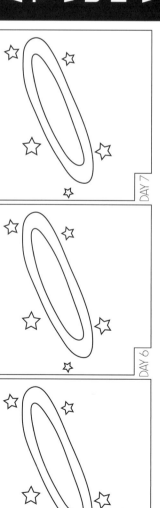

Think carefully about something "good" you want to achieve during the week; it might be a bad habit you want to break, or a job you have been putting off doing, or it might be visiting or writing to someone you love, or being nice to someone you don't like. Plan one thing for each day. If you do other good things as well, they are a bonus!

This sheet has been completed by ....

© Redemptorist Publications, Alphonsus House, Chawton, Hants GU34 3HQ. To be used solely as part of FaithMap Programme.

Family Sheet

To do at home with your family

For parents: Weekly Thought

Jesus wants us to be a light to help other people to be close to him. We do it best when we remember that what we do for other people we are doing for him.

FAMILY PRAYER

Help us to keep awake, ready for all the chances to serve you which will come (came) today. Thank you for your presence always with us. Amen.

Make a lantern

Take some paper, half a sheet of A4 will do – decorate it in any way you like. Fold it in half and cut straight up from the folded edge to within 3 cm of the top and bottom. Open out the paper and glue some orange/yellow/gold paper inside. Then glue it together at the side. Fasten a handle at the top to carry your lantern.

At home

Children do best what they see their parents doing. If we look for God's presence each day, giving time to others cheerfully, they will learn from what we see, not what we tell them.

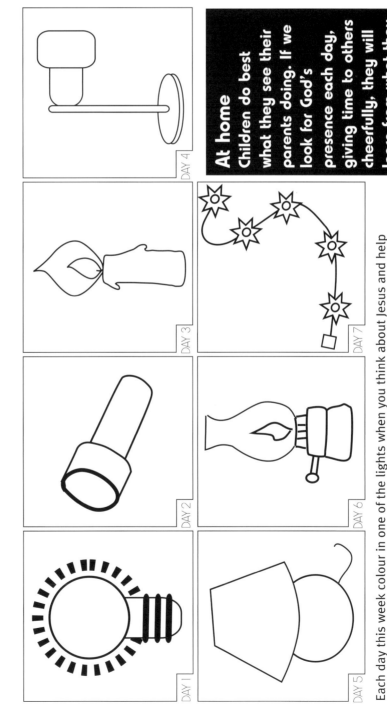

DAY 1

DAY 2

DAY 3

DAY 4

DAY 5

DAY 6

DAY 7

Each day this week colour in one of the lights when you think about Jesus and help someone else.

This sheet has been completed by ....

© Redemptorist Publications, Alphonsus House, Chawton, Hants GU34 3HQ. To be used solely as part of FaithMap Programme.

Family Sheet

To do at home with your family

For parents: Weekly Thought

Our God gave us the good gift of our children, let us enjoy that gift even when their talents seem to be for night-time wakefulness, reluctance to tackle homework, creating huge piles of washing; they always give us the gift of being themselves.

FAMILY PRAYER

Father in heaven, thank you for giving us to each other. Help us to share the talents we have with the people we meet. Help us to enjoy the talents they share with us. Amen.

TO DO

When we have shared our gifts and talents, God will say to us:

"WDEKLGLO DZOXNFEH MOYK GEOSOTDB ACNYDI FVAHIPTQHWFOUNLM SDEJRLVNARNWT"

Break the code by starting with "W" then using every other letter.

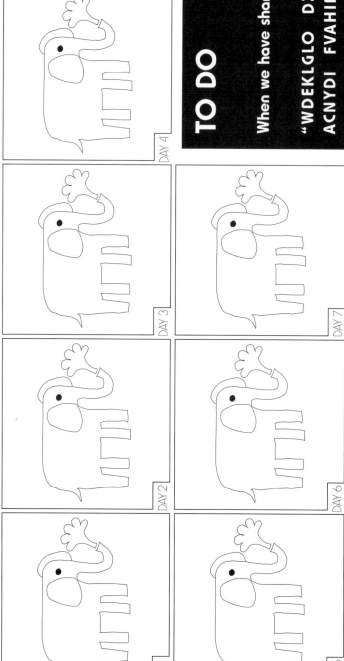

DAY 1

DAY 2

DAY 3

DAY 4

DAY 5

DAY 6

DAY 7

This week colour in the elephants each day as you remember to thank God for the talents he has given to you.

This sheet has been completed by ....

© Redemptorist Publications, Alphonsus House, Chawton, Hants GU34 3HQ. To be used solely as part of FaithMap Programme.

Our Lord Jesus Christ, Universal King

Family Sheet

To do at home with your family

For parents: Weekly Thought

In the chaos that is family life, we serve our king when we serve each other. If we can look outside the family and still find ways of being helpful we shall serve our king in even more ways. Try to involve the children in service – they have responsibilities, not just rights.

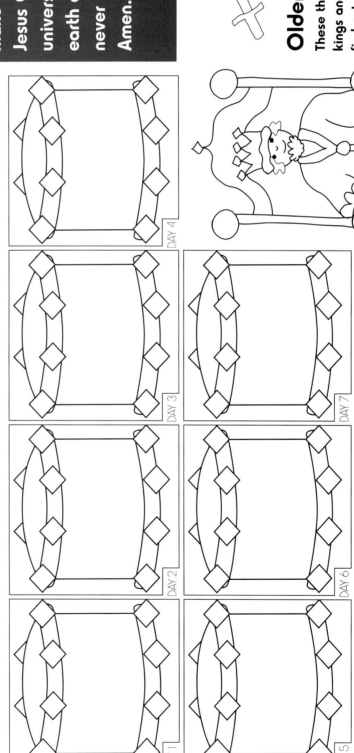

DAY 1

DAY 2

DAY 3

DAY 4

DAY 5

DAY 6

DAY 7

This week, colour a crown each day you try to help someone else and thank Christ our king for the opportunity to do it.

This sheet has been completed by ....

© Redemptorist Publications, Alphonsus House, Chawton, Hants GU34 3HQ. To be used solely as part of FaithMap Programme.

FAMILY PRAYER

Almighty and merciful God, you break the power of evil and make all things new in your Son Jesus Christ, the king of the universe. May all in heaven and earth acclaim your glory and never cease to praise you. Amen.

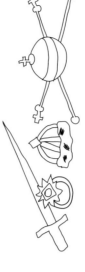

Older children

These things are all used at the coronation of kings and queens. They are symbols. Can you find out what they stand for?

Younger children

Colour the picture of the king on his throne. What do you think Jesus is saying?

The Most Holy Trinity

Family Sheet
To do at home with your family

FAMILY PRAYER

Very special Jesus, this prayer is for some very special people – us. Help us to have special love for each other on special days and lots of ordinary love for each other on ordinary days. Help us to have enough ordinary love so that we have some to spare for others we meet outside our family.
Thank you, Jesus. Amen.

For parents: Weekly Thought

How much ordinary love is there in your life for your family and for those outside your family? We have been talking about Jesus our brother and how love is important in a family. We show special love on special days like birthdays but there should also be ordinary love for ordinary days. We can show we care. We can notice the ordinary things that people do for us, and help in the ordinary things that need doing at home. Love can be special but love can also be ordinary.

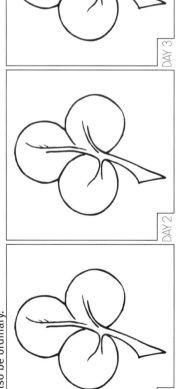

DAY 1   DAY 2   DAY 3   DAY 4

DAY 5   DAY 6   DAY 7

Colour the shamrock each day when you have done something loving for someone in your family.

This sheet has been completed by ....

THE TRINITY
A Thought

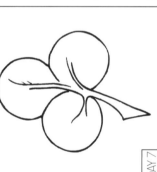

St Patrick used the shamrock to explain the Trinity. Other cultures have used natural objects, like the egg, to explain the three persons in one God. The egg has its yolk, surrounded by the albumen (the white) which is surrounded by the shell; three separate parts but one whole egg. Coconuts are also used to give the same sort of explanation.

Can you think of other things from the natural world that would work just as well?

© Redemptorist Publications, Alphonsus House, Chawton, Hants GU34 3HQ. To be used solely as part of FaithMap Programme.

The Body and Blood of Christ (Corpus Christi)

Family Sheet

To do at home with your family

For parents: Weekly Thought

Family meals are often hard to fit into our routines these days. Parents are busy working and may not have time or energy to start cooking when they get in. Children with after-school activities may need lifts and then want to relax with the television or computer. But sharing a meal was one of the key places for Jesus to share his teachings. Eating and drinking together, as well as sharing conversation, can help in building relationships, getting to know each other better, sharing joys and overcoming disputes.

If you are able to share meals regularly, rejoice and continue to make them an important part of your family's life. If not, see if it might be possible once or twice a week and enjoy some simple family time around the table.

FAMILY PRAYER

You might like to use this prayer before meals:

"God of all creation, bless this food which the earth has given, farmers have cultivated, and people have prepared for us to enjoy. As we enjoy our meal together, we ask you to bless those who will be hungry today. Amen."

Soda bread

This bread is delicious with butter and jam. Ask an adult to help you as the oven is very hot and you will need to use a knife.

RECIPE

250g/9oz plain flour
1 level teaspoon salt
1 level teaspoon bicarbonate of soda
2 teaspoons soft brown sugar
175ml/6 fl.oz milk
50ml/2 fl.oz plain yogurt

Method

1. Heat the oven to 200C/400F/Gas 6. Grease a baking sheet with a little oil or lard.
2. Sift the flour, salt and soda into a large mixing bowl. Add the sugar.
3. Stir in the milk mixture with a wooden spoon, then bring it all together with your hands. It should feel soft and firm, not sticky. Add a little more flour if it feels too wet.
4. Knead the dough lightly for 1 minute on a floured surface, and shape it into a ball. Put it on the greased baking sheet. Cut a deep cross in the top of the loaf with a knife.
5. Bake for 20-30 minutes until bread is brown and sounds hollow when tapped on the bottom.

DAY 4

DAY 3

DAY 2

DAY 7

DAY 1

DAY 6

DAY 5

Colour in a loaf for each day as you remember Jesus and how he chose bread as a sign of his gift of everlasting life.

This sheet has been completed by ....

© Redemptorist Publications, Alphonsus House, Chawton, Hants GU34 3HQ. To be used solely as part of FaithMap Programme.

The Presentation of the Lord

Family Sheet

To do at home with your family

For parents: Weekly Thought

You are a light to your children; they imitate you.

FAMILY PRAYER

Dear Jesus, when you were a baby, Mary and Joseph went to the Temple and offered two turtledoves to say thank you to God. Sometimes we don't feel like we have very much to offer. Help us to remember that the best thing we can offer God is our love for Jesus and for each other. Amen.

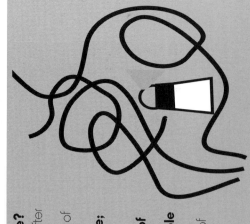

Can you find the path to the lighthouse?

Simeon's song is also called 'Nunc Dimittis' after its first words in Latin.
This prayer is prayed by the Church as part of its Night Prayer.

"Lord, now let your servant go in peace; your word has been fulfilled: my own eyes have seen the salvation which you have prepared in the sight of every people: a light to reveal you to the nations and the glory of your people Israel."

Older children may like to learn the words of Simeon's song.

DAY 4

DAY 3

DAY 7

DAY 1

DAY 2

DAY 5

DAY 6

This week colour one of the candles on this sheet every time you light the candle you decorated last week and speak to Jesus, the Light of the World.

This sheet has been completed by ....

© Redemptorist Publications, Alphonsus House, Chawton, Hants GU34 3HQ. To be used solely as part of FaithMap Programme.

The Birth of St John the Baptist

Family Sheet

To do at home with your family

For parents: Weekly Thought

Today we celebrated the birthday of John the Baptist. He prepares the way for Jesus in the same way as all the Old Testament prophets. He is, however, the only one of them to witness the fulfilment of his own prophecy.

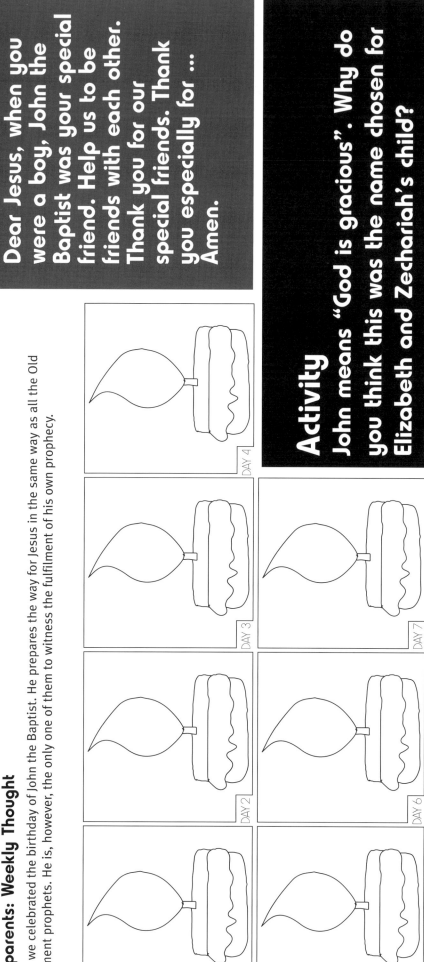

DAY 1

DAY 2

DAY 3

DAY 4

DAY 5

DAY 6

DAY 7

Families can be hard work, especially when there is a new baby. Each day do a job to help your mum or dad or your carer. Colour in a candle on the cake when you have done it.

This sheet has been completed by ....

© Redemptorist Publications, Alphonsus House, Chawton, Hants GU34 3HQ. To be used solely as part of FaithMap Programme.

FAMILY PRAYER

Dear Jesus, when you were a boy, John the Baptist was your special friend. Help us to be friends with each other. Thank you for our special friends. Thank you especially for ...
Amen.

Activity

John means "God is gracious". Why do you think this was the name chosen for Elizabeth and Zechariah's child?

What does your name mean? Visit your library, or do a web search to find out.

Ss Peter and Paul, Apostles

Family Sheet

To do at home with your family

For parents: Weekly Thought

We are not alone in caring for our families. Christians worldwide pray for our families. Christians worldwide pray for each other. When you remember to pray for others, you can be sure that, somewhere, you are being held in prayer.

FAMILY PRAYER

Dear Lord, keep this family safe in your love. Be with those families around the world who know fear or hunger, especially those who do not know you as their loving Father. Amen.

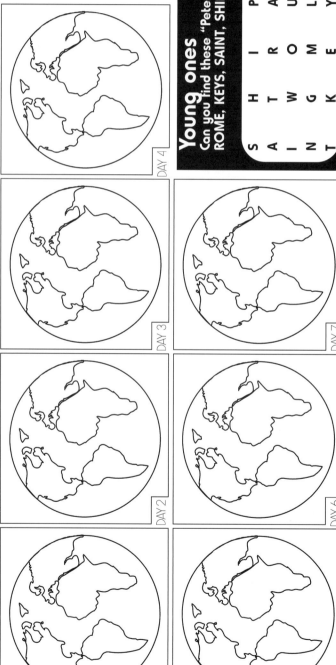

DAY 1

DAY 2

DAY 3

DAY 4

DAY 5

DAY 6

DAY 7

Young ones
Can you find these "Peter and Paul" words?
ROME, KEYS, SAINT, SHIP, TRAVEL, PETER, PAUL

S	H	I	P	Z	P	N
A	T	R	A	V	E	L
I	U	O	Q	T	P	
N	G	M	L	S	E	K
T	K	E	Y	S	R	B

Older ones
How did people in Britain learn about Jesus?
What can you find out about: St Augustine, St Columba, St Patrick, St Ninian?
Next week tell your teacher what you found out.

Colour in a globe each day you remember to pray for another part of the Christian family around the world.

This sheet has been completed by ....

© Redemptorist Publications, Alphonsus House, Chawton, Hants GU34 3HQ. To be used solely as part of FaithMap Programme.

The Transfiguration of the Lord

Family Sheet

To do at home with your family

For parents: Weekly Thought

In the thin air of the mountain top, our sense of God can be more acute, enhanced no doubt by the sense of exposure, isolation and revelation as all is laid out before us. It is in such an exposed, rarefied space that Jesus chooses to reveal himself. This was the briefest and most secret of glimpses into his transcendence and the Gospel makes the point that "they came down from the mountain". Although we may not find it quite so thrilling, the experience of God in the mundane and ordinary is just as authentic.

FAMILY PRAYER

If you have created a praying place, and it is not private to the child, it might be helpful to gather there for family prayer this week.

Dear Jesus, please bless this place where we pray. Help us to make time to be with you, and to enjoy being with you. Amen.

Activity

Think a little more about your prayer space. Is there a place in your home that you could use for this?

Try and spend a few minutes there each day this week. You can pray with words if you like, or just sit there, enjoying being with God in your special place.

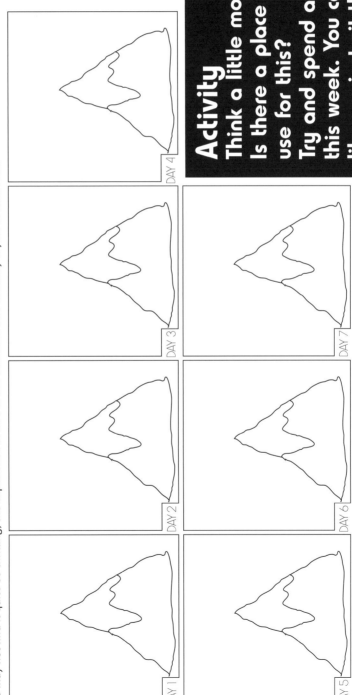

DAY 1

DAY 2

DAY 3

DAY 4

DAY 5

DAY 6

DAY 7

Each day, draw someone you love on top of the mountain and say a prayer for them.

This sheet has been completed by ....

© Redemptorist Publications, Alphonsus House, Chawton, Hants GU34 3HQ. To be used solely as part of FaithMap Programme.

The Assumption of the Blessed Virgin Mary

Family Sheet

To do at home with your family

For parents: Weekly Thought

When we see the immensity of God's love for us, it is hard not to praise him and exult in his power and love for us.

FAMILY PRAYER

Father in heaven, we praise you, we bless you, we thank you. Amen.

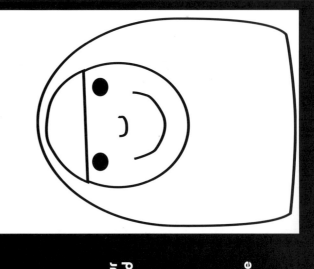

Young ones
Here is a picture of Mary, our queen in heaven, colour it and put a crown on her head.

Older ones
Can you find out some of the titles we give to Mary? You already know some of them, "Our Lady" for example. Write them down to take with you next week.

DAY 4

DAY 3

DAY 7

DAY 2

DAY 6

DAY 1

DAY 5

This week colour in a star each day when you remember how glad Mary was to praise God for all he is.

This sheet has been completed by ....

© Redemptorist Publications, Alphonsus House, Chawton, Hants GU34 3HQ. To be used solely as part of FaithMap Programme.

The Triumph of the Cross

Family Sheet
To do at home with your family

For parents: Weekly Thought

Today's feast celebrates the "Lifting up" of Jesus on the cross as a moment of revelation and triumph. "When you lift up the Son of Man, then you will realise that I am he, and that I do nothing on my own, but I say only what the Father taught me" (John 8:28). In today's Gospel, Jesus likens himself to the serpent in the desert that was lifted up to heal the stricken Israelites. Jewish tradition understood that the healing came about, not directly through looking at the serpent, but through the act of looking upwards – shifting their gaze from themselves to God. It was their renewed focus on God that healed them.

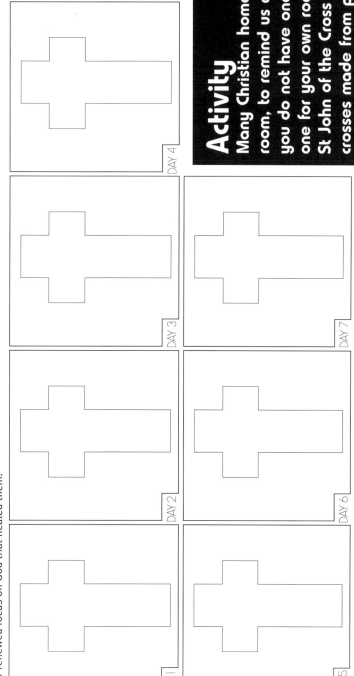

| DAY 1 | DAY 2 | DAY 3 | DAY 4 |
| DAY 5 | DAY 6 | DAY 7 | |

FAMILY PRAYER

Concentrate simply on making the sign of the cross together. If there are any little ones in your family then you can help them to practise.

Activity

Many Christian homes have a cross or crucifix in each room, to remind us all the time of Jesus' love for us. If you do not have one, this would be a good time to make one for your own room. It does not have to be elaborate; St John of the Cross decorated his first monastery with crosses made from paper and sticks. Decorate the crosses in your home this week as we give them special honour. Also a good week to have hot cross buns again: you can help to make them!

Decorate a cross each day when you have said a thank you prayer to Jesus for his great love.

This sheet has been completed by ....

© Redemptorist Publications, Alphonsus House, Chawton, Hants GU34 3HQ. To be used solely as part of FaithMap Programme.

Family Sheet

To do at home with your family

For parents: Weekly Thought

We often think of saints in terms of those whose heroic virtues have led to their being canonised and recognised by the Church as saints. Today's feast gives us a chance to redress the balance in favour of the countless thousands, whose lives are not as famous but are no less praiseworthy for being hidden but holy. We can try to remember those people we know, and celebrate their virtues and pray for them, forgiving where we can, and asking God to draw them ever closer to himself.

DAY 1

DAY 2

DAY 3

DAY 4

DAY 5

DAY 6

DAY 7

Beside the saint in the boxes, draw or write something good that you might do each day to help others.

This sheet has been completed by ....

FAMILY PRAYER

God of heaven and earth, you love everyone, for you created them.
We thank you for all those who have lived lives that can inspire us.
Help us to follow their example and seek to become closer to you. Amen.

All Saints, All Souls and the month of November

All Saints: the day we remember those who have died and are now in heaven.
All Souls: the day when we pray for those who have died and are on their journey to heaven.
November: the month when we remember everyone who has died. We think especially of people who have died in the last year. Remembrance Day (11 November): we remember all those who have died in war. Wear a poppy to remember people who have died or been seriously injured in war, and for those left behind who mourn them. Some churches have books for the names of people who have died. We pray for them during November.

© Redemptorist Publications, Alphonsus House, Chawton, Hants GU34 3HQ. To be used solely as part of FaithMap Programme.

The Commemoration of All the Faithful Departed (All Souls)

Family Sheet

To do at home with your family

For parents: Weekly Thought

Today we explore a little further the idea of purgatory and our role in praying for those who have died. In the catechism it is written that all who die in God's grace and friendship, but still imperfectly purified, are indeed assured of their eternal salvation; but after death they undergo purification, so as to achieve the holiness necessary to enter the joy of heaven. From the beginning the Church has honoured the memory of the dead and offered prayers for them ... so that thus purified, they may meet God face to face.

FAMILY PRAYER

Dear Jesus, when we die we want to come to live with you in heaven. Today we pray especially for ... We know you love him (her) as much as we do. We pray that you will bring him (her) into heaven to live with you and be happy for ever. Amen.

This would be a good time to visit the grave of somebody you know who has died; you can help to tidy up their grave, maybe take flowers or plant some bulbs to come up in the late springtime. When you have finished, take some time to look at the other graves, read about the people who have died and say a prayer for them.

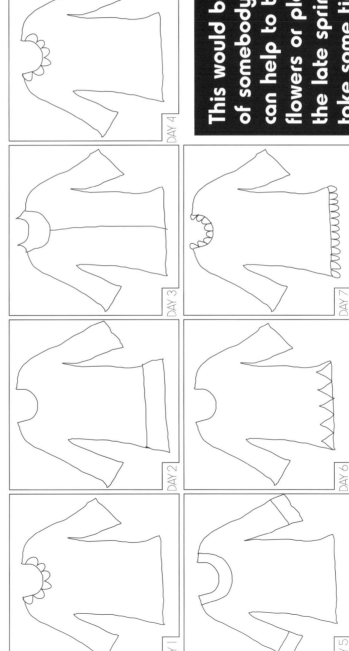

DAY 1

DAY 2

DAY 3

DAY 4

DAY 5

DAY 6

DAY 7

Each day decorate one of the white garments for somebody you know who has died.

This sheet has been completed by ....

© Redemptorist Publications, Alphonsus House, Chawton, Hants GU34 3HQ. To be used solely as part of FaithMap Programme.

The Dedication of the Lateran Basilica

Family Sheet

To do at home with your family

For parents: Weekly Thought

Our church buildings can provide us with oases of calm. They can also be places of stress especially when you are with small or reluctant children. Thank God for the times of calm, put the problem times in his hands. Be grateful for the special places there are which help to see us through the special times in our lives.

FAMILY PRAYER

Thank you, loving Father, for leading us to meet you in special places. Help us to keep them special for everyone who is there now and in the future. Amen.

Older children

What do you know about the special places of other faiths? What are their special places called? What can you find out about the Basilica of St John Lateran or your local diocesan cathedral or Canterbury Cathedral? Tell your catechist or teacher next week.

Younger children

Draw a picture of a place that is special for you. You may like to show it to your teacher next week.

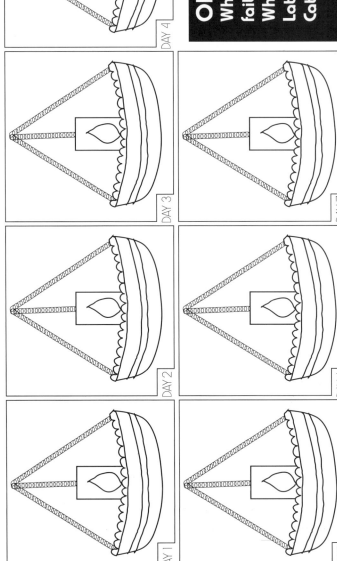

DAY 1

DAY 2

DAY 3

DAY 4

DAY 5

DAY 6

DAY 7

This week colour in a "sanctuary lamp" each day you remember how Jesus is always present with his people.

This sheet has been completed by ....

© Redemptorist Publications, Alphonsus House, Chawton, Hants GU34 3HQ. To be used solely as part of FaithMap Programme.

St David, Bishop

Family Sheet

To do at home with your family

FAMILY PRAYER

Dear Jesus, thank you for St David and for all the other saints who give us good ideas about the way to live, and who pray for us. Amen.

For parents: Weekly Thought

St David, patron saint of Wales, was very much a man of his era. His ascetic lifestyle will seem excessive to our modern outlook. In fact, even in his day it was considered to be notable. He was known as the Man of Water, because he is reputed to have drunk only water for the whole of his life. Today we think about the principles underlying his way of living. What did he do to ensure that Jesus remained the centre point of his life? How can we apply his wisdom so it is relevant for us?

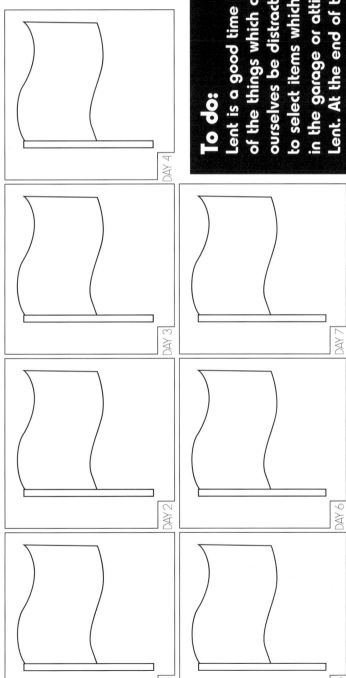

DAY 1

DAY 2

DAY 3

DAY 4

DAY 5

DAY 6

DAY 7

To do:

Lent is a good time for asceticism: for clearing away some of the things which clutter our lives and not letting ourselves be distracted by them. One way of doing this is to select items which we feel preoccupy us and store them in the garage or attic for the duration (or the rest) of Lent. At the end of that time we can get them back if we want, or we might discover that we have lived quite happily without them and choose to pass them on to a charity shop instead.

In the United Kingdom we have flags for St George (England), St Andrew (Scotland), St David (Wales) and St Patrick (Ireland). Use the first four days to draw and colour in these flags. Ask a grown-up to help you find three more countries that have flags for their patron saints. Draw and colour these in as well.

This sheet has been completed by ....

© Redemptorist Publications, Alphonsus House, Chawton, Hants GU34 3HQ. To be used solely as part of FaithMap Programme.

St Patrick, Bishop

Family Sheet

To do at home with your family

FAMILY PRAYER

God of all creation,

thank you for sending St Patrick to us – and for all the people who have passed on the Good News about Jesus.

Help us to be the kind of people who continue to spread that Good News.

Amen.

For parents: Weekly Thought

The Irish people have given the world a great deal of their Christian heritage. As they travelled to all parts of the world, whether as a result of famine or the search for work, they took their faith and, even today, they are among the foremost missionary countries.

Our children are blessed that people have passed on the light of faith. In a way you are a missionary to your child, passing on the faith you have inherited in words and ways they can understand. Even today, the spirit of St Patrick lives on through us.

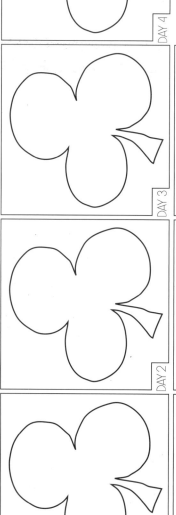

DAY 1
DAY 2
DAY 3
DAY 4
DAY 5
DAY 6
DAY 7

Colour in a shamrock each day. Think about St Patrick telling people about the Good News of Jesus. Try to find a way of showing people that being a Christian makes you happy.

This sheet has been completed by ....

A CELEBRATION CAKE TO MAKE

Apple cake from the county of Kerry

150g/6oz butter.   150g/6oz castor sugar.   2 eggs, beaten.   200g/8oz self-raising flour.

2 medium cooking apples, peeled, and chopped.   1tsp lemon rind.   Mix together 2tbsp demerara sugar, pinch of cinnamon and nutmeg.

1. Preheat oven to gas mark 4/180 C/350 F.
2. Grease and line a 900g/2lb loaf tin.
3. Cream together the butter and castor sugar and gradually add eggs and flour.
4. Stir in the apples and lemon rind.
5. Pour into the tin and sprinkle the top with the demerara sugar and spices.
6. Put it in the oven and bake for 1-1¹/₂ hours.

© Redemptorist Publications, Alphonsus House, Chawton, Hants GU34 3HQ. To be used solely as part of FaithMap Programme.